Playing Dolly

Millennial Shifts

A Series Edited by
E. Ann Kaplan, Helen Cooper, Román de la Campa, and Sandy Petrey
Robert Harvey, Managing Editor
The Humanities Institute at the State University
of New York at Stony Brook

*Playing Dolly: Technocultural Formations, Fantasies,
and Fictions of Assisted Reproduction,*
edited by E. Ann Kaplan and Susan Squier

The Politics of Research,
edited by E. Ann Kaplan and George Levine

Playing Dolly

Technocultural Formations,
Fantasies, and Fictions
of Assisted Reproduction

EDITED BY
E. ANN KAPLAN
SUSAN SQUIER

RUTGERS UNIVERSITY PRESS
New Brunswick, New Jersey, and London

176
P723
1999

Library of Congress Cataloging-in-Publication Data

Playing dolly : technocultural formations, fantasies, and fictions of
   assisted reproduction / edited by E. Ann Kaplan and Susan Squier.
        p. cm. — (Millennial shifts)
   Includes bibliographical references and index.
        ISBN 0-8135-2648-5 (cloth : alk. paper). — ISBN 0-8135-2649-3
   (pbk. : alk. paper)
        1. Human reproductive technology—Social aspects.   2. Human
   reproductive technology—Moral and ethical aspects.   I. Kaplan, E.
   Ann.   II. Squier, Susan Merrill.   III. Series.
   RG133.5.P62 1999
   176—dc21   98-48454
                                                                          CIP

British Cataloging-in-Publication data for this book is available from the British
Library

Manufactured in the United States of America

Contents

Part 3   Fictions

Acknowledgments

We want to thank our authors who participated in the two conferences that gave rise to the papers in this volume, namely that on "Reproductive Technologies: Narratives, Gender, Culture," and the follow-up conference on "Gender/Technology," both held in The Humanities Institute at Stony Brook. We thank these scholars for contributing to the success of the conferences and now for revising their papers for this volume. Other authors were eagerly pursued as we expanded our purview and as our ideas grew. Their contributions nicely complement those of the original conferences.

Thanks also to the staff at The Humanities Institute who gave so much of their time to making this volume a reality: special mention goes to Robert Harvey, managing editor for the book, for work on the volume in 1998, and to Adrienne Locke, Humanities Institute administrative coordinator, who took over many of Robert's tasks during his leave in spring 1999. Meanwhile, we especially want to thank Eva Woods and Leanne Warshauer, HISB graduate assistants for publications, who did most of the legwork. Without their unflagging efforts, there would have been no book.

Thanks also goes to Julie Vedder and Christina Jarvis, research assistants at Penn State University and themselves students of literature and science, who helped with the preparation of the final manuscript. Thanks, too, to the Society for Literature and Science for providing a stimulating community of scholars committed to thinking across disciplinary boundaries.

As always, we needed the support, advice and insights of the HISB Editorial Board—Helen Cooper, Román de la Campa and Sandy Petrey—in making this book come about. We also gratefully acknowledge the State University of New York at Stony Brook and the College of Arts and Sciences for their continued, steadfast support of our endeavors.

Finally, we want to thank Leslie Mitchner, editor in chief at Rutgers University Press and Paula Kantenwein, as well as Brigitte Goldstein and Grace Buonocore for their editorial work on the book, and their patience with the

somewhat complex processes involved in the book's production. We are grateful to Rutgers University Press for their imagination and energy to bring the
fruits of the HISB research to a wider public.

E. Ann Kaplan and Susan Squier

Playing Dolly

Introduction

E. ANN KAPLAN
SUSAN SQUIER

THE DAY we began writing this introduction, NBC-TV aired its "Sunday Movie Original," the suspense thriller *Cloned*. This drama—no doubt inspired by the stunning news of Ian Wilmut's cloning of the Finn Dorset ewe in the Roslin Institute earlier the same year (1997)—provides a serendipitous point of entry to the multiple meanings that "reproductive technology" (RT) holds for the writers in this volume and for us as its editors.[1]

Set in postmillennial 2008, *Cloned* adapts to the world of for-profit health care many of the stock aspects of other thrillers about reproductive technology— the forbidding high-tech company with its ethically compromised CEO, the naïve physician-researcher whose only concern is "helping people," the innocent and endangered woman, the posse of corporate goons. However, the remarkable aspect of this mass-market narrative is not what it protests but what it accepts. As it raises the alarm about cloning in response to the Roslin laboratory's accomplishment in February 1997, it normalizes a birth technology, ectogenesis, that was the focus of strenuous debate between scientists, novelists, and public intellectuals in the early years of this century.[2] These thinkers discussed whether ectogenesis would lead to the production of debased human beings tailored to the demands of industrial production; whether it would reduce human suffering by improving the species, lead to the development of a feminist master sex, or be abandoned by a careful society because the children did not thrive.

No such debate is figured in *Cloned*. That reproductive technology has moved from a revolutionary breakthrough to a routine medical procedure is the premise of the program. *Cloned* invokes the circuit of meanings traveled

by the term *reproduction*—biological, economic, informatic—in the late twentieth century. Such a circuit of meanings is central to this collection of essays, which incorporates research presented at two conferences held at the
Humanities Institute at the State University of New York, Stony Brook: the
1992 conference "Reproductive Technologies: Narratives, Gender, Culture,"
and the 1996 conference "Gender and Technology." At the first conference,
a group of scholars, professionals, and activists came together for an intense
three-day period to discuss the broad sociocultural implications of such issues
as gamete ownership, prenatal sex selection, surrogacy, and techniques of genetic intervention. While not necessarily the first of its kind, our event was
unique in its bringing together—in these early days for such conferences—
medical doctors involved in biotechnology, reproductive endocrinology, and
genetics; people using the technologies; social work and for-profit surrogacy
providers; lawyers; and an interdisciplinary group of academic scholars in literary and cultural studies, historiography, and religion.

Listening to tapes of some varied voices from that conference, we can
hear the circuit of meanings again and note the predominance of ethical concerns. Dr. Jordan Cohen, then dean of the medical school at the State University of New York, Stony Brook, observes, "The topic you are engaged in is one
of the most riveting examples in contemporary society of a timeless dynamic,
namely the impact of technological advancement on the broader society, public
policy and ethical questions." He goes on to note, "The fact is, we are confronted with capabilities that are beyond our ethical thinking in many cases.
We need to struggle to relate what we can do to what we should do."

This sentiment was echoed by others, including Father Robert Smith, then
director of the Institute for Contemporary Medicine at the Stony Brook Medical School. Commenting on prenatal testing in the context of a heart-rending
video on Huntington's disease, he wondered "if this is morally significant
knowledge. What's the moral significance in passing from a possibility to a
probability to a certainty that x will happen? . . . Even if it becomes a certainty,
does that settle the moral question of what we should do?"

Listening, one hears the degree to which such processes in 1992 were still
cutting edge, unfamiliar, and therefore looked on with some trepidation: Smith
is concerned about the social and ethical costs of our new high-tech capabilities. He noted that "we have catapulted ourselves into a situation of having
some kind of knowledge we simply don't know what to do with as humans."
It seemed to him that "the central thing is to develop pluralistic moral communities. That is to say, communities in which people have a real stake in
one another."

Lawyers, too, were anxious and wary in the early 1990s. Isobel Marcus
said she was "concerned about the social implications of what we are under-

taking and the extent to which we have the social consensus . . . to resolve them." She noted that "we cannot set aside the social context in which we think about reproductive technologies, in which we make policy, and in which the law is involved," and she argued that RT is every lawyer's and social policy maker's nightmare because it polarizes profound issues. In a postmodern world, social issues compete with biology, and law tries to make coherence out of fragmented realities, Marcus said. She concluded that American society should try to regulate surrogacy.

Perhaps predictably, those at the conference already deeply involved with surrogacy—either as doctors, as directors of agencies, or as successful surrogate mothers—were anxious to dispel ethical worries and defend what they were doing morally. Dr. Daniel Kenigsberg, who practices in an in vitro fertilization clinic, defined surrogacy, distinguished altruistic from commercial surrogacy, and described how he managed a specific case. Rather than addressing ethical or moral implications of surrogacy, Dr. Kenigsberg concluded with a warning about surrogacy's medical contraindications, which included anatomical ones (e.g., being born without a uterus), acquired ones (e.g., a medical condition, like pulmonary hypertension, severe renal disease, HIV infection, or having had a hysterectomy), and, finally, genetic disorders, like overly flexible connective tissues.

Dr. Betsy Aigen, director of a surrogacy agency in New York, testified movingly to the pain of infertility and noted that surrogacy is usually a last and desperate option. She discussed her careful screening of surrogates-to-be, her counseling of all parties, and her efforts to "match" people to ensure success. Two women who were then current surrogate mothers in her agency accompanied Dr. Aigen to the conference. They confirmed how carefully Aigen did her screening and testified to the positive experience of surrogacy.[3]

Although these transcripts from the 1992 conference reveal overriding concerns with the moral and ethical issues that new birth technologies, including prenatal testing, evoked for people at all levels, in contrast, as we planned this volume in 1997, ethical questions seemed less urgent—to the general public, to the scholars and researchers whose work we included, to us as editors. Where ethics emerged, it concerned the uses to which reproductive technologies were put in realms beyond the obviously reproductive. In regard to 1992 issues, it seems that some U.S. scholars have crossed a certain boundary in their thinking, or that in undertaking further research the "newness" of the issues we raised in 1992 is no longer central. This is because enormous changes have taken place in the way that reproduction is represented, understood, and discussed, whether in biomedicine, informatics, or both simultaneously—as the NBC movie *Cloned* suggests is increasingly the case.

Our collection documents this shift in the public construction, and positioning, of reproductive technologies. The essays included reflect the change in public and scholarly attitudes toward reproductive technology that has occurred in less than a decade. Not only do the essays testify to the increasing normalization of reproductive technology, and the resulting reduction in concern over the ethical issues raised by intervening technologically in a natural process; they also mark the link between the technologies that serve biomedical reproduction and those that carry out other forms of reproducing image and content, from visual to textual. The latter issues were highlighted in the second conference in 1996, when scholars reconvened at the Humanities Institute at Stony Brook to study gender and technology. This second conference, linked to that on birth technologies, now pursued issues relating to bodily technologies of reproduction—in the sense of reproducing one's own body, as against reproducing another body. We invited people who had worked on bodily self-fashioning in terms of sex change and fleshly reshaping. Participants addressed these technologies of reproduction in various ways, as we explain below.

Because we understand reproductive technologies to be a subset of a larger phenomenon, extending beyond biomedicine to the global risk culture of modernity, we have organized the essays in this volume in three parts, tracking the reverberating effects of an assault on the unique individual body from the biomedical, to the informatic, and finally to the global. The first two parts, "Technocultural Formations" and "Fantasies," build on the Humanities Institute conferences and exemplify the linkage between biomedical and visual reproduction. The third, "Fictions," departs from those conferences and is organized instead around a work of fiction. Before going on to describe the issues raised by the contributors to each part, we want to explore our rationale for the section on fiction. The generic departure—from the analytic essay to the work of fiction—reflects our sense that the form of knowledge production crucially shapes what we can know. Moreover, in its content, this fiction links the specific subject of reproductive technology (addressed in the first part) to another global context, this time not global information technologies but global trade in rare animals.

Despite their manifold differences of technique and context, all three versions of reproductive technology (human, visual/informatic, and xenobiological) challenge the notion of a unique body. The central image of the NBC Sunday movie exemplifies that challenge to embodied uniqueness in the photographs of cloned children that, in the story, proliferated on the Internet in response to the mother's query about her cloned son. Moreover, her horrific discovery of the cloned embryo harvested for body parts invokes the "real world" instance that triggered the television drama: the Roslin Institute's successful cloning of Dolly, the Finn Dorset ewe.

From the mass-market newsmagazines to more specialized publications, the press coverage of this event was remarkably homogeneous: it featured multiple identical images of sheep. The cloning of Dolly and the proliferation of images of a clone are linked in more ways than the analogy between reproduction at the biomedical level and that at the photographic or digital level. Both participate in a general movement to privatize commercial "life": that is, to take biological and intellectual properties out of the public domain and hold them for private industry—a phenomenon Vandana Shiva has explored.[4] Both of them are linked to the risk culture of late modernity.[5]

To put it tersely, a simultaneous process of intellectual and biological enclosure is occurring, in response to risk, at the end of the twentieth century. This simultaneous process of enclosure is illustrated by the plot of *Cloned* in its emphasis not on the replicative effect of cloning but on the use to which it is put: the provision of organs for transplant.[6] With the shift in focus from the specific population of consumers of reproductive technology to the far broader pool of current and potential consumers of transplant technology, which could, in fact, be anyone, we have arguably made the transition into risk society: a specific historical epoch dominated by the calculation of how "the risks and hazards systematically produced as part of modernization [can] be prevented, minimized, dramatized, or channeled."[7] Of course the techniques of producing children by in vitro fertilization and other high-technology forms of fertilization can be understood as the medical response to the increased risk of infertility arising from environmental pollution introduced by modernization. Yet with the move into the organ transplant market, the risk calculus now applies to everyone, and everyone joins the pool of at-risk individuals and potential organ transplant recipients.

The link between reproductive technologies and technologies of reproduction can also be explained in terms of the new risk calculus: the exchange of information becomes a crucial component of the risk-assessment, -management, and -abatement strategies central to this new risk society.[8] Risk-management discourse, then, proliferates: it is a new expert discipline that cordons off any real response to risk by authorizing as acceptable only those risks that lie within the parameters of scientific rationality. Disciplinary limits and expert systems with clear borders thus actually function to keep things running as they were before: the processes of modernization that gave us risk can continue unshaken. This is where fiction comes in.

Some fiction, and other forms of nonscientific testimony including psychoanalysis, are nonexpert, extradisciplinary responses to risk that may escape and thus threaten the reflexive, self-replicating status quo. Like other forms of nonexpert, nonprofessionalized knowledge, fiction (principally avant-garde forms) resists the increasing scientificity of our risk society. Fiction speaks—

testifies—to the risks that the expert risk-management discourses leave out because of the scientistic, disciplinary bias that is built-in. Thus avant-garde fiction, perhaps ironically, becomes a crucial site of resistance to the enclosure movements paradigmatic of modernity, whether we are talking about the enclosure of ideas in the process of disciplinary specialization; the enclosure of biological life-forms (gametes, embryos, organs, transgenic animals) for the production of profit, by industry or biomedicine; or the attempts by commercial media to limit what stories can be told, what ideologies stories will manifest. While parts 1 and 2 of our volume provide a range of theoretical responses to "Technical Formations" and "Fantasies," part 3, "Fictions," takes as its centerpiece a work of fiction that both articulates the drift from reproductive technology to technologies of reproduction, from the individual to the global, from the human to the interspecies, and embodies—and reproduces—a powerful act of resistance to it.

Part 1: Technocultural Formations

Ranging from a Euro-American to a Javanese context, and from the historical to the contemporary, to the utopian future, the essays in part 1 differ in the extent to which they protest or affirm the effects of reproductive technology. They share an attention to the differing ways in which reproductive technologies are used and discussed and to their different meanings, depending on their historical, cultural, and geographic contexts. Dion Farquhar's essay critiques the aspect of reproductive technology she names "gamete traffic": that is, the donation, exchange, or sale of eggs and sperm. Farquhar's position on reproductive technology falls between affirmation of its emancipatory possibilities and wariness of the ways it can be used to oppress women. Her metaphor includes the notion of a traffic in, or between, discourses, bodies, or subjects:[9] Farquhar argues that gamete traffic both reinscribes and challenges "prior cultural and material constructions of gender." Exploring how a reproductive regime saturates culture, involving a set of symbolic effects as well as technologies, Farquhar shows how gamete traffic calls into question a whole set of discursive anchors: kinship, nature, individuality, ownership, intention, and bodily integrity. Gamete traffic, she argues, cannot be constructed "along a binary model—either as inherently repressive or liberatory."

Unlike Farquhar's assessment of gamete traffic, which at least some of the time gestures toward a time and space of utopian possibilities, the essays by Leslie Dwyer and Angela Wall assess the use of Norplant in Indonesia and in specific low-income communities in the United States, Bangladesh, and Zimbabwe, respectively. Examining how contraception in Java is enacted, interpreted, and given meaningful form from "within a lattice of culture and piety,"

Dwyer explores "how reproductive technologies shift meanings as they move across flows of information and interpretation and become enmeshed in local, state and transnational concerns." Dwyer explores how women co-opt the state language of biomedical modernity to assert the right to reject so-called advanced birth control methods. In so doing, they resist the reproductive politics of the state. Arguing that the debate over the moral status of Norplant is a struggle over the role of women in modern society, Wall traces how Norplant functions paradoxically to insert women who use it into a circuit of less freedom while promising more freedom. Wall introduces the valuable concept of zoning—that is, the regulation of access to reproductive and contraceptive technologies by class and ethnicity. She suggests that social and economic institutions shape women's needs so that certain options are closed out. Both essays explore how women exercise power through the use of contraceptive technologies: Dwyer focuses largely on the crucial role of nationalism in the decision to adopt or resist contraceptive technologies, but Wall concludes with an analysis of Norplant's promotion to a U.S. audience as a disturbing way to solve social problems by intervening in women's bodily choices.

In "Selling Reproduction," Pamela L. Moore analyzes the extensive advertising campaigns on which select health care providers sometimes spend as much as $1.20 billion. Moore's research establishes continuities between present representations of reproductive technology and earlier discourses. Instead of worrying directly about either the ethics of reproductive technologies or the risk to the species, Moore analyzes the commercial and cultural forces that have put pressure on infertile couples and the larger culture to accept reproductive technologies as routine: infertility, Moore shows, is seen as having the potential to be an infinite growth market. According to Moore, "in health care advertising . . . fertility treatment seems more like a regular part of a healthy woman's pursuit of 'wellness' than a remarkable feat of mythic proportion."

Thus, partly as a result of changes in the health care system—now a commercial proposition—technologies like reproductive ones have become naturalized in the time between our 1992 conference and our writing in 1997. Readers will recall how Robin Cook in his novel *Vital Signs* goes so far as to fantasize the harm to infertile individuals and couples of the sale of illegally harvested female eggs grown into an international mafia-dominated criminal underground enterprise.

Anne Balsamo's essay, "Notes toward a Reproductive Theory of Technology," nicely sets the stage for the essays in part 2 by focusing on how technology has become, in Teresa de Lauretis's words, "our context, political and personal."[10] The issue of technology has been taken up by all disciplines in one way or another, and, Balsamo notes, "there are few places in the world

that exist 'outside' the technological reach of multinational capitalism."
Balsamo usefully outlines debates about the proper definitions of technology
from Aristotle to Heidegger, to contemporary thinkers like Webster Hood and
Zoë Sofoulis, and on to cultural theorists and feminist scholars. Balsamo stresses
the specifically *reproductive* formation of technology and argues that the essays in parts 1 and 2 address how "the new reproductive technologies are implicated in the reproduction of ideologies of the gendered, race-marked, and
class-positioned body." The project is "feminist," she argues, in being less concerned with the ontology of technology theory than with "trying to think
through the technological conditions of possibilities of social transformation."

Part 2: Fantasies

While the first five essays deal with reproductive technologies as an intervention whose significance shifts in relation to the locale and the historical period,
the second part begins with Susan Squier's essay comparing historical changes
in the representation of the fetus/mother relationship with current changes in
the representation of human/animal boundary related to cloning Dolly. Squier
shows how historical changes in the representation of the fetus reflect an increasing tendency to pit fetus and gestating woman against each other as legal and medical opponents. These changes have produced an image of the
new fetal subject constituted increasingly in reaction to an objectified mother.
Squier addresses the new discourse of the "fetus at risk" that increasingly facilitates medical, legal, religious, cultural, community, and even culinary interventions on behalf of the fetus (and against the will of the gestating
woman).[11] Some fiction expresses the surplus meaning ungrasped by the logic
of the risk society: the disturbing implications of this discourse emerge, Squier
argues, in literary texts that image the apocalyptic excesses of the new fetal
subject. However, such fictions not only figure forth the contemporary privileging of the fetal position, but they can also be read against the grain to cata-
lyze a shift in reader identifications that draws attention to the predicament
of the silenced mother-to-be. Squier's essay demonstrates that like the fetal/
maternal boundary, the human/animal boundary, too, is destabilized by assisted
reproduction and its biomedical sequel, the assisted reproduction ushered in
with the cloning of Dolly. Both boundaries are subject to a range of interventions that produce and manage them unevenly, reflecting the ideological
struggles of different contexts.

    By contrast, E. Ann Kaplan and Kay Torney and John Wiltshire explore
the voices of gestating and adoptive mothers in differing surrogacy cases.
Kaplan focuses on the loud voices of gestating and adoptive mothers, as they
struggle for possession of the fetus and then baby, in her comparison of late

1980s representations of surrogacy, in magazines and on TV, with recent images in texts by a video artist, an anthropologist, and a Taiwanese film director. Kaplan categorizes 1980s popular stories as idealizing and negative, and in her study of differing visual materials she argues that the popular melodrama form—despite its semiotic and narrative traditions—at least offers space for the passionate and conflicting emotions rarely detailed in public discourse. Other texts offering interesting contrasts in imaging surrogacy include Emily Liu's film detailing an entirely different sensibility toward surrogacy in the Taiwanese Los Angeles community. Kaplan argues that even in 1997 surrogacy is still a difficult psychological process for those involved. Unconscious fantasies, projections, envy, and desire to control remain obstacles given our still predominant U.S. cultural organization in the nuclear family. Kaplan is ultimately interested in the links between narratives circulating in popular culture and women's lived experiences: she concludes that, as feminists face the millennium, we need subtle and complex narrational and visual forms so that we can imagine differently and extend, rather than limit, what we can experience.

Torney and Wiltshire focus on an early Australian surrogacy case and the narrative of it later written up by the participants. Writing as two scholars who have worked extensively on issues of literature and medicine, and who teach at the University of Melbourne (near where pioneer in vitro fertilization doctor Alan Trounson worked), Torney and Wiltshire analyze the strange unconscious fantasies at work in the Kirkman family's idea to have a sister bear a child for her sibling. The family members take this opportunity to release unconscious incestuous sexual desires in a fascinating way. Perhaps, we might hypothesize now, such unconscious wishes and fantasies account for the distrust with which surrogacy and in vitro fertilization were regarded in the early days.

Like the cultures from which the technology issues, discrete instances of innovation in reproductive technology tend to be thought crucial when they happen in the United Kingdom (with Edwards and Steptoe) or the United States (as with the Mary Beth Whitehead case) but to be seen as marginal (and in particular marginal to the developmental trajectory of the technology) when they happen in Australia. Yet like those two earlier cases, the Australian case of sister-sister surrogacy, as it was called, between Maggie and Linda Kirkman received widespread publicity for its legal and public policy implications. Perhaps there is a similarity between Australia's role in the development of in vitro fertilization and the role Scotland may play in the development of cloning. In each case, a former British colony destabilizes the national hierarchy by an innovation that accomplishes the preemptive enclosure of the presumptive subjects of a new realm. "Offshore," in the margins of the official disciplinary and political centers, more maverick methods can emerge.

Yet if these maverick methods are liberating at the margins, they may in-deed provoke discomfort at the psychological centers of the new scientific empire. Vivian Sobchack moves discussion to a reproductive technology of a new kind, namely, reproducing one's own body through cosmetic surgery and cinema. This time the technology is to reproduce "youth"—to magically turn back time and reproduce how one looked thirty or forty years ago. Such re-production technology, Sobchack argues, can be found in the linked devices of cinema and cosmetic surgery. "Cinema is cosmetic surgery," she argues, "its fantasies, its 'makeup,' and its digital effects able to 'fix' (in the doubled sense of repair and stasis) and to fetishize and to reproduce faces and time as both 'unreel' before us." She goes on to show that, equally, "cosmetic surgery is cin-ema, creating us as an image we not only learn to enact in a repetition com-pulsion but also must—and never can—live up to."

Without actually using the word, Sobchack seems to be saying that both cinema and cosmetic surgery enact a kind of cloning. In cosmetic surgery, one re-creates one's face of forty years ago. But, as in cloning proper, one can never in fact be that same person. Hence, one can "never live up to" (in the sense of being the same as) that earlier face, any more than a clone of myself could actually be the same person as me. Yet, as Fay Weldon has demonstrated in The Cloning of Joanna May, a less negative view of cloning is possible: one could watch oneself starting out again in the same image but becoming some-thing different. Commercial cinema, through new digital technologies, now shares with cloning the power to reproduce images of actors long dead or aged yet moving in youthful form in completely new stories on film. An actress watching a re-created youthful self on the screen might feel very much like someone watching a biologically "cloned" physical self.[12] Between the cin-ematic narrative and the biological replotting, the power of cloning (like the power of film) lies less in its material reconfiguration than in the way it alters how we see things. As Sobchack points out, "With or without medical sur-gery, we have been technologically altered, both 'seeing' differently and 'seem-ing' different than we did in a time before either cinema or cosmetic surgery presented us with their reversible technological processes of immortality and figurations of 'magical' self-transformation." And narrative—the telling of stories—is central to that process of seeing.

Susan Stryker explores a bodily reproductive technology of a rather dif-ferent kind, namely, reproducing a new gender. A similar crisis to that which birth technologies provoked in the 1980s emerged in the 1950s in response to Christine Jorgensen, one of the first women to become a transsexual. Stryker links the "ambivalent hopes and fears" inspired by the atom bomb in this pe-riod to those also evoked on a mass scale by a transsexual body "corporealizing the transformation of human existence through scientific technology." For

Stryker, what she terms "Jorgensen's Atom Bomb" marked a moment of passage "into the hyperreality of postmodern conditions," for transsexual bodies, like bodies produced through reproductive technology, stage questions of truth, falsity, authenticity, and imitation. Like those writing about reproductive technology today, Stryker is not interested in the morality and ethics of transsexuality, in whether it is right or wrong to alter the body's anatomical sex signifiers through the use of hormones and plastic surgery. Rather, she wants to explore how the possibility of transsexual modes of embodiment has arrived in twentieth-century Euro-American culture. As with assisted reproduction, Stryker argues that transsexual surgery creates the opportunity for the production of new material selves that result in avenues for a new cultural/historical episteme.

Concluding part 2 is Karyn Valerius's essay, "The Monstrous Genealogy of Assisted Reproduction." The essay nicely returns us to reproductive technology discourses in our 1992 conference, since Valerius argues that in positing the unintelligibility of reproductive technology as a high-tech phenomenon that breaks with the past, analysis is precluded of how assisted reproduction is informed by existing power relations, in both its use and how the public perceives it. She goes on to show that, far from representing the end of history, "the issues raised by in vitro fertilization and related practices . . . have precedents." Historically, reproductive issues have stimulated debates about the boundaries of the natural, but the register of marvels and miracles used to describe assisted reproduction has a long history in Western European/Anglo-American traditions of monstrosity.

If Valerius is right, why did uses of the new technologies create such a crisis in contemporary U.S. culture? And why has that crisis subsided somewhat in the years since our 1992 conference? Is it simply that the usefulness of the technologies—their being of such help to infertile couples—has led to people simply opting for them quite routinely? Could the practicing of the technologies, despite ethical and policy ambiguities, rather have put at bay the ethical questions that so troubled many of us in 1992? That is, have the practical needs for the technologies managed to outweigh individual couples' and the larger society's ethical worries? Further, changing social roles for women together with pollution of the atmosphere have increasingly negative impacts on fertility. More birth defects and miscarriages add to fears for the species and the need for avenues alternate to old-fashioned reproduction.

Part 3: Fictions

Charis Thompson Cussins's short story, "Confessions of a Bioterrorist: Subject Position and Reproductive Technology," ponders the following questions:

Who and what gets to reproduce where and under what conditions? Why are resources committed to enhancing some human and nonhuman reproductions and to restricting or obliterating others? Responses to this story by Richard Nash and Gabriele Schwab highlight some of the themes it addresses: the racialized politics of reproduction, the resilient Enlightenment narrative built into its religious metaphor, the phantasmatic surplus of science that the story articulates. The Cussins short story, like the commentaries on it, embodies the broader context in which reproductive technology is increasingly understood at the end of the millennium, namely, as applicable to both humans and animals; as linked to Western fertility politics and xenogenesis; to biological, digital, and cinematic forms of reproduction; and to the myriad risk-management strategies that take reproduction as their site of intervention in the struggle to preserve endangered species or to preserve patriarchy against the threat posed by marginalized "others."

In forcing a confrontation with the underside of reproduction—with monstrosity, hybridity, and narcissism—Cussins's short story also returns us to the drama broadcast the day we began this introduction, the NBC movie *Cloned*. Cussins tells us the story of a biotechnology worker who goes against her bosses to liberate a bonobo embryo from its status as object of national property in a contest over who gets to reproduce what and where; the NBC movie tells us the story of another biotechnology worker whose embryo is stolen in order to produce biotechnological profit. In the contrast between Mary's bonobo embryo and the NBC film's cloned children we can read the contradictory potential of reproductive technologies, either to destabilize or to advance the enclosure movement: of gametes, of seed lines, of land, of intellectual property.

In closing, we suggest that this volume does more than document a changing cultural response to reproductive technology. It also documents a crucial shift in the response to technology by academics involved in the social critique of knowledge. From initial anxiety about the seemingly inherent oppressiveness of these new technologies, the essays (and fiction) in this volume move to an appreciation that technology has no more of an inherent essence than does "nature" or its principles: gametes, embryos, animals, human beings. However, technology—now most often "managed" by mainstream institutions and biomedical forces—needs to be opened up to, and its control shared by, usually marginalized communities whose bodies and lives are most affected by the technologies.

Notes

1. Since 1994, the field of reproductive endocrinology has refused the term *new reproductive technologies* for the range of medical practices it offers to infertile patients. Reasoning that these technologies are no longer "new," the American

Society for Reproductive Medicine seems to be gradually eliding its technological aspect, choosing instead to call them "assisted reproductive technologies," often shortened to "assisted reproduction" (Farquhar, 1996, 193). We preserve the old term, *reproductive technologies*, because for us it captures a specific convergence: the nexus of medical technologies associated with reproduction (both conceptive and contraceptive technologies), visualization and informatics technologies like film, television, and video that reproduce information, and a range of reproductions of human life beyond its temporal and taxonomic boundaries.

2. *Ectogenesis* refers to the formation of embryos outside the womb. Thinkers debating this between 1923 and 1929 included Aldous Huxley, J.B.S. Haldane, Anthony Ludovici, and Vera Brittain. Extrauterine gestation, or "ectogenesis," was the epitome of futuristic science to J.B.S. Haldane, pioneer popular science writer who first surveyed the cultural effects of reproductive technology. See Squier, *Babies in Bottles: Twentieth-Century Visions of Reproductive Technology* (New Brunswick, N. J.: Rutgers University Press, 1994).

3. See E. Ann Kaplan's essay in this volume, where she discusses these women's testimonies in more detail.

4. See Vandana Shiva lecture, "Women, Biodiversity, and Biotechnology," Pennsylvania State University, 21 April 1997.

5. See Ulrich Beck, *Risk Society: Towards a New Modernity* (London: Sage Publications, 1992).

6. John Travis, "A Fantastical Experiment: The Science behind the Controversial Cloning of Dolly," *Science News* 151, no. 14 (5 April 1997): 214.

7. Beck, *Risk Society*, 19. Beck discusses, in addition (51–84), the practices of scientific risk management that serve to delimit, and thus perpetuate and even increase, risk: the insistence on elevated criteria for the validation of risk causality, the notion that acceptable levels of risk exist, the failure to address the issue of risk holistically (i.e., by considering the synergism of toxic substances), and the tendency to extrapolate from animal studies to human reactions. In our conclusion to the volume, we deal more with issues having to do with risk management.

8. Think of the mother in *Cloned* using the replicative and reproductive aspects of the World Wide Web to find out whether her son had been cloned and to mobilize the parents of the cloned children to close the cloning project down.

9. The term *gamete traffic* refers to an increasingly microcosmic sphere of activity and has been linked to a feminist genealogy from Gayle Rubin (via Lévi-Strauss) to Donna Haraway.

10. See Teresa de Lauretis, *Technologies of Gender: Essays on Theory, Film, and Fiction* (Bloomington: Indiana University Press, 1987), 167.

11. Stephen Katz, personal communication.

12. Indeed, Fay Weldon uses precisely that image in her novel, as the cloned Joanna May imagines meeting her four clones for the first time: "What woman of sixty would want to meet herself at thirty: rerun of some dreary old film, in which she gave a bad performance, like as not, and split-screen technique at that." Fay Weldon, *The Cloning of Joanna May Fay Weldon* (New York: Penguin Books, 1991), 112.

Part 1

Technocultural Formations

Gamete Traffic/
Pedestrian Crossings

DION FARQUHAR

It is precisely from the disarticulation of the body that the
idea of dissemination derives its force.

David Wills, *Prosthesis*

A HOST OF unprecedented prosthetic medical interventions engage, mark, and manipulate the human body, producing and revisioning it in multiple, often contradictory ways. Donor-assisted reproduction, organ transplantation, brain-dead cadaver donors, postmortem maternal ventilation, and transgenic medical, pharmacological, and agricultural applications have provoked a generalized crisis of embodiment both historically and philosophically. Reproductive technological interventions and prosthetic extensions are either represented by panic narratives about monstrosity and hubris or simultaneously naturalized and deified, just like "natural" unassisted conception.[1]

While only a minority of people are directly involved in reproductive technologies in general or gamete traffic in particular as either users or providers, everyone knows about their existence and potential. What everyone knows is that conception can occur without sex and that a woman can now have a baby without a man. The resultant ubiquity of dissemination of knowledge and lore about reproductive technologies—gossip, debates, legal struggles, and scholarly and popular representations—supports anthropologist Marilyn Strathern's contention that "these ways of thinking are now available to everyone."[2] Technological challenges have disrupted the self-evidence of such nodal discursive anchors as kinship, nature, individualism, ownership, intention, bodily integrity, and so on.

Only new reproductive stories can make sense of the contemporary radical dispersions and reorganization of bodies, nature, and kinship. The traffic in gametes both demands and allows changes in traditional narratives about how reproduction is understood. Whatever their differences, they all assumed that gametes, in the case of ova, inhere within their bodies of origin and do not travel and, in the case of sperm, that they only travel via sexual intercourse. It is to some of the consequences and possibilities of this unprecedented gamete mobility and obviation of intercourse that this essay looks.

Donna Haraway's introduction of the figure of the cyborg to facilitate a politics of heterogeneity remains useful in revising our understandings of embodied corporeality, kinship, and nature.[3] Cyborg practices, like reproductive technology, entail "transgressed boundaries, potent fusions and dangerous possibilities,"[4] generating new material and discursive sites of recuperation *and* resistance. Gamete traffic is cyborgian because it fuses and confuses boundary guarantors such as artificial/natural, public/private, masculine/feminine. While modern gametes are unprecedentedly mobile, traveling far and indifferently from their bodies of origin, they are not the first or only indexes that maternities and paternities are mobile and mobilizable. Contemporary gamete traffic has routinized, commercialized, and medicalized—and in so doing, expanded— the reproductive mobility and multiplicity of childbearing and child-rearing practices in Western modernity. Indeed, gamete traffic drives home the inexorability of gametes' historicity, discursiveness, and social embeddedness.[5]

This essay examines one constellation of contemporary reproductive practice—gamete traffic—and the conflicting desires, rhetorics, and representations that underwrite its importance for contemporary social relations. Vehicles (e.g., cars, buses, semis, scooters, bicycles, and skateboards—assuming land travel), drivers (documented as well as unlicensed), passengers, cargo, hitchhikers, runners, walkers, and animals constitute some of the circulating elements of contemporary traffic. Recently mobilized body parts are subject to similar vicissitudes of organization, disruption, transfer, routing, administration, integration, and expulsion as their internal combustion analogues.

Like the traffic generated by four-wheeled engines and their spin-offs, gamete traffic is sustained by the circulation of (essentially) unrelated and newly related bodies and body parts. Part pattern, part random, it is a kaleidoscopic caravan of intersecting and colliding strangers, not kin. That gamete traffic is a public circulating space shows reproduction to be inexorably political. How access is policed, by whom and what, how regulation generates transgression and appropriation, and what individual and social tolls are imposed are some of the essential contestations raised by mobile gametes.

Gametes (from the Greek *gamein*, to marry)—eggs and sperm—are presumed by scientific narrative to be coupled in an inalterable natural matrimony. The technological capacity, now routinized in institutional and quasi-institutional donation practices within infertility medicine, is about moving gametes around—from bodies of origin to recipient bodies. Gamete traffic is the intentional, and unintentional results of the transfer of human sperm, ova, and embryos from the endogenous bodies that generated them to other bodies that lack them.

Difference Driven

Gamete traffic admits both sperm and egg donation as equal participants in its busy thoroughfares. Now sperm and ova are the equally necessary components of and contributors to human reproduction as male and female germ cells. Yet curiously, male and female gametes are normatively laden with multiple gender, class, and race inscriptions. Even as one tries to describe the donation process as neutrally as possible, asymmetrical gender difference is invoked. Although recipients may be constructed as an individual, couple, or institution, and although donation may result from either elective individual private negotiation (friend or family member donor) or the institutional commercial mediation of a sperm bank, donor egg program, or embryo donation medical network, *all* gamete recipients are ultimately women. Even a preliminary elaboration of gamete traffic evokes asymmetrical relations of gender and sexual difference, which is to say, sexed bodies in history.

Regardless of the difference of its routes and despite its origins in the male and female bodies that act as its vehicles, the ultimate terminus of all gamete traffic is women's bodies. Sperm donation supplies effluvia (semen/sperm) from a donor male's body, while ovum donation supplies a body part(s) (ova) from a donor female's body. Sperm is then subsequently transferred—immediately in the case of fresh sperm and later via cryopreservation—to a woman through vaginal or uterine insemination. The decision to utilize donor sperm is usually based on either the woman's partner's sperm deficiencies or her own social "deficiency" of lacking a male partner (single heterosexual or lesbian). Ova, on the other hand, are both donated by and extracted from a donor woman, manipulated in a laboratory, and then transferred to a recipient woman whose own ova are deficient or absent.

Like other instances of biomedical prosthesis, gamete traffic is driven by difference—the circulating, supplementing, and hybridizing desires, fantasies, and identities of their multiple users, suppliers, and administrators. It is the possibility and availability of prosthetic intervention that determines the degree of deficiency.[6] The real or imagined or desired prosthetic solution proffered by gamete traffic constructs the precise nature of the need or lack it will ameliorate, often expanding on the initial intended application. Technophilic promises of intervention and assistance through prosthesis construct "nature" as defective. However, this degradation of "nature" also destabilizes the conceptual role it occupies on the "nature" side of the binary nature/culture bor-

der. By inviting and justifying technological intervention, the discursive production of an ailing nature in need of technological assistance disarticulates
"nature" from not only ontological but also epistemic, foundational status.
Whether this is a somatophobic degradation of the body or an enabling victory narrative, or both, is an open question.

So, for example, the technique of ovum donation stimulates new demands
and desires—for instance, for peri- and postmenopausal pregnancy—which in
turn steer themselves into the flow of gamete traffic, seeking resolution through
the expansion of childbearing capacity offered by prosthesis. The relation
between desire and technology, however, is reciprocal. While desire for technology sometimes exacerbates the development of a technology, an existing
technology also always stimulates and proliferates essentially unpredictable
desires and fantasies along with resistances and backlash.[7]

The routes, detours, and dead ends that facilitate or block gamete traffic
are relatively unmapped, unpatrolled, and inconsistently traveled. Contemporary gamete traffic interpellates millions of disparate users (recipients and
donors) as well as crews of providers (medical-legal) and pedestrians (popular
reception). This crew of facilitators includes the usual hierarchy: professional
administrators, designers, transportation experts, and researchers (reproductive endocrinologists, gynecologists, embryologists, laboratory technicians,
pharmacologists), an array of toll takers, materials suppliers, repair people, regu-
lators (state licensing boards, insurers, inspectors, safety standards administrators), and road builders (nurses, sonographers, receptionists, accountants,
laboratory equipment salespeople, instrument and machinery manufacturers,
assembly line workers, and so on).

These users and providers modify and contest the emerging routes and
sites of gamete traffic with their partial affinities, divided loyalties, hybrid identities, and shared borders. Regardless of whether gamete traffic facilitates
smooth, efficient flows or causes crippling, artery-jamming stalls and crashes,
the conceptual and material space of its postmodern mapping is ambiguous,
ephemeral, and crisis-ridden.[8] Gamete traffic generates a number of under-
acknowledged political, social, and cultural conundrums (conflicts about access, right of way, illegible signs, speed limit) that complicate the binary logics
supporting atavistic traditional discourses.

The postmodern collapsing, unhinging, and blurring of seemingly inevitable progressions and associations, relationships, and definitions of the body
in general, and reproduction, sex, and kinship in particular, cuts both ways.
While gamete traffic threatens to remove reproduction from its heteronormative context (love, marriage, sexual monogamy), it can also fuel its recuperation. However, it is not the checkpoints and roadblocks or hazards and
social costs that attend all postmodern trafficking that this essay attempts to

map. Rather, my focus is the underthematized circulation of open-ended democratizing opportunities as well as the resistances, popular appropriations, and effects that flow and backfire from the always insecure logic and history of self-identity.

Gamete traffic is best envisioned as a two-way street—not only a constellation of shifting postmodern effects of medical technological capacity crossed with social and economic trends but also an unpredictable stimulus to new social ways of embodied being (a parent, kin). It produces and proliferates—extending bodies' capacities and relations at the same time that it circumscribes them. Incipient revisions in traditional reproductive narratives *result from* technological capacities like the mobilization of gametes at the same time that they are *required by* them. The crisis of such foundational categories as motherhood, family, kinship, and nature identified by some feminist analysts is linked to the massive anxiety that postmodern practices like assisted reproduction have generated.[9]

The obsessive requirement of authorial signature for reproduction—be it genetics or heterosexual intercourse—can never signify stably or singularly. This fact invites individual and institutional practices of countersignature, forgery, and substitution. The ontology of "natural" biogenetic married heterosexual reproduction depended on its binary other of "unnatural" sterility—the "case" of physiological or social pathology (homosexuals, unmarried people, and so on). Now, a new "other" to "natural" reproduction has been introduced by biotechnology—"artificial" donor-assisted asexual reproduction—and it quickly must work to erase its otherness lest it betray its dependence on its binary "natural." It does this by claiming *its* alliance with the "natural"—helping would-be parents have their "own" biogenetic child, an instance of what Avital Ronell aptly calls "retrofit[ing] the technological prosthesis to a metaphysical subject."[10]

Scandalous Travel

Just as the norms of clinical medical practice have relied on teratology (classification of anomalies), the stabilization of reproductive normativity is produced by racialized and gendered reproductive difference. As David Wills notes: "Thus the 'signs' of prosthesis—canes, amputees—are effects of a prosthesis that, in being a reading, signs, and, in being a signature, countersigns, and in countersigning, signs *counter* to what it signs."[11] Gamete traffic ostensibly operates under the sign of *origins*, preserving the markers of embodied difference (sex, race, ethnicity), but it countersigns prosthesis in the sense that it potentially scrambles, redistributes, and obliterates these markers.

Practices of gamete circulation and commodification also interrogate, challenge, and contravene a geneticized and totalizing kinship discourse. At the very moment when the requirement of paternity/authorship devolves into the signature of genetics as sameness/identity, predictor and guarantor of health, and so on, the ensuring logic unwittingly invites alterity and indeterminacy, undermining and loss. It is increasingly socially incoherent to define *parent* or *child* solely on the basis of genetic relations. The contemporary geneticization of culture works to stabilize, disavow, and contain the myriad competing institutional countersignatures of a historically unprecedented post-1950s social, economic, and geographic mobility. Historical shifts involve considerable realignment of parenting arrangements and a massive hybridization of sex-affective relations (through divorce, adoption, fostering, step-, blended, and reconstituted families, chosen families, and the like).

Never before were more people involved in the social rearing of children entirely separated from genetic parenting; nor were as many people unsure and guaranteeless about their genetic forebears. The separation that gamete donation effects between genetic and social parenting, however, is intentionally organized prenatally rather than postnatally.[12] Likewise, once the requirement of parental authorship is obsessively contracted onto the signature of penile-vaginal intercourse, the sameness of reproduction as genetic self-perpetuation that was so anxiously ensured is simultaneously undermined, dispersed, and lost.

Both gamete donors and recipients and their enablers are unauthorized traffickers in genes. Donors scandalize the economy of endogenous essence in their willingness to give away or sell their sacralized germ cells. Egg donors become as consequence-free of obligations for maternal nurture as do sperm donors for paternal support of their genetic offspring, and this leveling of gender asymmetry also collapses conservative assumptions about sex difference. Recipients, on the other hand, ignore or flaunt the importance of genetics in childbearing, declaring themselves willing to call their "own" child one who is not genetically related to them.

It is not merely its technological-organic hybridity or breaching of species boundaries, however, that marks gamete traffic as liminal. Rather, its essential randomness, instability, and circulation of difference mark the traffic in gametes as indeterminate. Any technological-organic synthesis breaches borders traditionally held to be stable, inviolable, and necessary.[13] Gametes have been traditionally represented as dormant and hidden in the *recesses* of the individual bodies (testicles and ovaries) that produced them. Formerly, their fusion in fertilization could occur only as a result of a contiguity following male orgasm and ejaculation achieved through penile-vaginal intercourse occurring during ovulation. Gamete traffic makes the physical transmission of eggs joining sperm (and vice versa) far more powerful and wide-ranging, though no less material than when they get there through heterosexual intercourse.

Now gametes can be viewed, scanned, measured, and photographed as well as extracted, then manipulated in the laboratory, and cryopreserved. Their abstraction and their removal as well as long-distance mobility are inseparable components of their historicized materiality. However, it is the *social* effects of reproduction with donor sperm and donor egg that gamete traffic's "cyborg liminality"[14] unwittingly exacerbates. The now-routine deracination and acoital extraction of gametes from their bodies of origin is both a technological and a social achievement bearing complex signifying effects for donors, recipients, and providers as well as the procreative process. Gamete traffic materially incorporates new routes of relation and kinship as well as revolutionizes the signification of reproduction.

Gender Routing

While gamete traffic entails the extraction and transfer of both male and female gametes, there are important material and symbolic differences that resist efforts at collapsing them into equivalents. Although officially unmarked by gender, the practices and discourses of gamete traffic are thoroughly gendered. Likewise, gender difference marks everyone involved in gamete traffic—not only women. As feminist analyst Mary Ann Doane argues, "when technology intersects with the body in the realm of representation, the question of sexual difference is inevitably involved."[15]

The genetics of male and female gametes may be sex-blind because they are equivalent germ cells, but nothing else about the technologies of extraction and transfer is. That these technologies are solely gamete-driven and technically indifferent to the gendered social relations, power differentials, and ideological practices of their donors, providers, and recipients is an accepted axiom of Western medical discourse and practice. Material social effects are represented as ontological givens. The result is that the relative symbolic and cultural capital that sperm hold over and above eggs is presumed to belong to the sphere of science, not politics.

As we move deeper into the congested loops of gamete traffic, I want to insist on the conceptual distinction between two aspects of ovum transfer: egg *donation* and *extraction*. While consensually donated, ova are extracted via an invasive high-tech pharmacological, medical, and parasurgical in vitro fertilization (IVF) protocol. This difference doubly invests ova with contradictory attributes: donation signifies female agency, will, self-constitution, even rigor, whereas extraction signifies feminine passivity, penetrability, and submission to the clinical practices of reproductive medicine. On the other hand, the equivalent distinction cannot be made of sperm donation because, except for practices of electro-ejaculation for men with spinal cord injuries, sperm donation *is* sperm (self-)extraction.

Both male and female gamete donors are interviewed, examined, classi-fied, and surveyed (both fill out many pages of forms on personal health, medi-cal history, and so on).[16] However, men (and men's bodies) are relatively casual transients in the donation protocol. Women (and women's bodies), on the other hand, are the longer-term medical clients who traverse a protocol of stressful, risky, and invasive procedures. Although the male body may be scru-tinized, the female body is amenable to far greater surveillance.

At the same time that female bodies are hypermedicalized, male bodies and their effluvia are unabashedly inscribed in the main institutional and medi-cal framework supporting the spermatic economy—commercial sperm banks.[17] Egg donation is less commercialized only because of the relative scarcity of ova, in part because it necessitates high-tech professional medical interven-tion as its ontological condition of possibility. Whereas a minority of sperm donors and recipient women (and their partners) are motivated solely by ties of altruism and friendship and practice sperm donation informally in a non-commercial, unregulated private domestic setting, *all* egg donors and recipients—even if united by noncommercial altruistic donation motivation—must pass through institutional reproductive medicine because of the technical IVF re-quirements for egg procurement.[18]

The female homosociality of egg donation is exploited by the official dis-course on egg donation that repeats an axiom of essentialist female sexual dif-ference. Egg donation, according to the discourse of femininity, as altruism and nurturance is a woman-to-woman process of giving and receiving aid. Yet egg extraction, fertilization, and transfer even when discursively packaged as techno-altruism remain sutured to high-technology interventions. Both representationally and materially, women's bodies inconsistently resist imper-sonal phallocentric centralization at the same time they suffer its organizing, controlling, and disciplining thrust more than men's.

In addition, whatever mediations sperm and ova pass through in enter-ing the flow of gamete traffic, it is women, as noted above, who are the uni-versal recipients of both sperm and egg donation. Women are reproductive subjects in ways that both bind and free them. A closer look, however, re-veals not only differences of gamete travel direction or telos (women's bod-ies) but also differences in the kind of travel each undertakes. Sperm are heterosocial travelers (from men's bodies to women's), and ova are homosocial travelers (from women's bodies to women's). Sperm cannot be transferred homosocially from donor man to recipient man but is only reproductively meaningful if it reaches the body of a woman. Sperm heterosociality can gen-erate masculinist gender narratives that may be read as heroic, expansionist, even conquering, a mythos of men's "natural" alterity. Ovum homosociality, on the other hand, can be read as a feminine narrative of insular conservatism, a limitation of expansionist imagination, or a failure to confront alterity.

Shifting Gears

At the same time, however, ovatic narratives can also be read as politically bidirectional. A homosocial telos for ova may be taken as autonomous self-direction or cautious peer bonding. However, the homosocial traffic in ova is not direct and unmediated. Although ova do not move heterosocially, as do sperm, their homosocial route is multiply marked by the overdetermined masculinist detours and checkpoints of biomedicine and embryology. Ova must first be fertilized. Only then can the resulting preimplantation embryo be transferred to a recipient woman. The patterns of gamete traffic are thus complexly overdetermined by prior cultural and material constructions of gender at the same time that they challenge them.

The fact that donor sperm have a heterosocial route and ova a homosocial one may be used to fuel essentialist gender ideology as well as challenge and undermine it. The ephemeral and casual aspects of sperm production associate it with masculinity, whereas its sensual aspect (link to orgasm and pleasure) links it to feminine sensuality. The heterosocial terminus of sperm can be interpreted as another heroic gender victory narrative of adventuring gamete explorers who risk venturing far from their origins to found new lineages. However, sperm heterosociality may equally be read as a narrative of defeat and loss, a failure of masculine self-sufficiency and autotelism and capitulation to heterodomesticity because of lack of skill, autonomy, and so forth to survive without women.

Put another way, donating one's gametes for flexible accumulation earns one a different ticket, depending on gender. So, the female gamete gets to travel for the first time in her life, although she must earn her passage by surmounting the dangerous obstacle course of donation (and gets no sex out of the deal). The male, on the other hand, donates easily and harmlessly and gets to see his gametes well dispersed but suffers a proscription on his fucking.

In addition to feminine altruism or reticence, the homosocial trajectory of ovum donation may be read as a masculinist practice, also normatively equivocal. Women who willingly donate their eggs possess skills and attitudes that are prototypically masculine: willingness to take risks, stoical endurance of pain and discomfort, perseverance, rationality, and organization. In addition, and far more scandalous, is donor women's willingness to make public and (relatively) indiscriminate what was once tied to an intimate scenario of eggs accessed by sperm supplied only through husband intercourse. The contemporary dispersion of ova can be viewed as a flagrant but deliberate scattering of their eggs (making them accessible to a public institution rather than a "private" husband) and taking money for it as well.

While the work involved in egg donation is ephemeral (compared with the work of surrogacy), it continues to be an ethical scandal. As a condition of its traffic, female genetics is detoured around reproduction, materially separating the formerly inextricable: the biogenetic. In addition, it makes reproductive consequences as irrelevant for female donors as it does for males. Egg donors are as socially and legally consequence-free of obligations of maternal support as are sperm donors for paternal support of their genetic offspring. Since patriarchal reproductive norms encode maternal support as nurturance and paternal support as economic provision, this gamete equivalence is an unnatural horror.

After all, women who can snap the glass tops off drug ampules, load a syringe, and give themselves a daily intramuscular shot in the buttocks with a three-inch needle for two weeks of their stimulation cycle—not to mention accurately calibrating a baroque medication schedule and keeping an array of medical appointments, including having their blood drawn three times a week for two weeks—are not flighty wimps or passive dupes. Equally, however, ova's homosociality may be essentialized positively or negatively: romanticized as greater connectedness and capacity for empathy and nurturance or dismissed as the hesitant conservatism of self-protective homebodies.

In comparison to the baroque protocols of female gamete donation, male gamete donation is simple, nonrisky, and noninvasive. Sperm is produced by donor masturbation. Because sperm provision requires semen and semen is provided through ejaculation, it is usually associated with male orgasm. The provision of ejaculate through masturbation leaves intact male gamete donation's association with at least orgasm, though not coitus. The requirement of masturbatory ejaculation not only materially separates sperm donation from the body of a woman but also symbolically separates it from any "higher" reproductive telos.

Institutional sperm donation socially constructs the donor as a paid public masturbator even though ejaculate is provided in a private room of a sperm bank or clinic. While all institutional Western medicine normalizes the permeability of the boundary between public and private—strangers are authorized to view and touch the bodies of strangers—through its clinic protocols, institutional sperm donation intensifies this breach by introducing sex, or one variant of it, into the medical setting.

Female gamete donation, on the other hand, ostensibly because of the vicissitudes of the physiology of egg production, entails no equivalent sexual or protosexual associations. Egg production coincidentally upholds the norms of feminine sexual subjectivity—reproductive but not pleasure-centered. It is always an asexual, medically managed physiological event. It is, in short, chaste. After pharmacologic stimulation to produce multiple eggs, retrieval requires the transvaginal passage of a micro catheter into the ovary. The female gamete donor, whether out of love for an infertile friend or as a recruited anonymous donor in a donor IVF program, is an asexual gynecological patient, albeit a temporary and a paid one. She is nevertheless subject to institutional medical protocol and control—the organization and manipulation of high-technology reproduction. Conversely, high-tech institutional reproductive medicine is hyperinvested in the female body not only as an object to be manipulated and inserted into its protocols but also as a subject to be interpellated, seduced, and educated into the promises of its techno-world.

The differential sociomedical processes of gamete procurement line up isomorphically with the facticity of physiology, thereby validating the gendered binary cultural assumptions that produced them in the first place.[19] The social process of egg provision is represented as asexual, as is the biology of egg *production*, and the social act of sperm provision is represented as ineluctably sexual, as is biological sperm *production*. The hypersexual and the asexual— both social norms—are all too easily mapped onto male and female physiological sex difference. Gamete procurement recapitulates phantasmatic representations of sexual difference by constructing sperm as sex-driven, promiscuous, and lusty and representing ova as sexually disinterested, relational, and asexual.

That the spermatic economy is one of plenitude overdetermines reception both individually and institutionally. The traffic in sperm offers donors, recipients, and medical providers relatively easy, prolific, and low(er)-cost opportunities for provision, supply, exchange, and storage. Despite its telos in the dispersion of biogenetic paternity *and* the social effect of creating a surplus spermatic economy, sperm donation's tie to the physiology of male masturbation—its individuality, control, and autonomy—functions to bolster phallic unicity *as well as* to undermine it.

That these qualities are not equated in an ovatic economy constrained by relative scarcity, expense, difficulty of procurement, and perishability (unfertilized ova are intractable to freezing and thawing) bears scrutiny. The confounding indeterminacy, opacity, and unrepresentability of the female body demands relentless medicalization—probings, visualizations, and penetrations. Egg provision remains a matter of *extraction* via high-technology protocols.

In addition, most gamete traffic is routed through the embryology laboratory. Certainly, all ovum traffic and most sperm traffic (except for instances of simple sperm donation between friends) is supported, worked on, graded, and even disposed of by lab personnel. Here, too, ova and sperm are treated quite differently. Egg retrieval as well as laboratory manipulations of ova are usually done in low lighting conditions that are intended to replicate the maternal uterine environment.[20] Sperm, on the other hand, are handled in normal lighting and are subjected to many rigorous procedures; they are probed and poked, timed, and measured, separated from the rest of their ejaculate, spun in a centrifuge, and finally cryopreserved, a procedure from which they emerge unharmed and viable, unlike their more delicate gamete fellow travelers. Yet sperm robustness and ovum delicacy are not essential attributes of body parts but residual patriarchal cultural ascriptions that have become self-justifying science.

At the same time, however, there can be some strategic advantages to the normative insistence on female maternal identity and the underrepresentation of female desire. Despite the resistant hermeticism of the ovum to extraction, female gamete provision, no less than male provision, technologically enables the social effect of distributing and dispersing maternal identity and responsibility, thereby destabilizing its unicity. Perhaps this historically unprecedented monstrous fragmenting of maternity can only be allowed *if* it is shown to be the effect of disciplining and torturing a recalcitrant and chaste female body. As long as egg extraction is represented as coaxing or flushing out a reluctant nested ovum into the visibly chaotic and cacophonous arteries of a (dangerous) high-speed public domain, the full monstrosity of mobilized ova is contained. After all, a fem would only go butch under duress.

However, narratives that represent egg donation as the masculinist perversion of feminine essence must contend with competing ones that construct egg extraction equally essentially as the telos of proper femininity—redemptive nurturance and woman-to-woman aid through suffering and sacrifice. Egg donation does not evoke the *casual* masculine agency of autonomous or promiscuous sperm donation but is linked (more than sperm donation) to the baroque and public coordination and institutional relaying of female informed consent, perseverance, and commitment. It makes a certain ironic sense that the weightier essence of maternity cannot be casually challenged but only tortuously confronted, materially and ideologically, whereas the ephemeral quality of paternity is reflected in both the relatively facile procedures and widespread acceptance of sperm donation.

The deracination and debiologizing of ova from the female bodies that produced them and their transfer to other female bodies that desire them technically makes possible what has always obtained socially—the circulation of partial elective maternities. Professional medical providers as well as many feminists consider this technological instantiation of distributed maternity so bizarre as to necessitate disavowal.[21] Fundamentalism must defend itself against its own desires, hence its reiterative denigration of desire and refusal to acknowledge the ontological role of desire in the complex social construction of "infertility." Feminist fundamentalism's relentlessly universalizing and acontextual crude antinatalism dismisses the sometimes desperate desires of women for biogenetic maternity: "what is desire created in the context of mandatory motherhood."[22] Such mobile and mobilizable maternity may send female agency careening off in ambivalent and indeterminable directions.[23]

Even the most axiomatic misogynist principles and subject positions are intrinsically unstable, always defended against excess, deviation, and implosion. Ovum traffic creates expanded social possibilities, disseminating and proliferating maternal identities, making it more difficult to pass off an identity as stable than before. When the technological achievement of maternity distributed among genetic (ovum-providing), gestational (uterus-providing), and social-legal (nurturance-providing) mothers is lamented by social conservatives as scandalous fragmentation, its many unintended and unpredictable effects are ignored or suppressed along with ambivalence and difference.

Distributed maternity, like "natural" unitary maternity, can be "good," "bad," or "indifferent"—depending on the actors' social circumstances and histories. Neither has an essential ahistorical "natural" meaning that exists apart from the uses to which it is put. Feminist theorist Mary Ann Doane notes that maternity poses many terrifying boundary-confusing questions (the distinction between self and other, subject and object) at the same time that it also threatens paternal signification systems based on differentiation by its flaunting of maternal-fetal symbiosis as well as by its guarantee of knowledge of paternity.[24]

Border Crossings

Gamete traffic is paradoxical because it both fragments and unifies, enables and excludes. Although it can bolster class and race inequality, dispersing procreation from dyadic heterosexual coitus extends the conjugal dyad into a widened circle of actors, foregrounding its socialization. Sexual conservatives recognize the defamiliarizing tendencies that gamete traffic's dispersion facilitates. For others, the differentiation of family from kinship, creating a "field of procreators whose relationship to one another and to the product of conception is contained in the act of conception itself and not in the family as such," is welcomed. These effects "add new possibilities to the conceptualization of intimacy in relationships."[25]

When it is foregrounded for the as yet unassimilable differences it makes—as the unprecedented cyborg transformations they are[26]—rather than romanced and recuperated as only more of the same, gamete traffic can stimulate and challenge traditional epistemic and ontological parameters of origins and histories.

At the same time, liberal medical discourse's hypocrisy and class bias can be seen in its exclusion of very poor people from donation, although there are industrywide de facto exceptions to the prohibition against allowing donation by the desperate poor.[27] Pious caveats against accepting indigent donors attempt to deflect criticism of crass commodification. The vast majority of poor and working-class people, the cohort most in need of treatment, are excluded from using reproductive technologies for several de facto reasons. Insurmountable excluding factors are inability to pay high out-of-pocket medical costs, lack of high-end medical insurance, and/or lack of informational or cultural familiarity with high-technology reproductive options like gamete donation.[28] Gamete traffic has unapologetically linked the public sphere of economics (paid donor remuneration and marketed gametes) to the private realm of sex/love and body interiority.

The economics of gamete provision is an exemplary site of contemporary biomedicine's denial of any economic motivation on the part of providers and health care delivery institutions. Biomedical ambivalence toward its own essential alliance with commercialization, however, is not driven exclusively by profit and biomedical empire building or contravened by donor altruism and identification with infertile couples. Gamete traffic practices starkly force the subtext of class within biomedicine to the discursive surface—from which it can be contested and confronted.

Heterosex

Donor procreation attempts to recuperate the biogenetic family by intervening to aid conception that did not occur as a result of private dyadic heterosex, "for the same technologies that enable some infertile people to become genetic parents also place the whole notion of genetic parenthood in jeopardy."[29] No longer does heterosex have a material or symbolic monopoly over procreation. Gamete donation is invoked as a solution to the problem of failed biogenetic parenting, though it itself is a bypass rather than a solution of an intractable problem. While parasitic on the desire for genetic parenting, gamete traffic also subverts the very drive toward geneticization that rationalized its development. Intended parent(s), gamete donors or recipients, also displace the desire for heterosex with desire for a child. "Thus, reproductive technologies carry the threat (or the promise) of delegitimating genetic parenthood, and even of fracturing commonsense understandings of what 'the biological' is."[30]

Through reprotech's prenatal, indeed preconception, interventions, donor gametes radically displace the biogenetic family with myriad unintended effects and new ontologies—both social and corporeal. Parenthood is expanded to include "a number of contributions from parties previously uninvolved in the conception of new persons."[31] Once reproduction has been expanded to include "noncoital means of conception"[32] despite efforts to limit this expansion to infertile couples, it necessarily broadens the definition of "mother" to include those for whom "coital conception" is not a possible *or desired* route, that is, to those whose bodies cannot *or will not* conceive through heterosex. Heterosexual desiring parents who use gamete donation have often acknowledged that their desire for genetic connection to their offspring is subsidiary to their desire for a child. Marilyn Strathern argues, "If finally what remains intact is the intention or desire to have a child, then that desire is what the child 'reproduces.' So in becoming a means to fulfill such a desire, procreation itself ceases to be the crucial reproductive moment. We might see that moment as instead the acting out of intention or desire."[33]

Gamete Circulation

While medical, commercial, and "private" routes of gamete traffic are anything but anarchic, they are equally neither predictable nor deterministic. The emerging history of gamete donation is marked by continuous contestation and shifting realignments among participants. Gamete donors, recipients, professional providers, marketers, and bystanders differ in their interests not only from one another but also within any self-identified group. Ambivalence, exclusions, and the vicissitudes of circulation make gamete traffic, like "natural" procreation, porous and unstable. We have seen how gamete traffic projects traditional gender assumptions *and* enables their disarticulation, facilitating a diversity of possible reproductive experiences including oppositional and erased ones. For example, a feminist advocate of gynogenesis (the still experimental and speculative fusing of the genetic material from the ova of two different women) notes both its collusion with geneticization as well as its violation of the biological familial norm of one man and one woman.[34]

This continual reciprocal interaction of conflicting appropriations among providers, recipients, and donors continues to relay its permutations and uneven developments. For example, the increasing suturing of sperm donation to state-regulated licensing and regulation of institutions within capital-intensive biomedicine is marked by contested and shifting resistances—innovations, ambivalences, and redefinitions—on the part of both donors and recipients.

Gamete provision by anonymous donors and the use of donor gametes by intended parents articulates with differentials of social, economic, and political power, both between donors and recipients and within each group, as well. Because medicalization is a historical process, its always contested status complicates any universalizing analysis (e.g., that all donors are exploited, or all recipients are privileged). Critics of medicalization often represent contemporary institutional medical practice as totalizing and monopolistic.[35] If high-technology biomedicine is a historical outcome,[36] it should not be reified into an eternally inhering one. The contemporary forms of procreative medicalization continue to be debated, modified, negotiated, and resisted—both within and outside professional medicine. The contemporary shape of gamete traffic is a result, but it is also an element of its next wave.

Hybrid appropriations and applications of donor technologies can transform prosthetic procreative supplementation of kinship and family into enhancements or enlargements of deficient democracy and shrunken social possibilities (in need of assistance)—or they can be the somatophobic (dreamed of) transcendence of deficient (female) nature. Misogyny may be more the ally of technophobia rather than technophilia.

Put another way, to theorize about whether gamete donation practices in particular and body prostheses in general can ever be merely supplementary or are always also additive raises the issue of power within gamete provision and use—for recipients, donors, providers, and, in the case of procreation, offspring. Gamete donation practices embody a plurality of repercussions that are both recuperative and disruptive of conservative kinship ideology. While gamete traffic can produce alienating effects, including the gynophobia charge leveled by many feminists,[37] it *also and at the same time* can stimulate the radical revision and hybridization of social relations and identities. It is impossible to construe gamete traffic along a binary model—as either inherently repressive or liberatory.

Because of the relative mutability of its flows and its indeterminate openness, the safety and beneficence of gamete traffic is essentially unensurable, for better and for worse. There are no liberatory guarantees or totalizingly repressive outcomes. Rather, there are multiple consequential disruptions of *one*, private, unified body—potentially co-optable, resistant, *or* both. Gamete traffic can be either normalizing or disruptive of stereotypic sexual difference, depending on the positions and histories of its travelers.

Ironically, it is the experimental or "language" poets and their theorizing bedfellows who know this: "Isn't otherness otherness, Stein might say? And isn't an other a how as much as a what? Shouldn't how and what make common cause?"[38] Gamete traffic might also be a *way*, a how among many otherings that is also a way of being fruitful and multiplying the wonder and terror and promise that drive the hard bargain of being human in fin de siècle postmodernity. Whether it becomes a way out of present conundrums—and a way into new ones—remains to be seen.

Notes

1. See Sarah Franklin's discussions of the naturalization of technological intervention and the reconstruction of assisted reproduction as crisis-laden and miraculous. "Making Miracles: Scientific Progress and the Facts of Life," in *Reproducing Reproduction: Kinship, Power, and Technological Innovation*, ed. Sarah Franklin and Helena Ragoné (Philadelphia: University of Pennsylvania Press, 1998), 106.
2. Marilyn Strathern, "Displacing Knowledge: Technology and the Consequences for Kinship," in *Conceiving the New World Order: The Global Politics of Reproduction*, ed. Faye D. Ginsburg and Rayna Rapp (Berkeley and Los Angeles: University of California Press, 1995), 352.
3. Donna Haraway, "A Cyborg Manifesto," in *Simians, Cyborgs, and Women: The Reinvention of Nature* (New York: Routledge, 1991).
4. Ibid., 154.
5. Judith Butler understands that "to invoke matter is to invoke a sedimented history of sexual hierarchy and sexual erasures." *Bodies That Matter: On the Discursive Limits of Sex* (New York: Routledge, 1993), 49.
6. Mark Wigley notes: "In a strange way, the body depends upon the foreign elements that transform it. It is reconstituted and propped up on the 'supporting limbs' that extend it. Indeed, it becomes a side effect of its extensions. The prosthesis reconstructs the body, transforming its limits, at once extending and convoluting its borders. The body itself becomes artifice." "Prosthetic Theory: The Discipline of Architecture," *Assemblage* 15 (1991): 8–9.
7. Rosalind Petchesky, arguing against simplistic theories of passive female victimization, notes: "Women throughout the nineteenth and twentieth centuries have often *generated* demands for technologies such as birth control, childbirth anesthesia, or infertility treatments, or they have welcomed them as benefits." "Fetal Images: The Power of Visual Culture in the Politics of Reproduction," in *Theorizing Feminism: Parallel Trends in the Humanities and Social Sciences*, ed. June C. Herrmann and Abigail J. Stewart (Boulder, Colo.: Westview Press, 1994), 413 (original emphasis).
8. By "postmodern" I mean the contested, ambivalent, antifoundational, and undecided character of our contemporary cultural practice of gamete provision, exchange, donation, sale, and symbolization. I invoke the modifier "postmodern" to signify the essential contestability, uncertainly, and insecurity inhering in a practice's evocation of diverse adaptations, emendations, appropriations, and resistances.
9. See Sarah Franklin, "Postmodern Procreation: A Cultural Account of Assisted Reproduction," in Ginsburg and Rapp, *Conceiving the New World Order*, 323–345.
10. Avital Ronell elaborates: "In other words, the technological prosthesis would merely be an amplifier and intensifier borrowed by a centered subject whose fragmentation is, as they say, a simulation—that is, a device for *disavowing* fragmentation, selflessness, or, on another register, castration" (her emphasis). "A Disappearance of Community," in *Immersed in Technology: Art and Virtual Environments*, ed. Mary Anne Moser et al. (Cambridge, Mass.: MIT Press, 1996), 120.
11. David Wills, *Prosthesis* (Stanford, Calif.: Stanford University Press, 1995), 60 (original emphasis).
12. Even liberal ethicist John Robertson notes this distinction. *Children of Choice: Freedom and the New Reproductive Technologies* (Princeton, N. J.: Princeton University Press, 1994), 121.
13. Technophobes rue the invasion of the "once sacred texts of life" (viii), the enormity of "enclosing and commodifying the human body itself, the last ecological invasion" (ix), the "colonization of the human body" (ix). They exhort us to "per-

form the exorcism" (x). Jeremy Rifkin, introduction to Andrew Kimbrell, *The Human Body Shop: The Engineering and Marketing of Life* (San Francisco: HarperSanFrancisco, 1993).

14. Franklin, "Postmodern Procreation," 337.

15. Mary Ann Doane, "Technophilia: Technology, Representation, and the Feminine." In *Body/Politics: Women and the Discourses of Science*, ed. Mary Jacobus et al. (New York: Routledge, 1990).

16. A critic of egg donation who posed as a donor and underwent the intake process at a New York fertility clinic asserts a gender difference in donor selection criteria. "Programs for egg and sperm donation emphasize drastically different attributes, suggesting a classic double standard: virtually no attention was given to my intelligence; academic achievement was not focused on in the course of the interviews, nor was I subject to any intelligence tests, which are de rigueur at some sperm banks." Sharon Lerner, "The Price of Eggs: Undercover in the Infertility Industry," *Ms.* (March–April 1996): 28–34.

17. Institutionalization is not a technical requirement for sperm donation, itself a relatively low technology procedure. For a discussion of the ways semen banking establishes a hierarchy of power among men as it, at the same time, potentially disrupts it, see Matthew Schmidt and Lisa Jean Moore "Constructing a 'Good Catch,' Picking a Winner," in *Cyborg Babies: From Techno-Sex to Techno-Tots*, Robbie Davis-Floyd and Joseph Dumit, eds. (New York: Routledge, 1998).

18. Once ova are obtained from a donor, they are examined in an embryology lab, and select ones are either fertilized in a petri dish (in IVF) or placed in the fallopian tube with sperm in gamete intrafallopian transfer (GIFT).

19. I can imagine/theorize that should women's bodies ever come to be less bounded by the naturalized norms of a heterosexist sexual economy, the "scientific" methods of ovum extraction will also be different (perhaps as simple, noninvasive, and painless as cutting a fingernail).

20. Charis Thompson Cussins notes that the laboratory provision of a putatively maternal environment contrasts with the retrieval's instrumental invasion of the woman's body. "This crossover of the properties of techniques to the women's body and woman-as-mother to the lab creates the matrix in which reproduction can be conceived of and produced medicotechnically." "Producing Reproduction: Techniques of Normalization and Naturalization in Infertility Clinics" in Franklin and Ragoné, *Reproducing Reproduction*, 93.

21. For an example of typical feminist worship of maternal-fetal symbiosis as a model of community, consider Barbara Katz Rothman's universalizing hagiography of pregnancy: "We have in *every* pregnant woman a walking contradiction to the segmentation of our lives: pregnancy does not permit it. In pregnancy the private self, the sexual, familial self, announces itself wherever we go." *Recreating Motherhood: Ideology and Technology in a Patriarchal Society* (New York: Norton, 1989), 59 (my emphasis).

22. Robyn Rowland, *Living Laboratories: Women and Reproductive Technologies* (Bloomington: Indiana University Press, 1992), 272.

23. A new bash-feminism genre appears in infertility memoirs and treatment guides that emphasizes the regrets of those middle-age women who rejected marriage and family in their reproductive youth. One writer's unreflective social and epistemic conservatism channels her ambivalence into repeated essentializing of maternity: "Is it sweet, the height of sisterliness, all this sharing of bodies and body parts? Or is it a transgression of some basic order, of nature itself, herself, and of the very notion of maternity?" Anne Taylor Fleming, *Motherhood Deferred: A Woman's Journey* (New York: G.P. Putnam's Sons, 1994), 96–97.

24. Doane, "Technophilia," 170, 175.

25. Strathern, "Displacing Knowledge," 352, 353.
26. The assisted-reproduction pre-embryo that is fertilized in a laboratory petri dish and then grows in that culture environment for the next forty-eight to seventy-two hours until transfer to a woman's uterus is an embryonic cyborg, a human-machine hybrid. Likewise, the multiple ova (ten, twenty, thirty, or more) that are removed from a woman whose ovaries have been pharmacologically stimulated can be thought of as cyborg ova and the hyperovulating woman as a cyborg ovulator.
27. Surrogate brokers and agencies are particularly sensitive to the charge of capitalizing on women's economic desperation. See Helena Ragoné, *Conception in the Heart* (Boulder, Colo.: Westview Press, 1994), chap. 1.
28. In a chapter designed to acquaint users with the exact (range of) costs of specific infertility treatments "to avoid misconceptions, and to prepare [them] for future financial demands as [they are] about to embark on treatment" (347), Richard Marrs, M.D., ultimately loyal to his provider colleagues, is never critical or apologetic about astronomical costs or militant in calling for universal economic access. He is even and rational: "Because costs can mount up so quickly, it is extremely important at this stage of your decision-making process to get a complete picture" (353). Before going on to lament the lack of national guidelines in insurance coverage, he concedes, "So expensive, in fact, that unless a large portion of the cost is borne by a couple's insurance carrier, many can't afford to even try it" (363). Richard Marrs, *Dr. Richard Marrs' Fertility Book: America's Leading Fertility Expert Tells You Everything You Need to Know about Getting Pregnant* (New York: Dell, 1997).
29. Michelle Stanworth, ed. *Reproductive Technologies: Gender, Motherhood, and Medicine* (Minneapolis: University of Minnesota Press, 1987), 21.
30. Ibid.
31. Franklin, "Postmodern Procreation," 336.
32. Robertson, *Children of Choice*, 6.
33. Strathern, "Displacing Knowledge," 355.
34. Elizabeth Sourbut, "Gynogenesis: A Lesbian Appropriation of Reproductive Technologies," in *Between Monsters, Goddesses, and Cyborgs: Feminist Confrontations with Science, Medicine, and Cyberspace*, ed. Nina Lykke and Rosi Braidotti (Atlantic Highlands, N. J.: 1996), 228–229.
35. Radical feminist critics of the medicalization of childbirth narrate its successful (98 percent of U.S. births occur in hospitals) appropriation from woman-assisted midwifery. What they omit, however, is both the accompanying demand of middle- and upper-middle-class white women for medical school admission and changing norms of male-female mixing. The professional male obstetrical victory over midwifery entailed changes in perceptions of modesty and appropriateness of male physicians' being present at birth, a formerly all-female social and cultural event. The admission of male obstetricians to birthing, however, also required the discursive disarticulation of female genitalia from sex and seduction. Likewise, the attending male obstetrician's disinterestedness had to be secured by disclaimers of sexual interest in the birthing woman's genitalia.

 The transformation of birthing from a private, female-centered natural process into a medical event presided over by the male professional, however, also represents a revolutionary shift in gender norms—by bringing female genitalia (out of the home) into the public space of the male obstetrician and his institution, the hospital. While nineteenth-century state regulation of childbearing was also tied to industrial capitalism's labor needs, the historical intentions of primary actors are never exhaustive or stable and do not isomorphically determine effects. Emergent feminist struggles for the unprecedented public mixing of women and men in all formerly homosocial spheres of production, including medical school and the practice of obstetrics, strategically utilized the imputed desexualizing of women that produced it.

36. Paula A. Treichler, "Feminism, Medicine, and the Meaning of Childbirth," in Jacobus et al., *Body/Politics*, 118.

37. See Michele Stanworth for a useful summary of feminist opposition to assisted reproduction. "Birth Pangs: Contraceptive Technologies and the Threat to Motherhood," in *Conflicts in Feminism*, ed. M. Hirsch and E. Fox Keller (New York: Routledge, 1990), 289.

38. Jonathan Monroe, "Poetry, the University, and the Culture of Distraction," *diacritics* 26, nos. 3–4 (fall–winter 1996): 7.

"God is Stronger Than Medicine"

LESLIE DWYER

Islam and the Cultural Politics of Contraception in Indonesia

ONE AFTERNOON in Java, as the monsoon rains fell heavy and hard, I sheltered with a friend under the plastic tarp of a sidewalk restaurant. Over cakes of fried tempe and sticky bottles of Fanta soda, my friend Dewi, a student at one of Java's most prestigious universities and a devout Muslim, exchanged stories with me about our families. Our mothers had each had six children, we discovered. She was surprised by this, she told me, because she had expected that in America, a "developed" country, families would no longer be so large. And I had thought it probable that in the years since 1970, when the Indonesian state's intensive population program began in Java, a middle-class family such as hers would have limited itself to a size somewhat smaller, if not to the "two children are enough" encouraged by family-planning sloganeers. I asked her about this, and she replied, "Oh yes, in fact my mother was one of the first people in her village to follow family planning (*keluarga berencana*, or KB). She took the pill for fifteen years." At my look of astonishment she continued, "God wanted her to have a big family, and God is stronger than medicine."

Puzzling over this conversation later, I tried to interpret what Dewi had said. My first thoughts were that Dewi's mother must have been doing something wrong, forgetting to take her pills or taking them at other than the recommended intervals. Steeped in the biomedical discourses of my own culture with their emphases on symptom and cure, risk and cause, I wondered with concern about her health and that of her children. But as I heard similar claims repeated by other Javanese Muslim women, I began to explore different ways of listening to these narratives. These were not stories of what Westerners might call contraceptive failures. The women who told them did not seem to take them as evidence of a "problem" to which blame needed to be attached so it could be "fixed," nor did they appear to question overtly the efficacy or appropriateness of contraception more generally. The most important issue at stake was not, I began to believe, whether these women's contraceptives were "working" but in what contexts and for what ends.

This essay explores how we might interpret stories such as Dewi's. Addressing contraception's complicity in discourses of Javanese culture, Islamic piety, and nationalist and international ideologies and technologies of "development," it examines how different frames of analysis highlight particular aspects of women's experience. My aim is not to offer a definitive reading of my friend's statement, for I would argue that such closure or analytic mastery runs counter not only to the partiality inherent in cross-cultural translations but also to the perspectives of Javanese Muslim women themselves, embedded as they are in a contested and unstable discursive field. Rather, I use these stories as a starting point for trying to understand how reproductive technologies shift meanings as they move across flows of information and interpretation and become enmeshed in local, state, and transnational concerns. My argument is that instead of seeing reproductive technologies working *on* a universal, generic "body," we can understand contraception to simultaneously work *through* and construct processes of embodiment in ways that are at once biological, cultural, and political. As Javanese women move through their lives, certain ways of constructing embodied experience become foregrounded and backgrounded, leading not only to changing perspectives on what it means to use contraception but also to ways of combining birth control and bodies that have particular cultural and political effects. By contextualizing contraception within these relations of significance and power I hope to offer ways of hearing Javanese women's narratives that are attuned to their local resonances, while introducing a creative note of dissonance into the way these technologies are normally understood in Euro-American practice and thought.

Contraceptive Contexts

I tried family planning, but it was not a success. The first time, I used the spiral [IUD] and I became pregnant with twins, but later I miscarried. Twins, that would be hard, wouldn't it? The second time, I was given the injection [Depo-Provera] and afterward I had my daughter. She was born very large—four and a half kilos. But my body is strong, stronger than family planning. My husband says I am like a buffalo. God created me strong to bear these children.[1]

Anthropologists have long been faced with the task of trying to explain utterances and practices that seem from within their own systems of belief and behavior to be inaccurate or misleading, while at the same time taking seriously the cultural meanings and effects of these discourses. For those concerned with sickness, healing, and other embodied experience, it is tempting to resolve this tension by positing "the body" to be something upon which culture "writes" but which it does not fundamentally change. Bodies are imagined, narrated, or translated, attended to through practices of therapy, ritual, or aesthetic modification, but these actions are ultimately categorized as interpretations or adornments of a generic reality, that shared ground of the humanist dictum that we are all the same, under the skin. Following this logic, one could categorize these stories of "God and medicine" as culturally bounded symbolic elaborations of a reality more accurately apprehended through the investigative and explanatory techniques of modern biological science. Like the Azande in Evans-Pritchard's classic discussion of non-Western "rationality," these women could be seen as filling in gaps in cause and effect created by a lack of developed scientific "knowledge" with cultural "belief."[2] Provided with the relevant facts about contraception and its effects on the body, these women would come to see that, God notwithstanding, the workings of medicine transcend their experiences of it.

It is this type of framework that has been commonly relied on and promoted by aid organizations in formulating population control projects in Indonesia and other places identified as "underdeveloped." According to development experts and state planners, there are two kinds of birth control in Indonesia now: modern, technological methods of contraception developed in Western laboratories according to culturally neutral scientific criteria, and "indigenous" methods of birth spacing. These "indigenous" methods (a label that ignores the tremendous diversity to be found in multiethnic, multireligious, multilingual Indonesia) are, in population control discourse, tied to (at best) "tradition" and (at worst) "ignorance." Culture, power, and history are seen as immaterial to biomedical contraception, while they are conversely viewed as "factors" to be overcome or manipulated in the case of nonbiomedical fertility regulation. As the World Bank, in a report entitled *Strategies for Family Planning Promotion*, advises: "A . . . program implies a long-term commitment to the family planning program client. It must recognize that *behavior change is evolutionary* and affected by many determinants, facilitated or hindered by *factors in the client's environment*. Interventions must go beyond persuasive messages to directly address the *barriers to behavior change*."[3] In these kinds of narratives, local meanings of sexuality, bodies, reproduction, health, gender, or indeed development itself are reduced to "environment," a static, timeless, premodern state that can be overcome only by an "evolutionary" advance to a universal modern.

One could point out many flaws and dangers with these kinds of discourses.[4] But one of the most obvious problems with applying this line of reasoning to the stories of Javanese women is that many of their narrators are quite conversant with ideas of the biomedical body. Dewi, for instance, is a member of Indonesia's educated elite, schooled in basic sciences and comfortable seeking care from Western-trained doctors rather than practitioners of Javanese healing techniques. She is also an adherent of a modernist Islam supportive of the project of science; indeed, on other occasions she told me that the Qur'an anticipated Western discoveries, containing within it predictions of humans reaching the moon and developing atomic weaponry. To call her relationship to "rationality" and biomedical explanation one of simple ignorance or even rejection would be to disregard her positioning within networks of religious allegiance, local culture, and a transnationally inflected modernity. A more nuanced understanding of how, why, and when contraception "works" for Javanese Muslims is necessary to understand her story.

How, then, might we otherwise approach narratives like Dewi's? One framework anthropologists have used to explain similar conjunctures is the concept of medical pluralism.[5] Rather than positioning "traditional belief" and "Western medicine" as stages on a progressive time line, different systems for understanding bodies and their workings are seen as possibilities available for people to draw on as they seek care or explanations. And indeed Javanese women have a wide variety of choices, from high-priced private hospitals to public health clinics to assorted traditional and not-so-traditional healers, available to them as options for the organization of bodily experience. But as they navigate these choices, creative conjunctures occur that escape the intentions of the producers and distributors of contraceptive devices and blur the boundaries between these sites.

Although in Java family planning has an overwhelming presence in public culture, owing primarily to massive promotional campaigns, for the most part state programs have not focused on offering explanations of the functioning of various contraceptives. In the absence of hegemonic understandings of how birth control works—or, more accurately, because of a focus primarily on family planning's *political* effects as part of a broader state development apparatus rather than its *biological* operations—interpretations of its functioning differ widely. For instance, the IUD, I was told, works by killing a man's semen on contact, an opinion that prompted some religious women to question whether it was permissible given Qur'anic injunctions against infanticide. And when I spoke with women about the contraceptive injection Depo-Provera, I frequently heard that its effect was to make a woman's body confused or capricious (*kacau*), bleeding at the wrong times or sometimes not bleeding at all, thus making the otherwise orderly process of conception impossible. Other women told me they preferred the "calendar method" because there was no chance that it would destroy living matter, it inculcated religious *disiplin* by encouraging one to abstain periodically from sexual indulgence, and it provided women with a sanctioned means of regular escape from a husband's unwanted attentions. Likewise, the birth control pill is thought by many women not only to be an effective means of preventing pregnancy or, through its daily discipline, increasing one's faith or power but to be a way to halt unwanted bleeding. Within Islamic doctrine, menstruation is considered to be a state of impurity during which women are prohibited from performing the five daily prayers, fasting, or other religious observances. Women who make the hajj pilgrimage to Mecca often take the pill in order to be able to perform their religious obligations in a state of purity (although the propriety of this practice is disputed), while in some areas of Indonesia the pill has even been promoted by the government as the "Ramadan pill." Women, it was hoped, would try the pill in order to block menstruation and complete their Ramadan fasting and would then continue using it as a means of birth control.

What these hybrid tales tell us is that the question of how contraception "works" produces culturally situated answers. Javanese women's reasons for choosing particular contraceptive technologies or for using birth control more generally differ depending on their circumstances and desires and involve much more than a calculation of an optimal number of children. Although women speak of "following family planning" (*ikut* KB), they do make choices that modify the scripts offered them by state, corporate, or development plans. Given this, even speaking of "contraception" is to borrow a particular way of coding embodied experience that parcels out certain experiences for emphasis and others for repression or erasure. Contraceptive manufacturers (like other drug manufacturers) separate out "therapeutic effects" from "side effects," defining the former as the prevention of conception and the latter as anything else the intervention might incidentally do to the body.[6] But here it becomes difficult to sustain such categorizations. The notion of a contraceptive working or failing to work shifts along with ideas of what contraceptives are considered to do or to be good for. When Javanese women assert that the contraceptive injection works to cause a woman's body to become confused, that the pill fortifies religious discipline or enables women to perform religious obligations, or that the rhythm method organizes their sexual lives in ways they find more pleasurable, their understandings might be seen less as a failure to distinguish appropriately between "correct" functioning and "side" effect and more as particular ways of parsing out from the interweaving of biological, religious, political, and cultural elements what constitutes such reproductive technology and how one should approach it. This is not to say that Javanese women do not use contraceptives in order to prevent pregnancy. It is to say that contraception becomes much more complex than birth control and that culture becomes not merely the "context" for the body but, in very concrete ways, constitutive of it.

These women's stories also, however, need to be framed within religious discourses. As pious Muslim women influenced by recent movements to intensify the practice of Islam in Java, they often narrate bodily experience through the lens of an Islam that provides them with a set of assumptions about the world that take ultimate precedence over their knowledge of science or the body. "God is stronger than medicine" not because medical explanations or techniques are seen by them to be false, irrelevant, or culturally variable but because they do not exist in a self-contained universe independent of divine logic. Many women whom I asked about these stories responded with references to various hadith (sayings of the prophet Muhammad) that supported their statements in these terms. Several days after our conversation, Dewi showed me the following hadith cited in a popular Indonesian book of advice for Muslim families: "There was a man who came to the Prophet and asked, 'There is a woman slave of ours who waters the date garden and I take turns with her (to have sex) but I don't want her to become pregnant.' The Prophet said, 'Practice coitus interruptus ('azl) with her if you like, because indeed what will happen to that woman is what Allah has predestined for her.'"[7] I also, on other occasions, heard similar hadith cited, including: "A man came to the Prophet and asked about coitus interruptus. The Prophet said, 'Even if you spill seed from which a child was meant to be born on a rock, God will bring forth from that rock a child.'"[8] These Islamic texts emphasize the power of God to order human existence, to bring forth or withhold life according to his scheme. Human agency in the world is not only possible but essential; however, the ultimate effects of one's actions are not predictable or comprehensible solely by employing rationality or science. Islamic theories of predestination (takdir) are invoked through these hadith not to discount the explanatory mechanisms of biomedicine but to render them, in the end, subordinate to God's will. Within this framework, contraceptives are not judged simply according to their efficacy or failure rate at preventing pregnancy but are understood to combine with bodies in ways that are opaque to the minds that occupy them.

When contraceptive practices are viewed within the frame of Javanese Islam, Western analytic categories appear ripe for revision. In this context, "belief" is not merely an after-the-fact elaboration of a universal reality ultimately accessible through scientific techniques or rational investigation. God's plan provides such a transcendental logic, but it is one that is not transparent to human analysis. The vocabularies Westerners use to discuss contraception, including freedom of "choice" and the "planning" of families, begin to seem insufficient for capturing the complexity of the Javanese Muslim context.

But just as local knowledge of the body or of reproduction is not easily extractable from the crossing currents of transnational biomedicine, development, or science that flow through Java, Islam does not exist in women's daily lives as a set of pristine textual truths. The positions Javanese women articulate and occupy as Muslims within a state focused on particular forms of economic and social development are politicized and subject to constant pressures and negotiations of power. Understanding contraception in Java to be a culturally and religiously located phenomenon is a first step away from oversimplistic evolutionist analyses of reproductive technologies. Following the networks of power that weave their way through these women's lives can take us further toward a more sensitive and nuanced reading of their narratives and the experiences they describe.

The Politics of Planning

The IUD, the injection, the pill, nothing could stop those children. There was the sign on my door saying that I was following family planning, but I told them [the village officials] when they asked me why I kept having children, what I want or what you want is not what God wants.[9]

Contraception in Java, I have argued, does not exist simply as a discrete set of technologies but is made meaningful within a lattice of culture and piety. The terms we are faced with in trying to understand this are, however, more complex than "Islam" or "Javanese culture" versus "biomedicine." Contraceptive practices are enmeshed in networks of power and politics, tied to nationalist narratives and transnational discourses of development and global inequality.

This was illustrated for me most recently while perusing the Internet.[10] Reading a bulletin board devoted to Islam in Indonesia, I found passionate debates under way over family planning. In these exchanges, Islamic theology, state policy, economic and social development, and global politics were all being brought to bear on the meanings of contraception. One author, after quoting a lesser-known hadith comparing coitus interruptus to the burying alive of infants, questioned the relationship of the Indonesian state to Islam, arguing that the government's family-planning policy ran counter to Islamic doctrine: "Don't let the practice of family planning be carried out in Indonesia. . . . At first the *ulama* [religious experts] of Indonesia unanimously said that family planning was forbidden. Now that conviction has changed.

What happened? Has there been a new Qur'an and commentaries [*tafsir*]? Or have the *ulama* had money troubles? Muslim people must return to the pillars of Islam, not to Pancasila or the pillars of the State." Here a temporal state power is posed against the transcendental truth of Islam, and the role of Muslims in supporting family planning is cast as corrupt politicking. The official Indonesian state ideology of Pancasila, or "five precepts," is cast against the "five pillars" of Islam as a usurper of authority. Other commentaries, however, defended family planning, stressing the responsibility of Muslims to participate in economic development:

> In terms of the totals, the Muslim community already numbers in the hundreds of millions. But unfortunately, most of them are still poor and ragged. Imagine how sad the Prophet Muhammad would be to witness us: hundreds of millions but full of rows of beggars and *becak* [pedicab] drivers. My opinion is that it's better to talk about adoption and childrearing than to busy ourselves prohibiting family planning. It's time to use the brains given to us by Allah to develop strategic programs to improve the standard of living of the Muslim community. . . . We need to analyze how nations that used to be poor like Korea and Taiwan now have moved forward to become economic dragons.

Other contributors to this debate cast their opinions in light of what they perceived to be global inequalities and oppression of Muslims. In one commentary, the author frames issues of family planning not within the discourse of development offered by Indonesian nationalism but in terms of a struggle between a world "Muslim community" and its "others":

> As Muslims, certainly we must try to become rich in the world and in the afterlife. It is not enough to be rich in the afterlife and poor in the world. That is only opium, so that we the Muslim community will keep quiet if we are oppressed, so that we can be dragged off without a sigh. Why isn't it best if we are rich in the world and in the afterlife? Then there will no longer be a stereotype that Islam is identical with a lack of education and poverty and finally we will conquer unbelief. God says that the livelihood of a person He also makes certain. But this is not the same meaning as sitting in the house waiting for our livelihood to fall from the sky. We still need to make efforts. Isn't it true that according to their nature, humans cannot fly? However, with the use of reason given them by God, can't we make airplanes that make it possible for us to fly? What would happen if we stopped this, saying that according to our nature it is only birds that fly? We must ask, then, who wants to forbid family planning. It is not God, nor is it the Muslim community.

As these exchanges show, the question of whether family planning "works" is not simply a question of whether it can be depended on to prevent pregnancy. Questions arise as to *how* family planning might be working *for* particular agents and goals. Is it working for the progress of the Indonesian nation on the road to a zero-growth-rate modernity or economic dragonhood? Is it working for a community of believers, the boundaries of which cross state borders and redraw lines of allegiance? Or are state development programs and the Muslims who support them working for those imagined to be enemies of the Muslim community? The evocation of Allah's promise to provide for believers and the mystery of his plan for them is posed against the responsibility to work for one's own and one's community's success, a responsibility that technological innovations such as family planning are argued to assist or hinder. Theological debate around predestination and human effort (*takdir/ikhtiat*) is framed in terms of the Indonesian nation and the Islamic *ummat*, or community of believers, posed as compatible or competing. Bodies are argued to be not generic and interchangeable but politically inflected and subject to change, able to fly or forced to go hungry.

How, though, are these intellectual debates over family planning relevant in the lives of Javanese women such as Dewi and her mother? What power relations are sedimented in these stories of contraception and what political effects are there to their telling? In Java, where women have traditionally been active participants in family and community decision making and in economic affairs, many women are indeed vitally and publicly concerned with the meanings of nationalism, transnational Islamic solidarity, and the impact of "development" and "Westernization" on their lives.[11] But even for those many others who do not (or, in a climate of political repression, cannot) directly participate in the sort of debates taking place on the Internet, family planning leaves traces of power in their bodies and their lives.

Under the post-1965 "New Order" government founded by President Suharto, development (*pembangunan*) has become the cornerstone of Indonesian nationalism, and family planning has been embraced as one of development's crowning glories and as one of its most concrete, measurable manifestations. Under Suharto, Indonesia implemented a population control program that international aid organizations have hailed as one of the most successful in the world, in terms of both a dramatic increase in numbers of birth control "acceptors" and an effective integration with local cultural, especially Muslim, values. Indeed, major development agencies have used Indonesia's program as a model, supporting its exportation and implementation in dozens of other "third world" nations. Since 1970, Indonesia has trained thousands of delegates from more than eighty countries in its methods.[12] In the words of the World Bank, Indonesia has undergone "one of the most impressive demographic transitions within the developing world," owing to what, according to the United States Agency for International Development (USAID), is a "'success story' unrivaled in family planning history."[13] In Indonesia, population control has become both a politically charged icon of what it means for a nation to be "modern," and an extremely direct writing of state-sponsored nationalism on the bodies of Indonesian citizens, especially women.

The impact of these state family-planning programs on women's lives has been tremendous, in ways both overt and more subtle. Critics of Indonesia's policies have challenged the state's use of coercive methods to increase the numbers of contraceptive users and to maximize influence over which methods they employ. They have publicized practices such as the aptly named "safaris" in which National Family Planning Coordinating Board (BKKBN) workers descended on rural or isolated villages, military or police escorts in tow, to present lectures on the benefits of contraception and to offer free insertion of long-term, non-user-dependent devices such as Norplant or IUDs,[14] and they have called attention to situations in which needed agricultural loans, access to high-yield rice varieties, hybrid coconut seedlings, or school scholarships are given only to those who practice family planning.[15]

The Indonesian state has, however, in recent years outwardly appeared to respond to some of these critiques. In keeping with a shift in international development rhetoric away from the language of "population control" toward the language of "women's health" and "community based initiatives," it has renamed the safaris "service operations" (*operasi bakti*), trained local midwives in contraceptive insertion and prescription, and instituted "cafeteria plans" that, working within a consumer idiom of "choice," purportedly make a wider variety of birth control options available, especially to those who pay for services at private clinics.[16] As the former state minister for population claimed, "We don't treat our culture roughly. . . . It is like giving flowers to your wife before asking for a kiss. Eventually you get what you want."[17] Who, after all, could object to the state throwing a family-planning "party" with the Jakarta poor as invited "guests," especially one that combined needed health services such as immunizations with traditional entertainment and information on family-planning possibilities?

It is, however, crucial to understand how power takes the form not only of coercion but of attempts to remake experience by managing the meanings of gender, sexuality, reproduction, and citizenship. While the Indonesian program has frequently been effected by threats of force and of economic and political marginalization, it has more often operated by means of campaigns designed to produce desire for a planned family. By creating spectacles—public cultural displays of images designed to simultaneously engage viewers and to inculcate them with certain emotional and ideological dispositions—the Indonesian state at once offers compelling cultural narratives and positions itself as the primary author of national representation. By staging these spectacles, the state works to create a regime in which people monitor themselves and their practices to accommodate to public displays of gender, sexual, or reproductive "normalcy."[18]

Examples of these state-sponsored spectacles are numerous: encouraged by the government, Muslim leaders deliver sermons on family planning and female anatomy and sexuality in mosques; discussions about contraceptives and sexual morality are held in religious groups, state schools, and Boy and Girl Scout meetings; and billboards and television commercials blare the benefits of condoms, birth control pills, or "small, happy, and prosperous families." "Model couples" who have been using contraceptives long enough are paraded before national media audiences; those who have been "acceptors" for five years are offered a commemorative plaque or batik shirts decorated with the spiral pattern of an IUD, and after ten years they are eligible to win an all-expense-paid trip to Saudi Arabia for the hajj or to be brought to Jakarta to have tea with the president flanked by lights and cameras. Children's television shows present songs and skits for preschoolers telling how "two children are enough," while puppeteers who present shadow plays are recruited by the government to add contraception to the sexual scenes of the dramas they present. Reproductive practices are also made visible when state university students perform mandatory community service as "family-planning motivators" in rural villages; when the state conducts a national family-planning survey that attempts to assess the contraceptive knowledge and behavior of every home in the country; or when some civil servants are delivered their paychecks on different days of the week depending on what contraceptive method they use. These power relations are made even more overt when the government requires the posting of signs on the doors of houses indicating the contraceptive "acceptor" status of the inhabitants,[19] or when village maps are posted in many Indonesian "town halls" indicating birth control users, color-coded by contraceptive method—the same sorts of maps that Clifford Geertz describes being used to show the location of former Communist households in the years following the New Order's ascent to power.[20]

These nationalist sexual spectacles encode a gender politics, as well, by positioning women as both privileged spectators and primary targets of family planning. Women's behavior is placed under surveillance, but it is also rendered spectacular through the repeated exhibition of idealized female figures. These may include the regional leaders of Dharma Wanita, the mandatory organization for the wives of civil servants that assigns women a rank based on that of her husband, or, in the pages of a glossy women's magazine, the smiling, modest housewife standing in front of her Westernized house beside her suited husband and two happy children. Closer to home, villagers may be confronted with the woman who, by becoming a participant in KB Mandiri—independent, private-sector family planning—has received a plaque announcing her status to be placed on the outside of her house. Positioned as consumers of these spectacles, Indonesian women are, in Althusserian terms, interpolated, "hailed" with a potential identity as (non)reproductive citizens. They are offered a place as participants in the process of nation building by becoming guardians of family morality and national development through the acquisition of fertility-controlled bodies. Although Indonesia is certainly not unusual in its identification of women as the primary users of contraception—the majority of research and funding for contraception worldwide is for birth control methods that work on female bodies—what is instructive in this case is the extent to which the cultivation of a particular kind of embodiment and the ascendance to "citizenship" are intertwined and made to seem interdependent.

Can we, then, read Javanese Muslim women's narratives of contraceptive "failure" as coded defiance of these state exhibitions of and incursions into their bodies and lives? Are Dewi and others like her arguing for a power stronger than medicine that is, by extension, stronger than state control? Are they evoking an alternative to the ideologies of state nationalism, using "religion" as "resistance"? The sexual and gender politics of the Indonesian state are not, certainly, complete and coherent in their agency and effects. Resistances to reproductive interventions take many forms in Indonesia, although identifying and analyzing them offers theoretical and methodological challenges. What to a Western observer might seem to be agreement may, from a local standpoint, be viewed as an alternative to or protest against dominant modes of ordering experience. And what might appear from one perspective as refusal or challenge might not be articulated—or indeed articulable—in such oppositional terms.

Explicit protests against family-planning policies or hegemonic state versions of reproduction are rare in Indonesia. In large part because of state willingness, backed by military might, to regularly and rigorously denounce alternatives as "political," and thus antinational, Indonesian women are seldom able to critique family planning publicly as a system of practices or representations. This does not mean, however, that women simply acquiesce to state policy or state rhetoric. Quite often women will refuse to use particular forms of birth control, especially the more invasive hormonal methods that the state favors, on grounds of "health risk," co-opting a state language of biomedical modernity to assert their right to reject these "advanced" methods. And, more frequently, women rework state discourses through their participation in family planning to create new ways of representing embodied experience.

Looking at the ways women interpret and transform the meanings the state attributes to their bodies, we find that, despite the ease with which Indonesians generally discuss family planning—it is not, for example, considered impolite to ask a relative stranger what kind of contraceptive she uses—women frequently resist attempts to bring reproduction into a public domain of *nationalist* discourse. Rural women may, for instance, refuse to use condoms because they must be requested from a state-appointed family-planning official—in villages typically the wife of a local political leader—who could possibly gossip with others about the frequency of one's sexual activity. In the cities, where condoms can be bought in pharmacies only after showing a government identification card or a marriage certificate, women are similarly wary of exposing themselves to state control and neighborhood knowledge. Through such refusals Indonesian women assert a connection between family planning, sexuality, and local politics, subverting attempts to depoliticize or desexualize these technologies. Women also position themselves outside state discourse by using contraceptive "acceptor club" and women's group meetings officially about family planning to discuss other issues of concern to them, including lack of sexual fulfillment, methods of keeping a husband from taking another wife, or ways to gain a prospective partner's interest. For example, at one government-sponsored meeting I attended, the ostensible purpose of which was to disseminate information about the benefits of Norplant, the divisions between nationalist ideology and local interests became blatantly apparent. As the chair of the meeting lectured women about how they could participate in the development of Indonesia as a modern nation by switching to a more "modern" contraceptive technology, most of the women were chatting and laughing with one another along the edges of the room. Only when the chair asked for questions did anyone seem to pay much attention. After a long silence one younger woman called out, "I have read in a magazine about orgasm. Could you tell me what it is and how I can get one?" After the meeting, the chair complained to me that the major problem with the family-planning program these days was that women were getting information from one another, rather than from the appropriate experts. "They come to the meetings and gossip, and then after they leave they gossip again." While the state's intention may be to promote "planning," these women can, to an important extent, fill the discursive space created by the population control program with their own concerns.

"Participation" in family planning also has other unintended effects. In Java, by representing and positioning women as the primary "planners" of their families, able to control their sexuality through rational calculation, the state often ironically undermines its own social policies by invoking the cultural values many Javanese attribute to ascetic control. As Brenner argues, Javanese women consider themselves to be less susceptible than men to the vicissitudes of passion, a quality they say justifies their participation in economic activities and community decision making.[21] The state's attributing to women an ability to domesticate their sexualities and reproductive potential through family planning may galvanize women's understandings of their own power, countering government rhetoric that seeks to confine women's influence to the home. I frequently heard that just as women were more suited to be "planners" of their families by using contraception, they were more able to "plan" other activities ranging from economic decisions and purchases to smoothly run social activities and community organizations.

In overtly Islamic contexts, as well, Muslim "participation" in family planning is often directed toward goals other than those articulated by the state. Although 85–90 percent of Indonesia's population identifies itself as Muslim, Indonesia is not an Islamic state. Negotiating with Muslims has been crucial for the government, not only because of Islam's increasingly prominent role in Indonesian public culture but because success at deflecting potential Islamic opposition to family planning has been high on the agenda of international development organizations interested in using the Indonesian case as a model for export to other postcolonial countries.[22]

A number of Muslim groups do, in fact, run Islamic family-planning clinics, hospitals, and schools to train women in midwifery and family-planning medicine. However, in so doing they have challenged the gender politics of the state by expanding opportunities for women as trained professionals. Many Muslim women medical students told me they felt it was religiously mandated (*wajib*) for them to use their intelligence and skills to become physicians devoted to the care of women. And although Muslim organizations officially support the family-planning program, many have done so using logic very different from that of national development. For instance, Muhammadiyah, Indonesia's largest modernist Muslim organization, decided in 1968 that although contraception violates Islamic doctrine, it is permissible "in case of emergency" with agreement by both husband and wife and respect for Islamic values; for example, abortion and permanent sterilization are prohibited, and IUDs should be inserted by female doctors or nurses.[23] "Emergency" has been broadly defined by Muhammadiyah not only to respond to the state's neo-Malthusian declaration of an Indonesian "population emergency" but to include the need for Muslims to have small, economically stable families that will "create healthy, intelligent, and religious children,"[24] able to compete in the national arena with non-Muslims, especially the ethnic Chinese, whom many perceive to be controlling much of Indonesia's economic resources and political power. Muhammadiyah has been careful to distance its support for family planning from Western "individualist" attempts to *limit* births for personal convenience. Its leaders have defined *planning* as an attempt to improve Muslim economic and social standing that favors the community over the individual, as expressed in the insistence on speaking not of birth control (*pembatasan kelahiran*) or of family planning (*keluarga berencana*) but of family welfare (*keluarga sejahtera*) when discussing contraception.

These sentiments were echoed in my discussions with individual Muslim women. One nineteen-year-old university student who had recently decided to try to live a more orthodox Islamic lifestyle told me:

> Your body does not belong to you. It does not belong to the govern-ment. It belongs to God. Therefore you have to take care of it, continue along with it the way it was given to you naturally. You can't use family planning like the spiral [IUD] or the injection [Depo-Provera]. You can use the method where you check what days it is safe to have sex, or if your husband agrees you can use condoms. Yes, you can follow family planning, but not because you are afraid of becom-ing poor if you have many children. You have to trust God that you will be able to take care of your children. But you can follow family planning so that the children that you have will be able to be more educated and better taken care of. If you only have two children the attention that you are able to give them will be more concentrated. It will be stronger. The Muslim community will then become stronger.

While by no means do all Muslims share such sentiments, at least a third of those I asked told me that they believed only the rhythm method to be permitted by Islam, even though they were aware of government statements to the contrary. On another occasion, at the wedding of two Muslim student activists, guests were asked to offer congratulations and advice to the couple on videotape. Many of the younger women urged fruitfulness on the newly married couple. "Don't just have two children!" one exhorted. "Have many children who can go out and protest with us!" Here the benefits of family plan-ning accrue not to the individual engaged in rational planning in order to create a maximally convenient lifestyle, or to a nation as an abstract, united entity. Family planning ideally creates community, but one with particular moral and religious values that indeed may be in tension with state priorities. What is articulated as "natural" here is not the linear move toward the kind of progress or modernity stressed by state nationalism, nor is it a notion of the body as a unit in a population count. Bodies are sites for the deployment of ethical and political values, and "development" is articulated in moral and cultural terms, not in assertions of technical virtuosity.

Conclusion

Returning, then, to the stories of Dewi and other Javanese Muslim women, we might interpret their statements as narratives of resistance. By framing their bodies not as grounds for the inscription of nationalism or the implementation of state or international development programs but as religiously marked and meaningful, sexual, and sensitive to relations of power, these women could be seen as articulating their opposition through the most direct means at their disposal. In the absence of options for more overt and organized rebellion, they could be understood as engaged in a sort of political somatization, couched in Islam as a practiced and culturally valid framework for dissent. The "failure" of birth control could be viewed as a "triumph" over attempts at control of their bodies and lives.

There are, however, serious pitfalls to an easy triumphalism when looking at these stories. "The romance of resistance," as Abu-Lughod terms it, may seduce us into underemphasizing the ways in which women do willingly participate in family-planning programs, even as they reshape the discourses that come packaged with contraception.[25] We need also, I would argue, to keep in mind that women's resistances to family planning, or practices and narratives that can appear to be resistances, can have profound and unanticipated impacts on their lives. As the Indonesian state, bolstered by international aid agencies' policies, moves increasingly toward contraceptives that cannot easily be controlled by the individual user, such as Norplant (which is implanted under the skin and is effective for five years) and Depo-Provera (which is injected once every three months), these stories of Javanese Muslim women may provoke increased scrutiny and regulation of their bodies. Despite their unequal access to information and their marginalization from political decision-making processes, these women can make creative movements within development and biomedical discourses, but this same disenfranchisement limits their abilities to perceive and act on the range of relations of power pertinent to their lives.

Writing about the contraception stories of Javanese Muslim women cannot, then, be simply a descriptive or intellectual undertaking. It is a political endeavor shot through with practical implications, some foreseeable and some opaque. It is also one that highlights both the ways in which bodies interact with biotechnologies in historically particular ways and how connections are forged between Euro-American categories and practices and those elsewhere. Not only are Javanese women impacted by discourses of development, biomedicine, women's "choice," and family "planning" current in the West, but their challenge to the category of "contraceptive failure" carries connotations for Western feminist politics. As Western women grapple with new reproductive technologies and abortion politics, simply doing away with such a category to focus on women's agency carries serious implications for women's rights to make decisions about their bodies. Contesting descriptions of women whose contraceptives "fail" as irresponsible or ignorant of biotechnologies while opposing abuses such as forced sterilization or Norplant insertion that have been perpetrated upon women deemed "noncompliant" is an endeavor fraught with tension.

The stories of these Javanese women also challenge us to explore the possibilities for cross-cultural understandings of women's experiences of reproductive technologies. When I began this essay, a friend asked me, "Yes, but what do *you* believe? Do you think that Dewi's mother was *really* taking her pills?" And indeed it is a feature of anthropological analysis, and perhaps all disciplines that seek to "explain" phenomena in the world, that we tend to focus on and write about what we think we understand. How, then, can I analyze something—here the statements of Javanese women about God and medicine—in a way that translates both something about embodied meaning and its negotiation in Java as well as my continued inability to master and mold their words to make them "make sense" in any one compelling way?

By exploring the various ways in which contraception can be framed in Java, purposely avoiding any easy closures, I am not trying to abdicate any possibility of explanation or any responsibility for an informed reading of these narratives. By emphasizing the range and intricacy of the issues involved in these stories and their telling, I hope to give a sense of the ways in which different analytic approaches to reproductive technologies bring to light certain aspects of women's lives while shadowing others. But I am also hoping to show how, for Javanese Muslim women themselves, contraceptive technologies are discursively contested and variously embodied. Dewi and others who tell such stories are foregrounding and backgrounding different interpretations and experiences in a variety of contexts and in response to multiple forces. Contraception in Java is made locally meaningful, and it is also rendered religious in dialogue with Muslims in other parts of the world. It is a matter of faith and a matter of science. It is personal, at work in intimate spaces of the body and behind closed doors, and it is political, offering women public roles as planners and as participants in nation building, while at the same time it erases the dividing line between such domains. Contraception can organize resistance to development ideologies as well as encode the power of the state to shape the bodies of its citizens. It can provide a stage for the struggle of Indonesia to find its place in a world of economic dragons and provoke a search for alternative ways to be "modern." None of these framings alone can account for the complexity of contemporary Java, yet offering them in their tangled connection runs the risk of blurring our focus. This is, however, a risk that Javanese women run regularly. Navigating the complexity of contraception

in their everyday lives, Javanese Muslim women are subject to a dizzying combination of forces that both shape their bodies and provide spaces for the articulation and debate of meaning. If, as Donna Haraway suggests for Western
biological sciences, "the body is theorized as a coded text whose secrets yield
only to the proper reading conventions," the stories of Dewi and other Javanese
women urge us, I argue, to multiply our reading strategies to account for other
ways of imagining, articulating, and embodying reproductive technologies.[26]

Notes

This research is based on fieldwork in Yogyakarta, Central Java, Indonesia, funded
by Fulbright IIE, the American Association for Asian Studies Southeast Asia Coun-
cil/Luce Foundation, the Spencer Foundation, and the MacArthur Foundation/
Center of International Studies, Princeton University. For helpful comments and
criticism on drafts of this essay I thank Vincanne Adams, Lauren Leve, John
MacDougall, Elizabeth Oram, and Degung Santikarma.

1. Author's field notes.
2. E. E. Evans-Pritchard, *Witchcraft, Oracles, and Magic among the Azande* (New York:
Oxford University Press, 1937). For a discussion of the uses of "belief" and "knowledge" in studies of non-Western medical systems, see Byron Good, *Medicine, Rationality, and Experience: An Anthropological Perspective* (New York: Cambridge
University Press, 1994).
3. Phyllis T. Piotrow, Katherine A. Treiman, Jose G. Rimon III, Sung Hee Yun, and
Benjamin V. Lozare, *Strategies for Family Planning Promotion: World Bank Technical
Paper Number 223* (Washington, D.C.: World Bank, 1994); emphases added.
4. For critical discussions of development from an anthropological perspective, see
Arturo Escobar, *Encountering Development: The Making and Unmaking of the Third
World* (Princeton, N.J.: Princeton University Press, 1995); James Ferguson, *The
Anti-Politics Machine: "Development," Depoliticization, and Bureaucratic Power in
Lesotho* (Minneapolis: University of Minnesota Press, 1994); Mark Hobart, ed., *An
Anthropological Critique of Development: The Growth of Ignorance* (New York:
Routledge, 1993).
5. Ferzacca explores the limits of a medical pluralism model in his study of Javanese
discourses of disease and modernity. See Steve Ferzacca, "In This Pocket of the
Universe: Healing the Modern in a Central Javanese City" (Ph.D. diss., University of Wisconsin, 1996).
6. One example of this is provided by the Upjohn Company in its patient information literature for Depo-Provera. According to the manufacturer, "Depo-Provera
Contraceptive injection acts by preventing your egg cells from ripening. . . . [It]
also causes changes in the lining of your uterus that make it less likely for pregnancy to occur." See "Important Information for Patients" brochure (Upjohn Company, 1996). In a separate section, Upjohn lists the "most common side effects" of
Depo-Provera: "irregular menstrual bleeding, amenorrhea (no menstrual bleeding),
weight gain, headache, nervousness, stomach pain or cramps, dizziness, weakness
or fatigue, decreased sex drive." The last item, especially, seems somewhat ironic
as a "side effect" for something whose purpose is premised on sexual activity. Interestingly, Upjohn does not mention Depo-Provera's increasing use in the United
States as a method of "chemical castration" for male "sex offenders."
7. Translated from the Indonesian volume by H. Abdul Qadir Djaelani, *Keluarga
Sakinah* (Surabaya, Indonesia: PT Bina Ilmu, 1995).
8. The English translation of this hadith is from B. F. Musallam, *Sex and Society in*

Islam (Cambridge, U.K.: Cambridge University Press, 1983). Musallam's book also contains very useful information, including hadith and arguments made by Muslim jurists, about contraception in the medieval Arab world.

9. Author's field notes.

10. The Internet has, in recent years, become an extremely popular medium for political expression for many Indonesians, especially given the restrictions on the press and on public discourse under the New Order. Indonesian Muslims have created a large number of discussion groups and Web pages devoted to religious propagation and debate. While this is, certainly, a technology most prevalent among the elite and well educated, in the urban Javanese city where I worked there are computers capable of accessing the Internet in cafés and post offices, and there are a phenomenal number of inexpensive computer rental shops lining the streets.

11. On gender in Java, see, for instance, Laura Sears, ed., *Fantasizing the Feminine in Indonesia* (Durham, N.C.: Duke University Press, 1996); Suzanne Brenner, "Why Women Rule the Roost: Rethinking Javanese Ideologies of Gender and Self-Control," in *Bewitching Women, Pious Men: Gender and Body Politics in Southeast Asia*, ed. Aihwa Ong and Michael Peletz (Berkeley: University of California Press, 1995); Diane Wolf, *Factory Daughters: Gender, Household Dynamics, and Rural Industrialization in Java* (Berkeley: University of California Press, 1992); Barbara Hatley, "Theatrical Imagery and Gender Ideology in Java," in *Power and Difference: Gender in Island Southeast Asia*, ed. J. Atkinson and S. Errington (Stanford, Calif.: Stanford University Press, 1990); Ward Keeler, "Speaking of Gender in Java," in Atkinson and Errington, *Power and Difference*; and Hildred Geertz, *The Javanese Family: A Study of Kinship and Socialization* (Prospect Heights, Ill.: Waveland Press, 1961). On gender and Islam in the Javanese context, see Suzanne Brenner, "Reconstructing Self and Society: Javanese Muslim Women and 'the Veil,'" *American Ethnologist* 23, no. 4 (1996): 673–697.

12. Barbara Crossette, "A Third-World Effort on Family Planning," *New York Times*, 7 September 1994, 8.

13. International Bank for Reconstruction and Development (The World Bank; hereafter cited as "IBRD"), Indonesia, *Family Planning Perspectives in the 1990s* (Washington, D.C.: IBRD, 1990); United States Agency for International Development (USAID), *AID's Role in Indonesian Family Planning: A Case Study with General Lessons for Foreign Assistance*, AID Program Evaluation Report Number 2 (Washington, D.C.: USAID, 1979). Some scholars have challenged whether a reduction in population growth rates in Indonesia can be directly attributed to the family-planning program or if it is attributable instead to other social changes. See Terence Hull, "Population Growth Falling in Indonesia," *Bulletin of Indonesian Economic Studies* 27, no. 2 (1991): 137–143, and Geoffrey McNicholl and Masri Singarimbun, *Fertility Decline in Indonesia* (Yogyakarta: Gadjah Mada University Press, 1986).

14. See Kathryn Robinson, "Choosing Contraception: Cultural Change and the Indonesian Family Planning Program," in *Creating Indonesian Cultures*, ed. Paul Alexander (Sydney: Oceania Publications, 1989), for an account of a "safari" in South Sulawesi. Susan Greenhalgh, "Controlling Births and Bodies in Village China," *American Ethnologist* 21, no. 1 (1994): 3–30, notes a similar preference by the Chinese government for contraceptive devices whose operation does not rely on the control of the user, who can "forget" to take pills or who can pull out an IUD.

15. See Robinson, "Choosing Contraception," and Betsy Hartmann, *Reproductive Rights and Wrongs: The Global Politics of Population Control* (Boston: South End Press, 1995).

16. On "women's health," see Ines Smyth, "The Indonesian Family Planning Program: A Success Story for Women?" *Development and Change* 22 (October 1991): 781–

805; on "community based initiatives," see Escobar, *Encountering Development*; on "service operations," see Margot Cohen, "Success Brings New Problems," *Far East Economic Review* 151, no. 16 (18 April 1991): 48–49. Despite this shift in rhetoric, however, Indonesia has moved increasingly toward long-term contraceptive methods. In a 1976 survey of contraceptive users in Java and Bali, 56.7 percent were using the pill, 6.8 percent condoms, and 0.8 percent Depo-Provera. In a 1987 survey, 31.4 percent were using the pill, 3.5 percent condoms, 21 percent Depo-Provera, and 0.8 percent Norplant (IBRD, *Family Planning Perspectives in the 1990s*). A 1995 survey reported 32 percent using the pill, 32 percent Depo-Provera, 22 percent IUDs, 8 percent Norplant, and 6 percent sterilization. See "Family Planning Participants Spurn Comfy Contraceptives," *Jakarta Post*, 12 July 1996, 2. These figures are weighted even more heavily toward non-user-controlled methods in islands other than Java and Bali.

17. Crossette, "Third-World Effort."
18. For a more detailed discussion of the relationships between nationalism, sexuality, and family planning in Indonesia, see Leslie Dwyer, "Spectacular Sexuality: Nationalism, Development, and the Politics of Family Planning in Indonesia," in *Gender Ironies of Nationalism: Sexing the Nation*, ed. Tamar Mayer (New York: Routledge, forthcoming).
19. Described as also occurring in West Sumatra by Evelyn Blackwood, "Senior Women, Model Mothers, and Dutiful Wives: Managing Gender Contradictions in a Minangkabau Village," in *Bewitching Women, Pious Men: Gender and Body Politics in Southeast Asia* (Berkeley and Los Angeles: University of California Press, 1995). Blackwood notes that these placards also reinforce the state's gender ideology by requiring inhabitants to list "household head" and "wife," despite the matrilineal culture of the area.
20. Clifford Geertz, *After the Fact: Two Countries, Four Decades, One Anthropologist* (Cambridge: Harvard University Press, 1995).
21. Brenner, "Why Women Rule the Roost." Brenner's argument counters previous analyses that describe ascetic power as primarily the province of men. Brenner argues that while Javanese men may see themselves as paragons of control, Javanese women may perceive the situation quite differently.
22. For an official government history of the negotiations between Muslims and family planning officials, see BKKBN, *The Muslim Ummah and Family Planning in Indonesia* (Jakarta: BKKBN, 1993). In one World Bank report, the authors relate how Indonesia's family-planning success was unexpected because of its "large areas of Muslim fundamentalism." See IBRD, *Population and the World Bank: Implications from Eight Case Studies* (Washington, D.C.: IBRD Operations Evaluation Department, 1992), 27. The state's dealings with Muslims are listed as one of six main reasons why the Indonesian program has succeeded.
23. BKKBN, *Muslim Ummah*.
24. Ibid.
25. Lila Abu-Lughod, "The Romance of Resistance: Tracing Transformations of Power through Bedouin Women," in *Beyond the Second Sex: New Directions in the Anthropology of Gender*, ed. Peggy Sanday and Ruth Goodenough (Philadelphia: University of Pennsylvania Press, 1992).
26. Donna Haraway, "The Biopolitics of Postmodern Bodies: Constitutions of Self in Immune System Disorders," in *Simians, Cyborgs, and Women: The Reinvention of Nature* (New York: Routledge, 1991), 206.

Biting the Magic Bullet

ANGELA WALL

Reproductive Freedom and the Promise of Norplant

I_N HER STUDY_ of abortion rights activists, "Different Voices, Different Visions: Gender, Culture, and Moral Reasoning," Carol Stack stresses the importance of ethnography in the analysis of reproductive politics. She suggests that in addition to the divisions existing across race, culture, class, and gender, differences exist also in the moral voices and practices people adopt in public spaces: "We must study side by side, both discourse, and course of action. This brings us face to face with the difference between interpretative studies of moral voices, and ethnographies of gender that regard moral reasoning in the context of everyday activity."[1] This dissonance between public acts and private thoughts provides a preliminary framework from which to attempt a critical inquiry into developments in reproductive technology. Recent advances in medical research, particularly birth control technologies such as Norplant, pose certain bioethical questions about the effects of new technologies on women's lives. Who are the true beneficiaries of these medical technologies: pharmaceutical companies, affluent women, women of lower economic status, state welfare systems, third-world women? At the same time, the broadening scope of reproductive options suggests women now have greater choices in their reproductive decisions. While these new technologies offer greater choice, developing alongside is a rapidly growing commercial industry in managing reproduction. Thus the business of being a family is what Marilyn Strathern has termed a thriving "enterprise culture."[2]

In this inquiry, I do not want to promote belief in a conspiratorial system of medical bureaucracy in which women have little or no power, nor do I want to celebrate outright a contraceptive device that seems literally to figure the

female body as a site of potential reproduction in need of medical management.[3] Rather, I want to work between these modes and examine the specific
ways in which the Norplant implant functions to insert women who use it
into a circuit of less freedom while promising them something called "more
freedom of choice." In other words, the important questions to raise in a discussion of Norplant are not those centering on whether the implant is good
or bad; rather, the use of the implant needs to be addressed in terms of its
contradictory functions. Furthermore, by interpreting the impact of Norplant
via its multiple uses and potentially unsettling consequences, we can assess
the cultural climate out of which this technology emerges to unravel how
women are variously positioned—and position themselves—in relation to their
reproductive bodies.

Perceptions about women's relationships to reproductive technology are
formulated in a range of cultural locales extending from medical studies to
popular magazine articles. These various discursive tales offer multiple ways
to make sense of science and medicine, and if we, as feminists, are to examine the implications of new technologies on women's lives, we need to account for the varied ways such technologies emerge. The Norplant implant,
for example, exists in the news media as a contraceptive technology that is
very different for white, middle-class women than for mothers on welfare. Al-
ternatively, medical journals tell a completely different story about Norplant's
contribution to world health care than do popular magazine interviews with
young teenagers. Only by cross-referencing these various configurations can
we scrutinize the cultural impact on the women whose lives they have arguably been designed to improve.

Bruno Latour analyzes such configurations in terms of a "network." For
Latour, a network "indicates that resources are concentrated in a few places—
the knots and the nodes—which are connected with one another—the links
and the mesh: these connections transform scattered resources into a net that
may seem to extend everywhere."[4] The contradictory aspects of new medical
procedures—their capacity to offer more freedom to women while at the same
time binding women to a particular system of reproductive practices—need
to be contextualized (my term) or located within a network (Latour's term) if
the different configurations of various technologies in women's lives are to be
recognized in all their complex formulations. The discursive canals that chan-
nel interpretations of medical technological approaches—magazine articles,
medical journals, TV commercials, information videos—construct what appears to be a single, dominant way of understanding reproductive medicine.
When these discursive channels are closely examined, however, a network
comprising a particular understanding of reproductive technologies is revealed.
Such networks bring together contradictory methods of perception. Thus a

relationship exists between discursive practices for channeling information and the production of knowledge that categorizes the significance of these technologies on the lives of particular groups of women. When these relationships are examined in terms of networks, a system of understanding can be detected and used to assess the development of terms such as *knowledge*, *choice*, and *reproductive freedom*.

For example, generational and racial differences between women manifest themselves in how women practice motherhood. On the one hand, changes in education, labor force participation, and postponed marriage and childbirth may enable many white, middle-class women to maintain at least the illusion of control over their own lives to a degree unprecedented for other groups. On the other hand, in many African American and Hispanic communities women have filled the dual role of mother and worker for generations and continue to do so. As a result, "reproductive control" is often readily ascribed to advances in medical science, rather than to the complex set of material conditions that enable a particular decision-making process to take place.[5]

Ontological differences are important to remember when we interrogate the emergence of new medical technologies, as these distinctions shed light on the processes by which particular lifestyles are promoted over others. In the case of emerging reproductive technologies, while we might not be surprised that medical practitioners show little concern over ontological shifts of what constitutes motherhood, monitoring such shifts would seem a plausible way for the medical community to meet more actively the needs of a diverse body of patients.[6] An investigation of the systemic structures out of which discourses about reproduction emerge necessarily leads one to look at the social epistemology of specific knowledge constructions regarding women, reproduction, and rights.[7] Discursive constructions of women and childbearing are foundational to an examination of how reproductive technologies are understood within a framework of competing discourses and "knowledges" about women. In addition, such analyses demonstrate how the utilization of technology continues to ensure the engendering of the body.[8] The debates that have emerged around the use of Norplant suggest that a discussion about the moral status of Norplant becomes a struggle over the role of women in modern society and how technology—in this case reproductive technology—maintains a gendered body that remains tied to culturally held values concerning sexuality, economic status, ethnicity, premarital sex, motherhood, and marriage. Thus the implementation of this new birth control device provides an opportunity from which to engage the role of women in global capitalism.

The implant is increasingly prescribed in the United States for the "protection" of young women who "get pregnant" out of "ignorance." These women are typically women of color. With the introduction of Norplant, abortion as a remedy to unwanted pregnancy becomes less a medical option than a means to blame women further for their irresponsibility—"Why are they still getting pregnant when Norplant is available?" As a result, physicians and legislators become the protectors of women's best interests, authorizing abortions only when "medically needed." Furthermore, the contraceptive choices made available to low-income white women and women of color are significantly reprioritized in the eyes of the state when Norplant is available through Medicaid—the state can look forward to further unburdening itself from child care responsibilities for five years at a time. Thus issues of class and race contribute to the ways medical and scientific practices authorize practices working for the "greater good of all." Removing the implant, a costly medical procedure performed by doctors under limited criteria, subjects a woman's reproductive choices to further medical surveillance.[9] As a result, Norplant inserts motherhood into the broader cultural framework whereby one's suitability for motherhood is assessed in terms of how the decision to have a child will affect the greater good of society, the economy, and the nation as a whole.

Yet such connections between the benefits of advancing technology in an industrial world and reproductive "rights" confuse the activity of birth control with the techniques through which it is achieved. New contraceptive methods contribute to a decline in the birthrate as a result of their techniques, marketing, and information dissemination; however, in the process they continue to gender the body female, suggesting that broader cultural issues are always already wrapped up in the implementation of technological practices. As a result, one's body—marked by its sexuality, class, ethnicity, and gender—becomes a combination of cultural access codes that determine one's entry into the spaces offered by new reproductive technologies. However, as Rosalind Petchesky's work shows, these spaces are becoming increasingly zoned: certain classes and ethnicities are being denied access to some technologies while being encouraged to access and "take advantage" of others.[10] Such zoning practices are evident in the popular media's coverage of Norplant's usage as a prophylactic against pregnancy among women financially dependent on the state.

In February 1993, *Newsweek* magazine announced Norplant's popularity as a "cure not only for teen pregnancy, but also for welfare dependency, child abuse and drug-addicted mothers."[11] Norplant, as an antidote to pregnancy, offered a limit to the major drain on U.S. economic resources, a means to treat the "epidemic" of welfare problems by controlling the ability of low-income women to have children. Furthermore, it offered a means to punish "abusive mothers" under the guise of prevention and to limit the availability of abortion services to underprivileged women.[12] Under this system, the problem of providing accessible and affordable alternative services to women (ranging from pregnancy termination to adequate child care) becomes a secondary issue. Many states initiate Norplant trials while remaining reluctant to increase child care support or loosen stringent abortion laws. Are we witnessing a growing awareness of women's needs here or a strategic endeavor to control pregnancy at the least cost?[13]

The ability of low-income women on welfare to exercise reproductive rights is significantly reduced under this system. "Rights" for women who obtain Norplant under judicial conditions are displaced in the name of preventative medicine. As a form of coercive birth control to "solve" teen pregnancy and stem the "epidemic of drug-addicted babies," Norplant is made available under a rhetoric of reproductive freedom and improved rights.[14] Yet this promise of greater choice ignores the compulsory manner in which the procedure is prescribed. Many women are literally implanted with state-sanctioned reproductive freedom: their reproductive rights are constituted by the site of state regulation that their bodies have become.[15] Still, we must be mindful not to position women who opt voluntarily for Norplant as dupes of the medical system: Norplant is an economic benefit to women who cannot afford another child or who do not want to confront the alternatives to another pregnancy. The decision to receive Norplant involves a complex negotiation among women and medical, legal, and scientific institutions. However, the role a patient's race, class, and economic background plays in the prescription of Norplant is unsettling.[16]

One Body Fits All: Clinical Trials and the Global Construction of Womanhood

Much of the initial research on the efficacy of Norplant is based on early clinical trials performed in third-world countries. In such countries, women make up a considerable percentage of the labor force, yet the potential economic benefits of this new technology are not addressed in trial reports, and as a result many questions emerge unanswered. If women no longer need time away from work to accommodate their roles as child bearers and parents, will this make them available to work longer hours? If not, will they be allowed more leisure time? Will a change occur in how women are treated in terms of career advancement in the workforce? Will Norplant increase minority executive hiring in the United States given that women of color constitute a significant percentage of the target group for the implant? Even as many of the studies take place in countries populated by people of color, the issues of race, cultural ethnicity, and class fail to inform test trials for Norplant's approval in the United States. Such an absence serves as a stark reminder that while the purpose of the trials is to determine the effectiveness of Norplant after prolonged use, the lack of concern shown for the diversity among the women directly affected by these trials reveals an unsettling, if obvious, modus operandi: rendering safe an implant that will enable the international marketing and production of another contraceptive device in a highly lucrative global marketplace.[17]

Inconsequential to the suitability of Norplant are the varying lifestyles women lead. Although many of the trials conclude with comments that relate Norplant's efficacy and suitability to the specific community in which the trial took place, a direct connection is rarely made between the cultural, social, and racial specificity of the trial group and the potential efficacy of Norplant for U.S. women. Commentaries frequently make culturally specific references to a trial group: "The findings presented suggest that the Norplant system is a highly effective, safe and acceptable method *among Bangladeshi women.*"[18] Yet they fail to acknowledge the differences that exist between such a group and the women who will eventually use Norplant in the United States. Although such a lack of hindsight remains unsurprising within a commercial operation whose bottom line is to profit, the criteria utilized to assess the viability of Norplant within a given community of women relies on the cultural and ethnic specificity of that group. What makes this suitable for "Bangladeshi women," the researchers write, is that

> there were no post-insertion pregnancies after Norplant insertion and that after five years of Norplant implant use, there was no clinically significant change in body weight, systolic or blood pressure. . . . Less than 3% of the women ever reported significant medical problems such as migraine, respiratory or cardiac problems during the study. . . . The two most frequently reported reasons for discontinuation during the study were menstrual problems and desired pregnancy.[19]

The recognition of national differences is acknowledged in accounting for the success of a particular trial group yet plays no part in determining inevitable cultural differences among trial participants. The results of this inconsistent recognition of racial diversity become the means to access a broader economic market. Racial differences do nothing to point out the fallibility of concepts such as a universal female body, and instead the female body is read as a universal concept: what's good for one group of women is good for all—one body fits all. Success among the Bangladeshi women is based on lack of harmful side effects, maintenance of "body weight," and the device's effectiveness as a method of birth control. Interestingly, "menstrual problems" or discomfort are not listed as a side effect; rather, they are termed a reason "for discontinuation." Although the general health of trial participants is monitored, the priority of the trial is the production of a relatively secure, highly marketable form of birth control. If one incentive to develop long-term, effective methods of birth control is to enable women to lead fuller lives, then this development takes place simultaneously with the lucrative profits to be gained from the successful marketing of a new contraceptive product—one that can boast universal and global appeal. The betterment of some women's lives might be a by-product of Norplant, but this improvement is not central to its promulgation. As a result, and it perhaps comes as no surprise, women are the indirect, partial beneficiaries of these clinical trials, and the need—both our own and that of medical researchers—to regulate our reproductive bodies makes possible business as usual.

The findings of a study in Zimbabwe offer a similar story: acceptability and efficacy were high, and no significant side effects were observed. Although three implants were removed because of "local infection," on the whole Norplant "is highly acceptable as a long term contraceptive."[20] An early "multicentre trial carried out in 1980 in Egypt has lead to date [the article was published in 1993] to more than 3,000 women [receiving] the contraceptive" at one of the primary research centers, the Assiut University Clinic; the overall five-year cumulative continuation rate is "51 per 100 women" with a pregnancy rate of "1.8 per 100 women." The report goes on to state that Norplant in "our community" has indicated no "deleterious effect on the lipid profile liver, functions and blood coagulation system." The overriding conclusions drawn from these trials represent Norplant as a drug tested with cultural specificity in mind and implies that the drug's efficacy lies in its transnational, transcultural solution to the global problem of women getting pregnant.[21] Norplant can be made available for the common good of all women. Yet to benefit the "common good," the implant requires a universal rhetoric that gives the biological body precedent over the cultural body; however, such precedents shore up women's similarities at the cost of ignoring their differences.

The need for awareness of differing cultural practices is highlighted in the studies conducted in Egypt. The importance in Arab and Muslim cultures of prolonged breast-feeding means that "the initiation of Norplant use shortly after delivery" cannot have any "unfavorable effect on lactational performance, or on physical or psychomotor development of the breast-fed infants." As a result, this study draws several conclusions: (1) in order to assess users' attitudes toward Norplant, several cultural considerations need to be emphasized; (2) Norplant provides a suitable answer to the problems of a culture, like Egypt's, in which "there is a special need for long term methods of contraception" and in which neither abortion nor sterilization is socially acceptable for women. In Egypt, an implant birth control enables the regulation of women's reproductive systems in a manner that maintains current traditions. However, in light of the role self-actualization plays in the reproductive decisions made by many U.S. women, the extent to which Egyptian cultural practices of motherhood echo the very traditional standards of motherhood from which many Western women are trying to depart provokes troubling insights rather than positive affirmations as to the consequences of the drug's introduction into the United States.

One Trial Fits All: Norplant and the Universal Patient

Traditional methods of constructing a universal female body in terms of its medical management can be disrupted only when what has typically been considered to be "natural" to the female body can in fact be shown to be situationally specific. For example, Nelly Oudshoorn writes that the institutionalization of specific medical practices concerning the female body made women an accessible source of research material. Oudshoorn's research on the "success" of clinical trials involving the contraceptive pill demonstrates how such tests were more or less "successful" because scientists were able to make the "context fit the demands of the testing, for example, by enrolling trained medical staff and by selecting trial participants who may be made into ideal test subjects but who are not representative of the whole population."[22]

Norplant's appeal to many women is its offer of greater "choice." Yet in this rhetoric of reproductive choice, the promise of more choice becomes the promise of more control over our bodies, which in turn leads to a better life: if a woman's reproductive capacities can be regulated satisfactorily, then women will be able to attain a higher standard of living and quality of life. One researcher notes that "the high contraceptive efficacy, lack of serious side effects, reversibility and the convenience of long-term unattended use explain the high acceptability of Norplant."[23] Norplant's "convenience" is a crucial factor to its overall success in clinical trials. But the criteria for success—efficacy, acceptability, and convenience—are established by research professionals.

In the contemporary United States, convenience is often available more readily to those in positions of privilege. Given that Norplant offers an easier lifestyle to those who would typically be excluded from this group—it enables women who are financially unable to raise a child the chance to prevent pregnancy—the concept of what counts as success becomes complicated. Current methods of trial assessments leave Norplant promising both a global answer to current population problems, another weapon in the battle to control the excessively reproductive female body, and the answer to the "modern woman's" desire to defer pregnancy in favor of a successful career. Yet what costs accompany such promises and how do we assess the nature of this cost?

Marilyn Strathern suggests that new reproductive technologies open up new options as well as offering a vision of biology under control. This vision means that the possibilities for human fulfillment are enlarged and procreation can be "thought about" as subject to personal preference and choice in ways never before imagined. Strathern's work locates the discourse of choice within a broader economic context to examine the concepts of choice in terms of an analogous relationship to the market economy. Choice and the possibilities of "reproductive freedom" are highly subjective terms reliant upon a broader context of accessibility and affordability. One's "freedom to choose" is not a "right"; rather, it is bound up in a consumer culture that involves pharmaceutical companies and health care agencies and insurance providers as well promotional and advertising budgets.[24]

Norplant is marketed by the medical establishment to women who are (socially positioned as being) in need of a method of long-term and effective contraception through the use of precisely the rhetoric of freedom developed by the "pro-choice" movement. Indeed, in the 1990s, the Norplant implant system enters into this predisposed circuit as a method that is already marked as compatible with modern lifestyles.[25] Reshma Memon Yaqub, a freelance writer in Chicago, exemplifies how the rhetoric of Norplant's marketing has enabled it to "fit the needs" of modern women. She writes, "I am one of the 500,000 women who have opted for Norplant. . . . Although it's the right choice for me right now, it's not for everybody."[26] She acknowledges that her ability to choose is embedded in a social and economic environment in which women are able to self-actualize. "If it is properly managed," she writes, "it can open doors to women. But we must make sure it remains just that—a fully informed and conscious choice." Drawing from the language of choice, Norplant becomes a means of class, cultural, and ethnic leveling: one technology to solve the problem of child prevention regardless of nationality, race, class, religion, sexuality, and economic stability.

However, discussions of how Norplant is used in the United States consistently illustrate women's options as firmly rooted in the traditions of their historical and cultural environments: exercising control over one's body is contingent on the practices of one's cultural community. As Yaqub writes, this ability clearly differs according to one's social and economic status. For example, a study in Texas among 678 women implanted with Norplant shortly after it became available in the United States suggests:

> The majority (56%) had tried the implant because they were dissatisfied with their previous contraceptive method. 44% . . . indicated that the implant was one of the first contraceptive methods they had used and that they had only recently decided to prevent unplanned pregnancy. The average number of children per woman was 1.2, and

one-third of the [participants] had [all had] at least one abortion.
While 37% said they wanted no more children, 63% said they were
using the implant as a spacing method.[27]

However, reasons for "choosing the Norplant implant and concerns about it
[vary] according to the user's age, educational level and race or ethnic group."
As a result, some women use Norplant as a financially effective birth control,
while for other women it enables a greater degree of self-fulfillment. With
Norplant, economic status is mapped onto the body in the form of an implant that makes reproductivity contingent on medical technology: medical
surgery literally facilitates a transference of power. As it is currently employed
in the United States, Norplant necessarily invokes discussion of the height-
ening of status differences among women. As Norplant is increasingly tied to
issues of welfare dependency, drug abuse, inadequate child care, teenage pregnancies, and limited abortion services, a woman's decision to reproduce can
no longer be separated from her economic class and cultural status. Reproductive choice in this context is increasingly defined by the needs of the industrial labor force and national economic policy. For many low-income
women in the United States, this translates into the typical rhetoric of welfare "dependency," drug "abuse," and unacceptable child care/abuse—all of
which may be defined as the failure to adhere to socially prescribed family
values. Such values and their strong work ethic, coincidentally, are exactly
the values on which global capitalism relies.[28]

Norplant in the United States: The Panacea to Teenage Pregnancy

A *Time* magazine survey of 21,276 U.S. women who received Norplant through
Planned Parenthood states that the vast majority, 89 percent, were under thirty,
and 22 percent were nineteen or younger. Norplant is "teenage-proof," an in-
terviewee boasts: "We need long-term methods like this because failure rates
are high for younger women using other forms of contraception," says Laurie
Schwab Zabin of the Johns Hopkins School of Hygiene and Basic Health. In
support of this, a study of adolescents aged eighteen years or under gave convenience as the most frequent reason for selecting Norplant. But convenience
for whom?

Norplant is convenient for the state, too. Emerging as it is, Norplant will
exist as the socially responsible option for teenagers "at risk." As such, the
state will no longer have to support women on welfare who cannot work because of the lack of affordable day care, or women who prefer to care for their
child rather than join the professional labor force. However, Norplant is certainly convenient for sexually active teenagers for whom high school gradua-

tion can be put in jeopardy through pregnancy and inadequate child care facilities. Furthermore, Norplant reduces the embarrassment of having frequently to address the issue of contraception with possible sex partners: it provides adolescents with a way to avoid facing social disapproval that accompanies over-the-counter birth control purchases. In short, Norplant could relieve many teenage anxieties surrounding sex. Yet this means of anxiety relief is troubling. Instead of using new reproductive technologies to incite a greater sense of social ease with sex, under this process of implementation, it works to brush sexuality further under a rug of secrecy and moral deviance.[29]

The appeal of Norplant, or rather the appeal of its success, derives from its promise of convenience for all who encounter it: distributors, medical practitioners, and patients alike. Yet, if women's needs are to be addressed specifically, if reproductive freedom for women *is* the issue here, the conjuncture between women's reproductive practices and the systemic technologies that provide the semblance of reproductive freedom and convenience needs to be examined carefully.

In 1990, Norplant was introduced into the Baltimore high school system as part of a rigorous attempt to curb the escalating number of teen pregnancies.[30] The failure of condoms and other methods of birth control produced a need for "extra measures."[31] In January 1990 school clinicists began offering Norplant and recommending "abstinence as the best way to avoid pregnancy." Positive responses are typical among many of the young women interviewed about the introduction of Norplant into inner city schools. Primarily, responses reiterate the role Norplant plays in easing many teenage anxieties about sex. One seventeen-year-old student suggests in the *Economist*, "I was on the pill, but I couldn't remember to take it every day, and then I got pregnant. I just decided if I got this everything would be a lot easier.[32] A *Los Angeles Times* story quotes an eighteen-year-old Hispanic woman, Gracie Ramirez: "I didn't want to have children so young. . . . A lot of my friends have kids, and I see what it has done to them. I didn't want to end up like that."[33] Ramirez explains that she has future plans: she wants "to be a veterinarian and does not want a pregnancy to ruin her chances of finishing school." For Ramirez and many young women, anxieties about sex seem based not on embarrassment but on the probability of becoming pregnant. Pregnancy is equated with a ruined life and failed ambitions, and Norplant promises a way out. When contraception is available, getting pregnant is avoidable, and unmarried, low-income women can finally take responsibility for their actions. Under these conditions, an unwanted or unplanned pregnancy is no longer a matter for social concern. Instead, an individual woman becomes responsible for taking precautions against "screwing up" her life.

Once again, the choices promised by Norplant come at a significant cost to some women, and once again the criteria that enable some of us to describe Norplant as a contraception that increases our reproductive "freedom" and offers us "control" over our bodies involve a recognition of the differences in status that exist among women. Norplant offers us control over our bodies for five years at a time. During this period, we can turn off our reproductive capabilities without having to remember to take a small pill each day. But it comes at the cost of inserting women's reproductive choices into codes according to economic and ethnic standing. The extent to which the control offered by Norplant differs from the control offered by other reproductive technologies remains to be seen in the degree to which Norplant actively begins to change the conditions in which women live and work.

From Trials to Lifestyles: U.S. Women's Stories

The potential of Norplant to resolve the social "problems" caused by teen pregnancies typifies many of the stories that make their way into the popular presses. An educational video made by the Emory University Summer Program in Family Planning and Human Sexuality is frequently cited in such discussions.[34] The tape is distributed to sales representatives, doctors, and family-planning clinics and opens with a young woman smiling into the camera: "'I love my Norplant.' The next says shyly, 'You don't have to worry about having a child for five years.' A third volunteers, 'For me, Norplant is the ideal method.'"[35] These sound bites are most often quoted.[36] However, the comments of the young women are interesting when positioned in relation to a larger cultural script that puts Norplant in the role of potentially duping women. The Los Angeles Times uses these quotes to support the claim that Norplant is different from previous contraceptive drugs: "The promise of Norplant as a foolproof, longstanding contraceptive that requires little thought and works for almost everyone is so seductive, so longed for, that the message has spread with amazing speed among young women and policy makers since the Food and Drug Administration approved it for public use in December, 1990."

A detailed discussion follows between two women currently using Norplant. Sondra is a second-generation inner city welfare mother in the "drug ridden northeast of Washington D.C." By association, if not by implication, she lives among drug users and is possibly a user herself. She had her first baby at fifteen and her second at sixteen. Now seventeen, she tells the two Times reporters that she can't really say why she didn't use birth control before: "I don't want to be on welfare, I want to give my kids things. That's why kids go out and sell drugs. Because their parents can't afford to buy them things." Sondra desires a "no hassle," "problem free" contraceptive. In response to this the interviewers write: "Sondra is precisely what policy-makers have in mind when they propose offering Norplant at the school-linked clinics or conditioning welfare payments to its use: a young woman who just needs information, a little technology, a little push to get herself together and off the welfare rolls. A dream solution. A magic bullet." After this disclosure, Smith and Easton reveal that Sondra "hangs out with an assortment of men" and has "sex with as many as half a dozen men a month, many of them drug dealers," and of whom at least one was HIV positive. Sondra, they state, "says no-one at the clinic she visited counseled her about the importance of also using a condom to protect herself from sexually transmitted diseases." She weighed 180 pounds and had high blood pressure when she was given the implants and has since gained an additional 20 pounds. She has no regular health care and has not been back to the clinic in four months.

Sondra's case leads the journalists to conclude: "Norplant seems to have an exaggerated appeal, leading some to wonder whether its very success signals deeper trouble for the women who use it. Not only are the health risks of poor young women a matter of concern, but also, as politicians continue to push the long acting contraceptive, the expectation seems to have vanished that these women might learn to manage their sexuality and be responsible for their own reproduction." Sondra's need for a foolproof contraceptive method is made apparent by her lifestyle. However, she is economically disadvantaged in a society that values financial self-sufficiency. The two journalists recognize the potential problems heralded by Norplant. Unlike the earlier discussion that cited clinical trials and utilized the rhetoric of welfare dependency and drug (as well as child) abuse to pass judgment, these journalists hesitate to draw positive conclusions about Sondra's case. Furthermore, the clinical trial in which Sondra has been involved brings to light many of the cautionary suggestions raised during some of the clinical trials conducted on third-world women—suggestions that have been recorded but not addressed by pharmaceutical companies and medical practitioners. Still, the rise in the number of homeless women and welfare-dependent women who are testing HIV positive means that while Norplant may reduce the risk of pregnancy, it will do little to reduce the spread of HIV infection among women for whom HIV diagnosis and treatment are already sparse, if available at all. Again, Norplant's increasing popularity as a social panacea comes at the cost of effacing women's needs as they are differently distributed according to race and class even as it reinscribes them further into these categories.

Carol, the second woman whose experience with Norplant appears in the *Times* article, is "one of the many young women eager—desperate even—to try Norplant." She is twenty-five and has had five abortions, a fact that, according to Smith and Easton, even this "wide-eyed, redhead can hardly

believe . . . herself, [weeping] at the memory as she sits on the clinic table waiting for a nurse practitioner to insert the rods into her upper arm." This is
Carol's second attempt to get the implant. When she tried a year earlier, it
was not subsidized, and as a member of an "itinerant performing troupe, she
could not afford it without the subsidy." Once in receipt of the subsidy, she
went to Santa Monica's Planned Parenthood with "$52 and some change bor-
rowed from her boyfriend to help pay for the inserts." The procedure takes
five minutes and, "starting within 24 hours, will prevent Carol from becoming pregnant until she is 30." As she is heading out of town, she is told by the
nurse-practitioner that if she wants to get the rods removed, she needs to ensure the health care worker is familiar with the procedure: "Make sure they've
done it at least once." The removal of the rods is a procedure that patients
are not encouraged to go through. However, the tacit suggestion that medical practitioners are not all adequately trained in the procedure of removing
Norplant rods is alarming: women are literally offered the implant with little
thought or planning given to its removal.

Carol's suitability for Norplant is interestingly constructed. The first few
lines of her narrative—those recounting her abortions—read like an Operation Rescue success story. Norplant saves Carol from future abortions. She
avoids being written off as a "bad girl" because she repeatedly attempts to obtain Norplant so as to avoid further abortions. Furthermore, she is deeply re-
pentant of her past lifestyle. Her story ends with the offer of a new beginning.

The closing words of advice offered to Carol by the nurse-practitioner
and the context in which these words are delivered become increasingly more
problematic if they are considered in the light of a historical context of perceptions of women's needs and reproductive technologies. Although Carol's
numerous abortions indicate that pregnancy and motherhood are not positions she wants to occupy, the assumption underlying her Norplant implant
is that eventually Carol will want to occupy that position: "starting within
24 hours . . . Carol [will be prevented] from becoming pregnant until she is
30." Even though Norplant is a device that has been created to impede pregnancy, the discourse of this reproductive technology coupled with the difficulty involved in getting the rods removed suggests that this technology still
operates in a familiar framework: woman equals motherhood, even if a five-
year transitional gap has been opened up between subject positions. In the
post–Reagan-Bush years, with their emphasis on family values, this perhaps
comes as no surprise. To borrow from the logic of Kristin Luker, it would indeed appear that a decision about the suitability of a new contraceptive implant is an implicit statement about the role of children and women in modern
society.

Although the women interviewed in the Emory video are a different set of women from those interviewed by the *Los Angeles Times*, the Emory video advocates the suitability of the implant for young women. Dr. Melinda Miller, who introduces herself as a physician with a particular interest in teenage pregnancy, suggests that a number of factors make teenagers good candidates for Norplant. She firmly states that as a group who have "peer pressures" and "a lot going on," other forms of contraceptive are undesirable and inefficient. Norplant does not require a woman to "coerce or force her partner to participate in the act of contraception."

In addition to its suitability for teenagers, Norplant's reversibility is emphasized throughout the video. All the young women talk about the importance of wanting to put off having any children or, if they are already teenage mothers, of not having any more children so they may achieve their goals. One woman suggests that "Norplant can contribute to your life plan." The video devotes considerable time to familiarizing viewers/potential clients with the minor surgical procedure involved in receiving the implant. This process of familiarization ranges from young recipients displaying their implanted rods to the camera while describing the painlessness of the procedure to a few scenes in the doctor's office in which a young woman's arm is prepared for the implant. Despite this attention to detail, no suggestions are offered as how to get the rods removed or what to do if one suffers from side effects—indeed, the removal of the rods is a concern that remains consistently unaddressed. The makers of the video include the reactions of the women to their first six months using the implant, but any spotting, weight gain, headaches, or decrease/increase in the menstrual cycle is addressed more as an inevitable consequence that will gradually lessen rather than a worrying side effect. Most of the women seem thrilled about their implant and exclaim that they have encouraged all their friends to take advantage of this method of contraception. Precisely because Norplant requires so little aftercare it is considered a suitable and desirable—almost "popular"—form of birth control.

Yet concerns over the affordability of the implant as well as its availability appear contingent only on the choice and willingness of the individual: both issues remain unaddressed throughout the tape. The compilation of interviews, procedural explanations, recognition of drawbacks, and suitability makes this a persuasive tape: persuasive and effective at relieving the "fears of pregnancy" that many young women have—particularly the young minority teenagers who are featured in the video. Norplant's reliability is unabashedly marketed as a possible magic bullet in the war against teenage pregnancy: Dr. Miller asserts on several occasions that it is the most effective form of birth control available, and many of the young women express relief at not having to worry about getting pregnant for "the next five years."[37]

The relief evident in the comments of the young women is worthy of serious attention. That Norplant meets the needs of certain women should not be overlooked; however, the emergence of Norplant and its efficacy for a particular group of women need to be considered in multiple contexts. An analysis of the comments of Julia R. Scott, director of the National Black Women's Health Project, shows how perceptions of U.S. women's needs in the 1990s are patterned in familiar ways. Scott doesn't "think that Norplant is necessarily a bad method. We are very much in favor of alternatives, but the operative words are safety and choice."[38] Scott is careful also to point out that poor women have specific health conditions, such as obesity, high blood pressure, or diabetes, which could make Norplant disproportionately risky. However, she continues, "there's not a pill or an implant that's going to solve the teen-age pregnancy problem. That's going to come when this country decides to be committed to children." However, Scott doesn't address the need for a national policy of commitment to *women's* reproductive needs. Similarly, Rosetta Stith, principal of Laurence Paquin School for expectant or parenting adolescents in Baltimore, a school positioned at the center of a national controversy over the moral and ethical implications of giving a birth control implant to young adolescents, states that with widening choices, perhaps young women—and men—of the 1990s will start to hear the "drums of prevention." She believes that "if we teach morality and self-esteem to toddlers, giving children character-building experiences, when they reach puberty they will understand the importance of delayed childbearing and the value of abstinence." That Norplant expands our methods of contraception is obvious. That it markedly relieves low-income women of the financial, emotional, and mental burden of another child and mouth to feed is undeniable. These two factors are of crucial importance in any discussion of reproductive technologies as they materially improve the lifestyles of low-income white women and women of color.

Yet the potential misuse of this technology is alarming. Reproductive technologies that can be used as a punishment or used as a means by which the government can evade social responsibility for a generation of unplanned children are clearly in the business of reproducing a particular taxonomy of social order—one that is simultaneously profitable. Reproductive technologies that fail to educate young teenage women of the risks of sexual activity beyond pregnancy work against broadening the reproductive options available to women. However, if reproductive technology is truly to benefit women's lives, then discussions of reproductive technologies need to take place within frameworks that extend beyond defining women in terms of motherhood. Any attempt to suture concepts of sexual activity, pregnancy, and motherhood only reinscribe such practices into a discourse that denies women positions of multiple subjectivity. Indeed, we return to the old formula of sex = pregnancy = motherhood.

While the problems with Norplant are many, these final points are of great significance and should not be ignored. If the material effects of the implant on women's lives are to be examined productively, then these examinations need to take place in the contexts of women's lives. In the version of the story that we are offered by the popular press, we are given such a context from which to begin to address the multiple ways in which women's bodies are constructed by medical practices. The failure of much medical research to acknowledge the importance of cultural differences among women is a point to be lamented; however, we need to work within as well as outside this capitalist framework in order to utilize emergent reproductive technologies successfully. Although we need to examine technologies and be wary of the ways in which they continue to position women as mothers under the guise of greater reproductive freedom, we need to be aware also of the ontological differences that inform notions of motherhood within the lives of different women. In outlining and examining new technologies we find ways to identify the limitations of current technologies in the context of women's lives while pushing toward a system of improved health care and reproductive provisions that allow women multiple ways to improve their lives. The language of choice and greater freedom from which we often draw in our discussion of reproductive technologies is fertile with the strains of exclusion and discrimination; yet from our varying positions as feminists we must continue to make use of what's available and illuminate the dangers in emergent possibilities. We need to draw on our collective knowledge and experience to affect the design of public policies; we need to pay attention to the application and prescription of new technologies; and we need to start creatively imagining what a future of reproductive freedom might actually look like from a multifocused vantage point.

Notes

1. Carol Stack, "Different Voices, Different Visions: Gender, Culture, and Moral Reasoning," in *Uncertain Terms: Negotiating Gender in American Culture*, ed. Faye Ginsberg and Anna Lowenhaupt Tsing (Boston: Beacon, 1990), 26.
2. I would like to extend a huge thank you to Susan Squier for bringing the work of Marilyn Strathern, among others, to my attention in this context. Susan Squier, E. Ann Kaplan, and Andrew Rivera demonstrated tremendous patience, confidence, and intellectual inspiration during the revising of this essay. Working with them has been and continues to be a sustaining experience.
3. Norplant and its method of implant are variously described. In an attempt to provide as lucid a definition as possible, I have borrowed from many sources in what follows. The implant typically used is composed of six rubbery, "match-stick like rods" filled with a powdered synthetic progesterone. They are inserted in a fan-like pattern just beneath the skin. The insertion takes approximately ten to fifteen minutes using local anesthetic. A two-millimeter incision is made on the underside of the upper arm. A metal tube is loaded with one of the cylindrical

implants and nudged into place beneath the skin. The other five rods are sequentially inserted. The tube is removed and the incision pressed together and closed with a bandage wrapped around the arm. Once in place, the progesterone leaks through the semiporous walls of the capsule into the bloodstream. It is then carried to the pituitary gland in the brain, which within twenty-four to forty-eight hours will stop producing luteinizing and follicle-stimulating hormones, both of which are necessary for ovulation. Without this hormonal cue, the ovaries fail to release an egg.

4. Bruno Latour, *Science in Action: How to Follow Scientists and Engineers through Society* (Cambridge, Mass.: Harvard University Press, 1987), 180.

5. In her analysis of amniocentesis, Rayna Rapp illustrates the importance of delineating cross-cultural discursive differences as part of an ongoing study on the impact and cultural meaning of prenatal diagnosis in New York City. Rapp uses ethnographic interviews and observations to uncover a tension between the "universal" abstract language of reproductive medicine and the personal experiences pregnant women articulate in telling their amniocentesis stories.

   Rapp notes that in amniocentesis counseling sessions between pregnant women and health care workers, a "negotiation" takes place between women's everyday discourses and the discourse of scientific technology: a negotiation that has the power to influence and rewrite the languages previously used for the description of pregnancies, fetuses, and family problems and values. As a result, social, cultural, economic, and racial differences emerge at this intersection as prescribed ways of understanding a particular scenario come face to face with how such prescriptions are lived. For example, among white, middle-class women, the decision of whether or not to carry a pregnancy to term after amniocentesis is negotiated amid a running battle over the question of selfishness and self-actualization. As more women "self-actualize" in late Western capitalism, the age for which high risk is attributed to pregnancy is gradually being lowered: women of thirty-five or thereabouts are now considered to be in the "at risk" age group for fetal abnormalities. As a result, more women are subject to "medical technology" in the name of advanced medical science. Rayna Rapp, "Constructing Amniocentesis: Maternal and Medical Discourses," in Ginsberg and Tsing, *Uncertain Terms,* 28–42.

6. Sarah Franklin discusses the construction of fetal personhood in terms of teleology and ontology in "Fetal Fascinations: New Dimensions to the Medical-Scientific Construction of Fetal Personhood," in *Off-Centre: Feminism and Cultural Studies,* ed. Sarah Franklin, Celia Lury, and Jackie Stacey (London: HarperCollins, 1991), 190–213. Franklin articulates a twofold dimension to a struggle in the abortion debate over the cultural definition of a key set of "natural facts." "First," she writes, "biology as a force, in and of itself, displaces the social as evident in the concept of biological viability as a criterion for fetal personhood, independent of any social considerations. Second, what is occurring is the replacement of social categories with biological ones, such as biogenetic fetal individuality and personhood. Biology thus not only obscures social categories, but it becomes the basis for their cultural production. It is this double move, of displacing and replacing the social with the biological, that enables a woman's pregnancy, the work of nurturing a child, the meaning of personhood (in terms of kinship, identity, naming, reciprocity, interdependence, etc.) all to be reduced to one dimension, which is that of biological life" (200).

   In a related analysis, "The 'Word-Made' Flesh," Faye Ginsberg considers how pregnancy, childbirth, and motherhood act as transitional moments for women in American culture. "Pregnancy," she writes, "(especially first conception) places women in a liminal status, a temporary condition in which the subject is in transition between two structural stages" ("The 'Word-Made' Flesh: The Disembodiment of Gender in the Abortion Debate," in Ginsberg and Tsing, *Uncertain Terms*, 70). These transitory moments typically inscribe onto women's bodies a particular version of social reality—pregnancy = childbirth = motherhood—that gets culturally read as natural. This "natural" role of women and pregnancy is then inscribed with a highly significant role in the maintenance of the cultural order.

Prior to the legalization of abortion, the inevitable outcome of pregnancy for a woman resulted in her ascribed status of motherhood. Deviations from this assigned script were either kept secret or punished and as such served to confirm the prescription for women of the dominant discourse. Ginsberg argues that the legalization of abortion "subverted a prior associational chain that pregnancy 'must' result in childbirth and motherhood." In other words, when abortion became a possibility at least in terms of the law, the "dominant and oppositional discourses regarding the place of pregnancy and abortion in women's lives were suddenly reversed" (70). Antiabortion supporters do not consider termination as an option, yet "their viewpoint exists within this new social and discursive context created by abortion's legalization" and is clearly framed oppositionally: prior to the legalization of abortion, pregnancy and motherhood were pretty much a given. However, in postlegislation discourse, the concept of motherhood put forward by antiabortion supporters is forced to divide the terminal equation of pregnancy and motherhood by the possibility of a third term, "non-motherhood." Hence a woman's decision to see a pregnancy to term is viewed as *an achievement* in the face of and despite adverse material and social circumstances.

The existence of a law that enables women to access abortion does not produce a systemwide introduction of Ginsberg's "third term" to all women. The slogan "a woman's right to choose" operates within a structure of meaning whereby the outcome of one's choice is still highly contingent on the ways in which women are variously positioned and position themselves within a given community.

7. In *Abortion and the Politics of Motherhood* (Berkeley: University of California Press, 1984), Kristin Luker locates issues of reproductive rights for women and the abortion debate firmly within a context of advancing medical technology. As reproductive technologies advance and the heartbeat of the embryo can be detected earlier, the viability of a fetus as an individual with a right to life, medically speaking, is increased. Luker offers a way to analyze this situation in her discussion of the positions defended in the abortion debate. She suggests that different positions in this debate are influenced in terms of differing "world views:" "A decision about the moral status of the embryo is an implicit statement about the role of children and women in modern American society" (7). Placing the reproductive rights debate in a historical context, Luker considers the various positions on abortion in relation to the representation of women in a changing economic and domestic world. She writes, "The past twenty years have seen the emergence of two very different constituencies of women [with regard to the issue of a woman's right to have an abortion], two groups that have different experiences in the world and different resources with which to confront it" (8). In addition, Luker analyzes medical journals, particularly the emergence of the American Medical Association (AMA) medical journal in 1849 and the subsequent availability of "new scientific evidence," to account for the shift away from the formerly sanctioned practice of abortion. The professionalization of medicine through the emergence of the AMA journal meant that more than one doctor had access to "new research" that demonstrated that the embryo was a child from conception onward. Thus "new research" spread among the profession. Luker suggests that this epistemological shift over the viability of the fetus enabled physicians to assert that women practiced abortion because they were *ignorant* of the biological facts of pregnancy. As a result, physicians' control over reproduction was solidified. Inevitably, this raises im-

portant epistemological and political questions about the criteria employed to determine what kind of knowledge counts and what kind doesn't—what kind of knowledge counts as ignorance? whose knowledge counts only as ignorance?

8. The best account I have come across so far of how the body is gendered in its interactions with technology appears in the work of Anne Balsamo in her recent book *Technologies of the Gendered Body: Reading Cyborg Women* (Durham, N.C.: Duke University Press, 1996).

9. This assertion is primarily based on popular accounts of Norplant. See, for example, "Norplant: A Three-Year Report," *Glamour* (July 1994): 154–157; Lynn Smith and Nina J. Easton, "The Dilemma of Desire," *Los Angeles Times Magazine*, 26 September 1993, 24–42; Stephen Findlay, "Birth Control," *U.S. News & World Report*, 24 December 1990, 58–64; and Barbara Antrowitz and Pat Wingert, "The Norplant Debate," *Newsweek*, 15 February 1993, 37. Overwhelmingly, women of color are consistently represented as the lower-income recipients of Norplant. The Norplant Foundation does offer a sliding scale system whereby the device can be implanted or removed for free. However, potential clients are carefully screened and must provide a written letter from their general practitioner as to—in the case of the implant's removal—why the device needs to be taken out.

10. Rosalind Petchesky, *Abortion and Woman's Choice: The State of Sexuality and Reproductive Freedom* (New York: Longman, 1984).

11. "The Norplant Debate," *Newsweek*, 15 February 1993, 37.

12. The term "abusive" here spans a variety of actions. It typically ranges in its application from working mothers who leave their children alone or with underage babysitters because of the absence of available day care, to mothers who use physical violence on their children, to mothers who are habitual drug users.

13. A *Glamour* magazine report in 1994 suggests the cost of Norplant ranges between $465 and $625. It suggests an additional $35–$125 for a gynecological exam that is not included in the cost of the treatment. If a woman has the implant inserted at a Planned Parenthood clinic, she can expect to pay a total of $500; privately the cost can be upwards of $800. The estimated manufacturing cost of the drug in 1994 was $16. At an average of $365 an implant, in the United States Norplant costs more than in "developing" countries, where it can be as low as $23. Elsewhere in the world, the top price for the implant and its insertion is approximately $120.

14. "Sure-Fire Birth Control, for Five Years," *U.S. News & World Report*, 12 November 1990, 15.

15. The cases and examples of how Norplant is enabling literal state enforcement of contraception easily support this fear of coercion. In Tennessee, for example, officials wanted to pay women on welfare five hundred dollars to get Norplant and fifty dollars a year for each year they kept it in. Walter Graham, a state senator in Mississippi, proposed that his state require the contraceptive for women with at least four children who wanted any kind of government support. His legislation did not pass. A California judge tried to make Norplant a condition of probation for a mother of five convicted of child abuse. She appealed. And a judge in Texas ordered a convicted "child abuser" to use Norplant. She didn't appeal but developed medical problems and had the implants removed. A tubal litigation was performed instead.

16. A glance back over medical history shows that shifts in the reconstruction of women's reproductive rights and bodily integrity are contingent on a changing social climate that rarely has improving the lot of women as its primary incentive. For example, Thomas Laqueur writes in his essay "Orgasm, Generation, and the Politics of Reproductive Biology" that whereas prior to the eighteenth century the male sex organs were considered to be the norm—the female sex organs the in-

version of the norm—by the middle of the century biological differences and distinctions between men and women were virtually mandated not just at the level of the body and soul but "in every physical and moral aspect" (2). Laqueur insists that more than scientific progress is at work here. Rather, oppositions and contrasts between the sexes are evident throughout much of history, but until such differences became politically significant, little interest was expressed. The new biology that emerged, with its "fundamental differences between the sexes and its tortured questioning of the very existence of women's sexual pleasure," did so at a moment of social discord when "the basis for a new order of sex and gender became a critical issue of political theory and practice" (4).

Laqueur's work is pertinent in light of contemporary developments in reproductive technologies. By tracking the language and terms used to discuss reproduction, he is able to assess one of the ways in which the womb and reproductive organs come to be a synecdoche for woman. Useful for understanding both recent debates on women's reproductive freedom and advancing technologies in the field of "reproductive science," Laqueur's analysis illustrates the need to make connections between the practice of the "science" of reproduction, the construction of women's rights, and the contingent shifting attitudes toward sex and sexuality in social, cultural, economic, and global spheres. Thomas Laqueur, "Orgasm, Generation, and the Politics of Reproductive Biology," in *The Making of the Modern Body: Sexuality and Society in the Nineteenth Century*, ed. Catherine Gallagher and Thomas Laqueur (Berkeley: University of California Press, 1987), 1–41.

17. Very few personal interviews with women involved in the global trials are available. The interviews that are readily accessible tend to be confined to the popular press in the United States at least. I could find no formal ethnographies of the effects of Norplant in the United States or elsewhere, so I am basing much of my analysis in this essay on interviews taken from the U.S. press and magazine articles. These range from sources such as the *Los Angeles Times, U.S. News & World Report, Newsweek*, and *Time* to glossy women's magazines such as *Glamour*.

18. Emphasis added. H. Akheter et al., "A Five Year Clinical Evaluation of Norplant Contraceptive Subdermal Implants in Bangladeshi Acceptors," *Contraception* 47, no. 6 (1993): 569–582.

19. Despite the fact that this study is careful to specifically locate itself culturally, a universalizing construction of women's actions based on a model of woman = pregnancy = motherhood is established: one of the most frequent *given* reasons for discontinuation is "desired pregnancy."

20. J. Kasule, T. Chipato, A. Zinanga, M. Mbizvo, and J. Maigurira, "Norplant in Zimbabwe: Preliminary Report," *Central Africa Journal of Medicine* 38, no. 8 (1992): 321–324.

21. M. Shaaban, "Experience with Norplant in Egypt," *Annual of Medicine* 25, no. 2 (1993): 167–169.

22. Nelly Oudshoorn, "A Natural Order of Things?: Reproductive Science and the Politics of Othering," in *Future/Natural: Nature, Science, Culture*, ed. George Robertson et al. (New York: Routledge, 1992), 128.

23. H. B. Croxatto, "Norplant: Levonorgestrel-Releasing Contraceptive Implant," *Annual Medicine* 25, no. 2 (1993): 155–160.

24. Marilyn Strathern, *Reproducing the Future: Anthropology, Kinship, and the New Reproductive Technologies* (New York: Routledge, 1992). Her particular focus is IVF programs whereby women become consumers in order to access these new choices. Given the high cost of many assisted-reproduction programs, choice is contingent on financial access. Thus the concept of greater "freedom to choose" as the ultimate outcome of new reproductive technologies works, according to Strathern, a little like money that "in differentiating everything makes itself the only source

of difference" (35). Choice is imagined as the only source of difference. "Prescriptive consumerism dictates that there is no choice but to always exercise consumerism" (38).

25. A study reported in *Current Opinion in Obstetrics and Gynecology* corroborates this: "International development of biodegradable and nonbiodegradable implants and 1, 3, and 6 months injectables continues. These injectables and implantable contraceptives promise diversity in contraceptive options to match diversity in contraceptive need and lifestyle" (V. E. Cullins, "Injectable and Implantable Contraceptives," *Current Opinion in Obstetrics and Gynecology* 4, no. 4 [1992]: 542). While environmental concerns may well be affecting pharmaceutical companies, a new contraceptive that in the 1990s fails to provide some form of barrier method protection against the spread of HIV and other STDs raises a concern as to what extent "diversity in contraceptive need and lifestyle" and thus sexual practices are acknowledged.

26. Reshma Memon Yaqub, "The Double-Edged Sword of Norplant," *Chicago Tribune*, 24 January 1993, sec. 6, 11.

27. M. L. Frank, A. N. Poindexter, M. L. Johnston, and L. Bateman, "Characteristics and Attitudes of Early Contraceptive Implant Acceptors in Texas," *Family Planning Perspective* 24, no. 5 (1992): 208–213.

28. One examination of how Norplant is experienced in an inner city population comprises a diverse group of people among whom Norplant is already well accepted. This study suggests that intensive counseling about side effects, especially menstrual changes, is crucial for patient satisfaction. The researchers state that "phone calls and unscheduled visits [to deal with] problems were frequent," and "adequate counseling about side effects obviates the need for a routine follow-up visit one month after insertion." Norplant success here rests considerably on patients' being able to make unscheduled doctor's visits and/or phone calls, as well as being able to schedule such visits and phone calls into their lives. Patients on Medicaid are less likely to be able to have the time to make visits or phone calls, nor are Medicaid patients encouraged to assume their rights to make such unscheduled demands of their health care providers. V. E. Cullins, "Preliminary Experiences with Norplant in Inner-City Populations," *Contraception* 47, no. 2 (1993): 193–203.

29. Although a discussion of pregnancy prevention does not implicitly involve a discussion of HIV transmittance, I think that AIDS activists have taught us that in the "age of AIDS" we need to rethink the cultural impact of medical practices: it is important to consider emerging contraceptive technologies in light of the extent to which they are utilized by a diverse group of sexually active people and thus how they contribute to safer sex practices. At a time when sexually active teenagers are among the highest numbers testing positive for the AIDS virus, any means that exacerbate social anxieties toward sex are problematic, especially as Norplant does not provide a barrier against STDs. Studies on the efficacy of the implant frequently conclude that adolescents "may be especially suited for this method of contraception because of its long duration of action and lack of dependence on patient compliance for efficacy." I would argue that failure to educate young women on HIV transmittance during sexual activity continues to buy into the myth that women can't transmit HIV—a myth that has positioned women, particularly young women of color, as the highest group testing positive in recent years. A. B. Berenson and C. M. Wiemann, "Patient Satisfaction and Side Effects with Levonorgestrel Implant (Norplant) Use in Adolescents 18 Years of Age or Younger," *Pediatrics* 92, no. 2 (1993): 257–260.

30. The Laurence G. Paquin School is most notorious of the Baltimore schools for the national controversy it stirred. The school opened in 1966 and "caters for more

than 1,000 girls between 13 and 20, 90 percent of them are black and all of them either pregnant or caring for an infant." "Ending Child Labour," *Economist*, 30 January 1993, 27.

31. "Radical Prophylaxis," *Time*, 29 November–5 December 1992, 23.

32. "Ending Child Labour," *Economist*, 30 January 1993, 27.

33. Tracy Kaplan and John Johnson, "District Defends School Clinic Offering Norplant Contraceptive," *Los Angeles Times*, 26 March 1993, B3.

34. The video is entitled *Planning for the Future: Norplant, A Contraceptive Option for Young Women* and is distributed for educational purposes by the Bridging the Gap Foundation in Decatur, Georgia. Bridging the Gap is a nonprofit organization attempting to inform young women about available contraceptive choices. They distribute a CD-ROM designed to "help people decide between the currently available contraceptive options." The catalog advertising the various videos also includes a 1–800 number for "emergency contraception" as well as offering a video detailing the "Emory method for rapid Norplant removal." The catalog itself seems to be aimed at educators and health care providers.

35. Smith and Easton, "Dilemma of Desire," 24–42.

36. The video is very focused in its aim at young women, particularly young women of color. All the women interviewed are either young high school teenagers or college students and are either African American or Hispanic with the exception of one white woman, who is clearly an Emory student. On occasion throughout the tape, the women are reminded quietly from the sidelines of further points to make: "Oh! yes," remembers one young woman, giggling in response to a muffled voice off camera, "I have no children and with Norplant that's something I don't have to worry about for a while. I know I'll have at least five years to decide whether or not I want to have children and that even when I'm ready, I can just have the Norplants removed and I can become pregnant."

37. Several of the recipients, as well as Dr. Melinda Miller, readily point out that Norplant offers no protection against STDs, particularly HIV. The video makes clear that to be an effective barrier against such diseases, condoms must be used in conjunction with Norplant: "I'd advise anyone, everyone, to use a condom," says one woman.

38. Smith and Easton, "Dilemma of Desire," 42.

Selling Reproduction

PAMELA L. MOORE

COLUMBIA/HCA, a nationwide hospital chain, launched its first national brand equity campaign in 1996. Its multimedia barrage included a full-page print ad that summarizes both the Columbia mission and the modern state of health care. "Forceps . . . Scissors . . . No. 2 pencil. (Hmm, what would happen if someone ran a hospital like a business?)," the headline reads. The tag line proudly announces, "Health care has never worked like this before."

It's hard to argue with that. Subsequent scrutiny by the Office of Inspector General muted Columbia/HCA's later messages but has done nothing to change the fact of the matter.[1] Columbia/HCA had it right in 1996; health care has changed. More than ever, the medical industry professes its commonplace business practices and profit motive. We still speak of physician-patient relationships and deride the most powerful cost controls. But have no doubts—America can't afford old-style payment systems, and we're not about to accept a more socialized method, as the Clintons found out. Managed care, and the business ethos that informs it, are here to stay.

However, academic discussions of medicine have not kept pace, especially in the area of reproductive medicine. Academic discussions of the new technologies center on ethics, global politics, and cyborgian bodies. Meanwhile, the industry moves on, driven in large part by an economic model that looks for profit, not righteousness or postmodern play. Economics are not, I think, a final determinant. My point is merely that the economic part of the picture goes missing too often, a shortened perspective that seems especially odd in light of the financial terms in which the medical industry sees itself.

This essay considers reproductive medicine as an industry. Particularly, it provides an analysis of the way the medical economy presents itself to consumers through advertising for assisted-reproduction technologies (ART).

Marcus Welby Is Dead

The first thing to notice about ART advertising is its existence. Medicine used to be conceptually separate from the capitalist concerns that make advertising necessary. As the Columbia/HCA ad comments, health care as a business is a new idea.

People used to go to doctors and hospitals when they got sick; they were treated because of an ethical imperative. Hippocrates was in fashion. So were indemnity insurance plans that liberally compensated providers for whatever tests and treatments they deemed necessary. In this world, health care advertising was an oxymoron.

Now, insurers offer employers low prices while contracting with providers to cut the costs of treatment through consolidation, elimination of staff, use of gatekeepers, shorter hospital stays, fewer tests, and preventive care.

Physicians too are accepting capitation contracts. These policies give doctors a set payment per month to care for each patient in the physician's patient pool. If expenses to treat the patients exceed that amount, the physician loses money. In short, providers are taking on risk and have a direct incentive to control costs.

Infertility: The Last Great Market

In this world of controlled cost, fertility treatment is a welcome reminder of the good old days. Infertile couples are perceived as an underserved, infinitely expandable market, a market willing to supply substantial out-of-pocket funds when denied access by insurers or managed-care organizations.

The new importance of profit to hospitals and other providers can help explain why, although donor insemination and other procedures have been possible for many years, they only recently have come into widespread use. It may also help explain why infertility only now is being so loudly hailed as a health problem of concern to all, although infertility was equally widespread in previous generations.[2]

The medical establishment is not shy about discussing the economic benefits of promoting ART. Reporting on a meeting of the American Fertility Society, the *Journal of the American Medical Association* comments eagerly that "by one estimate, IVF procedures alone . . . are a \$30 to \$40 million market."[3] Another source notes the potential clientele for IVF is 1 million people with an estimated annual income of \$2 billion; yet another source points out that "infertility affects . . . about 10 percent of the reproductive age population."[4] Approximately 4.9 million women aged fifteen to forty-four report infertility, but only 1.3 million people seek treatment, observes Mark Hornstein, director of the IVF program at Brigham and Women's Hospital, citing statistics from the National Survey of Family Growth. "There are more infertile patients than there are people seeking treatment," he concludes hopefully.

Of course, patients have to be willing to pay for the industry to succeed. Currently, twelve states—Arkansas, California, Connecticut, Hawaii, Illinois, Maryland, Massachusetts, Montana, New York, Ohio, Rhode Island, and Texas—have legally addressed insurance coverage of ART. But not even in these states is coverage guaranteed. In Arkansas, for example, HMOs are exempt from the law, and other insurers can limit coverage to a very small lifetime maximum of $15,000. In all Arkansas cases, a woman's ovum can only be fertilized with her husband's sperm.

For the most part, then, patients who want the service pay for it themselves. Thus, providers are not concerned about providing care cost-effectively to meet the demands of HMOs or avoid risk under capitation. More patients simply equals more money.

Estimates of revenue vary widely. One study says a live birth from IVF ranges between $66,667 and $114,286, depending on the number of times the treatment has to be repeated. Older couples can pay as much as $800,000 per delivery, the study says.[5] Newsweek reports that couples using ART "spend at least $10,000 and as much as $100,000 on diagnostic tests and fertility drugs and . . . assisted-reproductive techniques."[6] A retrospective study of all ART procedures at a California HMO revealed the average cost per delivery as $37,816.[7] USA Today says the average cost for one attempt of IVF is $9,990.[8]

Many individuals are willing to accept such financial burden. One survey found respondents willing to spend between $170,000 and $1.7 million of their own income, savings, or bank-loaned money for IVF. More than 60 percent of respondents to another survey would pay more than one year's earnings or $100,000, assuming a success rate of 25 percent to 100 percent per cycle.[9]

If patients can pay the price, a good part of the proceeds is pure profit for the provider. George Annas, professor of health law at Boston University, estimated in an interview that fertility clinics realize a margin of 37.5 percent per procedure.

Providers are, for obvious reasons, reluctant to reveal exactly how much profit they make from ART, but it seems possible to incur very few expenses. Excluding some surgeries, there is no need to feed, bed, and otherwise care for long-term patients. While some larger providers pay to hire famous physicians or build new facilities, many simply begin performing and marketing procedures. Only about half of the fertility clinics in the United States are associated with hospitals; the rest are independent physicians or physician groups.[10]

The bottom line is that infertile women willing to pay out of pocket are a key audience for the new breed of medical marketers, as the growth of female-targeted advertising demonstrates. Hospital and health plan advertising rose 50 percent and 95 percent, respectively, in 1996–1997 over 1995–1996 levels.[11] Nearly all ads in the field are "image" ads, designed to create general confidence rather than a demand for specific services—a strategy meant to keep the expensive ill away. The few exceptions are services patients are willing to pay for out of pocket—especially ART.

Infertility for Everyone: The Naturalization of Reproductive Technologies

It's striking that advertising for ART exists and is growing. It is bizarre that the ads appear in mass-market publications. Standard marketing procedure would suggest that advertisers use direct mail or at least make media buys in female-targeted publications. Instead, the ads collected here all appeared in general newspapers. Increasingly, ART is portrayed as a natural, expected part of womanhood, not as a high-tech miracle for the few.

As Janice Raymond has remarked, stories about reproductive medicine are usually "eschatological": "Reproductive technologies get portrayed as technological breakthroughs. Images of progress pervade the print and electronic media representation of these technologies."[12] To some extent, ART remains within this narrative trajectory. In health care advertising, however, fertility treatment seems more like a regular part of a healthy woman's pursuit of "wellness" than a remarkable feat of mythic proportion.

Trigon Blue Cross Blue Shield, for example, offers a women's health program, a "wellness and disease prevention program" designed to keep up with the "predictable changes in every woman's life." Some of the "key health issues" that "every woman" may find "predictable" are "preconception, postpartum care, parenting, gynecological surgery, cancer prevention, domestic violence, osteoporosis, and menopause."

"Preconception" fits easily into the category of what every woman can expect. It is no technical miracle.

Harvard Pilgrim Health Care similarly recognizes women's "special health care needs," including "planning a pregnancy." "Planning a pregnancy" used to be code for using contraception or spacing births. Now it's a matter of medically induced pregnancy.

Even the techie-sounding Center for Reproductive Endocrinology explicitly refutes miraculous stories of progress in its advertising, replacing them with stories of caring and hope. "You know the cold, hard facts," its headline reads over a photograph of a bee and flower. "Now how about some nice, warm answers? We're here for you every step of the way," the copy continues comfortably. ART is not even as cold and hard as the birds and the bees; it's a simple part of health care.

All this buzz to naturalize ART is part and parcel of changing conceptions of the role of (white, wealthy) women and of the role of reproduction in modern society. But it is also part of a shift in what medicine is about. The "miracle" babies of yesteryear must be the "normal" babies of today if providers are to be able to exploit the lucrative market they see, and partly created, in infertility.

Madwoman in the Fertility Clinic?

It is ironic to consider medical marketers' machinations to get women into fertility treatment. The media insist that there are growing crowds of aging women mewling desperately for children at any cost, women serviced, thank god, by a self-sacrificing medical team. Medical advertising implies something quite different. Who's desiring whom?

Advertisers recognize infertile women as a tough audience. They are skeptical and knowledgeable, not crazy. Terri Langhans, president of First Strategic Group, a health care marketing consulting firm based in Whittier, California, says infertile women are "more educated than any other consumer in the marketplace." Because the standard definition of infertility is a full year of unsuccessful attempts to conceive, patients already have been dealing with the medical issues involved for some time before seeking treatment. During that time, women tend to read voraciously, says Langhans. By the time they see an ad and are ready to respond, they are probably frustrated, technically knowledgeable, and in no mood for condescension.

Aware of their audience's knowledge, many advertisers try to woo patients with implicit promises of pregnancy. The Federal Trade Commission has banned explicit guarantees, filing eleven cease-and-desist orders against fertility clinics between 1991 and 1995. Saint Barnabas Medical Center, for example, offers "pregnancy rates that are among the highest in the nation." Michael Reese Fertility Center similarly states, "Our clinical results consistently deliver one of the highest rates in the nation. . . . " "Pregnancy is possible for more than half of all couples who seek treatment," reads an ad bordered by stylized sperm. However vague, such claims dispel the image of manic women. The ads assume an audience that is comparing rates and calmly going where the chances are best.

Even more revealing are ads that promote a facility based on fairly sophisticated knowledge about its staff or treatment options. Saint Barnabas Medical Center, for example, introduced its Institute for Reproductive Medicine and Science with the headline "World Leaders in Fertility Treatment Are Now at Saint Barnabas Medical Center," specifying that Dr. Jacques Cohen is at the center. Cohen was already well known for his work at Cornell Medical Center. Prospective patients, the ad's creators assumed, recognize his name. The Fertility Clinic of Northern New Jersey similarly announces the presence of Dr. David Navot. There are almost no other instances in medical advertising in which a physician's name is the message. Patients generally don't know one expert from another.

Often, they also don't know one form of treatment from another. The Genetics & IVF Institute, however, ran an ad in the *Philadelphia Inquirer* and other large-market papers with the eye-catching headline "ICSO for Male Infertility Donor Egg IVF Non-Surgical Sperm Aspiration Ovary Cryopreservation." It sounds like an article from a specialized medical journal, but it was intended for a "lay" audience. The institute could assume that prospective patients knew exactly what the ad promised.

Advertising for fertility services, in both its very presence and its messages, debunks assumptions about infertile women. It also reveals the changing economics that inform so much of what happens in hospitals and clinics today. Readings, ethical discussions, and other musings on ART should turn at least part of an eye to the way the medical community sees itself, that is, increasingly, as a business.

Notes

1. Although Columbia/HCA serves here as a paradigmatic instance of health care as business, its practices are not distinct in the industry, only more widely recognized. The kickback and Medicare fraud cases leveled against it, for example, also have been successfully launched against leading research institutions, including Thomas Jefferson and University of Pennsylvania, which are popularly believed to have patients' best interests at heart. The federal government's interest in Columbia and others has much more to do with making money and stopping fraud than it has to do with suspicion of the intersection of business and medicine. See, too, Robert Kuttner, "Columbia/HCA and the Resurgence of the for-Profit Hospital Business," pts. 1 and 2, *New England Journal of Medicine* 335, no. 5 (1996): 362–367; no. 6 (1996): 446–451. Kuttner's article derides for-profit medicine but concludes by admitting that there is very little difference anymore between it and not-for-profit health care.
2. A 1901 study claimed that 20 percent of married women were sterile, up from 2 percent in "preceding generations." This study was motivated by concern over women entering academics (straining their reproductive systems) and growth in the lower-class and immigrant populations. See George J. Englemann, "The Increasing Sterility of American Women," *Journal of the American Medical Association*

37 (1901): 890–897, quoted in Brian Pace and Micaela Sullivan-Fowler, eds., "JAMA 95 Years Ago," *Journal of the American Medical Association* 276, no. 14 (1996): 1120. Today's diatribes are motivated by similarly suspect sexual politics but also, I claim, by the economics of the health care industry.

3. Chris Ann Raymond, "In Vitro Fertilization Enters Stormy Adolescence As Experts Debate Odds," *Journal of the American Medical Association* 259, no. 4 (1988): 464.

4. Robert Blank and Janna C. Merrick, *Human Reproduction, Emerging Technologies, and Conflicting Rights* (Washington, D.C.: Congressional Quarterly Press, 1995), and American Society for Reproductive Medicine, "Fact Sheet: In Vitro Fertilization," http://www.asrm.org/fact/invitor.html.

5. Peter Neumann, Soheyla D. Gharib, and Milton C. Weinstein, "The Cost of a Successful Delivery with In Vitro Fertilization," *New England Journal of Medicine* 331, no. 4 (1994): 239 and 242.

6. Sharon Begley, "The Baby Myth," *Newsweek*, 4 September 1995, 38–47.

7. D. A. Hidlebaugh et al., "The Cost of Assisted Reproductive Technologies for a Health Maintenance Organization" (paper presented at the annual meeting of the American Society for Reproductive Medicine, 1995), http:///asrm.abstracts.org/1995toc.htm.

8. "Cost of IVF," *USA Today*, 7 April 1998, final ed., sec. D, 1.

9. Neumann, Gharib, and Weinstein, "Cost of a Successful Delivery," 242, and H. M. Shapiro, "Infertility, Quality of Life, and Cost-Effectiveness Analysis" (paper presented at the annual meeting of the American Society for Reproductive Medicine, 1995), http://asrm.abstracts.org/1995toc.htm.

10. "Infertility Clinics Need to Watch Ads," *Healthcare PR & Marketing News* 5, no. 4 (1996): 6.

11. Jane Hodges, "Direct Marketing," *Advertising Age*, 28 October 1996, s1–s2.

12. Janice Raymond, "The Marketing of the New Reproductive Technologies: Medicine, the Media, and the Idea of Progress," *Issues in Reproductive and Genetic Engineering* 3, no. 3 (1990): 253.

Notes Toward a Reproductive Theory of Technology

ANNE BALSAMO

Sɪᴛᴜᴀᴛᴇᴅ ᴀᴛ ᴛʜᴇ ᴇɴᴅ of part 1 of this book, this essay seeks to elucidate the contributions offered by the work collected here to the development of a reproductive theory of technology. I begin by presenting a set of assumptions about technology in order to establish a working definition of the term. By the end I suggest that even though "reproductive technologies" are the focal technological "objects" of these essays, the arguments that unfold describe the various ways in which all technologies reproduce cultural arrangements. In this sense, all technologies can be considered *reproductive* technologies. This assertion, discussed in different forms by feminist scholars such as Zoë Sofoulis, Donna Haraway, and Paula Treichler (among others), is one of the strongest insights to emerge from recent feminist studies of new reproductive technologies.[1] This insight has inspired my own work on the body and technology and in the construction of feminist multimedia; and just as this essay builds on the accumulated insights of other feminist scholars, so, too, will a more fully elaborated theory emerge from the collective analyses now going on in the name of feminist studies of science, technology, and medicine.

A Beginning Point

It is by now common to assert that technology must, first and foremost, be understood as a postdisciplinary object. This is to say that there is no discipline of study that has not taken up the issue of technology whether in its "object form" as an artifact, tool, or material practice or in its "subject form" as a topic of discussion, analysis, philosophy, or set of techniques. This assertion

87

echoes an observation made by Teresa de Lauretis more than a decade ago, that technology has become "our context"—regardless of how one defines the identity of "our" in that statement.[2] The differential distribution and use of technological resources across the globe do not negate this observation; more than a few cultural critics have noted that even with global disparities in access to technology and in levels of technological infrastructure, and indeed in the value placed on technology as part of an epistemological worldview, there are few places in the world that exist "outside" the technological reach of multinational capitalism. Given that this historically specific form of capitalism is significantly supported by the technologies of communication, command, and control—those networks of power Haraway calls the "informatics of domination"—we can see how right de Lauretis is in asserting that "technology is our context, political and personal."

To claim that technology is a postdisciplinary object suggests that it no longer properly belongs to the special few (the philosophers, the engineers). Instead this suggests that thinkers in several disciplines might have something important to contribute to our collective understanding of the "nature" of technology. In fact, this interdisciplinary influence is evident in the work of those who are considered to be the most noteworthy philosophers of technology: Jacques Ellul, for example, grounds his approach to the philosophy of technology in an analysis of modern society, offering a detailed sociological assessment of the way in which technology has become the defining characteristic of advanced industrial societies. Even though most contemporary philosophers have moved beyond thinking about technology strictly in relation to science, as marked by the formulation that once held sway that technology was "applied science," there is still significant debate surrounding the proper approach to defining technology: Should it be defined anthropologically as what human beings actually do, or sociologically as a consequence of particular social relations, or epistemologically as a specific form of knowledge? So even as philosophers themselves continue to wrestle with classic philosophical concerns pertaining to technology, concerns that address the ethics, morality, and metaphysics of technology, the field itself recognizes that the intellectual insights and habits of analysis required to understand technology may need to come from other places.[3]

If we review the insights drawn from the work of scholars in feminist studies, we encounter a different approach to the problem of defining technology. Less concerned with the elucidation of the underlying ontological or epistemological nature of technology or of *techne*, these scholars collectively suggest a slightly different, but in the end no less philosophical, definition as a starting point for the analysis of technology: technology is a manifestation of cultural values. Rather than debating an essentialist definition of the "nature" of technology as "tool," "means," or specific form of knowledge, this definitional statement expresses an understanding about the way in which technology manifests the material world. It is an antiessentialist statement in that although it is semantically structured as a definition (*technology is x*), by inserting the phrase "a manifestation of cultural values," this definition makes technology *not* an equivalence between *objects* but rather the equivalent of a *process* of making and revealing.

In one sense, this approach is consistent with Heidegger's view that technology is part of the existential structure of human "being." Moreover, it seems compatible with his notion of "technics," which for him is the term for a technological habit that can never be understood in isolation from human being but rather should be considered a means of "being-making." Zoë Sofoulis affirms Heidegger's view and its compatibility with a feminist theory of technology when she writes:

> Heidegger proposes that we cannot hope to properly reflect upon and understand the character of modern technology by merely staring at the technological. Instead we must inquire into what our technologies tell us about our ways of seeing and revealing the world, and be alert to the danger that we will ourselves be obliviously claimed by a technological ordering, will look on ourselves as available resources, and fail to see our own part in bringing the world and ourselves to this point. Likewise, we are mistaken to understand technological arts in terms of techniques and tools alone. Instead we must reflect upon what modes of revealing they present, what questions they pose about dominant forms of technological revelation, what glimpses of alternative configurations they offer.[4]

Here Sofoulis reminds us of Heidegger's concern that people can be "claimed by a technological ordering" when they begin to see themselves and their world through a technological optic. This warning hints at the complex nature of technological agency—a topic that I will return to at the end of this essay. But on the issue of the process of understanding technology, Sofoulis is right to point out that it was Heidegger who argued that we cannot "hope to understand the character of modern technology by merely staring at the technology." To this end, Heidegger suggests a broader definition of technology whereby technology is understood not as a set of techniques or even tools but rather as *a total arrangement of life*. In an article titled "The Aristotelian vs. Heideggerian Approach to the Problem of Technology," Webster Hood elaborates Heidegger's thinking on this point:

> Technics are never used in isolation; they always occur as members in a context of technics, a totality of tools, implements, machines,

materials, energies and other items of use. Such contexts include more
than technics and useful items; we will see later that science and
persons are also included. To emphasize the spatial function of
technics in experience, let us call an arrangement of technics a
"context-totality"—the expression being synonymous with the terms
complex, pattern, system. Heidegger gives no detailed explication of
contextual-totalities, but provides some examples: the carpenter's
workshop, the shoemaker's shop, a house with different rooms, a
railroad platform, a construction site, a street.[5]

If we consider the examples given, that is, the carpenter's workshop, a house
with different rooms, a construction site, a street, the definition of technology implied by Heidegger—even if it is not fully elaborated by him—is one
that includes much more than the object notions of tools or techniques. What
else is included can be gleaned from the examples listed: tools and techniques,
certainly, but also people, professional and artisanal activities, functions, in-
frastructures, points of circulation, and so on. Thus we can borrow from
Heidegger an insight about the phenomenological process of technology as
"being-making" and his sense of the character of technology as being multiform, that is, a pattern, a system, or an arrangement. The key insight Heidegger
offers to the project of building a feminist theory of technology is, as Sofoulis
suggests, the admonition to focus on "modes of revealing" presented by a technological arrangement, as well as the "glimpses of alternative configurations
they offer." This is consistent with and amplifies insights gathered from feminist studies of new reproductive technologies (NRT)—that the technological arrangements (of which NRT are a part of) reveal deeply embedded
ideological beliefs about the nature of the female body, the meaning of gender differences, and the privilege of heterosexuality. The practice of feminist
criticism is, in this sense, the act of making the "mode of revealing" evident
and of narrating the logic whereby some of the possible or "alternative configurations" are promoted and formally sanctioned, while other possibilities
are foreclosed and outlawed.

The key difference between Heidegger's view and a feminist definition
of technology is the extent to which technology is defined as a part of an unchanging "nature" of the human being, and the extent to which this "nature"
transcends history, erases gender and race, and obscures notions of positionality
and location. In this sense, what technology manifests or reveals, that is, cultural values, is not something reducible to objects or things, nor is it an essential and historically unchanging aspect of human "being." Rather, I am
suggesting that we consider technology as a complex cultural arrangement that
is determined by cultural forces that precede it, as it also organizes and reproduces those forces over time.

A Reproductive Model of Technology's Reproductive Mode

To assert that technologies manifest cultural values still leaves everything to say about the characteristic form of the manifestation and the meaning of the cultural values revealed. Drawing on recent work in cultural theory, especially work by Ernesto Laclau, Chantal Mouffe, Stuart Hall, and Jennifer Slack, a fuller elaboration of this definition explains that technologies are best thought of as an "ensemble" or an "articulated arrangement." As will be familiar to many readers, this assertion draws on Gramscian articulation theory and Raymond Williams's work on cultural formations. Articulation is defined as a process of meaning construction whereby one unit of the ensemble or formation acquires meaning in part through the relationship with or attachment to other units of the ensemble. The process of articulation—which is the process through which meaning is constructed by the forging of associations and of semiotic codings—expresses a nuanced similarity to the process of second-order signification discussed by Roland Barthes, where the meaning of any one sign within a system of signs is in part constructed through the association with other signs, both through associations of identity (equivalence) and difference (dissimilarity). In contrast to the Heideggerian sense of the technological totality as "contextual-totalities," where the examples included "the carpenter's workshop, a house with different rooms," and so on, this notion of articulation implies that a key dimension to the elucidation of any technological formation is the historical and cultural specificity of a particular arrangement.

The cumulative effect of the articulation or arrangement is the reproduction of specific cultural values. The central question that emerges from this formulation concerns the meaning of the term *reproduction*. As Michelle Barrett reminds us in her book *Women's Oppression Today*, there are at least three "analytically distinct referents of the concept [of reproduction]—social reproduction, reproduction of the labor force, or biological reproduction."[6] The project of thinking through the way in which technological formations serve to reproduce cultural values can take as a starting point any one of these referents. For example, Marilyn Strathern begins with a biological notion of reproduction to explicate the process whereby anthropology as an academic discipline will unfold in the future. In her chapter "Reproducing Anthropology," she offers an encapsulated account of the genetic theory of human reproduction as it involves two procreative processes: one the process of heredity, the other the process of development. Reproduction is the means whereby constitutive material (DNA in this case) has "an effect either when it is replicated (as a genotype or genome) or when the genotype is in turn expressed (as a phenotype)."[7] This dual process of replication and expression, of heredity and development, is at the heart of the "reproductive model" that Strathern is keen to elaborate in the aim of understanding the hopes that academics hold for the future of the field of anthropology. Although she is careful to situate this "reproductive model" in a particular Euro-American view of procreation, she notes that it offers an interesting approach to think about such issues as continuity, change, potentiality, and the future, both as these apply to the intellectual work of anthropology as a discipline and as they mark our thinking about the nature of human identity and individuality. In fact, throughout her discussion of the reproductive model, she draws explicitly on the discourse of reproductive technologies, especially statements made by Warnock and others in the debates that preceded the formulation of the 1990 Human Fertilization and Embryology Act.

Strathern's model identifies the processes that need to be elaborated in the project of understanding the reproductive dynamics of technological formations. These include the manifestation of continuity, of development, of change, and of potentiality. In addition to this list of *processes*, we can also begin to identify the *elements* that constitute a technological formation. These include:

- Devices and artifacts/tools and techniques
- Forms of knowledge (*techne* and technics)
- Reified human labor
- Material conditions of production/reproduction
- Forms of embodiment
- Cultural narratives
- Aesthetic properties
- Institutional forms and policies
- Economies (systems of value)
- Codified social relations
- Circuits of exchange or patterns of circulation

These elements itemize the multiform "nature" of technology. In this sense, what "counts" as a technology are the articulated elements of a particular formation. The reproductive dynamic of the technological formation will also involve those processes Strathern identified: the manifestation of continuity, of development, of change, and of potentiality. The nature of these processes are difficult to define precisely because they refer to differences that are manifested over time and understood relationally, either as a relation between two states—the meaning of continuity, for example, implies an equivalence between two states or moments—or, as in the case of the concept of potentiality, as a relation between what is possible and what is manifested. In addition to accounting for the actual processes of reproduction, a fuller elaboration of a reproductive theory of technology would also need to account for the way in which the elements are articulated—or "sutured"—one to another. Although such an account of the forces of articulation is beyond the scope of this essay, I would like to discuss this set of theoretical assertions in the context of the feminist work included in this collection. These essays not only describe the multiform shape of the technological formation of technologically assisted reproduction but also describe in more concrete and historical detail how specific cultural values are actually reproduced.

Reproductive Technologies as Technologies of Reproduction

Not surprisingly, the different projects represented here illuminate different aspects of the technological formation built around new reproductive technologies—some take as a starting point the "object form" of new reproductive technologies, others focus on the cultural narratives that invest these technologies with meaning. What they share is an attempt to understand the way in which the new reproductive technologies are implicated in the reproduction of ideologies of the gendered, race-marked, and class-positioned body. In the first essay in part 1, Dion Farquhar takes as her subject the circulation of human body parts in the form of gamete traffic. Although this is a highly specific set of practices bordering on the science fictional, what she also elaborates is an understanding about the institutional processes of technological reproduction—where what is being reproduced is not just bodies but also desires, cultural identities, and subject formations. Thus, in describing the gendered nature of gamete traffic, Farquhar describes how

> gamete traffic is driven by difference—the circulating, supplementing, and hybridizing desires, fantasies, and identities of their users, suppliers, and administrators. . . . So, for example, the technique of ovum donation stimulates new demands and desires—for instance, for peri- and postmenopausal pregnancy—which in turn steer themselves into the flow of gamete traffic, seeking a solution through the expansion of childbearing capacity offered by prosthesis. The relation between desire and technology, however, is reciprocal. While desire for technology sometimes exacerbates the development of a technology, an existing technology always also stimulates and proliferates essentially unpredictable desires and fantasies.

The focus of Farquhar's essay is on the unintended consequences of gamete traffic, including the production of new agents of reproduction, of new cultural "conundrums," and of new social ways of being. Thus Farquhar sets forth a reading that suggests how this technological formation produces change out of potentiality. The technological fragmentation of maternity into "genetic (ovum-providing), gestational (uterus-providing), and social-legal (nurturance-providing)" sets up new possibilities for kinship relations. In her discussion of the circulatory dynamic of gamete donation, she reminds readers that the process of reproductive medicalization is not monolithic—not only does it set up different possibilities for different participants, but the effects of the process are not totalizing: donors are not all victims, recipients are not all privileged, and physicians are not all empowered. Her strongest claim argues that "it is impossible to construe gamete traffic along a binary model—as either inherently repressive or liberatory." Rather, she argues for the need to appreciate the contestation that animates the technological formation and offers suggestions for tracking its dynamic unfolding.

With a similar sensibility, Angela Wall analyzes Norplant implants as a technological device that has contradictory consequences tied to its use by women who are situated in different networks of social and economic relations. As Wall explains, "Norplant is an economic benefit to women who cannot afford to have another child or who do not want to confront the alternatives to another pregnancy." At the same time, Norplant is also touted as a judicial tool that could assist in the state's regulation of the birth options of low-income women. Thus Norplant is simultaneously defined as a technique of empowerment and of disempowerment. What Wall shows is how the "meaning" of Norplant—as a device and tool—is a result of the articulation between the device, cultural beliefs about "worthy mothers" and "monstrous mothers," and forms of embodiment that themselves are a consequence of bodily practices, economic conditions, and cultural narratives about race-marked bodies.

Pam Moore's analysis of the industry of reproductive medicine offers a historically concrete description of the economics of infertility treatment and the way in which the reproductive medical industry exemplifies a post-Fordist logic of late capitalism. To this end Moore analyzes the role of advertising in the reproduction and naturalization of reproductive technologies. By investigating the marketing aspects of reproductive medicine, Moore addresses the interesting edges of the technological formation of new reproductive technologies where it intersects and collides with other cultural formations. For example, in discussing the claims made in certain infertility treatment center ads, she reports that the Federal Trade Commission had to step in and regulate the kinds of claims (about rates of pregnancy) that could be included in an advertisement. Apparently the FTC has banned the inclusion of explicit guarantees and now requires that advertised pregnancy rates be supported by reliable scientific evidence. This suggests one way in which the technological formation of new reproduction technologies reproduces the process of biological reproduction as a commodity that can be institutionally regulated just as are other commodities. The emergence of a reproductive medical industry attests to the fact that the business of life has never been better.

Susan Squier offers a clear analysis of one of the most potent and far-ranging consequences of the practice of new reproductive technologies: the reconstruction of new identities for fetuses and mothers, and the wholesale refashioning of the fetal/material relation. In tracing through the construction of these new identities, where the fetus is constructed as a subject with rights while the mother is cast as a threat to those rights, Squier is careful to remind us that this situation—of the increasing subjectification of the fetus and the desubjectification of the mother—does not result *simply* from the development and deployment of these new technologies; to argue thus would be to locate agency solely with the technologies in question. While she remains committed to the understanding that these technologies do play a significant role in the reconstruction of these identities and the reconfiguration of rights and ethics, Squier offers a more complex analysis of how these technologies acquire a determining force. She does this by reviewing the changing historical relationship between the fetus and the mother to suggest that it has long been the case that medical practitioners and indeed culture more broadly have had "notorious difficulty in ascertaining and accurately representing the subject position, desires, needs, and capacities" of gestating women. Moving from a consideration of literary representations of the fetus/mother relation, Squier turns her attention to an analysis of the 1994 Final Report of the NIH's Human Embryo Research Panel; in so doing, Squier illustrates the multiple ways that cultural narratives get constructed and circulate within literary genres as well as nonliterary forms. Specifically she draws our attention to a site where discourse meets materiality—where the discursive construction of maternal identity and fetal subjectification becomes materialized as panel reports get translated into policy statements that guide research practices and the development of (reproductive) technological protocols.

The role played by cultural narratives in the articulation of the meaning of new reproductive technologies cannot be underestimated. In her reading of "surrogacy narratives," E. Ann Kaplan addresses a different aspect of the technological formation—that of the ideological positions circulated in different surrogacy narratives. Kaplan describes two sets of popular narratives, ones where "sisterly motives abound" (where the motives for participating in a surrogacy relationship are expressed in terms of sisterly duty, devotion, or responsibility) and others (which Kaplan calls "negative" narratives) that "reveal antitechnology sentiments and dwell on 'unsisterly practices.'" She notes that these sets of narratives "set up a false binary" between competing polemics that fails not only to recognize the multiple positions that participants actually occupy but also to address the multiple lines of force (such as economics, class, and race) that determine and structure the surrogacy situation. Thus she illustrates how cultural narratives about women's experiences with a particular technology gain the status of myth and function to delimit what can be said and thought about the meaning of a new technology. Her essay also shows how the technological formation of new reproductive technologies reproduces received cultural values of an earlier arrangement through the articulation between cultural narratives and myths (of "mother-constructs," for example) and new mother-child configurations made possible by the application of new technologies.

Other projects offer a more historical approach to the study of the technological formation of new reproductive technologies and in so doing illuminate the processes whereby the formation both continues and revises previous articulations. For example, Karyn Valerius argues that the philosophical issues raised by the current practice of assisted reproduction and the recent deployment of reproductive technologies are best understood in relation to a set of questions that were answered in the nineteenth century. She situates the contemporary U.S. public discourse on assisted reproduction in relation to a historical understanding of Western traditions of monstrosity. The historical trajectory she traces includes early modern accounts of "monstrous births" as due to supernatural intervention as well as Aristotle's "imagination" theory that attributed monstrous births to the mental state of the mother during conception. Valerius suggests that the "imagination theory" of monstrosity was overturned in part because of broad epistemological shifts brought about by the rise of science and biologism in particular. Thus she offers an illustration of how this contemporary technological formation revives and revises—in effect, imperfectly reproduces—a particular epistemological worldview that is contradictorily scientistic and biological but also superstitious and irrational.

A Feminist Theory of Technology

If we take the work collected here as indicative of the range of scholarship going on in the name of feminist science and technology studies, we can see how it is a collective project that is less concerned with debating the ontological underpinnings of a theory of technology as it is with trying to think through the technological conditions of possibilities of social transformation. These feminist projects situate their "objects of study"—reproductive technologies—within a cultural matrix of social practices, discourses, and institutions. In so doing, they describe how technological devices are one—but only one—element of that matrix. More to the point, these essays illustrate the multiform meaning of the term *technology* and argue implicitly for the importance of developing a multimediated theory of technology. By multimediated I mean that the theory that is being constructed will necessarily take inspiration and guiding questions from various disciplines and intellectual methodologies. Even as this theory will be built across disciplinary traditions and through the application of different methods of analysis, the political horizon remains consistent with feminist work more broadly. This is to say that the ultimate aim of constructing such analyses of this technological formation is to illuminate the possibilities of transformation and reformation now and in the future.

Notes

1. Zoë Sofoulis, "Exterminating Fetuses: Abortion, Disarmament, and the Sexo-semiotics of Extraterrestrialism," *Diacritics* 14, no. 2 (1984): 47–59.
2. Teresa de Lauretis, "Signs of Wa/onder," in *The Technological Imagination: Theories and Fictions*, ed. Teresa de Lauretis, Andreas Huyssen, and Kathleen Woodward (Madison, Wisc.: Coda Press, 1980), 167.
3. Indeed, in the introduction to their edited collection called *Philosophy and Technology* (New York: Free Press, 1972), Carl Mitchem and Robert Mackey write: "But precisely because technology is intimately involved with practical affairs, the stimulus to develop a philosophy of technology is more than just philosophical. It also arises from economic, social, political and environmental problems" (30). In the end, they argue for the primacy of the philosophical approach, especially in the face of the judgment that "technology needs to be humanized": "the conception one has of technology ultimately determines whether, after philosophical issues have been exhausted, what remains is an economic, social or political problem. The issue of humanizing technology is, at its foundation, philosophical rather than simply social or political" (30).
4. Zoë Sofoulis, "Interdictions, Intersections, Interfacing: Women, Technology, Art, and Philosophy," Julian Branshaw Memorial Lecture, Sydney, Australia, 1993. Quotation is from page 11.
5. Hood cited in Mitchem and Mackey, *Philosophy and Technology*, 356.
6. Michelle Barrett, *Women's Oppression Today*, rev. ed. (London: Verso, 1980), 21. Although Barrett does address some of the theoretical problems attendant to the project of thinking about women's oppression in the context of these different forms of reproduction, her broader project is to evaluate the usefulness of Marxist theory in light of a gendered analysis of the nature of social reproduction. Thus she focuses on ideologies of gender, of class, and of the family and on the forms of gendered subjectivity as these are implicated in the processes central to the reproduction of the labor force. She reminds us of the critical insights offered by Louis Althusser on the nature of social reproduction and argues that his work that emphasized "the familial and ideological spheres—in contrast to classical Marxism's obsessional focus on production and the world of wage labor" offers a theoretical opening for "thinking gender" in the context of the reproduction of capitalism. This latter concern leads Barrett to evaluate closely and eventually dismiss theoretical claims made about women's role in the reproduction of capitalist relations of production based (solely) on their biological role in the process of human reproduction. For example, she rightly criticizes the biologism inherent in arguing that the gendered division of labor (which supports capitalist class relations) is a consequence of women's bodily experience with menstruation, pregnancy, lactation and child care.
7. Marilyn Strathern, "Reproducing Anthropology,"in *Reproducing the Future: Anthropology, Kinship, and the New Reproductive Technologies* (New York: Routledge, 1992): 163–182.

Part 2　　　　Fantasies

Negotiating Boundaries

From Assisted Reproduction to Assisted Replication

THE CASE OF Anna Johnson is a familiar one by now: the African American woman acting as gestational surrogate mother for Crispina and Mark Calvert decided during the pregnancy that she didn't want to surrender the child soon to be born. When she sued the Calverts to end her surrogacy contract, the courts decided against her, finding that the Calverts were the parents of the baby boy, since the embryo had been created from their gametes.[1] We may be less familiar with the case of Kawana Ashley. In 1994, in Clearwater, Florida, that nineteen-year-old girl shot herself in the stomach. Taken to the hospital, on March 27 she was delivered by emergency cesarean section of a baby girl. "After a week, [the baby's] underdeveloped kidneys began to fail and her body filled with fluids. She died April 11." According to newspaper reports, Ashley "claimed she didn't have enough money for an abortion." She was charged with third-degree murder and manslaughter: newspapers reported allegations that she killed her "6-month-old-fetus" "by shooting herself in the *womb* [my italic]."[2]

The Johnson/Calvert case is a classic example of assisted reproduction, while the Ashley case is not explicitly connected to the medical practices once called "the new reproductive technologies," and more recently referred to as assisted reproduction, a label that interestingly obscures technology in the guise of simple human assistance.[3] Yet I begin with these two cases because I see in both of them ways of thinking and behaving exacerbated by the practices of assisted reproduction: positing a fetal subject; thinking of the gestating woman as interchangeable object rather than unique subject; viewing the fetus and the mother as social, medical, and legal antagonists; and collapsing the broad range of activities and practices that are motherhood and fatherhood to the narrow fact of gamete contribution. Taken together, these tendencies reveal an increasingly ambiguous boundary between fetus and mother and an increasingly, troublingly narrow definition of parenthood.[4] In what follows, I will first examine the ways we are managing boundary ambiguity, returning in my conclusion to the issue of definitional precision.

As assisted reproduction has increasingly been naturalized, through law, commerce, and medicine, the distinction between fetus and mother has become an increasingly fuzzy one. With the breakdown of the firm line between inside and outside, between a potential future life and a current life possessed of social, legal, and medical status, the fetus *inside* is increasingly treated as if it were already *outside*, the rightful subject of medical, social, and legal intervention. Moreover, the mother-to-be is becoming less a civil, legal, or medical subject than the subject of policing by all three institutions.

While assisted reproduction is destabilizing the fetal/maternal relation, another boundary is also becoming more ambiguous—that between human and animal. Both boundaries were dramatically challenged in July 1996 by Ian Wilmut's cloning of Dolly, the Finn Dorset ewe, an event that called into question "nothing less than whether human procreation is going to remain human, whether children are going to be made rather than begotten," according to biochemist and philosopher Leon Kass.[5] Species and generation are boundary concepts, produced by the social and material technologies, institutionalized discourses, epistemologies, and critical practices that come together in assisted reproduction, including, should the technology be extended to human beings, in cloning.[6] In what follows I will consider how a variety of social technologies—literature, legislation, law—function to *produce and manage* the generational (fetal/maternal) and species (the human/animal) boundaries.

Generation

The two terms at the generational boundary—fetus and mother—are not symmetrical. We now have a great range of increasingly precise terms for the products of conception, ranging from zygote to pre-embryo, to embryo, to fetus, but we have no customary term that captures the in-between subject that is the gestating woman.[7] Two processes of subject formation occur in parallel during gestation: as the fetus is developing, so too the gestating woman develops, from a woman who may be pregnant, to a woman who is pregnant, to a woman who is carrying an embryo, to (after quickening) a woman who is carrying a fetus, and finally (with birth) to a mother. The term *mother* is relational in nature, carrying implications about a maternal subject as well as invoking the discourses of psychoanalysis, sociology, history, art, religion, and literature. Full as it is, however, it is also empty: when the gestating woman is known as the "mother," the term lacks any precision about the in-between state she experiences while the fetus gestates, granting her a subjectivity *in advance* of her condition (as any nervous first-time mother-to-be will attest). We lack a quick, specific term for her complex, liminal subject position.

Perhaps the asymmetry in these terms results from the increasing use of visualization technologies within reproductive technology. The different stages of embryonic/fetal life are more and more mediated by ultrasound and other fetal visualization technologies, as was first demonstrated by Rosalind Petchesky's groundbreaking study of the power of fetal images.[8] The proliferation of ultrasound "snapshots" of the intrauterine fetus in baby albums attests to the increasing role of medical and technological mediation in our mental conception of the fetus. And while this has received less emphasis or analysis, it is also arguable that the rising gynecological and obstetrical reliance on visualization technology has catalyzed a similar shift in our conception of the mother, perhaps including an increasing sense of her permeability. Routine as well as diagnostic ultrasound shapes the subjectivity of the gestating mother along with the visualization of the changing fetus, making the pregnancy seem "more real" and thus motherhood more immanent.[9] While both fetus and mother-to-be are equally mediated by the powerful visualization technologies used in contemporary reproductive medicine, in our turbulent new cultural imaginary we increasingly give more concrete social space and more subjectivity to the fetus than to the gestating woman.

One way of grasping the decreasing subject position available to the gestating woman of today is to consider how pregnancy has been represented and understood in earlier historical periods. Studying the medical case records of Dr. Johannes Storch of eighteenth-century Germany, Barbara Duden has found that in that earlier era a pregnant woman's experience had a central determining effect on how pregnancy was conceptualized. In Storch's era a woman's testimony that quickening had occurred established the existence of the pregnancy. However, that testimony more definitively constructed the woman as a mother-to-be than it shaped the contents of her belly as unquestionably a fetus, rather than a tumor, a growth, "wind," or any of a range of other possibilities. "Greater certainty came after the fourth month, when the fruit quickened in the womb . . . [but] the true thing hidden behind a big belly came to light only with the birth. Prior to that there were no certain prognoses."[10] Moreover, it was the woman's testimony and not the doctor's measurements or palpations that determined the pregnancy's anticipated duration and outcome. "Children were born from women; the womb had not yet become part of a reproductive apparatus."[11] Clearly, pregnancy was a far more ambiguous process prior to the nineteenth century than it is today, and Duden's work suggests that the sociomedical model for the fetal/maternal relation privileged the experience and testimony of the pregnant woman as a crucial guide through its complex territory.

The contrast between the pre-nineteenth-century understanding of pregnancy and our contemporary Western view reveals that once the pivotal experience of quickening is marginalized, so too is the role of the pregnant woman. Whereas once the interior space of the woman was unavailable to the scientific gaze and pregnancy was marked by the woman's testimony that she had felt the fetus move, now the woman's own experience of internal fetal movements is relegated to the unvoiced and unwarranted realm of private experience, while the interior space of the woman is available for all to see as part of the technologized state that Anne Balsamo has called "the public pregnancy."[12] Duden again is helpful here:

> The demise in the social status of quickening [is] an event that brings an important paradox to the surface: in the course of the nineteenth century, female innards and interiority become medically, administratively, and judicially public while, at the same time, the female exterior is privatized ideologically and culturally. . . . One the one hand, the newly discovered "naturalness" of domesticity and motherhood . . . place women in the "private realm" in law, education, and ethics. But at the same time, science discovers and professionals control and mediate her womb as a public space.[13]

One way of understanding the meaning of this shift from an emphasis on maternal testimony to a reliance on medical imaging and measurement is as a battle over representation. As David Theo Goldberg has demonstrated, post-Enlightenment moral culture increasingly shaped the notion of rights to the minimalist view that emphasizes equal opportunity and equal treatment over equality of result. In this view, based on the utilitarian calculus, "the rights of each becomes a matter of the power of and over the means of representation."[14] Goldberg's observation illuminates the increasing fetal/maternal disjunction and the consequent construction of fetus and gestating mother as social, legal, and medical antagonists. Constant improvements in fetal monitoring ensure the production of ever more accurate and detailed fetal representations and the increasing authority of such representations given medicine's investment—both monetary and psychic—in their continuous production. However, ever since Freud asked "What does woman want?" the medical community has had notorious difficulty in ascertaining and accurately representing the subject position, desires, needs, and capacities of woman—and that includes the gestating woman.

Representation always has an excess, however. Even while figuring the increasingly authoritative fetal subject, representation may also create a space reaffirming maternal subjectivity. An audaciously bitter comic novel published in the United States in the autumn of 1994, at roughly the same time as the Kawana Ashley case, figures the very conflict over the means of representation formulated by Goldberg, as it demonstrates technological management of the fetal/maternal boundary, made ambiguous by assisted reproduction. Pascal Bruckner's *The Divine Child* explores the philosophical and social implications of the battle between fetus and mother over the power of, and access to, the means of, visualization.[15] The plot of the novel is worth tracing in some detail, in order to demonstrate how visualization technology shapes its vision of assisted reproduction. Madeleine Barthelemey, a young woman nauseated by all forms of physical desire, marries Oswald Kremer, an elderly accountant whose obsessive-compulsive scientific monitoring of physicality promises her relief from the female sensuality, indeed the abjection, she fears. Kremer's appeal for Madeleine lies in his ability to account for, even to compass, *her* body with the precise taxonomies of medicine: "He was truly possessed with a mathematical itch, and in just a couple of weeks after his wedding he had already found his wife's equation: he was able to give the weight of her spleen, her kidneys, her liver, her bowels, and to gauge her average heartbeat over a twenty-four-hour period, and he also knew everything down to the circumference of her every last beauty spot and the diameter of her every last hair" (5).[16] As befits her need for control, Madeleine would have preferred "being inseminated by a great savant—say, a Nobel Prize winner, an elite mind" (5). However, that is impossible, and Madeleine finds herself pregnant by her husband. She is forced to play the genetic lottery, rather than selecting her "progeniture like an item in a department store" (7). While she thus escapes the traffic in gametes and fetuses that plays so large a part in reproductive technology, she has not escaped commodification entirely, for she decides to subject the fetuses to a rigorous course of prenatal education.[17] With the assistance of Dr. Fontane, her obstetrician, she feeds a barrage of information into her womb through a range of miniature speakers inserted in every available maternal orifice. The deluge of information finally catalyzes a response: one morning, when Madeleine is feeling "disheartened and miserable about birthing a garden-variety larva," she hears "two voices twanging and begging: 'More, more!'" (17). A sonogram confirms that she is carrying twins, and she immediately names them Louis and Celene, a detail that attests to the power of ultrasound and other visualization technologies to construct the fetal subject.

Although both fetuses are subjected to the same intense dose of prenatal education, it affects them differently. The female twin is vanquished; the male prevails. At the birth of little Celene, a would-be scientist already in the womb, the appalled audience of physicians, publicists, and the public watches her draw her first breath only to forget every last bit of her prenatal education: "Instead of the bewitching creature who was going to curtsy and then squeal, 'Where is the research program on the human genome?' they discovered a dreadful, mucus-covered mite with a wrinkled face. Terrified by the noise and the light, it could only stammer: 'Arrheu, Arrheu'" (46). The remaining fetus, Louis, has also been rendered preternaturally intelligent by his crash course in utero. Yet having seen what birth did to his twin sister, Celene, Louis is too intelligent to acquiesce in being thrown out of the maternal haven into the dangerous world. Instead, he refuses to be born. Staying in his cozy uterine control room, he aspires to control the world, relying on the same visualization technology that earlier was used to monitor him in utero: "His garret of mucus now resembled the instrument panel in a jet cockpit: several monitors, a video screen, earphones, dozens of flashing signal lights, a computer terminal, an ultrasophisticated radiophone, and a fax machine situated him at the center of a gigantic communications network, an immense nervous system that linked him to the four corners of the world" (100–101).

Bruckner's novel dramatizes the shift from the notion of the embryo as object of scientific control to the new notion of embryo-as-controlling-subject. "The introduction of new monitoring technologies has the consequence of bringing both the obstetrician and the pregnant woman into a system of normative surveillance," Balsamo has observed.[18] Bruckner's narrative takes the return of the gaze to its logical conclusion: not only does visualization serve as a means of control over the fetus, but now it acts as a means of control *by* the fetus, not only over the obstetrician and the gestating woman but over the world beyond her womb. Indeed, it is the fetus who has the best view of all, both of the world outside and of the inside of his mother's body:

> A small gadget, a miracle of microscopic engineering that some physicians lent to Louis, was to confirm him in his role of shepherd of the maternal flock. This doohickey consisted of a pair of infrared binoculars that combined the functions of a telescope, a magnifying glass, and a telephone: not only could you see things near or far, but also, thanks to an incorporated mike, you could speak to whatever the eyes picked up. With the help of these glasses not a particle of his mother's body would escape the tot; he could view the very core of any object, down to the nucleus of every cell. (131)

Standard medical practice increasingly subjects the pregnant woman's body, and her activities, to exhaustive, invasive scrutiny. We can recall the 1960s film *Fantastic Voyage*, in which a team of scientists led improbably enough by Raquel Welch journeyed into the bloodstream of a fellow scientist in order to cure him of some dangerous disease. Bruckner's involutional twist on this familiar paradigm reverses the direction of power. "Louis would have much preferred being miniaturized himself, piloting a bathyscaphe through Mom's veins, chugging through her tracheal arteries, tobogganing through her digestive tract. . . . However, since science was unable to shrink a human being to the size of a microbe or bacterium . . . Louis had to content himself with having only his gaze penetrate the maternal apparatus" (131). A shift in the site of privileged subjectivity has taken place. Now it is the fetus himself—rather than the physicians, miniaturized or not—who uses scopic power to penetrate the mother, colonizing her with all of the complex technological apparatus hitherto used on "the products of conception." Woman's subjectivity has been elided; instead, Bruckner gives us the embryonic or fetal subject whose rights exceed those of the already born, particularly of women.

Bruckner's embryo/fetus also reverses the direction of scopic power, from the fetus as object of scientific observation to the society as the object of critical fetal scrutiny. The modernist control aspirations articulated by geneticist Hermann Muller—"To gain adequate control over the world of things of our own size . . . we must first seek knowledge and control of the very small world"—are thus literalized with comic force in Bruckner's postmodern parable, as Louis's scopic invasion of his mother's private spaces enables him to achieve nearly total dominance of the world beyond the womb.[19] The scopic scrutiny leveled on the world by Bruckner's fetus resembles the increasing fetocentric position of the legal system, whose interventions reflect an almost panicky obsession with what must be managed in order to make things sufficiently safe for the not yet born.[20]

Yet such intrauterine safety has its costs. Finding to his horror that his body is gradually "fossilizing, returning to his embryonic state," Louis announces an impending apocalypse, planning to take the world down with him. "The defeat of the old world [is] slated for . . . the exact date on which Louis, five years earlier, had refused to be born, to lend himself to the human comedy. A shudder went round the world: What if the Super-Microbe were telling the truth?" (192). Now indeed fetus and mother *are* antagonists. Once more, visualization technology is integral to Bruckner's vision, but now the reliance on VT has an unexpected result. While it has generally been the case that "the same technological advances that foster the objectification of the female body through the visualization of internal functioning also encourages [sic] the 'personification' of the fetus," Bruckner's novel inverts this dynamic.[21]

Shaking off her lethargy, Madeleine works with her obstetrician to defeat the embryo's destructive intentions. They once again wire up "the still semibedridden genetrix . . . with cables and loaded down with cameras scanning every square inch of her belly" and subject Louis to the same technological barrage of information, sight, and sound that created him (205).

Overwhelmed by the cacophony, "the exhausted homunculus drop[s] into the maternal marsh to keep from hearing," sinking "into an interminable vortex" (209). Dr. Fontane then delivers the coup de grâce, subjecting the encysted fetus "to the type of high-frequency ultrasound normally used to crumble gall-stones and kidney stones. The mite explode[s] and disperse[s] in a thousand fragments. . . . Madeleine was delivered" (210).

From the very first page, through the apocalyptic excesses of the conclusion, Bruckner's novel invokes a resistant reader by the ways in which it images the new fetal subject and marks itself as fiction. By the novel's ending, we have been drawn to identify with the mother rather than her monstrous fetal tenant, affirm her subject position, and endorse the novel's critique of the contemporary mode of conceptualizing gestation and birth. In its fantasy of a willed regression to the power, centrality, and isolation of the fetus (a postmodern high-technology extension of Freud's "his majesty, the baby"), *The Divine Child* lays out some of the social implications of reproductive technology. Most explicitly, by the pun that links parturition with an end to persecution ("Madeleine was delivered") Bruckner's novel articulates the interconnections between high-tech gestation and growing maternal-fetal antagonism and reveals how the tendency to privilege the fetus, detached from an objectified maternal environment, develops from the increasingly conflicted and ambiguous state of the fetal/maternal boundary.

Species

If Bruckner's work of fiction shows us how assisted reproduction manages the generational boundary embodied in the fetal/maternal relation by privileging the fetus, which is accorded seemingly limitless rights and powers while the position or rights of the mother are ignored, a nonfiction government document reverses that dynamic, resurrecting maternal experience and claims. Created in 1994 by the director of the National Institutes of Health (NIH), the Human Embryo Research Panel was charged with considering "various areas of research involving the ex utero preimplantation human embryo" and providing advice "as to those areas that: (1) are acceptable for Federal funding; (2) warrant additional review; and (3) are unacceptable for Federal support."[22] The panel, which represented the disciplines of bioethics, medicine, medical research, cell and molecular biology, genetics, public health, law, philosophy, and sociology, as well as advocacy groups for the infertile and sufferers of sickle cell anemia, issued its final report on 27 September 1994. As its title indicates, the Muller Report (as it was known, after its chair, Stephen Muller, president emeritus of the Johns Hopkins University) addresses the management of two boundaries: the fetal/maternal and the human/animal.

The Human Embryo Research Panel focused exclusively, and explicitly, on what it calls the "ex utero preimplantation embryo" or "extracorporeal human embryos": a further step in the polarization of the fetal/maternal dyad. Yet there is a different valence to the relations this dyad encompasses. If in Johannes Storch's era that dyad was defined by maternal experience, and if in the modern era of high-technology gynecology and reproductive technology it is defined by an antagonism, mediated by law, religion, and medical science (so that maternal authority is in danger of being surpassed by fetal authority), the Human Embryo Research Panel might be seen to inaugurate a new era, in which the status of the embryo relies on its relation to the gestating woman. Two sorts of embryos are officially recognized in the Muller Report: the embryo authorized by its place in the fetal/maternal dyad, and the embryo that—unratified—may not be permitted to become a fetus.[23]

Observing that the "special moral status of the embryo" led to the formation of this commission to assess public attitudes toward embryo research, the Muller Report distinguished between "embryos intended for and not intended for transfer."[24] Relationship to a mother-to-be normalizes the embryo for the NIH panel: the status of an embryo was determined by whether it was to be transferred medically to the human uterus (and thus intended to develop into a human fetus) or was not to be transferred (and thus not intended to develop into a human fetus). Thus a potential subject position is available to an embryo if and only if it can be ratified as normal, acceptable, *transferable to a gestating mother-to-be*. Embryos not attaining such ratification—in the report, this group includes parthenotes, chimeras that are the result of intraspecies crossbreeding, clones—lose their teleological authority and become prey to chance during gestation.

In the NIH report, several different kinds of research were deemed unacceptable for federal funding: the cloning of human preimplantation embryos; studies designed to transplant nuclei into an enucleated egg; research beyond the onset of closure of the neural tube; research involving the fertilization of fetal oocytes; preimplantation genetic diagnosis for sex selection except for sex-linked genetic diseases; development of human-nonhuman and human-human chimeras with or without transfer; cross-species fertilization; attempted transfer of parthenogenetically activated human eggs; attempted transfer of human embryos in nonhuman animals for gestation; and transfer of human embryos for extrauterine or abdominal pregnancy.[25] The NIH document explains the decision not to fund such research methods on "scientific grounds," yet it is arguable that they are also declared off-limits because of the ways they shift and challenge the boundaries of the human self. If we revisit the lengthy list above, we will see that the following human definitional qualities are challenged or erased: the notion of individuality of each human subject (excluding twins, which are acceptable because a product of chance); the notion of the brain as an intact organ not subject to human manipulation (except through noninvasive environmental stimulation known as teaching, and parodied in Bruckner's novel); the notion of a distinct boundary between humans and other species and between humans and machines.

Two related procedures raise such clear problems that the NIH explicitly draws on extrascientific reasons for proscribing them: interspecies uterine transfer and the formation of chimeras. More than half a century earlier, philosopher Anthony Ludovici argued that interspecies uterine transfer would degrade the human species: "It is probable, therefore, that in the early days of extracorporeal gestation, the fertilized human ovum will be transferred to the uterus of a cow or an ass, and left to mature as a parasite on the animal's tissues. . . . And with this innovation, we shall probably suffer increased besotment, and intensified bovinity or asininity, according to the nature of the quadruped chosen."[26] In 1994, the creation of human-animal and human-human chimeras was disturbing to the Muller Report panel for very similar reasons:

> It is theoretically possible to make chimeras between human embryos and closely related primates, such as chimpanzees but . . . the fetus would have cells derived from both species in all tissues. It might be possible for the chimeric fetus to have large parts of the brain and/or gonads derived mostly from primate cells and other parts of the body derived mostly from human cells, a situation that would, from both a medical and ethical standpoint, be totally unacceptable.[27]

Although the panel specifies that "the fetus would have cells derived from both species in all tissues," the continuing discussion points to just what is threatening about this human-animal chimera: the possibility of either a brain or of gonads that are primate. While it is clear that there are strong scientific and social reasons why the creation of such a chimera would be problematic, the focus on the gonads and the brain suggests that the image generates specifically devolutionary anxieties. Although the Muller panel proposed prohibiting such research because of the possibility of immunological rejection, the importance of "maternal-fetal placental interactions," and the crucial "beginnings of mother-child bonding and of human relationship," only the devolutionary anxieties of the early years of this century can explain the powerful phrase with which the report concludes its assessment: "The Panel finds it repugnant to experiment with such *relating* between a human fetus and a non-human gestational mother."[28] The Human Embryo Research Panel puts the role of the mother in center stage, stressing her crucial role both during gestation and in early infancy. The Muller Report thus enacts a striking reversal of the tendency reflected in the Kawana Ashley case with which I began, and which I argued is nurtured by assisted reproduction: to privilege the fetus and ignore the mother.

How do we explain the interesting reversal in the value accorded the maternal position in these two examples of boundary negotiations associated with assisted reproduction? When the fetal/maternal boundary is under contestation, as in Bruckner's novel, the fetal position is privileged over the maternal. Yet as the Muller Report reveals, in the case of the human/animal boundary, the maternal position is resurrected in the guise of "maternal-fetal placental interactions" and "mother-child bonding," in order to protect a boundary that is perhaps even more highly charged: the human/animal. The strategic reversal marks which site of privilege is being challenged and which is seen as the abject category: in contrast to the categories "fetus" and "human being" (both seen as under attack), the categories "mother" and "animal" are inherently (if unconsciously) set as parallel, dangerous terms.

From Reproduction to Replication

I have been arguing that we fly the flag of convenience when we negotiate the generational or species boundaries under the auspices of assisted reproduction. When the interests of technological progress require it, we grant the fetus proleptic personhood, civil status, and medical and legal rights. But when the interests of species supremacy require it, we reverse the valence, affirming the rights of the "mother" and her crucial role in pregnancy and child rearing. Not only are the meanings of mother and fetus subject to negotiation and construction, so too are the meanings of "human" and "animal," as we see when we return to consider the cloning of Dolly.

Dolly was cloned not only in order to produce genetically engineered sheep whose milk would contain drugs targeted for humans but also to produce transgenic cloned sheep (and other animals) whose organs, less likely to provoke immune system rejection, could be transplanted into human beings.[29] As Ian Wilmut explained, "There are about 160,000 people a year who die before organs like hearts, livers, and kidneys become available to them." Cloning "will be an effective way of finding treatment for these conditions."[30] The implications of such transgenic animal-human organ transplantation, or *xenotransplantation*, had already been given serious consideration when Dolly was created. On 16 January 1997, only half a year after her birth on 5 July 1996, Britain's Advisory Group on the Ethics of Xenotransplantation, chaired by Professor Ian Kennedy, head and dean of the Law School, King's College, London, made plain the implications of such a program of farming genetically engineered organs: "We need to consider whether there is a basic identity in humans with which it is wrong to interfere and whether these procedures alter humans such that their identity, as humans, is altered."[31] The advisory group had been given its charge by the British secretary of state: to examine the ethics of transplanting organs from nonhuman animals to people. "If xenotransplantation proceeds and develops," the advisory group concluded, "with the genetic modification of animals with human genes and the transplant of animal tissue into humans, the distinction between humans and animals could be perceived, at some point, to break down."[32]

The cloning of Dolly threatens a border even more fundamental than the human/animal boundary, however. While current techniques in assisted reproduction challenge the boundaries of gender and species, the technique of cloning challenges another boundary, perhaps even more fundamental to our thinking than either generation or species, although implicated in both of them: the boundary between reproduction and replication.[33] We have gone from the binary model of reproduction common to humans and other animals to a model based on the proliferation of sameness, be it bacterial budding or rhizomic proliferation.[34] The technology of cloning, if applied to human beings, could arguably challenge not only our definition of "human" but also the broader dominions on which it rests: our membership and dominant position in the animal kingdom.

Yet here again, the management of boundaries produces curiously pragmatic and contradictory alliances, as we can see in the way the press managed the sequelae to Dolly's birth. The Roslin laboratory recently released the news that Dolly, the cloned ewe, had become a mother. As *Science News* reported it, this fact that Dolly has "had a little lamb" confirms "that she is able to breed normally and produce healthy offspring."[35] Even as the new technology of replication is celebrating its accomplishment, the social technologies of public relations and the print media swing into action, reinstalling the "natural" function of reproduction and affirming boundaries that Dolly's cloning so recently challenged, those of generation and species. With the reproductive norm reinforced, the sequence of generations and the dominance of the human species are reassuringly reestablished. An unspoken species hierarchy, enforced by the allusion to the nursery rhyme "Mary Had a Little Lamb," subordinates Dolly to her reproductive and social model, Mary. The human ownership of animals as property, and the notion of generational continuity, are sutured to this new commodified method of animal replication: once again, boundary relations have been redrawn to enable this new, potentially profitable technology of cloning to function without disrupting the system of hierarchized generational and species boundaries from which it originated.

Managing Boundaries through Representation

I would like to close with a thought experiment: let's return to the cases of Anna Johnson, surrogate mother for John and Crispina Calvert, and Kawana Ashley, the pregnant woman who attempted suicide—and consider them in relation to the birth of Dolly. Let's ask how these two cases would be different if the fetus with which each woman was pregnant had been cloned. Recalling Goldberg's observation that in post-Enlightenment moral culture "the rights of each becomes a matter of the power of and over the means of representation," we might initially find ourselves arguing against cloning, because of the way that new technology would produce an even more objectified mother, an even more subjectified fetus.[36] We might wonder how Anna Johnson could win even visiting rights, if the child to whom she gave birth were the identical clone of the commissioning mother or father; what Kawana's fate would be, if the fetus injured when she attempted suicide had an advocate—visually and genetically indistinguishable—*outside the womb*. The authority of a fetal subject—powerful enough in the imaginary to generate Bruckner's frightening "divine child" and to transmute Kawana Ashley's attempted suicide to attempted murder—would take on a whole new meaning if the fetus were genetically identical to someone already alive, someone with the power, status, or genetic excellence (by whatever measures) to merit cloning. And if through cloning combined with genetic engineering that child had been *enhanced* not only to prevent life-threatening diseases but also to extend life or broaden physical capacities, what sway would such a fetus have over the *unenhanced* woman carrying it to term?[37]

Different as this scenario seems from the stories of "natural" pregnancy and assisted reproduction discussed earlier, it shares with them the crucial power of representation in shaping our sense of options. At issue is not whether the fetus is genetically "superior" to, identical to, or simply just resembles the commissioning "parent" from whom it is cloned but the broader question of how representation leads us to understand the very terms *parent* and *mother*. Until the contribution of Kawana Ashley and Anna Johnson to the children they bear is factored into the definition of parenthood, until their experience is deemed as significant as the potential life experiences of their fetuses, the boundaries destabilized by assisted reproduction (even if it includes "assisted replication") will be restabilized to affirm the status quo. And there will be more Anna Johnsons and Kawana Ashleys.

Notes

Earlier versions of portions of this essay appeared in my essay "Fetal Subjects and Maternal Objects: Reproductive Technology and the New Fetal/Maternal Relation," *Journal of Medicine and Philosophy* 21 (1996): 515–535.

1. As *Time* magazine reported, "A California court rules that bearing a child is not motherhood." Susan Tifft, "It's All in the (Parental) Genes," *Time*, 5 November 1990, 77.
2. *Centre Daily Times*, 10 September 1994, 10A.
3. A significant act of elision, or black boxing, takes place in the change in terms, for the act of technological intervention is now represented, far more benignly, as simply human "assistance."
4. Recently, law and medicine have worked together to redraw that boundary, under the guise of managing it legally and medically, when South Dakota passed three laws designed to reduce cases of fetal alcohol syndrome. Under the statutes (which went into effect on 1 July 1998), "relatives or friends can commit pregnant women to emergency detoxification centers for up to two days," and judges can confine drinking women "to treatment centers for as long as nine months." Most far-reaching in its effects on our understanding of the fetal/maternal relation, the final statute "makes drinking while pregnant a form of child abuse." "Pregnant Drinkers Face a Crackdown," *New York Times*, 24 May 1998, 16 NE.
5. Gina Kolata, *Clone: The Road to Dolly, and the Path Ahead* (New York: Morrow, 1998), 14–15.
6. See Teresa de Lauretis, *Technologies of Gender: Essays on Theory, Film, and Fiction* (Bloomington: Indiana University Press, 1987), 2; Anne Balsamo, *Technologies of the Gendered Body: Reading Cyborg Women* (Durham, N.C.: Duke University Press, 1996), 9.
7. "Embryo: in humans, the developing organism from the time of fertilization until the end of the eighth week of gestation, when it becomes known as a fetus." National Institutes of Health Final Report of the Human Embryo Research Panel, 27 September 1994, 103 (hereafter cited as "NIH report").
8. Rosalind Pollack Petchesky, "Foetal Images: The Power of Visual Culture in the Politics of Reproduction," in *Reproductive Technologies: Gender, Motherhood, and Medicine*, ed. Michelle Stanworth (Minneapolis: University of Minnesota Press, 1987), 57–80. For a discussion of the role of visualization technology in the development of reproductive technology, see my *Babies in Bottles: Twentieth-Century Visions of Reproductive Technology* (New Brunswick, N.J.: Rutgers University Press, 1994).
9. Barbara Duden, *Disembodying Women: Perspectives on Pregnancy and the Unborn* (Cambridge: Harvard University Press, 1993).
10. Barbara Duden, *The Woman beneath the Skin: A Doctor's Patients in Eighteenth-Century Germany* (Cambridge: Harvard University Press, 1991), 160.
11. Duden argues that "the demise in the social status of quickening [is] an event that brings an important paradox to the surface: in the course of the nineteenth century, female innards and interiority become medically, administratively, and judicially public while, at the same time, the female exterior is privatized ideologically and culturally. These opposed but linked tendencies are both characteristic moments in the social construction of 'woman' as a scientific fact, as well as in the creation of the citizen in industrial society." *Disembodying Women*, 95. See also 28.
12. Balsamo, *Technologies of the Gendered Body*, 13–14.
13. Duden, *Disembodying Women*, 95.
14. David Theo Goldberg, *Racist Culture: Philosophy and the Politics of Meaning* (Oxford: Blackwell, 1993), 20.

15. Pascal Bruckner, *The Divine Child: A Novel of Prenatal Rebellion*, trans. Joachim Neugroschel (Boston: Little, Brown & Co., 1994). Subsequent page references for this work will be given parenthetically in the text.
16. Here Kremer recalls Edwin in Jolley's *The Sugar Mother*, who records all of his own physical changes in his "book of the body."
17. Dion Farquhar, "Gamete Traffic/Pedestrian Crossings," in this volume.
18. Balsamo, *Technologies of the Gendered Body*, 90.
19. Hermann Muller, *Out of the Night: A Biologist's View of the Future* (London: Victor Gollancz, 1936), 22.
20. In its sense of the world as too risky a place to be born into, Bruckner's novel echoes Laura Freixas's brilliant little short story "My Mama Spoils Me," in which a thirty-seven-year-old fetus refuses to be born because it's safer to stay in utero. Freixas's story explicitly and ironically contrasts that fetal-protection agenda with the lack of concern for human and animal rights its proponents reveal.
21. Balsamo, *Technologies of the Gendered Body*, 93.
22. NIH report.
23. Duden, *Woman Beneath the Skin*.
24. NIH report, 51.
25. Ibid., 94–96.
26. Anthony Ludovici, *Lysistrata, or Woman's Future and Future Woman* (London: Kegan Paul, Trench Trubner, & Co., 1924), 92.
27. NIH report, 43.
28. Ibid., 96; my italic.
29. Ian Kennedy, *Animal Tissue into Humans: A Report by the Advisory Group on the Ethics of Xenotransplantation* (London: Her Majesty's Stationery Office, 1996), 24–27.
30. S. William Hessert Jr., "Distinguished Speaker: Dr. Ian Wilmut," *State College* (March 1998): 31.
31. Kennedy, *Animal Tissue into Humans*, sec. 4.41, p. 68.
32. Ibid., sec. 4.42, p. 68.
33. Susan Squier, "Interspecies Reproduction: Xenogenic Desire and the Feminist Implications of Hybrids," *Cultural Studies* 12, no. 1 (1998): 360–381.
34. If any binary model of reproduction has an asymmetrical gender bipolarity as its shadow presence, thanks to the long-standing vitalism/mechanism controversy, cloning is shadowed by the fearful notion of machinic replication.
35. J. Travis, "Dolly Had a Little Lamb," *Science News* 153 (1998): 278.
36. Goldberg, *Racist Culture*, 20
37. Geneticist Lee Silver gives us a fictional scenario for such a process of genetic enhancement in the epilogue to *Remaking Eden: Cloning and Beyond in a Brave New World* (New York: Avon, 1977).

The Politics of Surrogacy Narratives

E. ANN KAPLAN

1980s Paradigms and Their Legacies in the 1990s

In our introduction to this volume, Susan Squier and I noted the change in social awareness and understanding of mother surrogacy since the first landmark cases in the early 1980s. The normalization of mother surrogacy is not so remarkable in the context of the much more dramatic technological advances in reproductive birth technologies in intervening years. Yet on the interpersonal, emotional, and psychological levels, things may not have "advanced" as much as we might imagine. In my study of 1980s narratives by and about mother surrogacy, I hope to remind readers of the extreme anxiety this practice evoked a decade or so ago. Although this anxiety is much less in the late 1990s, I will show that the perhaps inevitable emotional difficulties—especially those between the gestating and adoptive parents—continue today.

In their 1980s narratives, surrogate mothers (SMs) announce their motive for becoming such mothers as sisterly desire to help infertile women. Yet, in practice, surrogacy becomes the terrain for unprecedented hostility and violence between women. I am interested in the discrepancy between sisterly motives and unsisterly practice so prevalent in stories emerging in the first years of surrogacy. I will argue that such stories establish prototypes for narratives whose legacies remain in stories SMs tell in the 1990s. Since narratives are always discursively formed, I aim to understand what discourses produce both the women's stories narrated in 1980s popular journals and those continuing today: What audiences do they address? What effect does the context of their publication have on the form of the stories? What economic, political, and other social factors enter in? I am interested in how close the language and tone of the stories are to traditional melodrama. I will argue, first, that melodrama forms oversimplify the actual psychological, political, social, and economic contexts of surrogacy, while sometimes providing unconscious expression of female oppressions; and second, that women need to find more subtle narrative forms that can express multiple perspectives, ambiguities, contradictions, and undecidability: such forms are crucial as feminisms enter the new millennium and attempt to grapple with difference on new levels.

In this essay, I first explore some of the common structures and repeated themes in women's 1980s stories as they illuminate the paradox between sisterly motives and unsisterly practice. In the second section, I explore a 1980s TV miniseries and a feminist video—both about Mary Beth Whitehead's surrogacy case. For contrast, I look briefly at a 1996 video by an anthropologist about a couple and their surrogate to show changes between the mid-1980s and the mid-1990s, while emotional and psychological similarities remain.[1]

Surrogacy Narratives in 1980s Popular Magazines

Sisterly motives abound in popular 1980s narratives about surrogacy, and there is surprising uniformity in the basics of the story, even in the language used. Surrogate mothers discuss their pleasure in giving birth for another woman; they express sympathy for infertile women—wanting to give the gift of a child.[2] Some discuss having been fulfilled in having their own children and wanting other couples to share the same joy. For example, Mary Beth Whitehead represents herself as a woman devoted to being a mother and wanting nothing else in life than bearing and nurturing children. "Being a mother was always how I defined myself," she says. "Surrogacy was a way for me to help someone less fortunate."[3] In this story, surrogate mothering is represented as "a positive, multi-vocal symbol, pointing to previous barrenness and promised fertility."[4] The baby born of a surrogate is seen as both of the flesh and of the law—a member, by contract and law, in a "gift-relationship,"[5] rather than "baby-selling" on a shameful market, as in some of the negative narratives noted below. It is seen as a special celebration of birth itself.

Surrogacy, unlike many other reproductive technologies, is old and does not require medical sophistication. This may be part of its appeal: the historical and biblical precedent of Abraham, his wife, Sarah, and Hagar, Abraham's concubine, is sometimes quoted,[6] especially in stories dealing with women who give birth to a sister's baby. Surrogates and adoptive mothers who are actual sisters provide the most positive context for surrogacy in these narratives. Accompanying one such story are images of the sisters hugging, kissing, and crying. The surrogacy in this case is seen as a "family project."[7] In a similar story, the sisterly surrogacy is seen as paying the sister back for her love and support.[8]

In this story, the stress is on surrogacy as a community and family process, not in the hands of expert services and professionals: all members involved in the process meet, eat ritual foods, even if only coffee and cake, so as to establish celebratory aspects. In some cases, the artificial insemination is done with a turkey baster, to signify links with Thanksgiving rituals. These narrators represent insemination as another festive occasion, like Christmas, grandma's birthday, the Fourth of July.

In yet one more story, the SM says: "I'll never find a cure for cancer, but I'll always know I've done something important."[9] A surrogate husband, a rare voice in these narratives and about whom I would like to know more, says: "I rationalized that it was a medical experiment" (as if the medical "frame" suddenly legitimized surrogacy). ZIFT surrogacy (zygote intrafallopian tube transfer), in which the surrogate has no genetic claim to the child, is said in the same story to be made possible by God and thus acceptable.[10] In the more complex and still more unusual situation of gamete intrafallopian transfer (GIFT), one woman is described as gloating over her twelve eggs, ecstatic that her recipient and she were cycling simultaneously and likening the situation to being at war with each other (a telling metaphor that constructs comradeship between the women at this stage of things). The woman undergoing the transfer notes: "I almost didn't care if I had a baby—I just wanted to know what having life inside would feel like."

My second set of popular 1980s narratives—those I call "negative"—reveal antitechnology sentiments and dwell on the "unsisterly practices" I noted above. SMs whose experiences turned negative adopt narratives circulating elsewhere in North American culture (often originating in religious or right-wing contexts). One set of negative surrogacy concepts label it "baby-selling on a shameful market."[11] Other stories conjure up Orwell's *1984* to indicate the negative response. Surrogate reproduction is seen as cold and sterile because separated from love and family life.[12] "Babies born from frozen embryos will be cold the rest of their lives." Typical headlines for these stories are "Brave New Babies" or "Tales from the Baby Factory." "Baby Farming" is suggested, especially in relation to third-world women, and the figure of the surrogate mom as human incubator predominates.[13]

More negativity is evident in the way financial arrangements are highlighted in phrases like "womb rental fees." Mary Beth Whitehead's ten-thousand-dollar contract is detailed in her 1989 book, which gathered together negative motifs in earlier stories, setting the stage for more to come: "I have learned," she says, "that the rental of a woman's body for the sale of the child she bears is wrong. It violates the core of what a woman is."[14] The practice is often labeled "commercial trading in flesh" and articles assert that governments should outlaw surrogacy and the use of fetuses for medical purposes. If surrogacy is regularized, a class of breeder women would be created[15]—such as Margaret Atwood envisaged in *The Handmaid's Tale*[16]—women valued both for their biological fertility *and* for their unnatural ability to reject their own flesh and blood. Articles suggest that childless couples could abandon technological alternatives to give love to troubled young people and adopt "unadoptable" mixed-race, older, or disabled children.[17]

Quite often religious figures in the 1980s decried surrogacy: for instance, Richard A. McCormick, S.J., said that "the practice is morally unjustifiable, because a third party is introduced into the marriage of two who have become one flesh."[18] And a priest notes: "Procreation should not be divorced from the context of marital intimacy by involving a third party." Yet another priest told an adoptive surrogacy mother: "Your children have not sinned, but you have. You've used Michael's sperm in another woman's body" (74). Clearly, the medieval church's tolerance of concubinage to regulate the transmission of property is not viewed as applicable today.[19]

Unsisterly practices emerged in different narratives, or later on in the same narratives at the point where sisterliness changes to "women at odds." The drama of "women at odds" in the cases in which surrogates do not want to keep to the adoption contract dominates the negative surrogacy stories. Such drama was spelled out graphically in Elizabeth Kane's 1989 *Birth Mother*. Kane made a vivid plea against surrogate motherhood on the grounds of the birth mother's inevitable biological bonding with the baby that a surrogate carries.

Following Kane and popularized psychological studies, stories in commercial magazines assume automatic bonding of mother and child. Writers construct what they then call "the wrenching separation of the couple"[20] and dwell on negative psychological results.[21] Surrogacy is discussed as symbolic adultery, and the jealous competition between surrogate and adoptive mothers is emphasized. Authors lament effects of the process on other children in either family, along with the awesome psychological implications of signing a contract to give a child away.

A case is often made for the surrogate child as different from the adopted child, who is wanted by the birth mother who cannot keep it. In surrogacy, the gestating mother goes into the birth process intending to give the child up. Stories highlight how, indeed, some surrogates are making up for past acts, like abortion, or giving up a child to adoption.[22] From the perspective of the recipient couple, stories dwell on the psychologically heart-wrenching ordeal of couples who, through "hiring" a surrogate birth mother, are trying to have a child partly sharing their genetic inheritance. Narratives stress the "torture" such couples endure while waiting for their surrogate to be pregnant and the tension suffered during the period of the pregnancy. Legal and ethical issues are sometimes noted in popular stories,[23] although such issues are largely re- served for formidable, specifically legal literature.[24]

The two surrogate mothers who accompanied Dr. Aigen to our 1992 con- ference gave less sensational descriptions of their experiences but with com- ments surprisingly similar to those in the positive 1980s narratives. The first surrogate mother, Dawna (noted in the introduction to this volume), included many of the "set pieces" of the stories outlined above: (1) She gets the idea for being a surrogate mother from looking at a television program. (2) She is excited to share the baby's heartbeat and the changes in her own body with the parents-to-be. (3) She is fulfilled by the look on the parents' faces when she tells them they have a baby boy. (4) Her daughter's words when they have to part from the baby seem to capture her own feelings: "They're a family like us now," the child says. Several times Dawna notes how "special" surrogacy made her feel.

But an important difference in the 1990s is that Dawna was very aware of the negative stories about surrogacy, which she hastened to correct intelli- gently. For instance, she noted that no-one was "brainwashing" her or telling her what to do. She emphasized the importance of the contract as a protec- tion for all parties, and she noted that she was free to choose her own lawyer and that she had six months in which she could change her mind about giv- ing up the baby. Dawna also impressed on the audience that surrogate moth- ers were not "second-class citizens" doing this for the money; surrogacy, she said was not "public baby-selling," since one cannot put a price tag on a baby.[25]

Kathy, the second surrogate mother, departed in interesting ways from both Dawna's story and that of many narratives in books and magazines. She spoke without notes and began with a humorous comment about its being harder to get into a surrogacy program than into medical school. As a single woman without children, Kathy had at first been turned down by Dr. Aigen; her situation changed after an accidental pregnancy and the subsequent adop- tion of her baby, when Aigen matched her with a couple. Like Dawna, Kathy emphasizes her suitability for surrogacy because of her ability to give up a baby. Like Dawna, Kathy stresses that "this was something special I could do for someone." Kathy added an unusual note when she talked about the process of repeated inseminations: she is able to experience the prior disappointment of the parents-to-be trying to get pregnant in her own disappointment when her menstrual cycle begins. Like Dawna, Kathy insists on the excellent rela- tionship she developed with both the adoptive parents for her own child and now with the surrogacy couple.

Commentary, Discourses

I have always been suspicious of the sisterly pronouncements voiced in my first set of 1980s narratives and again by the women at the 1992 conference. I have been troubled equally by the polemical, self-righteous tone of the negative narratives. One of the things that makes me suspicious in both kinds of narrative is the lack of attention to the complex psychological relations between the couples and their surrogates: some jealousy and competition between the women is unavoidable, but the positive story is invested in showing only love, sharing, and generosity. Happy self-renunciation by the mother surrogate is always included. And the negative story, instead of dwelling on the "women-at-odds" angle, displaces these emotions into the loftier ones to do with shameful baby selling or "going against nature."

The two kinds of narrative set up a false binary that is inadequate for dealing with the actual psychological, political, scientific, economic, and racial aspects of increasing surrogacy practices. The multiplicity of positions is lost in the polemical arguments in both sets of stories. The *similarity* among the popular stories—the repetition of motifs of the gift, of doing something for infertile couples, of frustration, pain, ultimate joy to the adoptive parents, and so on—from as early as 1983 through 1992 is troubling. It demonstrates the limiting impact on what can be said of narratives and conventions already culturally in place—perhaps on what can be experienced in the first place. The surrogacy story, itself tied to prior mother constructs, gradually acquires the status of myth, with fixed characters, set verbal exchanges, and similar language and tone. After Mary Beth Whitehead's and Elizabeth Kane's 1989 narratives provided the full mythic account, there was less need for more stories, while these provided the blueprint for those that did appear.

The glaring absence of reference to the economic, class, and race issues in positive surrogacy narratives is an important structuring element. Just because money is rarely mentioned, one might suppose that financial gain (usually ten thousand dollars and all medical and other expenses paid for the surrogate) was the real, repressed motive. When the fee is mentioned, it is as enabling the SM to pay bills or buy necessities when a husband is laid off. (Is there guilt about receiving money for its own sake?) The main motive is always "to make infertile couples happy."[26] Although the financial surrogate arrangement may account for the class difference between surrogate and adoptive mothers, women need to show higher motives than financial ones. Perhaps religious or community values encourage this, as Mary Beth Whitehead's prototype story suggests: "I have always been religious," she says, "and I certainly prayed that if I did this for another childless couple, God would reward me by giving my sister a baby" (8). Although women rarely mention the financial part of the contract, I do not assume conscious duplicity. Future research will aim to discover, through interviews and other strategies, what social codes and pressures prevent women from mentioning finances.

Something more complex, psychologically and socially, is at stake than what emerges from either women's stories or my cynical questions. First, it is important that most of the surrogate mothers seem to be white and lower middle class, while adoptive ones *apparently* are white and middle class, with the rare publicized exception of Anna Johnson, a black surrogate mother involved in a custodial suit with the white biological parents.[27] Research on profiles of surrogate mothers is difficult because data are nearly impossible to obtain. Few narratives talk about either class or race, but the surrogate or recipient mothers touted in the media are rarely minority women.[28]

Also intriguing in narratives is why SMs do not anticipate the separation from the child, which they ultimately describe as "heart-wrenching," or anticipate that they may desire to keep the child despite their having had other children. Why doesn't the adoptive mother anticipate that the SM will have such a struggle? Each woman's desire to have the child produces the unsisterly practices—the hostility and the violence on both women's parts. Surrogates suddenly, and violently, declare they want the child they have just birthed, while the adoptive mother, having anticipated having the child for nine months, equally violently demands the child be handed over. It is as if the surrogates and adoptive mothers have started a story whose ending they have forgotten until they experience the ending: or as if they step into positions of women fighting women so common in film melodrama and TV soaps. Neither woman is self-consciously aware of the discursive forces shaping her experience and of how the stories are linked. The SMs violent desire to *keep* the child may be provoked precisely by the adoptive mother's urgent desire to *claim* the child, evidencing a negative symbiotic process.

I have wondered at my skepticism about the sisterly narratives with which I began: is it really so impossible for one woman to want to do something as disruptive of her own life as bearing and giving birth to a baby for another woman? What does sisterliness of these dimensions really mean? Perhaps I am missing something about what childbirth actually means to many women and simply do not understand the discursive frameworks within which surrogate mothers live: after all, having children is the main or only identity or life preoccupation for many women. Possibly really being able to contribute in a way conceived of as analogous to making scientific discoveries (as one narrator suggested) could motivate women.

The decision to become surrogates may be partly produced through media stories still stressing the self-sacrificial mother as what mothering is all about. Yet the idealized self-sacrifice function has become harder to fulfill for many reasons. Modern household devices give the appearance of mitigating housework, as does the new entry of fathers into domestic chores and even child rearing: women are reaching for new ways to perform motherly self-sacrifice and finding it in surrogacy.

But desire for self-sacrifice wills into being its binary opposite, the jealous, competitive mother, who wants to possess the child. Surrogacy provides a unique situation in which the binary mothers so common in North American stories can be made to merge—or where each woman can constitute herself alternately as the "angelic" and the evil "witch" mother. This narrative, I argue, excludes or marginalizes other stories, other experiences, because dominant culture is invested in the binary-mother fiction. The visual fictions discussed below will, I hope, demonstrate how "sisterly motives" (the ideal angel mother) subtly turn into "unsisterly practice" (the negative witch mother). Great effort is made to keep the "sisterly" fiction alive, but in different ways and to different degrees, cracks emerge in the fiction.

The ABC Baby M *Miniseries and Rosler's* Born to Be Sold

The traditional angel/witch mother figures in Western culture are obviously reworked in the metaphors and allusions in some stories outlined above. But one can isolate two main, linked strands through which this discursive mother formation returns in surrogacy narratives. A possible religious formation for the sisterliness (the angelic paradigm) may be found in some narrations. But another one—that of melodrama and soap opera (which has implications for the "women-at-odds" paradigm)—seems likely.[29] In order to explore this formation, I discuss two divergent fictional examples of Mary Beth Whitehead's well-known surrogacy narrative to show how the melodrama "genre" may be differently constitutive in both cases.

The *Baby* M miniseries continues the classical melodrama realism that TV soaps have adopted. It claims to be a window on the world and conceals its processes of selecting which images to show, which to ignore, and the illusory constructions at play. The series invites viewers to identify with the characters—named after their real-life equivalents. What is of interest is what identifications the miniseries solicits and what repressed perspectives are able to emerge unawares. As already noted, the TV miniseries genre is always ultimately *melodrama*. But unconscious desires are often at work, and the genre may provide a space for articulation of what cannot *be said*, what has to be repressed, but that is conveyed implicitly in the drama.

The miniseries focuses on the problem of *giving up the child*, which causes rivalry between the mothers: "women at odds," then, form the traumatic part of the surrogacy story. Here the story links up with nineteenth-century stage, and then film, melodrama, in which the adulterous mother is punished by having to give up her children.[30] Surrogacy in the commercial stories evokes this convention, albeit transferred to "unnatural" birth practices. The "women at odds" (or the women-to-be-at-odds) are established in deliberately contrasting ways in the opening sequences through careful selection of clothes, body language, physical location—signs that convey culturally loaded meanings. Betsy Stern (Dr. Stern, as well, professionally) is represented as stiff, proper, professional, well dressed, and in control of her emotions. Despite her emotional control, it's clear how upset Stern is about her inability to give birth.[31] Second, the motivation for Jewish Bill Stern's desire for a biological, not adopted, child is the loss of his mother and his being "all alone." While male figures are usually remote authorities or lovers in the melodrama convention, in this case Stern's behavior shows the impact of seventies women's movements.

The first image of Mary Beth Whitehead is in loud contrast to that of Betsy Stern. Stereotypical class signs predominate: Mary Beth is shown in an unattractive manner lying in bed, eating chocolates (sign of decadence, boredom?), watching TV in the afternoon. This is how she hears about a surrogacy case and thinks of becoming a surrogate. The following scene in which she persuades her husband is the only one in which money is mentioned (and then it's the last thing, an aside). Her main weapon is sex, and again this seems to be a class sign: Betsy's "virgin" to Mary Beth's "whore" represents a return to melodrama female types. Indications of Mary Beth's unreliability mesh with her sexual seductiveness (the whore is always unreliable). Mary Beth wears the wrong color suit to the restaurant (she changes her mind at the last moment, prefiguring her change of mind about the baby). She inappropriately brings her child, Tuesday, to an insemination session and plays loud annoying rock music in the car.

The miniseries, then, all but puts Betsy and Mary Beth into the classic female virgin/whore binary in terms of body types and emotional valence. Mary Beth is flirtatious with William Stern, fun-loving, and emotional, while Betsy is stiff, unsexy, and emotionally controlled. Betsy has fair hair, Mary Beth black hair. Mary Beth is plump and well contoured, Betsy thin and plain.

Narratively, Mary Beth becomes the witch when frustrated or unable to have her way. Within dominant gender codes, violent emotion in women still connotes irresponsibility and inability to function in the public sphere. Within the miniseries discourse, where motherhood is now part of a legal contract, this turns into unreliability as wife and mother. The discourse assumes old notions, namely, the mother as the calm, transcendent presence over the emotional turmoil of the children, who succors and nurtures her husband when he returns from the brutal battles of the public sphere. But in neither case is *she* allowed to be emotionally out of control. Betsy, as career woman, paradoxically also exemplifies the best emotional style to mother. She wins in terms of both class and emotional timbre. Presumably because William Stern is such a devoted father, Betsy's career is not seen to render her an inadequate mother. Indeed, given that she is a pediatrician, it possibly actually helps.

But while the miniseries apparently upholds Betsy as the best mother, some aspects of Mary Beth's own account reappear in the somewhat ambivalent depiction of Betsy. In telling her story in the ghost-written book, Mary Beth depicted Betsy as cold, unfeeling, and selfish—the fifties Hollywood stereotype of the career woman. Does the miniseries unconsciously collude in a critique of the yuppie Stern couple? Certainly, the scene when Betsy finds Mary Beth's dog distasteful could be cited as critiquing middle-class inability to let go and have fun, in contrast to the loose, fun-loving working-class family. William's middle-class stature is stressed through the scenes of the funeral for his mother. Interestingly, however, there seems something too pretty about William, something too WASP about Betsy Stern. A subtle critique underlies their representations.

The women-at-odds high-strung emotionality predominates in the miniseries once the baby is born and it is clear that Mary Beth will not relinquish her. Mary Beth becomes increasingly hysterical, wild, and unreasonable, Betsy increasingly despondent, depressed, silent, tortured. Their intense rivalry, competition, and even hatred override any consideration for each other, let alone the child. William Stern, and to some degree Rick, Mary Beth's husband, show some ability to distance themselves, but the series portrays the two women as locked in an intense competition to win the baby from each other. The baby is reduced to a "thing," standing in for all loss, absence, desire—the breast, the womb, the phallus. At some point, this raw female emotion gets out of control, and the authorities (the police, social agencies, and finally the Father, the Law) move in. Hysteria and jealous rivalry are displaced into the series of institutions the women have to move through in order to win each one's desire: the baby-breast-phallus.

Although I have put psychoanalytic labels on the women's desire in an effort to understand its intensity, the text does not produce concepts to explain the intensity of the jealous female rivalry over the baby. Such jealous rivalry in traditional melodramas is usually over the male lover: think of Betty Davis in *Jezebel*, Vivien Leigh in *Gone with The Wind*, or Olivia de Haviland in *The Heiress* competing to the death for their man. The similarities in the structure of the jealous competition in stories about male lovers and now about babies are significant and invite psychoanalytic explanations.

Ultimately, the miniseries is more complex than some of the surface semiotics might indicate. In line with feminist melodrama theory, the miniseries does represent a range of positionalities vis-à-vis surrogacy. Although one can read the images of Betsy and Mary Beth as conventional "witch/angel" polarities, the narrative does not automatically favor one of the women over the other, as traditional melodramas may do. The varying depictions of the women, and the varying positions spectators are invited to occupy throughout the drama, offer insight into the complexity of surrogacy.

Ironically, such complexity is less evident in Martha Rosler's video *Born to Be Sold: The Strange Case of Baby S/M*, independently produced by Paper Tiger Videos. Its genre and context of production offer different kinds of constraint than those of the miniseries: as a Paper Tiger production, the video has to be explicitly didactic. In this case, Rosler "reads" the *Baby* M miniseries, putting herself under the constraint of responding to the forms that the miniseries set forth, for Rosler's unconventional aesthetic form is determined by the need to break the conventional realist codes of the commercial series. She does this successfully and humorously by inserting herself as speaker in the text, first by reading a paper on camera and then using her own body to perform the various characters of the melodrama she is deconstructing. She also uses a familiar "collage" technique, inserting clips from Hollywood films and TV news programs to make her polemical points.

But most of the time Rosler comments on the TV miniseries. Hers is not a video *about the actual case*, as Maureen Turim seemed to indicate.[32] The specificities of the clothes and hairstyles mimic those in the miniseries, not the historical figures. As in agitprop street theater, Rosler acts out the various key moments in the miniseries melodrama with minimal props and comic, deliberate exaggeration.[33] Miniseries images are repeated in the background so as to prove Rosler's case. This direct camera address by the filmmaker avoids any attempt to hide the video's production or its producer. In this way, Rosler's work breaks the realist illusion of commercial melodramas and makes impossible identification with any of the characters, as such. In place of the multiple and alternating identifications of the miniseries, the spectator is lectured to even more deliberately than in some didactic drama.[34]

In contrast to the ABC miniseries, Rosler's video is a radical feminist reading of the case. And, as such, it is an important intervention. The video has been critiqued for reinforcing separation between women and showing that the only good women are from the lower class,[35] but this ignores the points Rosler is making about the power differential between the Sterns and Mary Beth, and about the coercive force of capitalist institutions. I am more concerned that the video ridicules the infertile woman in a simplistic reduction of the complexity of things. This complexity ironically *is* partly indicated in the commercial melodrama text, with its space for expression of emotions male culture normally excludes.

The difference, then, is not surprising: in a polemical critique of the miniseries, Rosler's video reverses the stereotypes to make its points and does not attempt to move beyond them. It corrects the commercial fiction's inability to critique class relations and its reduction of all to the level of the individual. But the video in turn repeats Mary Beth's own anti–careerwoman stance, which is close to right-wing positions. As much as the miniseries, the video ironically sides with the stance that the birth mother will "naturally" want to keep her baby, as if biological urges cannot be transcended. The video runs the danger of reflecting antimedical perspectives that too easily degenerate into antitechnology stances. These assume there is an unmediated "nature"—that "biology" is discursively neutral. Finally, while the idea of the central speaking subject, Rosler herself, breaks realist allusion, it is not questioned. In this sense, *Born to Be Sold* is a modernist, as against postmodernist, work. It does not argue for the plurality of voices for which feminists are currently looking.

Gillian M. Goslinga-Roy's 1996 video of a surrogacy case, *The Child the Stork Brought Home*, offers interesting contrast, within some continuity, to the prior two texts. As an anthropologist, Goslinga-Roy goes about her task in different ways, and for other ends, than either the ABC producers or Martha Rosler. A first motive was ethnographic documentation. Goslinga-Roy wanted to capture her subjects on tape so as to be able to analyze their words and facial expressions and to chart the changing relationships as the pregnancy continued. But, as a film theorist, I looked at the video in terms of its representational strategies—in terms, that is, of video techniques (Goslinga-Roy's choice of angles, her editing strategies, how she used music on the sound track), and in terms of the general mood or tone that the video projects. Two things in particular fascinated me: first, the discrepancy between Goslinga-Roy's academic paper about her ethnographic project (which I will refer to below) and the video about the same project; and second, how Goslinga-Roy unconsciously—and uncannily—reproduces some of the melodramatic features of ABC's *Baby M*.

The discrepancy between the academic paper and the video is not surprising. Feminist film theory has long been concerned with the difficulty of communicating abstract ideas on film.[36] Indeed, one might argue that the problematic aspects of Rosler's video arise mainly because of her effort to represent abstract Marxist ideas visually. Goslinga-Roy's careful Foucauldian framework, enriched by Donna Haraway's research, among others, enables her—in the academic paper—to communicate important understandings about how power works and about the difference between what she calls "biographical embodiment" and "biological embodiment."[37] The video, on the other hand, as a cinema verité documentary without voice-over commentary, cannot communicate these abstract ideas. It has to focus on the women's words, thoughts, and interactions as Goslinga-Roy follows their process.

Yet it is here that Goslinga-Roy slips into melodrama modes, first, in her choice of just which of all the many hours of tape to keep; then, in her editing techniques; and, most important, in her choice of nondiegetic music—mostly a well-known lullaby. This music, following Hollywood and commercial TV conventions, plays across the visual images and even, occasionally, across dialogue.[38] It is this music that projects the melodrama "mood" of both sisterly harmony and emotional conflict—the increasing stress between the women, their tension. Goslinga-Roy uses music to express the emotion she understood was underlying the relatively pleasant surface interactions. This creates a certain similarity with what I argued the ABC miniseries was also trying to do—namely, to confront the "unsisterly practices" that belie the easy surface talk about giving another woman "a gift." Only with Goslinga-Roy it seems a more deliberate strategy. For instance, the soothing lullaby accompanying a happy scene such as the baby shower will be terminated in the middle of a phrase, on a somewhat jarring note, rather than at the closure of the phrase. This suggests that all is not quite as the protagonists are trying to convey.

I do not want to overstate the melodramatic aspects of Goslinga-Roy's video, however. Since hers is a documentary (not a fictionalized version with actors), and since her "real" people are much more complex than any characters made for commercial TV, *The Child the Stork Brought Home* allows viewers to participate in a process that does not simply follow a preordained formula. Viewers are able to see the distance between the 1980s and the 1990s in the attitudes of both the gestational mother, Julie, and the genetic parents, the Martins. But most of all, viewers are given some of the complexity missing in either previous version just because these are not actors.

Editing the footage must have been a trying task. There is no space here to address in detail editing practices as they bear on the meanings the video produces.[39] In general, Goslinga-Roy adheres to a chronological ordering of the shots, and there are pleasant early shots of the "sisterly" relations between the two mothers. Goslinga-Roy attempts to avoid judgment or categorizing the two women, although by the end the viewer's sympathy cannot help but be more with Julie, for as the video advances, more shots show Julie's difficulties and hurts as the relationship between the two women becomes more complex.

A handicap in making this kind of documentary is the inevitable self-consciousness that the camera provokes. But, especially with repeated viewing, the tiny facial expressions, certain unconscious gestures, a slip of the tongue, or other apparently inconsequential details betray feelings, attitudes, conflicts that cannot be articulated within the women's self-conscious framework of love, caring, self-abnegation, and so on. A verité documentary can do so much more, even within the limits of its realist frames, than can anything scripted.

I marveled at the naturalness of most of the scenes. Goslinga-Roy had somehow enabled her subjects to "forget" the camera. But there was an interesting difference between the women: Julie evidently "bonded" more easily with Goslinga-Roy than did the genetic parents, so that her perspectives are more fully communicated than are those of the Martins. Indeed, the attitude of the gestational mother brings about one major difference from the 1980s narratives and visual productions. From the start, Julie seems quite clear about her motives and about her role in the process. Early on in the video she states that one of her motives is to have the pleasure of handing over a *live* baby to a mother. It's an emotional moment: Julie works with deformed babies and usually has to offer only a dead baby for the mother to grieve over.

Julie is more psychologically informed than the miniseries shows Mary Beth to be, and she is a complex person. The degree to which "Mary Beth" in the ABC series is an old stereotype of working-class women is highlighted by the contrast with the lively, intelligent, emotionally balanced and generally good-natured Julie. Also refreshing, narratively, is the apparently reasonable and friendly genetic couple, the Martins. There is no coding of blond/good versus black-haired/evil mothers, as in the miniseries (repeated in Rosler's tape). Both women happen to be light skinned and fair haired, even if Mrs. Martin is more blond than Julie.

Both Pamela Martin and Julie are complex people. Viewers of the video may find interesting Goslinga-Roy's academic, written analysis, which the video cannot, unfortunately, convey. Goslinga-Roy asserts that the real conflict was not about class or gender per se but about the different expectations of Julie, on the one hand, and the Martins, on the other. However, Goslinga-Roy is limited in the video by her realist codes and expectations of the audience, which prevent her from fully exploring what went wrong for Julie: there is no room to theorize or comment within the video's chosen form. The video shows Julie trying to express her hurt after the baby was born, but it makes little sense. Julie and her husband, Dallas, talk about the Martins' having missed a special moment, but the viewer is rather unsure just what that was.

Goslinga-Roy's academic analysis, on the other hand, makes excellent sense: Julie, she argued, wanted to "further expand the boundaries of her body/self to include the Martins and their child" (11)—what Goslinga-Roy calls "biographical embodiment." Julie knew that she was "loaning" her womb to the Martins but, according to Goslinga-Roy, thought that in sharing her body she could avoid being treated as simply "a cow." The Martins, however, held the more common understanding of "biological embodiment" in which there could only be one natural mother, the genetic, and one natural family, the nuclear private one. In this scenario, there was no place for Julie. Pamela Martin could not, in this view, "share" the pregnancy. Julie was only a means to an end for her. Julie's heartbreak at the end of the process came from this realization. It was not, as the Mary Beth and other 1980s narratives would have it, that Julie could not give up the baby. How her role was conceived by the Martins produced her upset and turned Pamela's actions into "unsisterly practices."

Nevertheless, paradoxically, the realist and melodrama genres—as I showed in some of the popularized magazine stories discussed in the first section—permit jealousy, envy, hate, spite, and even violence and aggression between women to be expressed, if not leaving room for analysis, theory, or critique. These are passions that childbirth and mothering elicit for many women and that rarely find public expression or validation. However, there is possibly a complex process at work such that the traditions of the melodrama genre construct or shape the form that women's stories take in the first place, including sisterliness becoming unsisterly: women at odds. As I noted at the outset, a main point here is to show how the prevalence of the melodrama form in women's lives itself conditions the modes through which women think their lives—even *experience* their lives to begin with. The genre may be constitutive of the experience as much as the reverse.

If Goslinga-Roy's ethnographic video is a start in the direction stated earlier—women needing to produce narrative forms that make possible the writing of different stories—then Emily Liu goes much further in her independent, fictional film *Kangaroo Man*. Liu imagines a very different kind of surrogacy, that in which, once the wife's pregnancy ends with loss of the baby and a hysterectomy, the husband, a fertility specialist, uses his resources and colleagues to experiment with implanting the couple's embryo in *his* womb. This is a last resort, however. Prior to taking that drastic step, the couple have tried to find an appropriate mother surrogate. The film presents a very different sensibility toward surrogacy within the Los Angeles Taiwanese community, in that the couple appear to go about advertising and finding a surrogate on their own, outside agencies or other institutions. There is a humorous series of interviews with would-be surrogates, rather few of whom make any reference to the "giving of the gift of life," and for most of whom this is a straight up-front economic arrangement. Once the husband decides to become the couple's own surrogate, the film develops into an interesting exploration of role reversal—far more creative and plausible than Arnold Schwarzenegger's pregnant man in *Junior*. Emily Liu works both with and against stereotypes of her Taiwanese community, and her main protagonists are carefully portrayed as warm, loving people. The husband, Michael, is an especially gratifying model of maleness, in his tenderness and gentleness while being an excellent fertility researcher and active in his profession.

Liu's film combines the virtues of the commercial melodrama and the independent film to ask viewers to imagine differently. But all three independent texts offered a different experiencing of issues surrounding surrogacy. Rosler challenges directly the biases of mainstream media accounts of surrogacy, while, as a feminist anthropologist, Goslinga-Roy's very act of following the surrogacy case and making the video opens up hitherto neglected possibilities for women to engage with one another across divisions of social role and class. Together, these texts begin the process of developing a plurality of stories, positions, and personalities that will open up more complex, nuanced, nonbinary possibilities that are crucial as feminism enters the nineties and attempts to grapple with difference on new levels.

Notes

This essay is an expanded and revised version of an essay in *Feminism, Media, and the Law*, Martha A. Fineman and Martha T. McClusky eds. London and New York: Oxford University Press, 1997, 193–202.

1. Research is still in progress and results of what I have been able to do are therefore tentative. I selected popular articles listed under the heading "Surrogacy" in the Reader's Digest Index throughout the 1980s. Materials quoted came from many magazines, including *Redbook*, *Good Housekeeping*, and *Women's World*. In addition, I looked at around twenty books about surrogacy, ranging from those aimed at quite a broad market to those more highly specialized, addressing legal or medical experts. Since writing this essay, I have read anthropologist Gillian M. Goslinga-Roy's 1995 unpublished paper, "Body Boundaries: Fictions of the Female Self," and seen the video she made of her ethnographic research with a surrogacy "couple." I have referred to her work in this revision of my 1992 paper.
2. See Elizabeth Kane, *Birth Mother* (New York: Harcourt Brace, 1988): 20–22–22; Mary Beth Whitehead, *A Mother's Story* (New York: St. Martin's Press, 1989), 7; Elaine Markoutsas, "Women Who Have Babies for Other Women," condensed from *Good Housekeeping* (April 1981), *Reader's Digest* 119 (August 1981): 71–72.
3. Whitehead, *A Mother's Story*, 89.
4. Mary Jo Deegan, "The Gift Mother: A Proposed Ritual for the Integration of Surrogacy into Society," in *On the Problem of Surrogate Parenthood*, ed. Herbert Richardson (New York: Edwin Mellen Press, 1987), 93.
5. Victor Turner, *The Ritual Process* (Chicago: Aldine, 1969).
6. See R. Lacayo and W. Svoboda, "Is the Womb a Rentable Space?" *Time*, 22 September 1987, 36; Henry M. Butzel, "The Essential Facts of the Baby M Case," in Richardson, *On the Problem of Surrogate Parenthood*, 7; David Neff, "How Not to Have a Baby: Surrogate Mothers May Create a New Class of Breeder Women and Further Confuse the Family Unity," editorial, *Christianity Today*, 3 April 1987, 14–15.
7. Sherry King and Elaine Fein, "'I Gave Birth to My Sister's Baby,'" in *Redbook* (April 1986): 34–38. This quotation, 34.
8. Karen Mills, "'I Had My Sister's Baby,'" *Ladies Home Journal* (October 1985): 20–22.
9. Suzanne Guinzburg, "Surrogate Mothers' Rationale," *Psychology Today* (April 1983): 79.
10. In future work, I will want to explore the framing contexts of "medicine" and "God" that speakers construct to legitimize surrogacy. The equivalence or not of these frames themselves is an important question, as well.

11. Note in what follows the repetition in different modes of this phrase from the negative stories in 1987. Mary Beth herself a bit later on, as readers will see, says that she has "learned" that this is baby selling. By 1992, surrogate mothers like Dawna and Kathy are ready to take on this criticism by stating that what they are doing cannot be "baby-selling" because the baby is not theirs to sell! Finally, in Goslinga-Roy's 1995 ethnographic study, Julie is quoted as saying precisely the same as Dawna and Kathy: "Whenever someone would accuse her of 'baby-selling' . . . she would confidently retort, 'How can I sell a baby which is not mine in the first place? I am not genetically related to this child. It is not mine to sell'" (Goslinga-Roy, "Body Boundaries").

12. Nelly E. Gupta and Frank Feldinger, "Brave New Baby," *Ladies Home Journal* 106, no. 2 (1989): 140–141.

13. See Neff, "How Not to Have a Baby," 14–15, and Julie Murphy, "Egg Farming and Women's Future," in *Test Tube Women: What Future for Motherhood?*, ed. R. Arditti, R. Dueilli Klein, and Shellen Minden (London: Pandora Press, 1984), 68–75.

14. Whitehead, *A Mother's Story*, xiv–xv.

15. Murphy, "Egg Farming and Women's Future."

16. See E. Ann Kaplan, *Motherhood and Representation: The Mother in Popular Culture and Melodrama* (London: Routledge, 1992), 213–215.

17. See diverse perspectives in Peter Montgomery, "Should Surrogate Motherhood be Banned?" *Common Cause Magazine* (May/June 1988): 36–38.

18. See Markoutsas, "Women Who Have Babies," 72.

19. See Neff, "How Not to Have a Baby," 14.

20. "Elizabeth: A Surrogate's Story of Loving and Losing," *U.S. News and World Report*, 6 June 1983.

21. D. Grogan, "Little Girl, Big Trouble: A Surrogate Birth, a Divorce, and a Tangled Custody Fight Mean an Uncertain Future for a Child Known Only as Tessa," *People*, 20 February 1989, 36–41.

22. Research shows that a high proportion of surrogate mothers at one time either gave children up for adoption or had abortions (Guinzburg, "Surrogate Mothers' Rationale"). The correlation of self-selection for surrogacy if a woman has had an abortion or given up a child for adoption is significant and will be pursued in my future research about surrogacy.

23. Jane Mingay, "The Furore over Surrogate Motherhood," *Maclean's*, 5 July 1982, 18; Mills, "'I Had My Sister's Baby,'" 20–23; Shona McKay, "A Media Judgement on Surrogate Birth," *Maclean's*, 14 February 1983, 41; Mary Thom, "Dilemmas of the New Birth Technologies," *Ms.* (May 1988): 70–72; Andrew H. Malcolm, "Steps to Control Surrogate Births Stir Debate Anew," *New York Times*, 26 June 1988.

24. E.g., Carole Pateman, *The Sexual Contract* (Stanford, Calif.: Stanford University Press, 1988).

25. My source for the comments of both Dawna and Kathy (following) is audio and video tapes made at the 1992 conference at the Humanities Institute, in which they participated.

26. David Gelman and Daniel Shapiro, "Infertility: Babies by Contract," *Newsweek*, 4 November 1985, 74–76.

27. See *Jet Magazine*, 1990; *New York Times*, 14 August 1990. Goslinga-Roy (in "Body Boundaries") quotes an interaction with the gestational mother, Julie (whose process as a surrogate she followed), in which Julie describes how horrified she is to find out that a Hispanic woman in her support group is pregnant with embryos from a black couple. She declares that she could never carry a black baby and discusses the social stigma it would cause along with her own thinly disguised disgust at the idea (2–3). Julie's spontaneous response speaks volumes about race relations in America today and possibly partly explains the few black women surrogates.

Issues are far more complex than I can address here. But Goslinga-Roy usefully notes that in claiming on the one hand that the baby is not *genetically* linked to her (their blood does not come into contact) yet being horrified at the idea of carrying a black fetus, Julie reveals that whiteness "was the invisible glue that held her narrative of gestational surrogacy together" (4).

28. Indeed, minority women and reproductive technologies seems a "taboo" subject. This is why the film *Made In America* was so interesting. In the film, the heroine, played by Whoopi Goldberg, has conceived her daughter by artificial insemination (AI). The plot relies on the consequences of the daughter finding out about her AI birth and that her father was apparently white for its comic effects.

29. However, Gordon was complaining about what she called "the soap-opera approach to reproductive conflicts" and the fact that this approach obscured the politics and the litigation (Linda Gordon, "Some Policy Proposals: Reproductive Rights for Today," *Nation*, 17 September 1987, 230). I believe she had the media accounts in mind more than the SMs' actual narratives. I am here more interested in how the availability of a form like melodrama in itself conditions the forms in which women think their lives and tell their stories.

It is also hard to determine how far the stories in the media account were themselves the product of editors and reporters, who may have turned what women said into familiar melodrama forms for marketing reasons. One would need to do extensive interviewing to see how women articulate experiences, but even the "telling to another" (the interviewer) may automatically make women "perform" the melodrama!

30. Such narratives (e.g., *East Lynne* [1861] is a well-known model: see Kaplan, *Motherhood and Representation*) dwell on the painful separation from the children—the years of yearning for them in exile, the tears over their loss, the poverty the mother succumbs to, her guilt.

31. Interestingly, neither the miniseries nor Rosler's experimental video deals much with the internal, psychological aspects of the adoptive parents for whom the surrogate is gestating the baby. Goslinga-Roy's video and essay are interesting in that by 1995 the adoptive mother has the language to articulate some of her concerns.

32. Maureen Turim, "Viewing/Reading *Born to Be Sold: Martha Rosler Reads the Strange Case of Baby S/M* or Motherhood in the Age of Mechanical Reproduction," *Discourse* 13, no. 2 (1991): 32.

33. I was most reminded of the agitprop techniques in a little-known early British feminist film, *The Amazing Equal Pay Show*, which Rosler may well have had in mind. This film, however, did mimic actual historical political figures and was not a reading of a commercial text, as is Rosler's piece.

34. I am thinking of theater like that of Berthold Brecht, from whose plays Rosler's techniques are perhaps drawn.

35. See Turim's essay, "Viewing/Reading *Born to Be Sold*," for similar arguments.

36. The most sustained effort to put theory on film may be found in British feminist independent films of the 1970s—films I termed "Avant-garde Theory Films" in my 1983 book *Women and Film: Both Sides of the Camera* (New York: Routledge, 1983). See chap. 10 for more on the difficulties and pleasures of these films.

37. See Goslinga-Roy, "Body Boundaries."

38. Space does not permit to go into the many reasons why Goslinga-Roy may have used this strategy. Often, filmmakers insert music to keep an audience's attention in "slack" parts of a film; usually, though, the music is intended to add meaning—to convey a mood, an emotional valence, and so on, as it does here.

39. In another essay, I hope to discuss Goslinga-Roy's video at greater length.

Reproductive Technology and the Unconscious

KAY TORNEY SOUTER
JOHN WILTSHIRE

An Australian Case

INFERTILITY AND its remedies confront us with ethical and philosophical tangles, but solving them does not put an end to the puzzles of high-tech baby making. Like everything else, infertility exists within a psychosocial context, and individuals who pursue the options offered by the new reproductive technology to provide them with children must be motivated to overcome considerable psychosocial difficulties—demands on time, energy, and financial resources, physical and emotional pain—and often repeated disappointment (Lasker and Borg 1989). Yet, despite this and despite the arguments of feminists and others against the exploitative demands of these practices (Rowland 1992), they continue to proliferate and flourish. Of these technologies, surrogate motherhood is the most controversial, the most surrounded by moral and social dilemmas. What, then, supplies the psychological resources required to engage in the protracted, as well as socially and legally fraught, processes of surrogacy? Rational cognitive processes seem scarcely to account for the tolerance of danger and discomfort that reproductive technology still causes all parties to such a transaction. We want to argue that it is only within the irrational, the contradictory, the space of the psychodynamic, that an adequate account of this phenomenon can be produced.

To test this proposition, however, poses immediate problems of access and ethics. If one supposes that the issue of surrogate motherhood turns on some of the deepest recesses of the self—recesses that may not be known to and can hardly be articulated by the individual subject—how can these be investigated with the tools of sociological or legal analysis? One option is to avoid interviewing or discussing real-life subjects and instead to approach their experience through an examination of their autobiographical self-representations, and materials certainly exist for such a project. Autobiography provides a text with ethical integrity and an existence that is independent of the researcher: it sidesteps the methodological dilemma by allowing access to less rationalized and defended positions than may be produced in, say, a short-answer questionnaire. Puns, parapraxes, analogies may be explored for contradictory and irrational impulses as they are in any text; and also as in any text, these productions exist in a sense independently of the historical figures who produced them. In this essay we substantiate our position by examining one of the many narratives of reproductive surrogacy, the book-length *My Sister's Child*, described as "a story of full surrogate motherhood between two sisters using in vitro fertilisation" by Maggie and Linda Kirkman (1988) in the title page blurb.[1] We argue that *My Sister's Child* is a considerable narrative achievement, since it documents in unmatched detail and with wit and flair a full history of surrogacy from the "conception" of the idea that one sister might carry the other's child, to the successful birth.

Contracted for two months into the pregnancy and published shortly after the baby's birth, *My Sister's Child* differs in important ways from other well-known narratives of surrogacy (as for example, Elizabeth Kane's and Mary Beth Whitehead's in the United States and Kim Cotton's in the United Kingdom); it is not ghosted, nor is it filtered through a journalist's or interviewer's medium, and it represents a family's decision to harness the media rather than a response to media exploitation. The book's very self-consciousness and self-possession, however, has another side. Its fullness and candor about its protagonists' emotions and motives allow, or in some instances demand, a reading that supplements these with other structures and drives, or inserts among them themes that remain out of the subjects' awareness. Reading against the grain in this way suggests itself not least because *My Sister's Child* is a joint narrative, fractured between two authors, and the fracture lines often provide insight into crucial issues. In other words, this narrative of surrogacy prompts a reading rather different from that which, we surmise, its authors intended in publicizing their actions. *My Sister's Child* does not, we argue, fulfill its authors' intention, to accept, even to celebrate, their joint achievement; rather, in regard to the psychological relations between the principals involved in a surrogacy arrangement, it prompts a troubling series of questions.

In Melbourne, Australia, where Monash University runs an important IVF clinic, a family group in the late 1980s planned and brought to fruition the birth of a new member via IVF conception and surrogate gestation. The mechanics of this surrogacy story (what one might call the "physio-surrogacy") go like this: Maggie Kirkman, the elder of the two sisters, has had a hysterectomy that has left her ovaries. Her second husband, Sev (the originator of the surrogacy plan), has a zero sperm count. The plan for Maggie and Sev to have a baby, without, as Maggie puts it, "a uterus or a sperm between them," is made feasible when Linda Kirkman, Maggie's younger sister, agrees to gestate a child for them, on the condition that her own ova are not involved. Ova from Maggie's ovaries are obtained, mixed with donor sperm, and inserted into Linda's uterus at the IVF center. A healthy daughter is delivered in May 1988, one month premature, by a cesarean section necessitated by a placenta praevia and a prepartum hemorrhage, badly disappointing Linda, who had hoped for another enjoyable vaginal delivery. Maggie breast-feeds baby Alice for twelve months via a Lact-Aid, fine tubing taped to her nipple and attached to a flat bottle of human milk. The milk is mostly provided by Linda; she produces up to a liter a day, and other women step in when supplies fall low.

This family, upper middle class, fond of each other, and conceptually sophisticated, believe they have worked out the perfect scheme for victimless altruistic surrogacy. Intellectual credentials are put forward as definitively important in the book's political intentions: Maggie Kirkman is a university teacher of psychology; Linda is a high school teacher; their father is a Melbourne doctor, which turns out to be important because he can administer some of the medical procedures. The family mixes socially with local politicians, society figures, intellectuals. They are used to directing society, rather than taking direction from it, and it is a very new idea for them to find themselves obliged to tolerate what they consider irrational and impertinent interference from the state. Indeed, most of the book's fundamental issues turn on the idea of "control," a slippery notion that moves between an idea of self-control or restraint of one's emotions and a somewhat different conception of outside power over one's future life. It is in the inevitable conflict between these two opposing ideas—self-restraint versus external dominance—that the Kirkmans' social position becomes relevant. This sense of family purpose is given an explosive impetus by their incredulous sense of outrage that what they think of as in all ways internal and well managed, thank you very much—control—should suddenly be presented to them as a matter for external jurisdiction—control! This is not a response that would be usual in a poor family or one of an ethnic minority, who are usually only too used to bureaucratic interference in their intimate family life, in who they sleep with, what they drink, what their babies eat, and where their adolescents play. Where Mary Beth Whitehead's response to state interference in her personal life is to turn fugitive, the Kirkmans enlist the political cavalry even before things get nasty, effectively throwing the first punch. My Sister's Child, then, is a bourgeois narrative, and like all bourgeois narratives, it rejects state interference: not (the book attempts to argue) primarily because of the injustices that are likely but because the family is paramount. The difference is more one of attitude than of fact, of course: the Kirkmans do fear the evils of state interference, but they attempt to argue their case from the high moral ground of absolute human rights, rather than from the relativities of actual harms suffered.

It is also a mark of the bourgeois narrative that the Kirkmans want their self-determination to be publicly acclaimed, not merely left unmolested: "We wanted the piquancy of our child's birth to be a matter of special pride, not shame, to be celebrated as a special family achievement," Maggie Kirkman writes. The enemy of this goal is the state government department responsible for adoption, the Department of Community Services Victoria, known as CSV, and its staff. It is this agency of the state that threatens, at every stage of the arrangements, to declare the Kirkmans' act illegal, to refuse to allow the commissioning parents to adopt the child, for instance, and even, perhaps, to take the newborn infant away, into state custody. It is demonized throughout the book in the form of "the social worker": "It would be much harder for a CSV social worker to play God with our family," notes Maggie, deciding to harness the media, "if we had public support for our actions." Social workers, represented as anonymous interfering bureaucrats, "unimaginative, inflexible tyrants" (Kirkman 1988, 266) "with entrenched ideological views" (235), threaten to violate the autonomy of the family, to take action against the benign and loving transaction it has engineered. The Kirkman family robustly challenges the right of the state to have opinions about what it might do in the privacy of its own bosom. "If only our legal problems were as trivial as our psychological ones" (204), Maggie Kirkman complains. *My Sister's Child*, in fact, presents unmolested family privacy as health, and state interference as illness. The interventions of government agencies cause the loss of precious internal control, unguarded emotions, and bodily anguish: headaches, catatonia, "frantic thoughts, fears and plans" (236) temporarily disturb the carefully managed poise of the diarist. When the sisters are secluded together after the birth, "the only barb from the outside world" comes in the form of an inquiry from the hospital social worker, and Maggie writes, "I immediately felt anxiety choking me" (301).

Psychological conflict within the family is thus minimized, and in the most ringingly ideological way. As an upper-middle-class family the Kirkmans seem at times to be arguing that it would be morally wrong for them *not* to defy state intervention in their reproductive lives. The struggle for power—a struggle for the baby—is displaced onto a concurrent struggle with a threatening external agent. "I have no wish to become a character in a play directed by an evangelical social worker" (234), sniffs Maggie Kirkman, in a tone reminiscent of a child whose grandiose belief in her possession of her mother is being challenged. These Oedipal complaints somewhat obscure the fact that it is the "evangelical" insistence of the Kirkman family on its own ideological correctness, its demand that it be not merely ignored but celebrated, that has meant that Maggie's private life has become the subject of meetings within the government department, that, in effect, "social workers" have become characters in a play directed by the Kirkman family. "I cannot help feeling," she laments, "as though we have become public property," which neatly reverses the fact that "public property," government departments and a public medical system, is pretty much dancing to the Kirkmans' tune. The strength of the resentment of the social worker, and its irrational and contradictory aspects, can be accounted for because the official, the social worker, does not simply represent an annoying functionary but takes on the power of the Lacanian father, the one who says "no," the marker of Oedipal division: she must be repulsed entirely because she threatens to break into and attempts to structure the happy, nondifferentiated world of family togetherness. If the demonized figure of the social worker is included, this story of a loving relationship between two sisters, this "extraordinary twelve months of family togetherness," is in fact triangulated, presenting a configuration of Oedipal tension and rivalry rather than dyadic fusion.

My Sister's Child thus encompasses a psychological narrative about external intrusions into perfect harmony that is much less overt than the book's theme of rational individuals making considered and benign choices. One sign of this is that, apparently unnoticed by the ostensible principals, Maggie and Sev, a bargain is being driven about the constitution of Maggie's motherhood. Linda Kirkman is a member of the Nursing Mothers' Association of Australia and, it is said, "a crusader for motherhood." When the proposal for her to become a surrogate is made, Linda is still "nursing" her two-and-a-half-year-old son, breast-feeding several times a day. Linda's advocacy of breast-feeding plays an important part in the subsequent narrative, and it is this that constitutes the unexamined bargain underlying the generosity and support that the sisters are represented as offering to each other. As soon as tests confirm that Linda is pregnant, she loads her sister with pamphlets from the Nursing Mothers' Association, and thereafter the narrative focus on the medico-legal vicissitudes of the pregnancy is counterpointed with Maggie's, as she struggles with various methods and devices, including at one stage a two-hour session of nipple stimulation (but not drugs, because of the unknown effect on the baby) to persuade her breasts to lactate. To be a mother, in this scenario, she must be a nursing mother, even though she can never be a gestating mother and may very well never be a lactating mother.[2] Breast-feeding constitutes the symbolic transaction that, in the sisters' eyes, serves to validate and legitimate Maggie's motherhood and the measures taken to ensure it. The book ends, not with the birth, but two months later, with Linda triumphantly expressing a few drops of milk from Maggie's reluctant breast. The traditional splitting of maternal function into wet nurse and gestational mother is reversed: the "real" mother is she who feeds, not she who gestates (or lactates); the breast/ Lact-Aid (not the uterus) becomes the sacred, inalienable site of motherhood.

A more important signal of hidden transactional realities, or what one might call an inner or unconscious narrative, is to be found in the book's main subplot. This is as Australian as the pioneer writers, the tale of rebuilding the family home after a bushfire. This story, which is apparently incidental and contingent—a mere happenstance background to the consciously engineered project of the surrogacy—in fact discloses a great deal of material that illuminates the account of the surrogacy. The bushfire story goes like this: on 16 February 1983, on what was by horrible coincidence Ash Wednesday of that year, southern Australia suffered its most destructive bushfires for two generations.[3] Mount Macedon, where Sev, the commissioning father of *My Sister's Child*, had grown up, was completely deforested, and a number of historic homes and gardens were destroyed. Sev, out fighting the Ash Wednesday fires himself, "returned to his beloved [family] house to find only charred stumps and chimneys." Even the nameplate on the ruined gate is stolen in a few days. He becomes determined to defy destiny, to build a house that will be a virtual fire-proof bunker. When, at the opening of the book, he first meets Maggie, he is living in a tin shed, and during the time frame of the narrative they complete the new house together. Much of the book is concerned with their subsequent trials and anxieties: the half-built house's vulnerability to intruders, its stored contents being ravaged by vermin, the physical indignities and exposure (outdoor showers, disgusting chemical toilets), and, especially, Maggie's irritation about all the other people who get to use the house before its hardworking owners (174).

This archetypal Australian narrative has particular resonance and consequence within this context. The attention that is given to it is not accidental, for *My Sister's Child* is, in fact, quite tightly structured. Other daily realities, such as Sev's complicated political aspirations, never get a mention; Maggie Kirkman's job as a lecturer in psychology significantly takes center stage only on occasions when it is unsettling her, when, for instance, she is evicted from her office while she is on extended leave and finds herself feeling "selfishly dispossessed and under attack" (193). Intrusion of nonsurrogacy material into the narrative generally represents the negative aspects of the surrogacy in general. The chronicle of the new house—its vulnerability to burglary, to attack by rats and vermin, the harassment by incompetent professionals who take months to do the simplest task and then stay only long enough to cause damage, the constant worry about whether it will work, whether its solidity wasn't what Maggie calls "overcompensation," whether they shouldn't perhaps have been contented with something simpler—represents an extended metaphorical condensation and displacement of thoughts about the surrogacy. It effectively "contains" the fear, exhaustion, and resentment of the principals in a way that allows the explicit narrative of surrogacy to focus on the joys of anticipation, to protect the "good" surrogacy experience by splitting off the bad into the other main creative task at hand. If there is a narrative about the horrors of displacement, of destruction from without and within, it is carried, and disguised, in the alternative history of the other enterprise of family consolidation, rebuilding the damaged family home.

To produce this reading of the psychological significance of the house subplot is to make a narrative rather than a psychological point. The Kirkmans' narrative functions as all narratives do, rather like the analytic hour, in which descriptions of subthemes are likely to be representations of major issues, in which everything that comes up is relevant, everything, however apparently coincidental, contingent, accidental, throws some light on everything else. The narrative of surrogacy, as a social, political, ethical, and familial act, is thus not completed until the psychological narrative is discerned. That rational worldview held by the principals of this surrogacy arrangement, as well as many of the commentators on reproductive technology, which insists that conscious and considered motives are all that need to be examined, may thus be loosened by such an analysis as this.

The notion of rational control is very important in this family: even the relationship of the sisters to the IVF program, and to their doctor's work within it, turns around this, as the individuals seek to maintain their legal and political autonomy. "Linda and I are not prepared to relinquish control over our lives" (190), they declare, speaking as one; "we are not prepared to be used as instruments to achieve the goals of other people" (192). Shades of J. S. Mill: "Over himself, over his own body and mind, the individual is sovereign."[4] This ideology (though control is different from sovereignty, defending against scarcely apprehended dangers), in its debased latter-day form "you are what you make yourself," is the official charter of the Kirkmans' freedom. To be "in control" of the body and the emotions is also represented as vitally important, a crucial aspect of control over personal destiny. "This pregnancy was requiring me to remain in control of myself and to be a rational person at all times," writes Linda Kirkman (216). "I've hardly shed a tear during the pregnancy in spite of all the recent distress because of the responsibility I've felt to be in control, to be ready to make decisions, or to act," echoes Maggie (264). In My Sister's Child, control is represented as another form of psychic splitting: maintained by defensive humor, "coping" with discomfort and emotional heights by deflection into facetiousness. The book displays, even flaunts, its own ability to perceive and ward off criticisms. The sisters are wary of, and quick to detect, their unruly emotions, quick to meet them in the name of this rational, purposive self.

But despite this repeated insistence on "the role of cognition," the narrative is preoccupied with the experience and enactment of psychic merging. In this text, bodies and psyches seem continually to be represented as interchangeable with each other, and identities and positions within the family constellation are malleable, temporary, imbricated one with the other. The moment of the actual proposal for Linda to carry the child is a striking instance: "I decided that after dinner would be an ideal time to present our proposition. I swear that my mouth was open to begin when Linda said: 'I'm sorry, but I couldn't be a surrogate mother for you.' It took a few breathless seconds before I could explain that, funnily enough . . . 'Oh,' said Linda, 'That would be all right then. It's different if you want to use your eggs'" (43–44). At a later point, Linda writes, "Maggie wondered aloud what breast milk tasted like. She was unable to bring herself to find out when I offered her some on a spoon, and collapsed in a heap of helpless laughter" (117). Before long, Maggie is feeding Linda as she lies prone on the couch of the IVF clinic waiting room (143). The intimacies between the sisters are extraordinary—massaging and manipulating the breasts in preparation for lactation provides many opportunities—though they are presented (and masked) almost always as comic. When their doctor father assists in the project by taking blood from her, Linda weeps. "Naughtily, the rest of us gave way to great mirth," writes Maggie, "when she concluded later that her tears had been inspired by what could be interpreted as symbolic incest." The blood is kept in the refrigerator in a mug labeled "Grandpa" (84). At four in the morning, before the scheduled "pick up" of ova, father (who has himself delivered Linda's obstetrician) gives Maggie an injection of HCG (91), or human chorionic gonadotrophin, to ensure her eggs ripen at the right moment. Mornings see Linda and Maggie leaping into bed with their mother and Linda's children, a nonspectacular but characteristic instance of the cuddles-all-round that this family enjoys. The most hilarious example occurs when the plumbing is fixed in the new house:

> The highlight of the weekend . . . was the inaugural bath. . . . The first sitting was for all three Kirkman sisters! It is a big bath, though not quite big enough for the demands being made upon it, so that protuberant parts of the anatomy emerged from the water in a way that focused all attention upon them. First we talked about [the baby], who formed the large mound above Linda and who seemed to enjoy the hot water, wriggling around in lively pleasure. Then Cynthia and Linda shifted their gaze to my breasts and began demonstrating how to express milk. Cynthia was able to produce drops of fluid from hers

and was immediately nominated as a wet nurse. Unfortunately, she as
swiftly declined the nomination. Both of my sisters then tried to
extract similar drops from me, but we all laughed so much we nearly
drowned. Sev saved me from further ignominy by bringing us champagne to celebrate the occasion, which seemed both luxurious and
decadent even though Cynthia drank all of Linda's and half of
mine. (205)

The fantasy of a "family body" is most clearly seen in this bathing scene,
a cheerful instance of polymorphous pregenital sexuality. The sisters share their
champagne, brought by the friendly husband of one of them, and then "nearly
drown" in amniotic gaiety. Such incidents are so characteristic of this family
and this narrative that they must be taken into, and interpreted within, any
comprehensive understanding of this surrogacy arrangement. One framework
in which to insert such material is offered by the French psychoanalyst Janine
Chasseguet-Smirgel (1985) in her examination of the determinants and meaning of perversion. "Perverse" in the usual sense of the word, of course, the
Kirkmans' behavior and psychology is not: it would be a crude and unhelpful
response indeed to the Kirkmans' project to dismiss it merely as selfish or transgressive. Another Parisian analyst, Joyce McDougall, points out that "etymo-
logically *per-vertere* means no more than a movement of returning or reversing.
Any dictionary will inform us, however, that this movement is invariably in
the direction of evil" (McDougall 1986, 246). "We never say," she has remarked, "that 'he was perverted to the good.'"[5] To remedy this situation,
McDougall proposes the term "neosexualities," which recognizes that in some
sense behaviors regarded as "perverse" are constructive and original solutions
to fears and fantasies. In the realm of the neosexualities, one might argue, corporeal reality becomes available as a space for manipulation and innovation:
like the sexual practices of the "pervert," these can at once express and contain
psychological proclivities, so as to organize the external life-world satisfyingly
and efficiently. It is in this sense that the thesis of *Creativity and Perversion* is
helpful in understanding the attractions of the procedures of reproductive technology. Chasseguet-Smirgel argues that "perversion is one of the essential ways
and means [that man] applies in order to push forward the frontiers of what is
possible and to unsettle reality" (1).

Her thesis articulates a relationship between the psychological dynamics
of the extended Kirkman family (as their narrative discloses them) and the
new "political" reality of surrogacy. Maggie Kirkman, Linda Kirkman, and other
supporters of IVF technology insist explicitly, in fact, that, with the conception and gestation of baby Alice, they are helping to bring about a "new social order . . . push[ing] forward the frontiers of what is possible." They decline
to remain in the technological closet. The Kirkmans' group celebration of the

technology that they were able to utilize to enlarge their family shows clearly that, in their case, the act of sister surrogacy was deeply ego-syntonic, that is, it was not simply a freely chosen rational act performed in the spirit of J. S. Mill but one that was deeply consonant with their psychic structure, a manic (and in this case, granted the wish to make a baby without a maternal uterus or paternal sperm, empowering) denial of Oedipal division. This explains why the Kirkmans are so ready to resent state interference with their family plans and what allows the Kirkmans to be so "generous" to each other. It is clear that the Kirkman family has elements in its joint history that allow it, in Chasseguet-Smirgel's terms, to activate the "perverse core" of limited differentiation in the search for new social and technological reality.

My Sister's Child documents the obliteration of difference whenever it suits, often to the accompaniment of gales of what Maggie calls "naughty mirth." The very title insists on the confusion of identities in the work; and Linda's title of Maggie's "baby sister" is milked for its ambiguities, ambiguities that it is hard to imagine would be apparent in many other families. Linda is represented not only as Maggie's favorite sister from birth but her surrogate daughter as well. Maggie has been a "surrogate mother" to both her sisters at times in their earlier lives: a sadistic mother who forces the barely toilet-trained Cynthia to pee *through* her heavy woolen knickers rather than shame Maggie by publicly lowering them; a loving mother in the case of Linda, eight years her junior. The sisters insist that genetic parentage (the production of the ova that go to make baby Alice) is vital in deciding that Alice is Maggie's baby, not Linda's, but genetic production of the sperm is irrelevant in deciding who is Alice's father. Linda herself, famous for her love of dogs, speaks of her newborn Heather's beautiful paws. Anyone can be your baby; your baby can be anything.

But the obliteration of difference cannot remain an idea; it will shade into the bodily reality of the self. The bathing scene, where all the sisters giggle and tweak one another's nipples, provides a sort of metaphor for the pleasures of merging. It all remains nonsexual—or at least pregenital. The hardened IVF specialist feels faint when told that Linda's obstetrician played the bagpipes at her thirtieth birthday, as if he feels that unethical professional intimacy can go no further. Maggie's body boundaries are not usually described as individual ego boundaries: they include her family. Maggie's doctor father warns her to protect her ovaries when she has her hysterectomy; Linda massages her nipples to encourage lactation. Maggie feels they literally keep her body together: "I have a sense of my family as a firm shell which prevents bits of me from being flung off the surface of my spinning life" (196), she declares. This describes a centripetal self, where the individual is not a cohesive unit and only an undifferentiated family group has strong enough boundaries to contain the individual's tendency to fragmentation. Altruistic sister surrogacy, with an intimate bodily involvement of parents, siblings, cousins, and friends, and indeed the cooption of the state, is the perfect project for such needs. Baby Alice is truly a family project.

The Australian philosopher and ethicist Max Charlesworth has praised the Kirkman sisters' initiative and enterprise as revealed in *My Sister's Child*. As literary critics we are not concerned to offer judgments as to the ethical rightness, the wisdom or unwisdom, of this arrangement. What we have been arguing, however, is that the narrative Maggie and Linda Kirkman jointly construct and publish tells more than they themselves can control, and undermines, or deconstructs, the very values that its protagonists use to give moral cogency and social legitimacy to their enterprise. We contend that this text, largely because it is so full and candid, calls into question the ideology of individuals making free self-creating choices that its protagonists consciously proclaim, and which is the rationale used to justify and underpin the promotion and proliferation of surrogacy. The account of the surrogacy shows that the interpersonal and personal-technological world of reproductive surrogacy has, as well as many pains and nuisances, a hugely pleasurable and rewarding side for the principals: it meshes with their needs and desires at a profoundly satisfying level. As the account of Linda's blood being taken by her father and left in the "Grandpa" mug seems to suggest, the surrogacy scenario offers extraordinary opportunities for safe and consensual quasi-incestuous intimacy and control: a technological and pre- or extragenital sublimation of sorts for transgressive Oedipal desires.

It seems likely that all surrogacy requires an acceptance of an undifferentiated world, where no Oedipal markers can be tolerated: in ways that recall de Sade's sequential and mechanical rupturing of prohibitions, the baby must be unparented or multiparented, the doctor must act in isolation from societal pressure, the parent must not be more potent than the child, the state must not be more potent than the parent. The case of the Kirkman family certainly shows these features,[6] and it may well represent the best possible "tapping" of the perverse core, where pleasure is had for regressive reasons, but exploitation of involved others is kept to a limit by a careful consideration of the rational complications. Reproductive technology and surrogacy arrangements use the hyperrational world of high technology to serve desire, conscious and unconscious and including polymorphous and perverse desire. Superimposing—if such a thing can be imagined—a poststructural analysis onto Millian ethics "might better able us to contest for meanings, as well as other forms of power and pleasure in technologically mediated societies" (Haraway 1991, 154). The altruistic nonexploitative contract of the Kirkman family does not settle all the objections about surrogacy, because the problems are not all to do with contract law and the exploitation of labor. It seems to us that central questions for further consideration of surrogacy issues will include such matters as how the intersubjective world of surrogacy is fitted into the desires and pleasures of the principals (including the child-to-be) and what the effects of this might be. These questions arise from the shift of perspective that encompasses the perverse—a perverse shift of perspective—and allows the critic to discern the limits as well as the benefits of the rational. Any discussion of reproductive surrogacy must account for its interpersonal, intersubjective, and unconscious rewards and consequences, as well as the material burdens and benefits.

Notes

1. In this essay we offer a reading of this text, and only this text: nothing we say should be taken as commentary on the personal attitudes or lives of the writers.
2. The trial of sterilizing the capillary tubing of the Lact-Aid for the frequent feeds of a newborn, plus the technical difficulties of getting a sterile source of donated human milk, storing it, thawing it, and so on, must be added to the inevitably drawn-out nursing sessions. It might be argued that, logistically speaking, feeding a baby with a Lact-Aid combines all the disadvantages of preparing safe bottle feeding with the sometimes wearisome need for the mother's permanent presence necessitated by nursing: neither ease nor freedom! In this sense, it could well be concluded that feeding via Lact-Aid is the most striking proof of maternal devotion.
3. In two states and many locations, more than seventy people died, several thousand houses were destroyed, and tens of thousands of livestock were killed. Extensive areas of national forest were devastated by firestorm and took more than a decade to recover.
4. The subjectivity instantiated by the Kirkmans has its roots in developments far earlier than Mill, of course. "The individual was seen neither as a moral whole, nor as part of a larger social whole, but as an owner of himself. The relation of ownership, having become for more and more men the critically important relation determining their actual freedom and actual prospect of realizing their full potentialities was read back into the nature of the individual. The individual, it was thought, is free in as much as he is the proprietor of his person and capacities" (MacPherson 1962, 3). The body in *My Sister's Child* is not continuous with, or a vessel of, the self but thought of as an object: its contents and products are exchangeable and salable. Linda also urges the need for women to have control over the birthing process. But, as we would argue, the notion of control is problematic. The idea of "control" in childbirth is not straightforward.
5. Joyce McDougall, public seminar, Melbourne, 1993.
6. Both in *My Sister's Child* and in subsequent interviews, the family asserts that the "normal" order of things can be changed to accommodate better the heart's desire: in an interview with a woman's magazine, Linda remarks, "My children . . . wanted a sibling, but I didn't really want any more children . . . so I thought, if I can't do a sibling, I'll do a cousin. It was a bit selfish—I wanted them to have a cousin." *Australian Woman's Day* (March 1993): 38.

On Morphological Imagination

VIVIAN SOBCHACK

*I once heard a man say to his gray-haired wife, without
rancor: "I only feel old when I look at you."*

—ANN GERIKE, "On Gray Hair
and Oppressed Brains"

*I'm prepared to die, but not to look lousy for the next forty
years.*

—ELISSA MELAMED, Mirror, Mirror: The Terror
of Not Being Young

It's science now. It's no longer voodoo.

—An advertisement for medical equipment in
a trade journal for cosmetic surgeons

W<small>HAT</small> FOLLOWS is less an argument than a meditation on the dread of middle-aging as a woman in our culture, rejuvenation fantasies in the American cinema, and the wish-fulfilling "magic" and "quick fixes" of technologies of transformation and display.[1] These technologies and the fantasies they engender and "realize" are themselves reproductive. That is, they reproduce both the appearance of female youthfulness that, in our dominant culture, signals sexuality and the biological capacity to reproduce, and those very cultural values that demonize the middle-aged and postmenopausal woman. Thus, as might be expected of a woman of fifty-eight with the privilege of self-reflection, I am struggling with the cultural determinations of my own middle age. Indeed, I despair of ever being able to reconcile my overall sense of well-being, self-confidence, achievement, and pleasure in the richness of my present with the problematic and often distressing image I see in my mirror. Over the past several years, I have become aware not only of my mother's face frequently staring back at me from my own but also of an increasing inability to see myself with any objectivity at all (as if, of course, I ever could). Within less than a single minute, I often go from utter dislocation and despair as I gaze at a face that seems too old for me, a face that I "have," to a certain satisfying recognition and pleasure at a face that looks "pretty good for my age," a face that "I am." I live now in heightened awareness of the instability of my image of myself, and I think about cosmetic surgery a lot: getting my eyes done, removing the furrows in my forehead, smoothing out the lines around my mouth, and lifting the skin around my jaw. But I know I will be disappointed. And so, while I don't avoid mirrors, I also don't seek them out. Rather, I try very hard to locate myself less in my image than in my (how else to say it?) "comportment."

It is for this reason that I was particularly moved when I first read in *Entertainment Weekly* that Barbra Streisand (only a year younger than I am) was remaking and updating *The Mirror Has Two Faces*, a 1959 French film about a housewife who begins a new life after plastic surgery. Barbra's update was to tell the story of "an ugly duckling professor and her quest for inner and outer beauty."[2] Obviously, this struck a major chord. Discussing the film's progress and performing its own surgery on the middle-aged producer, director, and star, *Entertainment Weekly* reported that the "biggest challenge faced by the 54-year-old" and "hyper-picky" Barbra

> was how to present her character. In the original, the mousy housefrau undergoes her transformation via plastic surgery. But Streisand rejected that idea—perhaps because of the negative message—and went with attitude adjustment instead. Which might work for the character, but does it work for the star? "Certain wrinkles and gravitational forces seem to be causing Streisand concern," says one ex-crew member. "She doesn't want to look her age. She's fighting it."[3]

Before I actually saw the film (eventually released in 1996), I wondered just what, as a substitute for surgery, Barbra's "attitude adjustment" might mean. And how would it translate to the superficiality of an image—in the mirror, in the movies? Might it mean really good makeup for the middle-aged star? Soft focus? Other forms of special effects that reproduce the work of cosmetic surgery?[4] And just how far can these take you—how long before really good makeup transforms you into a grotesque, before soft focus blurs you into invisibility, before special effects transform you into a vampire, witch, or monster? Perhaps this *is* the cinematic equivalent of attitude adjustment. The alternative to cosmetic surgery in what passes for the verisimilitude of cinematic realism is a change in genre, a transformation of sensibility that takes us from the "real" world that demonizes middle-aged women to the world of female demons: horror, science fiction, and fantasy.

Indeed, a few years ago, I published an essay on several low-budget science fiction/horror films made in the late 1950s and early 1960s that focused on middle-aged female characters.[5] I was interested in these critically neglected films because, working through genres deemed fantastic, they were able to displace and disguise cultural anxieties about women and aging while simultaneously figuring them "in your face," so to speak. For example, in *Attack of the 50–Ft. Woman* (1958), through a brief (and laughable) encounter with a giant space alien, wealthy, childless, middle-aged, and brunette Nancy achieves a literal size, power, and youthful blondness her philandering husband can no longer ignore as she roams the countryside looking for him wearing a bra and sarong made out of her bed linens. In *The Wasp Woman* (1959), the fortyish head of a similarly fading cosmetics empire can no longer serve as the model for her products and overdoses on royal "wasp jelly," which not only reduces but also reverses the aging process, although its side effects regularly turn the again youthful cosmetics queen into a murderous insect queen (in high heels and a sheath dress). And, in *The Leech Woman* (1960), blowsy, alcoholic June becomes her feckless endocrinologist husband's guinea pig and, taking a rejuvenation serum made from African orchid pollen mixed with male pituitary fluid (extraction of which kills the men, one of them her husband), ultimately experiences, if only for a while, the simultaneous pleasures of youth, beauty, and revenge. In these low-budget films, scared middle-aged women are transformed—not through cosmetic surgery but through fantastical means, makeup, and special effects—into rejuvenated but scary women. Introduced as fading females still informed by—but an affront to—sexual desire and biological reproduction, hovering on the brink of grotesquery and alcoholism, their flesh explicitly disgusting to the men in their lives, these women are figured as more horrible in, and more horrified by, their own middle-aged bodies than in or by the bodies of the "unnatural" monsters they become. Indeed, these films dramatize what one psychotherapist has described as the culture's "almost visceral disgust for the older woman as a physical being" and underscore "ageism" as "the last bastion of sexism."[6]

Transformed, become suddenly young, beautiful, desirable, powerful, horrendous, monstrous, and deadly, these women play out grand, if wacky, dramas of poetic justice. No plastic surgery here. Instead, through the technological "magic" of cinema, the irrational "magic" of fantasy, and a few cheesy low-budget effects, what we get is major "attitude adjustment"—of a scope that might even satisfy Barbra. The leech woman, wasp woman, and fifty-foot woman literalize, magnify, and enact hyperbolic displays of anger and desire, their youth and beauty reproduced now as lethal and fatal, their "unnatural" ascendance to power allowing them to avenge on a grand scale the wrongs done them for merely getting older. Yet, not surprisingly, these films also maintain the cultural status quo—even as they critique it. For what they figure as most grotesque and disgusting is not the monstrousness of the transformation but the "unnatural" conjunction of middle-aged female flesh and still youthful female desire. And—take heed, Barbra—the actresses who play these pathetic and horrific middle-aged women are always young and beautiful under their latex jowls and aging makeup. Thus, what these fantasies of female rejuvenation give with one hand they take back with the other. They represent less a grand masquerade of feminist resistance than a retrograde striptease that undermines the double-edged and very temporary narrative power these transformed middle-aged protagonists supposedly enjoy—that is, "getting their own back" before they eventually "get theirs." And, as is the "natural" order of things in both patriarchal culture and genre films of this sort, they do "get theirs"—each narrative ending with the restoration and reproduction of social (and ageist) order through the death of its eponymous heroine-monster. Attitude adjustment, indeed!

These low-budget films observe that middle-aged women—as much before as after their transformations and "attitude adjustments"—are pretty scary. In *Attack of the 50–Ft. Woman*, for example, as Nancy lies in her bedroom after her alien encounter but before she looms large on the horizon, her doctor explains her "wild" story away thus: "When women reach the age of maturity, Mother Nature sometimes overworks their frustration to a point of irrationalism." The screenwriter must have read Freud, who, writing on obsessional neurosis in 1913, tells us: "It is well known, and has been a matter for much complaint, that women often alter strangely in character after they have abandoned their genital functions. They become quarrelsome, peevish, and argumentative, petty and miserly; in fact, they display sadistic and anal-erotic traits which were not theirs in the era of womanliness."[7] Which brings us back to Barbra, whom it turns out we never really left at all. In language akin to Freud's, the article on the production woes of Barbra's film in *Entertainment Weekly* performs its own form of ageist analysis. The "steep attrition rate" among cast and crew and the protracted shooting schedule are attributed to both her "hyper-picky" "perfectionism" and to her being a "meddler."[8] We are also told: "Among the things she fretted over: the density of her panty hose, the bras she wore, and whether the trees would have falling leaves."[9] A leech woman, wasp woman, fifty-foot woman—in Freud's terms, an obsessional neurotic: peevish, argumentative, petty, sadistic, and anal-erotic. Poor Barbra, she can't win for losing. Marauding the countryside in designer clothes and an "adjusted" attitude doesn't get her far from the fear or contempt that attaches to middle-aged women in our culture. Perhaps she—perhaps I—should reconsider cosmetic surgery.

Around ten years younger than Barbra and me, my best friend recently did—although I didn't see the results until long after her operation. Admittedly, I was afraid to: afraid she'd look bad (that is, not like herself or like she had surgery), afraid she'd look good (that is, good enough to make me want to do it). Separated by physical distance, however, I didn't have to confront—and judge—her image, and so all I initially knew about her extensive face-lift was from e-mail correspondence. (I have permission to use her words but not her name.) Here, "in my face," so to speak, as well as hers were extraordinary convergences of actuality and wish, of surgery and cinema, of transformative technologies and the "magic" of "special effects"—all rendered intimately intelligible to us (whether we approve or not) in terms of mortal time and female gender. She wrote: "IT WORKED!" And then continues:

> My eyes look larger than Audrey Hepburn's in her prime. . . . I am the proud owner of a 15–year old neckline. Amazing—exactly the effect I'd hoped for. Still swollen . . . but that was all predicted. What this tendon-tightening lift did (not by any means purely "skin deep"—he actually . . . redraped the major neck and jaw infrastructure) was reverse the effects of gravity. Under the eyes—utterly smooth, many crow's feet eradicated. The jawline—every suspicion of jowl has been erased. Smooth and tight. I look good. The neck—the Candice Bergen turkey neck is gone. The tendons that produce that stringy effect have been severed—for ever! OK—what price (besides the $7000) did I pay? Four hours on the operating table. One night of hell due to . . . a compression bandage that made me feel as if I were being choked. Mercifully (and thanks to Valium) I got through it. . . . Extremely tight from ear to ear—jaw with little range of motion— "ate" liquids, jello, soup, scrambled eggs for the first week. My sutures extend around 80% of my head. *Bride of Frankenstein* city. All (except for the exquisitely fine line under my eyes) are hidden in my hair. But baby I know they're there. Strange reverse phantom limb sensation. I still have my ears, but I can't exactly feel them. I . . . took Valium each evening the first week to counteract the tendency toward panic as I tried to fall asleep and realized that I could only move 1/4 inch in any direction. Very minimal bruising—I'm told that's not the rule. . . . I still have a very faint chartreuse glow under one eye. With make-up, voila! I can't jut my chin out—can barely make my upper and lower teeth meet at the front. In a few months, that will relax. And I can live with it. My hair, cut, shaved and even removed (along with sections of my scalp), has lost all semblance of style. But that too is

transitory. The work that was done will last a good seven years. I plan
to have my upper eyes done in about three years. This message is for
your eyes only. I intend, if pressed, to reveal that I have had my eyes
done. Period. Nothing more.

But there's plenty more. And it foregrounds the confusion and conflation
of surgery and cinema, technology and "magic," of effort and ease, that so per-
vades our current image culture. Indeed, there is a bitter irony at work here
that perversely reminds me of listening to several computer-effects guys from
Industrial Light and Magic point to their incredible and "seamless" work and
bemoan the fact that no one can "see" all the time and labor they put into
creating it. Having achieved a "seamless" face, my best friend has lost her voice.
She cannot speak of the time and labor it took to transform her. The whole
point is that, for the "magic" to work, the "seams"—both the lines traced by
age and the scars traced by surgery—must not show. Thus, as Kathleen Woodward notes in "Youthfulness as a Masquerade": "Unlike the hysterical body,
whose surface is inscribed with symptoms, the objective of the surgically youthful body is to speak nothing."[10] But this is not the only irony at work here.
At a more structural level, this very lack of disclosure, this silence and secrecy, is an *essential* element of a culture increasingly driven—by both desire
and technology—to extreme extroversion, to utter disclosure. It is here that
cosmetic surgery and the "special effects" of the cinema converge and are
perceived as phenomenologically reversible in what has become our current morphological imagination. Based in the belief that desire—through technology—
can be materialized, made visible, and thus "realized," such morphological
imagination does a perverse, and precisely superficial, turn on Woodward's distinction between the hysterical body and the surgically youthful body. That
is, symptoms and silence are conflated as *the image of one's transformation* and
one's transformation of the image become reversible phenomena. These confu-
sions and conflations are dramatized most literally in the genre of fantasy,
where "plastic surgery" is now practiced through the seemingly effortless, seamless transformations of digital morphing.

In this regard, two relatively recent films come to mind, *Death Becomes
Her* (1992) and *The Mask* (1994). Technologically dependent on digital
morphing, both make visible incredible alterations of an unprecedentedly plastic human body and also render human affective states literally superficial.
The Mask, about the transformation and rejuvenation of the male psyche and
spirit, significantly plays its drama out only on—and as—the surface of the
body. When wimpy Stanley Ipkiss is "magically" transformed by the mask,
there is no masquerade, no silence, since every desire, every psychic metaphor is materialized and made visible. His tongue unrolls across the table

toward the object of his desire. He literally "wears his heart on his sleeve" (or thereabouts). His destructive desires are extruded from his hands as smoking guns. How, then, can one talk about the Mask's body in terms of hysterical symptoms when everything "hangs out" as extroverted id and nothing is repressed?

Death Becomes Her functions in a similar manner, although here, with women as the central figures, the narrative explicitly foregrounds a literal rejuvenation as its central thematic—youth and beauty the objects of female desire. Indeed, what's most interesting (although not necessarily funny) about *Death Becomes Her* is that plastic surgery operates in the film twice over. At the narrative level, its wimpy hero, Ernest Menville, is a famous plastic surgeon—seduced away from his fiancée, Helen, by middle-aging actress Madeline Ashton, whom we first see starring in a musical flop based on *Sweet Bird of Youth*. Thanks to Ernest's surgical skill (which we never actually see on the screen, a point I'll come back to), Madeline finds a whole new career as a movie star while Helen plots elaborate revenge. Seven years into the marriage, however, hen-pecked, alcoholic Ernest is no longer much use to Madeline. Told by her beautician that he—and cosmetic surgery—can no longer help her, the desperate woman seeks out a mysterious and incredibly beautiful "Beverly Hills cult priestess" who gives her a youth serum that grants eternal life, whatever the condition of the user's body. It is at this point that the operation of plastic surgery extends from the narrative to the representational level: the "magic" transformations of special computer-graphic and cosmetic effects instantaneously nip and tuck Madeline's buttocks, smooth and lift her face and breasts with nary a twinge of discomfort, a trace of blood, or a trice of effort, and reproduce her as "young." (What is said of the youth serum might also be said of the cinematic effects: "A touch of magic in this world obsessed by science.") This literalization of desire and anxiety is carried further still. That is, inevitably, the repressed signs of age return and are also reproduced and literalized along with signs of youth and beauty. When rejuvenated Madeline breaks her neck after being pushed down a flight of stairs, she lives on (though medically dead) with visible and hyperbolic variations of my friend's despised "Candice Bergen turkey neck." And, after Madeline shoots Helen (who has also taken the serum), Helen walks around with a hole in her stomach—a "blasted woman," however youthful. Ultimately, the film unites the women in their increasingly unsuccessful attempts to maintain and reproduce their peeling and literally "dead skin," to keep from "letting themselves go," from "falling apart"—which, at the film's end, they quite literally do.

In both *The Mask* and *Death Becomes Her*, cinematic effects and plastic surgery become reversible reproductive operations—literalizing desire and promising instant and effortless transformation. Human bodily existence is foregrounded as a material surface amenable to endless manipulation and total visibility. However, there is yet a great silence, a great *invisibility*, grounding these narratives of surface and extroversion. The labor, effort, and time entailed by the real operations of "plastic surgery" (both cinematic and cosmetic) are ultimately disavowed. Instead, we are given a "screen image" (both psychoanalytic and literal) that attributes the laborious, costly, and technologically based reality that underlies bodily transformation to the nontechnological properties of, in the one instance, a "primitive" fetish and, in the other, a "magic" potion. Of course, like all cases of disavowal, these fantasies turn round themselves like a Moebius strip to ultimately break the silence and reveal the repressed on the "same" side as the "screen image."

That is, on the "screen side," the technological effects of these transformation fantasies are what we want "in our face," so to speak. But we want these effects without wanting to see the technology, without wanting to acknowledge the cost, labor, time, and effort of its operations—all of which might curb our desire and despoil our wonder. Indeed, like my friend who wants the effects of her face-lift to be seen but wants the facts of her operation to remain hidden, our pleasure comes precisely from this "appearance" of seamless, effortless, "magical" transformation. On the other repressed side (one that becomes the "same" side, however), we are fascinated by "the operation"—its very cost, difficulty, effortfulness. There are now magazines and videos devoted to making visible the specific operations of cinematic effects, their tell-all revelations made auratic through a minute accounting of the technology involved, hours spent, effort spent, dollars spent. My friend, too, despite her desire for secrecy, is fascinated by her operation and the visibility of her investment. Her numeracy extends from money to stitches but is most poignant in its temporal lived dimensions: four hours on the operating table, one night of hell, a week of limited jaw motion, time for her hair to grow back, a few months for her upper and lower jaws to "relax," three years before she will do her eyelids, seven years before the surgeon's work is undone again by time and gravity. The "magic" of plastic surgery (both cinematic and cosmetic)—at least when it's not screened—costs always an irrecoverable portion of a mortal life.

And a mortal life must *live through* its operations, not magically, instantaneously, but *in time*. It is thus apposite and poignant that "offscreen" Isabella Rossellini, who plays and is fixed forever as the eternal high priestess of youth and beauty in both *Death Becomes Her* and old Lancôme ads, has joined the ranks of the on-screen "wasp woman," Janet Starlin: after fourteen years as the "face" of Lancôme cosmetics, she was fired at age forty-two for getting "too old." Unlike the wasp woman, however, Rossellini can neither completely reverse the aging process nor murder those who find her middle-aged flesh disgusting. Thus, it is also apposite and poignant that attempts to reproduce the fantasies of the morphological imagination in the real world are doomed to failure: medical cosmetic surgery never quite matches up to the seemingly effortless and perfect plastic surgeries of cinema and computer. This disappointment with the "real thing" becomes explicit in my friend's continuing e-mails:

> Vivian, I'm going through an unsettling part of this surgical journey. . . . When I first got home, the effect was quite dramatic—I literally looked 20 years younger. Now what's happened: the swelling continues to go down. The outlines of the "new face" (in quotes) are still dramatically lifted. . . . BUT, the lines I've acquired through a lifetime of smiling, talking, being a highly expressive individual, are returning. Not all of them . . . but enough that the effect of the procedure is now quite natural . . . and I no longer look 20 years younger. Maybe 10 max. . . . I'm experiencing a queasy depression. Imagining that the procedure didn't work. That in a few weeks I'll look like I did before the money and the lengthy discomfort. Now I scrutinize, I imagine, I am learning to hate the whole thing. Most of all, the heady sense of exhilaration and confidence is gone. In short, I have no idea any longer how the hell I look.

Which brings me back to myself before the mirror—and again to Barbra, both behind and in front of the camera. There is no way here for any of us to feel superior in sensibility to my friend. Whether we like it or not, we have all had "our eyes done." With or without medical surgery, we have been technologically altered, both "seeing" differently and "seeming" different than we did in a time before either cinema or cosmetic surgery presented us with their reversible technological promises of immortality and figurations of "magical" self-transformation—that is, transformation without time, without effort, without cost. To a great extent, then, the bodily transformations of cinema and surgery inform each other. Cinema *is* cosmetic surgery—its fantasies, its "makeup," and its digital effects able to "fix" (in the doubled sense of repair and stasis) and to fetishize and to reproduce faces and time as both "unreel" before us. And, reversibly, cosmetic surgery *is* cinema, creating us as an image we not only learn to enact in a repetition compulsion but also must—and never can—live up to. Through their technological "operations"—the work and cost effectively hidden by the surface "magic" of their transitory effects, the cultural values of youth and beauty effectively reproduced and fixed—we have become subjectively "derealized" and out of sequence with ourselves as, paradoxically, these same operations have allowed us to objectively reproduce and realize our flesh "in our own image."

Over e-mail, increments of my friend's ambiguous recovery from fantasies of transformation and rejuvenation seemed to be in direct proportion to the diminishing number of years young she felt she looked: "Vivian, I've calmed down, assessed the pluses and minuses and decided to just fucking go on with it. Life, that is. They call it a 'lift' for a reason. . . . The face doesn't look younger (oh, I guess I've shaved 5 to 8 years off), but it looks better. OK. Fine. Now it's time to move on." But later fantasy reemerges—for the time being, at least, with real and sanguine consequences: "Vivian, the response has been terrific—everybody is dazzled, but they can't quite tell why. It must be the color I'm wearing, they say, or my hair, or that I am rested. At any rate, I feel empowered again."

In sum, I don't know how to end this—nor could I imagine at the time of my friend's rejuvenation how, sans cosmetic surgery, Barbra would end her version of *The Mirror Has Two Faces*. Thus, not only for herself but also for the wasp woman, for my friend, for Isabella Rossellini, and for me, I hoped that Barbra—both on-screen and off—would survive her own cinematic reproduction. Unfortunately, she did not. "Attitude adjustment" was overwhelmed by "image adjustment" in her finished film: to wit, a diet, furious exercise, good makeup, a new hairdo, and a Donna Karan little black dress. Despite all her dialogue, Barbra had nothing to say; instead, like my friend, she silenced and repressed her own middle-aging—first, reducing it to a generalized discourse on inner and outer beauty, and then, displacing and replacing it on the face and in the voice of her bitter, jealous, "once beautiful," and "much older" mother (played by the still spectacular Lauren Bacall). Barbra's attitude, then, hadn't adjusted at all.

I finally did see my rejuvenated friend in the flesh. She looked pretty much the same to me. And, at the Academy Awards (for which the song in her film received the only nomination), Barbra was still being characterized by the press as "peevish" and "petty." I, in the meantime, have vowed to be kinder to my mirror image. In the glass (or on the screen), it is, after all, thin and chimerical, while I, on my side of it, am grounded in the thickness and productivity of a life, in the substance—not the reproduced surface—of endless transformation. Thus, each time I start to fixate on a new line or wrinkle, on a graying hair in the mirror, each time I envy a youthful face on the screen, I try very hard to remember that, on my side of the image, I am not so much aging as always becoming.

Notes

1. I am most grateful to the UCLA Center for the Study of Women for their research support. This essay is abridged from my "Scary Women: Cinema, Surgery, and Special Effects," in *Figuring Age: Women, Bodies, Generations*, ed. Kathleen Woodward (Bloomington: Indiana University Press, 1998).

2. Jeffrey Wells, "Mirror, Mirror," *Entertainment Weekly*, 12 April 1996, 8.
3. Ibid., 9.
4. It is relevant that developments in television technology have produced a "skin contouring" camera that makes wrinkles disappear. Using puns about "vanity video" and "video collagen," J. Max Robins, in "A New Wrinkle in Video Technology," *TV Guide* (Los Angeles Metropolitan Edition), 28 September–4 October 1996, tells of this "indispensable tool for TV personalities of a certain age" first used "as a news division innovation" (among its beneficiaries: Dan Rather, Peter Jennings, Tom Brokaw, and Barbara Walters). According to one news director, "it can remove almost all of someone's wrinkles, without affecting their hair or eyes." "The magic," however, "only lasts as long as the stars remain in front of the camera" (57).
5. Vivian Sobchack, "Revenge of *The Leech Woman*: On the Dread of Aging in a Low-Budget Horror Film," in *Uncontrollable Bodies: Testimonies of Identity and Culture*, ed. Rodney Sappington and Tyler Stallings (Seattle, Wash.: Bay Press, 1994), 79–91.
6. Elissa Melamed, *Mirror, Mirror: The Terror of Not Being Young* (New York: Linden Press, 1983), 30.
7. Sigmund Freud, "The Predisposition to Obsessional Neurosis," in *Collected Papers*, ed. Ernest Jones, trans. Joan Riviere (London: Hogarth and the Institute of Psycho-Analysis, 1959), 2:130.
8. Wells, "Mirror, Mirror," 8.
9. Ibid., 9.
10. Kathleen Woodward, "Youthfulness as a Masquerade," *Discourse* 11, no. 1 (Fall–Winter 1988–1989): 133–134.

Christine Jorgensen's Atom Bomb

SUSAN STRYKER

Transsexuality and the Emergence of Postmodernity

*A story which culture tells itself, the transsexual body is a
tactile politics of reproduction constituted through textual
violence.*

—SANDY STONE, "The Empire Strikes Back"

Another Manhattan Project

One afternoon in the closing months of 1949, the person who was becoming
Christine Jorgensen stepped up to the counter of a drugstore in New York City.[1]
At that moment she still answered to the name "George" and, by most standards, was a painfully insecure young man with a rather unsettled sense of individual identity. Jorgensen was twenty-three years old at the time, an aspiring
filmmaker born to Danish American parents and raised in unremarkable
middle-class circumstances in the Bronx. She was a draftee recently discharged
from the U.S. Army who had served her entire fourteen-month enlistment at
Fort Dix, New Jersey, processing demobilization paperwork for the combat
troops streaming home after the bombs had been dropped on Hiroshima and
Nagasaki and World War II had finally come to an end. Jorgensen was not
yet the woman who would make "transsexual" a household word, though she
was now taking the first practical step in the long process of becoming precisely that person.

During a directionless phase of life in 1948, after attending various photography schools, holding an unglamorous job in the cutting room of the RKO
motion picture studio in New York duplicating and cataloging stock film images, and failing miserably to make a break for herself in Hollywood, Jorgensen
happened upon a copy of popular medical writer Paul de Kruif's recent book,

The Male Hormone. It changed her life. Jorgensen read with fascination about
the structural similarities of testosterone and estrogen, the biochemicals whose
effects on moods and bodily morphology we have learned to interpret as signs
of the masculine and the feminine. A difference of only "four atoms of hydrogen and one atom of carbon" in each hormone, she learned, was all that
distinguished one substance from the other (71).

It seemed to Jorgensen that if indeed hormones determined one's status
as a man or woman, then an exceedingly fine border, a boundary measured
on a submolecular scale, was potentially all that separated the sexes. She rea-
soned that "there must be times when one could be so close to that physical
dividing line that it would be difficult to determine on which side of the male-
female line" one belonged (76). Perhaps, she thought, this newly discovered
scientific fact explained her effeminate mannerisms, her delicate facial features, her emotional attraction to men and her feeling that, whatever her genitals might seem to suggest, she was not really a man at all. Wasn't there woven
throughout de Kruif's narrative a tiny thread of recognition pulled from her
own private theories—that she might in fact be a woman in some real yet ill-
defined and largely unattained sense?

She abruptly enrolled in the Manhattan Medical and Dental Assistants
School, determined to learn more about endocrinology. She had already read
in the newspaper that virilization experiments using testosterone were being
carried out on chickens in New Haven, Connecticut. She knew from reading
de Kruif that there was "an uncanny ability in one of the pure female hormones to alter the lives and fate of man" (71). Now she began spending hours
in the library of the New York Academy of Medicine reading the technical
literature of fields she barely understood, and she came across references to
surgical "conversion experiments" being carried out in Europe—procedures
entirely unavailable in the United States. She sensed possibilities for herself
in this newly acquired and rapidly expanding body of knowledge. For nearly
a year Jorgensen had been cautiously approaching medical specialists, screwing up her courage to ask if they might help her explore the possibility of hormonal feminization, but all she yet had to show for her efforts was a psychiatric
referral. Still, she insisted to herself, to the question of her personal identity,
"There was an answer—somewhere" (76).

Through her reading, Jorgensen began to form a vague yet compelling
idea: "I would experiment on myself. But in order to do that, somehow I'd
have to get hold of that miraculous substance known as 'estradiol,'" a recently
synthesized version of estrogen (76). If Jorgensen found the "answer" she
sought in a chemical, she found her "somewhere" in a drugstore chosen more
or less at random where she could anonymously purchase the drug. She had
no idea clear what estradiol would do to her if she ingested it, but she was

compelled to find out. On that portentous afternoon in New York in 1949, Jorgensen drove around in her car until she found a pharmacy in an unfamiliar neighborhood of the city. According to her own account of the incident, she approached the unsuspecting pharmacy clerk and "adopted a tone of voice designed to convey my familiarity with things medical." She first ordered several unremarkable items—tongue depressors, perhaps, or an antiseptic solution and some cotton gauze—before asking nonchalantly for "high-potency estradiol."

> "That's a pretty strong chemical," the clerk replied. "We're not supposed to sell it without a prescription."
> "Well, I guess I could have gotten a prescription, but just didn't think of it. You see, I'm at a medical technicians' school, and we're working on an idea of growth stimulation in animals through the use of hormones."
> The clerk hesitated. "Oh, well, in that case I guess it's okay." (77)

Moments later Jorgensen was sitting in her car again, somewhat stunned by the ease with which she had accomplished a feat with such vast implications for her future. She unwrapped the package eagerly. "There at last, the small bottle lay in my hand. How strange it seemed to me that the whole answer might lie in the particular combination of atoms contained in those tiny, aspirin-like tablets. As recently as a few years before, science had split some of those atoms and unleashed a giant force. There in my hand lay another series of atoms, which in their way might set off another explosion" (77).

Jorgensen raced home. That night, and every night thereafter for the next several months, she took one of her little pills. Within a week she began to notice "a strange though not unpleasant feeling," a "sensitivity in my breast area and a noticeable development" (78). These changes quickly inspired her to form an even bolder plan—to go to Europe to find doctors who could administer the hormones more effectively to produce even more noticeable effects and who could perform the genital conversion surgeries that would allow her to "find [her] proper place in the world" (79). Jorgensen wrote in her autobiography years later, "No doubt these were radical thoughts, based only on my own desire and emotions, half-formulated ideas from scraps of medical information, but from then on, I was even more determined to follow the dream" (79). Using her last shred of savings, she purchased a one-way ticket and set sail in May 1950 for her ancestral Denmark, where she found the medical help for which she long had searched.

Jorgensen had little idea how big the "other explosion" she imagined outside the drugstore in 1949 would be until three years later, when, as she lay convalescing in a Copenhagen hospital, she learned that news of her recent "sex-change" surgery had been trumpeted to the four corners of the earth. Somewhat surprisingly given that the medical procedures involved were by then more than two decades old, Jorgensen was deluged with an unprecedented outpouring of media attention. She was promised tens of thousands of dollars for exclusive newspaper and magazine interviews, offered lucrative nightclub engagements, received thousands of letters and telegrams, and made banner headlines around the world. "It seems to me now a shocking commentary on the press of our time," Jorgensen recalled in her memoirs, "that I pushed the hydrogen-bomb tests on Eniwetok right off the front pages. A tragic war was still raging in Korea, George VI had died and Britain had a new queen, sophisticated guided missiles were going off in New Mexico, Jonas Salk was working on a vaccine for infantile paralysis—Christine Jorgensen was on page one" (130).

Through Jorgensen, the spectacle of transsexuality mushroomed into public consciousness during the early days of the Cold War with all the force of a blistering hot wind roaring across the Trinity Test Site. Transsexuality was nothing short of an atomic blast to the gender system, and a former boy from the Bronx found herself at ground zero. It's difficult now at the turn of the century, as transsexuality and other transgender phenomena become increasingly ubiquitous in media and culture, to appreciate the impact Jorgensen's story made in the early 1950s. Her return to the United States in 1953 garnered the kind of coverage usually reserved for movie stars and heads of state. Members of the medical profession debated the question of Jorgensen's "true sex" in highly public forums; the paparazzi dogged her heels, and the tabloid press hung upon her every utterance. The initial media frenzy that greeted her story subsided after a few months, but after achieving celebrity status Jorgensen was never able to resume an entirely private life. She eventually gave in to the inevitable and pursued a successful career in show business. She remained a cultural reference point for decades—constantly sought out for commentary on matters related to gender and sexuality from the 1950s through the 1980s.

What interests me most about Jorgensen, though, is not her remarkable career, which in any event is being researched by others with a great deal more scholarly attention to detail than I will attempt here.[2] Rather, I am more intrigued with the striking imagery of atomic bombs she repeatedly offers in metaphorical connection with transsexual medical technologies. She was not alone in making such an association. The weekly magazine *People Today* reported on May 5, 1954, after other transsexual stories had broken in the media, "Next to the recurrent hydrogen bomb headlines, reports of sex changes are becoming the most consistently startling world news."[3] The movie version of Gore Vidal's transsexual farce *Myra Breckenridge* later referenced this theme as well; Myra's opening monologue is spoken in voice-over narration as an image of a hydrogen bomb explosion in the Pacific fills the screen (Sarne 1970).

Because the bomb functioned as a master symbol for post–World War II American anxieties about the exigencies of existence in relation to scientific technology, it is hardly surprising that Jorgensen turned to it in her attempt to bring into language her own transformative experience with a new technology.[4] Nor is it surprising that a transsexual body, by corporealizing the transformation of human existence through scientific technology, should evoke on a mass scale some of the same ambivalent hopes and fears inspired by the bomb. I want to point out these associations by rhetorically conflating transsexual and atomic technologies just as Jorgensen did in her autobiography to construct a fanciful yet serious literary device: Christine Jorgensen's Atom Bomb, a figure intended to suggest that in the spectacular advent of Jorgensen's public womanhood we can discern a moment of rupture in the fabric of Western culture, a new event in our material circumstances, a point of ecstatic passage into the hyperreality of postmodern conditions.

Pomo/Euro/Techno Angst: The Transsexual as Cultural Fantasy Figure

"What could be more postmodern than transsexuality?" Julia Epstein and Kristina Straub posed this question in the introduction to their influential 1991 anthology, *Body Guards: The Cultural Politics of Gender Ambiguity* (11). The two editors elaborated their question no further, for the answer was apparently obvious to them: nothing is more postmodern than transsexuality. Epstein and Straub defined neither of their terms but clearly assumed them to be related in the form of a syllogism. My construction and deployment of Christine Jorgensen's Atom Bomb is motivated by the very questions the editors of *Body Guards* implied but left unvoiced. How can we begin to articulate the relationship between transsexuality and postmodernity and to complicate the syllogism they assumed? How are new technologies and cultural innovations implicated in the production of historically novel subject formations and subject positions? To what extent can transsexuality be considered a techno-cultural fantasy that helps map the contours of contemporary society? How might it be considered a type of "assisted reproduction" that spawns and sustains new forms of embodied subjectivity?

In *The Transparency of Evil*, Jean Baudrillard asserts that postmodernity is characterized by "a general tendency toward transsexuality which extends well beyond sex" into all other areas of cultural production (Baudrillard 1993, 7). Baudrillard railed against this "transition towards a transsexual state of

affairs' (12) but considered it the problematic culmination of sexual liberation discourses from previous decades that called for "the bursting forth of the
body's full erotic force." Baudrillard claimed that the historic exhaustion of
the sexual liberation "orgy" in the AIDS epidemic "left everyone looking for
their generic and sexual identity" but that in the postmodern aftermath of
failed humanist emancipation metanarratives few viable answers could be
found. Instead, people increasingly took their bodily pleasures not within the
context of sexual difference but rather from "playing with the commutability
of the signs of sex" (20). Transsexuality, which Baudrillard understands as a
refusal of sexual difference and a flight from the somatic body into technologically mediated body images fantasized as circulating within a dematerial-
ized "traffic in signs" (24), is thus symptomatic and characteristic of the current
era. Symbolically, Baudrillard claims, to the extent that we all necessarily participate in this semiotic (s)exchange, "we are all transsexuals, just as we are
all biological mutants *in potentia*" (21).

Throughout *The Transparency of Evil* Baudrillard's tone is vitriolic. He not
only ignores or erases the specificities of (dare I say it?) real transsexual lives;
he excoriates "symbolic" transsexuality as the embodiment of all he finds wrong
with postmodern conditions. He does so by means of highly offensive representations of AIDS, race, and (homo)sexuality. Michael Jackson, for example,
whom he considers to represent the tendency toward transsexuality that he
condemns, is described as a "genetically baroque" being, a "turncoat of sex,"
a "solitary mutant" with "Frankensteinian appeal," an ideal symbol for a
"miscegenated" society (21). What I find worth remarking in Baudrillard's
thoughts on transsexuality is not that he condemns it but rather that he uses
the figure of the transsexual to narrate a history of the second half of the twentieth century. I reject the trajectory of his plot—a further degeneration from
the postlapsarian knowledge of sexual difference into the gray entropy of
undifferentiation—but his underlying project is one with which I have considerable critical sympathy. The transsexual can, and often does, productively
figure in attempts to make sense of recent as well as prospective historical
experience.

As Rita Felski points out in "Fin de Siècle, Fin de Sex"—her own essay
on transsexuality, postmodernity, and the millennial shift—Baudrillard's work
can be situated within a more general cultural appropriation of "the figure of
transsexuality as a semiotically dense emblem in the rhetoric of fin de
millennium. . . . If ends of centuries serve as privileged cultural moments for
articulating highly charged myths of death and rebirth, senescence and re-
newal, in our own era such hopes and anxieties are writ large across proliferating representations of the transgendered body" (341–342). These same highly
charged myths are also articulated in current debates about the meaning (or

very existence) of "postmodern conditions," debates that can be understood to a certain extent as meditations on the meaning of contemporary history incited by the singular calendrical event of the year 2000.

There is a slight but significant distinction between "modernity and postmodernity" and "modernism and postmodernism" that seems useful to mark at this point. The first set of terms tend to refer to problems of historical periodization and to the dynamics of social, political, and economic change. They tend to be used when asking whether or not a new historical era has emerged that is as different in its worldview from the European Enlightenment as the Enlightenment was from the preceding period. The second set of terms tends to revolve around aesthetic considerations and styles of cultural production. They have something to do with pastiche, parody, appropriation, simulation, anachronism, and eclecticism. Charting various trajectories from modern conditions (in the historical sense) to postmodern cultural idioms (in the aesthetic sense), determining whether these changes are qualitative or quantitative and whether they represent a continuation of modernity or a profound discontinuity, assessing the moral and ethical significance of these developments, and formulating an appropriate political stance vis-à-vis them constitute the bulk of the "postmodern" debate. It will not be possible in this essay to delve too deeply into these matters, but my basic premises are that the advent of transsexuality as a cultural phenomenon capable of generating widespread attention during the immediate post–World War II period bears an important relationship to the emergence of postmodernity's preconditions, and that this "transsexual phenomenon" needs to be interpreted within the context of the postmodern debate.

A brief example drawn from the work of Fredric Jameson helps suggest the centrality to the analysis of postmodern conditions of the tendency Baudrillard metonymically reduces to "transsexuality." In an essay on postmodern architecture, Jameson writes:

> We are here in the presence of something like a mutation in built space itself. My implication is that we ourselves, the human subjects who happen into this new space, have not kept pace with that evolution; there has been a mutation in the object unaccompanied as yet by any equivalent mutation in the subject. We do not as yet possess the perceptual equipment to match this new hyperspace, as I will call it, in part because our perceptual habits were formed in that older kind of space I have called the space of high modernism. The newer architecture . . . stands as something like an imperative to grow new organs, to expand our sensorium and our body to some new, yet unimaginable, perhaps ultimately impossible, dimensions. (Jameson 1990, 38–39)

Like Baudrillard, Jameson advances a claim that recent cultural innovations compel the refiguration of both flesh and consciousness. Within Jameson's critical framework, however, this "neomorphic imperative" is not attributed to near-past historical antecedents. Rather, it is seen as deriving from a fundamental condition of human existence—that all Being (including forms of embodied subjectivity) is modulated through particular technological, political, and socioeconomic relations and is therefore always historically and culturally contingent. These changing modes of cultural organization are in fact the proper object of critical historical inquiry. Approached in this manner as a figure of the embodied subject embedded in and articulated through newly emergent biomedical and juridicolegal practices and discourses that have implications far broader than the construction of transsexuality, the transsexual body functions as something of an avatar of postmodernity. It becomes spectacle in the sense of which Guy Debord wrote: "a social relation among people, mediated by images," a "socially organized appearance" that is "nothing other than the *sense* of the total practice of a social-economic formation[,] . . . the historical moment in which we are caught" (Debord 1967, 4, 10, 11). Like media images, like architecture, transsexual bodies materialize, concretize, and render visible many of the structuring principles of the culture that produces them.

Ernest Mandel's characterization of the mid-twentieth century as a moment of quantum change between one organizational moment of capital and another helps explain the timing of transsexuality's appearance as spectacle through the vehicle of Christine Jorgensen's celebrity. In Mandel's view, this historical moment was partially determined by newly emergent power technologies and a concomitant shift from electricity and combustion engines to computers and nuclear devices. As other writers have suggested, it also involved a deepening crisis within the socially dominant empiricist epistemology of the modern West, specifically with regard to the problem of linguistic reference. In the atomic age, it has become increasingly difficult to think of representation as the mimetic reproduction for subjectivity of a stable, material objectivity that lies outside the subject (Jameson 1984, viii; Solomon 1988).

This complex cultural shift toward a non- or postreferential epistemology modeled by performative linguistic acts, generated in part by the advent of nuclear technology and by all the epistemological issues this technology raises, is primarily what I am referring to when I write of the emergence of "postmodern" conditions. Although postmodernism became a dominant aesthetic mode only in the early 1970s, it was in the late 1940s in the United States that postmodernity's necessary material preconditions initially established themselves—including nuclear war capabilities, a vastly expanded mass media and communications network, electronic computers, and a United States–dominated framework for international relations cobbled together from the wreckage of European imperialism. The semiotic environment produced by the postwar technoscientific transnational capitalist system is precisely what I intend to evoke by invoking the figure of Christine Jorgensen's Atom Bomb.

Atomic bombs and transsexual bodies are similarly ambivalent devices. On the one hand, they have perversely colluded with the fantasies driving contemporary culture, supplying evidence to modern Western subjects that their scientific worldview has triumphed over all. Anything from cold hard matter to the ineffable essence of a human identity can be engineered into or out of existence. Like the processes through which uranium is manipulated to set off a chain reaction of explosive changes at the atomic level, transsexual surgical and hormonal transformations represent the accomplishment of a desire for technical mastery over the material world. Metaphysical fantasies of transcendent power, like the old alchemical dream of turning lead into gold, apparently have been realized in nuclear technologies that could turn matter into energy, as well as in transsexual technologies that seemingly turned men into women (and women into men). On the other hand, this fantasy of total power precipitates its own inevitable anxiety-ridden crises. By attesting to a previously unimaginable potential for disrupting and refashioning the most fundamental attributes of existence, transsexual bodies and atomic bombs both confront modern Western subjects with the specter of their own dissolution by bearing witness to conditions in which the explanatory structures of modernity no longer suffice. They are both signs of an apocalypse of sorts that sets the stage for new forms of culture organized according to fundamentally different rules.

The parallel roles in recent history of transsexual bodies and nuclear bombs are rooted in the fact that both accomplish a literalization of modernity's representational crisis by abolishing the stability of material referentiality in a historically novel fashion. In doing so, they actualized the destruction of the modernist episteme. One end of modern history can indeed be found in a mushroom cloud, where meaning evaporates. Time and space lose all referentiality where Ground Zero and the Year Zero collide to mark the spot where reality evacuates itself into another dimension. Transsexuality, too, is posed as an impossible reality beyond the absolute limit of an incommensurable sexual difference, a liquidation of the body as a stable ground of meaning. It is the end of history in another sense, a space in which semiotic activity must mutate into new forms if it is to survive.

Like the bomb, the transsexual body is both a literal artifact and a powerful technocultural fantasy that offers us an opportunity to ruminate on and elaborate our concerns about our existential condition at a particular moment in history. They are simultaneously mirrors that reflect reality and hammers that shape it. It is relatively easy to see nuclear bomb technology as a force that shapes the world and less obvious that "nuclearism" has also been a lens through which to view the world. The reverse holds true for transsexuality. As I have been suggesting above, the transsexual has become a privileged figure in postmodern history, but as I will argue below, it is also an important vector through which postmodern conditions are themselves produced.

Points of Passage: Or, Christine in the Cutting Room

In a 1959 interview with television journalist Mike Wallace, Christine Jorgensen spoke about her lifelong fascination with photography in a way that opens out into broader discussions of the role of technology in (re)producing historically contingent forms of embodied subjectivity, and of the ways in which attention to transgender phenomena can help map postmodernity. If the atomic bomb has been the figure of technology that best represents the awesome impact of the new technocultural conditions that emerged in the mid-twentieth century, the cinematic apparatus is perhaps better suited for modeling the means through which these conditions continue to operate. In attending to Jorgensen as both photographer and visual image, we can perhaps begin to appreciate the mechanisms through which contemporary subjectivity has increasingly come to be understood as an effect of the visual performativity of bodily surface and how transsexuality exemplifies this process.

In the 1959 interview, Wallace asked Jorgensen a question about her nightclub performances, to which she began to reply, "I like performing very much. I—." Wallace, who throughout the interview seemed determined to put the worst possible construction on Jorgensen's every word, quickly interrupted: "Was there a great need in yourself for recognition? Is there possibly any of this involved in your going through with the surgery?" Jorgensen responded to the insinuation of crass publicity-mongering with characteristic graciousness:

> No, not with the surgery, not at all. But to say that I was not at all . . .
> interested in the theatrical world would be untrue, too. . . . I worked
> for RKO before [changing sex], in the motion picture industry. I was
> in the cutting room. I was a photographer. I believe that this is the
> reason why I went into the nightclubs—well, the reason I became a
> photographer was because I could work behind the cameras, because I
> was afraid to work in front of them.

When Wallace asked if the publicity surrounding Jorgensen's sex change gave her the show business break she'd always been looking for, Jorgensen insisted that she had taken up her career as an entertainer "for a very pure economic reason." Her unsought notoriety foreclosed other possibilities for living an unobtrusive private life, and by capitalizing on her celebrity status she could provide better for herself and her aging parents. Wallace persisted in looking for a vulgar motive in Jorgensen's choices, suggesting that supporting herself through nightclub appearances came "at a considerable price, in terms of exhibition of yourself." To which Jorgensen replied: "Exhibition is a very interesting word. I think every human being is an exhibition of themselves. We have a physical being which we are constantly showing to friends and people, because this is us. We have to carry it with us. Inside I believe there is another person. There is the thing that makes "you" you, and "me" me, and each person themselves" (Wallace 1959). Jorgensen's sense that there is an immaterial essential self that visually presents itself to others though the materiality of the body lies close to the heart of much recent theoretical work on transsexual subjectivity. As Jay Prosser argues in his recent book, *Second Skins: Body Narratives of Transsexuality*, it is the perceived discrepancy between the morphology of the transsexual's subjective image of the "bodily ego" and the reflected image of the transsexual's physical organism that launches the drive for somatic sex transformation (Prosser 1998, 61–96). Though Jorgensen did not rely on the technical psychoanalytic vocabulary that Prosser employs, she expressed in lay terms a compatible understanding of the process through which she shifted her subject position from man to woman. It seems that for Jorgensen, becoming a woman in the eyes of others was largely a matter of materializing and rendering objectively visible "the thing that made 'her' her." While she might well have described that "thing" as her soul, it could also be characterized as the projected image of her phantasmatic body, an image with which she made primary subjective identifications and through which she sought to situate herself as a speaker in language, an image whose acquisition and incorporation constituted the process through which "she" became instantiated as a subject in the first place.

Christine Jorgensen's reminiscence of herself as George at work in the cutting room of the RKO studios suggests ways in which cinematic modes of processing experience informed the construction of her transsexual identity just as much as did the medical techniques through which she made her self visible. Jorgensen's job in the cutting room required her to take film stock shot for RKO feature films and snip it into discrete images or short sequences (e.g., planes landing, lions hunting prey on the savanna) that could be recycled and incorporated into other film projects. She then filed the segments away according to a subject index of the images they contained, and reproduced the film stock as needed. As editor, archivist, and photographic copyist, Jorgensen occupied a position in which she necessarily learned both to fragment the visual representation of the world and to assemble those fragments according to any number of narrative structures. It seems likely that her extensive reading in medical literature allowed her to grasp how, through surgical and hormonal techniques, her own body could be "edited" in much the same way as film, its visual surface deliberately manipulated to capture the image of herself she saw in her mind's eye, and to produce and sustain the narratives that structured her identifications and desires. In applying cinematic insight to her own embodiment, Jorgensen moved herself from one type of cutting room to another. As she herself notes, it was this very transition that enabled her to become an object in front of the camera rather than merely a dis- (or mis-) embodied subject behind the lens.

The more one explores the emergence of transsexuality as a wide-scale phenomenon, the more readily it appears as part of a broader debate about the emergence of new epistemological conditions and a new aesthetic sensibility. In *The Postmodern Condition: A Report on Knowledge*, Jean-François Lyotard outlines several fundamental aspects of late-twentieth-century life, in addition to the aforementioned loss of the stable material referent, that are significant in assessing the relationship between postmodernity and transsexuality. These include the increasing extension of performative principles and criteria into new areas of social life, what he refers to as the "instrumentalization of knowledge," through which information is reduced to operational codes, and the proliferation of simulacra, where the difference between the original and the reproduction becomes increasingly irrelevant. Taken together, these various epistemological conditions focus attention on surfaces rather than depths, images rather than substances, "doing" rather than "being." Modernist notions of causality and narrative flatten out and break down in the face of a performatively defined present (Lyotard 1984, 3–67).

Transsexuality is "postmodern" according to each of these criteria. The sex of the body has, to a significant degree, become an object of the will—that is to say, the sexed appearance of the body has become more manipulable, so that the category of sex, rather than being an anchoring material referent of personal identity and social gender, has become an operationalized surface effect achieved through performative means. In this regard, transsexuality literalizes and renders visible the processes that postmodern performative theories of gender hold are the bases of all gender. In so doing, the naturalness of ontologizing bodily difference into social and psychical gender through the category of sex is called into question, and its destabilization is publicly displayed in spectacular fashion. The greater the skill in reproducing the semiotic codes that produce recognizable gender as their surface effect, the more indistinguishable the transsexual "simulacrum" becomes from "authentic" men and women. To the extent that transsexuality as spectacle has become one of the principal sites for encountering these new ways that bodies and gender can mean, transsexuality functions as a point of passage between modernity and postmodern conditions.

In suggesting that Christine Jorgensen was the prototypical postmodern transsexual I am not suggesting that either she or her doctors understood the project that drew them together as a harbinger of new cultural forms, new means of embodiment, new modes of establishing subjective identifications in the objective realm, or new ways for bodies to mean. But as Lyotard himself points out, the postmodern functions not only as a historical period but as modernism's avant-garde (79). Jorgensen was a modernist who accepted the metanarratives of Western science and believed science would discover the truth of her Being in its meticulous investigations of her material substance. When science pronounced her female, she had only to surrender to its verdict. This does not undermine the point I have been trying to make about her postmodernity. When I say that in Jorgensen's transition from man to woman we can see an emergence of postmodern conditions, I mean only that we can see at the microlevel of an individual life changes of more global significance, changes that have to do with new modes of semiotic production.

Consider again the question of hormones and the scenario at the drugstore that opened this essay. Jorgensen self-administered estrogen and subsequently received it from her doctors because she and they believed it contained the biological essence of the womanhood that she claimed to possess within her in some mysterious fashion. It's worth noting that science named the glands that produce hormones the "endocrine system," in that the Greek root, *krenein*, is a cognate of the Latin root for both "secret" and "secrete," and that *endo-* means "interior" or "within." Both Jorgensen and her doctors were fully caught up in a scientific discourse that conflated "internal secretions" with "inner secrets," and which thus conceptualized estrogen and testosterone as deep truths of the body waiting to be discovered and confessed, elaborated on, augmented, and publicized in a manner familiar to all readers of Michel Foucault. According to the views held by Jorgensen and her doctors, supplying the proper hormones to make a latent "true sex" more perceptible would represent a heroic scientific triumph, as would surgically altering the genitals of such persons. Through transsexual technologies, transgendered subjects could finally appear as embodied subjects within the heteronormative matrix. While the improper application of these techniques risked mismarking Nature's handiwork rather than magnifying its designs, their development and use could be fully justified within modernist narratives and discourses.

Within this modernist framework, however, postmodern conditions began to emerge. As noted previously, many of the important effects of estrogen on a biologically male body are visual. They are changes in skin texture
and fat distribution, surface changes in the appearance of the body. Genital
surgeries, too, have important visual effects in that they also change the shape
of the body and alter its appearance. To a significant degree, transsexuality
can be considered a technology that relies on hormonal and surgical manipulations of bodily surface to actualize in the visual (and therefore social) register psychical (and therefore private) identifications with specifically sexed
images of the body-ego. In acting out older notions of essences and depths, in
probing materiality to discover there the very projections they imagined as
their project's ground, Jorgensen and her medical team inadvertently
instrumentalized the very mechanisms through which the sexed appearance
of the body is performatively produced and through which it disappears again
into the fiction of a natural state of being. Precisely because the material body
is so readily taken as an ultimate form of truth, this instrumental knowledge
encoded within transsexual technologies has had the power to produce the
reality of the transsexual's gendered embodiment as one of its peculiar effects.
Somewhat ironically for Jorgensen and many other transsexuals who have followed her, modernity's quest to ground the meaning of gender in the flesh of
the human body began pointing beyond itself toward new, historically
postmodern ways for bodies and genders to mean. Pushed to its limit, the body
of scientific modernity collapsed into elsewhere, to arrive in a place where
the phantasmatic body of a transgender imaginary could warm itself beneath
the same sun that heated the surface of the skin.

Notes

Portions of an earlier version of this essay have been published previously as
"Transsexuality: The Postmodern Body and/as Technology," *Exposure: The Journal
of the Society for Photographic Education* 30, nos. 1–2 (fall 1995): 38–50, and are
forthcoming, in revised form, in Susan Stryker, *Ecstatic Passages: A Postmodern
Transsexual Memoir*, from Oxford University Press.

1. All information on Jorgensen in this essay is drawn from her published autobiography (1968), but see also Meyerowitz (1998) and Sirlin (1995) for more information on the historical context. The following anecdote about Jorgensen's
   transition is drawn from Jorgensen, 77–78, 130.
2. Sirlin (1995) offers a hostile account that stereotypically misreads Jorgensen as a
   closeted homosexual who went through surgery in order to appear heterosexual.
   Meyerowitz (1998), who is working on a book-length history of transsexuality, supplies a more nuanced perspective on her career and places her in a broader history of transsexual discourses and practices in the United States. Hausman (1995)
   devotes several pages to Jorgensen in her treatment of transsexual autobiography,
   as does Prosser (1998).
3. I would like to thank Joanne Meyerowitz for calling my attention to this source.

4. Transsexuality's relationship to "nuclearism" and cultural discourses of containment are explored in more depth in the extended version of this article forthcoming in my book. See Boyer (1985); Chaloupka (1992); Henrikson (1998); May (1988), chap. 4, "Explosive Issues: Sex, Women, and the Bomb," 92–113; Nadel (1995); Nye (1994), chap. 9, "Atomic Bomb and Apollo XI: New Forms of the Dynamic Sublime," 225–256.

The Monstrous Genealogy
of Assisted Reproduction

KARYN VALERIUS

In 1973 the director of OB/GYN at a Manhattan hospital destroyed an experimental in vitro fertilization that his subordinate was conducting without his authorization. If left uninterrupted, the experiment might have resulted in the world's first laboratory-conceived human embryo. A woman with blocked fallopian tubes and her husband had hoped this experimental method of conception would allow her to become pregnant with their genetic offspring. In the ensuing lawsuit, this director of OB/GYN testified that he interfered in the experiment because he feared the resulting infant might be a monster.[1] This panicked motive registers the extreme epistemological discomfort and accompanying moral outrage provoked by conception achieved in the laboratory. The doctor's testimony suggests a gothic tale in which excessive scientific ambition results in monstrous offspring that must be destroyed to restore an orderly world dictated by nature. By positing monstrosity as the object of fear, the doctor's testimony mobilizes multiple fears, including but not limited to a fear of the radically new; a fear of artificial methods of procreating; a fear of medical intervention causing physically deformed human beings; and a fear of technologically assisted generation producing nonhumans composed of human material.

It would seem the doctor's fears were disproved five years later in England when the quite human Louise Brown became the first child born following conception via in vitro fertilization. Yet twenty-five years later, assisted reproduction continues to provoke anxiety that technological intervention in procreation might compromise the humanity of humans, and monstrosity continues to figure prominently in the mediascape inhabited by high-tech assisted reproduction. Fictional thrillers create and exploit a fear that in vitro fertilization used in combination with other biomedical practices might produce monstrous, hybrid life-forms. The tabloids and the mainstream media alike invariably report success stories as "miracle babies," evoking the Christian tradition of signs and portents, while these same media deploy the "strange but true" mode of the freak show to describe the complicated host of legal disputes raised by various high-tech reproductive practices.[2] Frankenstein's monster, that icon of scientific hubris, remains an absent presence lurking behind the various public culture representations of assisted reproduction as unnatural conception with potentially hazardous results.

Alternately celebratory, incredulous, and fearful, much of the U.S. public discourse on assisted reproduction tropes on literary, popular, and religious traditions of monstrosity to position assisted reproduction as a fantastic and unprecedented departure from natural procreation. As Kelly Hurley's study of gothic literature argues, the fantastic is a productive mode.[3] In the case of assisted reproduction, fantastic representations constitute the natural through their elaboration of its violation. Inciting what Hurley calls "metaphysical estrangement" as the appropriate response to in vitro fertilization and related practices establishes natural procreation as an inviolable historical constant by contrast. This reactionary discourse elides the histories of birth control practices and other reproductive technologies like birthing chairs, forceps, c-section deliveries, and ultrasound; it also secures the normative status of the nuclear family, and it renders the status and function of male and female bodies in relation to generation self-evident, unchanging, and uncontested.

One means to contest this ahistorical discourse is to place it in relation to a historical understanding of Western traditions of monstrosity. The discussion that follows insists that the issues raised by in vitro fertilization and related practices—like questions regarding what constitutes a natural kin relation or the natural boundaries of the body—do have precedents. Of course, historically, reproductive issues have frequently been the impetus for intellectual and political debates about the boundaries of the natural.[4] More specifically, monstrosity has historically been an occasion to define and dispute what constitutes human embodiment and species identity, legitimate kinship relations, the boundaries of the natural, and the authority or ambiguity of signifying systems.

What Is a Monster?

Broadly speaking, monstrosity figures a failure of generation to reproduce a given species according to a normative standard. However, the definition of monstrosity and the significance attributed to it in the Western intellectual tradition change along with mutually reinforcing shifts in organizations of knowledge, political agendas, and shifts in the construction of nature. As Rosemarie Garland Thompson characterizes it, the history of monstrosity demonstrates "a movement from a narrative of the marvelous to a narrative of the deviant" that marks the "collective cultural transformations into modernity."[5] Across this history a corresponding movement can be traced from the soul to the body and the nuclear family as privileged sites of investment for contested cultural politics.[6]

From antiquity through the nineteenth century, *monster* was the term used by scholars and surgeons and common folk alike to refer to human births marked by death or deformity, as well as to abnormal plant or animal formations.[7] A range of phenomena from moles to miscarried fetuses to hermaphrodites and conjoined twins constituted monstrosity, and people attributed monsters to a variety of natural and supernatural causes. Ambroise Paré's *On Monsters* (1575) catalogs cases of monstrosity according to thirteen possible causes including God's judgment, Satan's interference, bestiality, and the influence of pregnant women's imaginations on their wombs.[8]

These explanations for monstrosity current from antiquity through the nineteenth century establish an economy of visible signs in which monsters indicate heresy or divine agency (Christian miracles and portents), inappropriate or excessive desire (maternal imagination), or inappropriate sexual conduct (adultery, consorting with the devil, or bestiality). Within the Christian tradition of miracles and portents, monstrous births were understood as material signs authored by God. Monstrous births figured prominently as evidence of God's judgment against apostasy in religious polemics during the period of religious and political unrest precipitated by the Protestant Reformation.[9] Both Protestant and Catholic writers identified monstrosity with heresy, drawing analogies between deformed or unnatural parts of a monster and the doctrinal errors of a given heresy.

Monsters continued to elicit scientific investigation and popular fascination into the nineteenth and early twentieth centuries, but as pathological bodies rather than as supernatural portents. In 1830 French scientist Isidore Geoffroy Saint-Hilaire named the scientific study of monstrosity *teratology*, and in the United States, the freak show emerged as a commercially profitable and immensely popular form of public entertainment by 1840.[10] Both developments were continuations of older practices: since antiquity individuals had traveled about, displaying themselves for profit, and seventeenth-century science initiated the investigation of monsters as natural rather than supernatural phenomena. However, in the nineteenth century, both popular and scholarly approaches to monstrosity were shaped by the emergence of biology, which directed attention to the anatomy and physiology of monsters, and by industrialization, which prompted a new threshold of organization for enterprises devoted to monstrosity.[11]

Freak shows employed a permanent staff of monstrous individuals and established standardized conventions for their display. To attract audiences, freak shows appealed to popular fascination with unusual bodies and novelty acts rather than supernatural associations.[12] Likewise, the significant difference of studies on teratology from previous studies on monsters is the classificatory schema they employ. These studies typically provide detailed descriptions of abnormal formations in plant or animal specimens or pathological human fetuses, classify these cases within categories established according to physiological traits, and attempt a medical explanation for each category.[13] This fascination with the physical bodies of monsters is one expression of a political investment in a physiological conception of embodiment for nineteenth-century Americans, an investment also apparent in newly theorized scientific explanations for race, gender, and sexual difference that similarly explained human difference in terms of pathological bodies.[14] Thus, by the nineteenth century, monstrosity continues to circulate in an economy of visible signs, but the monster functions as a sign of its own deviant embodiment, indicating disorder defined as an attribute of bodies rather than the effect of dissenting ideas or sinful conduct.

Now, at the end of twentieth century, changing terminology marks the effects of new biomedical knowledge and practices. In clinical and in popular usage the word *monster* no longer indicates congenital conditions in people or animals. A 1993 book explaining human genetics to a popular audience refers to the "genetically unfortunate" when dismissing Martin Luther's sixteenth-century evaluation of conjoined twins as monsters without souls.[15] Today the word *monster* more typically conjures up the potential for hybrid creatures created through the use of biotechnologies. Science has apparently replaced the supernatural and the natural as the agent of fantastic events. In current discourse, monstrosity functions to evoke the fear, curiosity, or wonder and awe characteristic of its historical significations only now in response to the pressure biomedical intervention in procreation places on organic notions of family and individual human identity.

Heretical Misconceptions

Monstrosity is the profane counterpart to what feminists have observed is the sacred import of the fetus in late-twentieth-century U.S. public culture. In contrast to the public fetus that Donna Haraway describes "as a kind of metonym, seed crystal or icon for configurations of person, family, nation, origin, choice, life, and future," monstrosity indicates biomedical technology's contamination of these same cherished ideals central to liberal democracy and American national identity.[16] Monstrosity similarly figures a threat to the concept of America in an incident from the United States' prenational history, the Antinomian Controversy (1636–1638). Conventional analyses of this colonial dispute, from the first colonial histories to the present, understand the antinomian as the paradigmatic example of the problem excessive individualism poses for sustaining community in a society paradoxically founded on individualism. Amy Schrager Lang argues for the central importance of gender politics and female embodiment to this controversy focused on the antinomian heretic Anne Hutchinson.[17] The monstrous generativity of the heretic embodied as a woman acquires additional relevance in the context of twentieth-century reproductive politics, in which conflicts provoked by assisted reproduction and abortion create a crisis in the liberal framework of individualism and natural rights.

In the Massachusetts Bay Colony, anxieties about the threat posed to civil order by dissenting religious fanatics manifested in the Antinomian Controversy. There is, of course, a vast body of scholarship on this intricate colonial dispute, but for my purposes here, the relevant focus of the controversy is Anne Hutchinson's monstrous offspring.[18] In 1638 the Massachusetts Bay Colony banished Anne Hutchinson for heresy. Four months later, she gave birth to monsters. The most notable account of her story, John Winthrop's *Short Story of the Rise, reign, and ruine of the Antinomians, Familists & Libertines* (1644), together with Thomas Welde's preface to Winthrop's *Short Story*, was written by her adversaries to justify the controversial decision against Hutchinson to the church overseas.[19] According to Welde, Hutchinson produced thirty monsters, "some of them bigger, some lesser, some of one shape, some of another; few of any perfect shape, none at all of them (as far as I could ever learne) of human shape" (214). In their narrative, Welde and Winthrop exploit the well-established associations between monstrosity and heresy to vilify Hutchinson. Their account inextricably binds Hutchinson's sexuality and monstrous procreativity with her positions on religious doctrine and with disrupted civil order.

In order to understand how monstrosity functioned to reestablish the authority of the orthodox Puritan position, an overview of the issues and events leading up to the monstrous birth is necessary. Hutchinson's theological error was that she subscribed to the Protestant doctrine of "free grace" too literally, insisting that deeds do not signify one's spiritual estate. Orthodox Puritans agreed with Hutchinson that redemption is a gift from God that cannot be earned, but the orthodox believed the state of grace would necessarily express itself in good deeds.[20] For her adversaries, Hutchinson's denial that visible signs necessarily signified invisible truths threatened to produce anarchy: if the community of saints did not have to worry about their actions in the world or obey the law, social mayhem would result, and certainly the work of colony building would be jeopardized.

More acutely, Hutchinson both transgressed her role as a woman and undermined the clergy's authority, while her able testimony at her trial frustrated her opponents, who could not successfully quell the ambiguous theological problem.[21] Hutchinson publicly criticized the clergy for preaching a covenant of works and argued for direct revelation from God. This claim invested each individual with authority to interpret Scripture and law and, therefore, rendered the clergy's role as spiritual advisers and biblical exegetes redundant. Orthodox Puritans feared direct revelation intimated total moral relativism because it emphasized the individual's personal relationship with God to the exclusion of communal claims for salvation as God's chosen people and denied any relevance of a person's actions for his or her spiritual status. Hutchinson disavowed the charges against the dangerous moral and social implications of her ideas, claiming her concern was solely with spiritual matters. Despite this, Hutchinson's opponents explicitly listed sexual misconduct, including adultery, sex outside marriage, and sex among women, as "dayngerous Consequences" of such relativism (371–372). To counter moral relativism and to maintain correct thinking and orderly behavior, the magistrates insisted on a direct relationship between signification and signs in all matters, religious and civil. Deputy Governor Thomas Dudley's rejection of Hutchinson's written recantation makes this clear: "Her Repentance is not in her Countenance, none can see it thear I thinke" (379).

Because the disputed relationship between signs and signification was a key issue in the Antinomian Controversy over visible evidence of divine agency and surrogacy, such a portentous event as Hutchinson's monstrous birth provided a fortuitous and quite powerful rhetorical tool for her opponents. Hutchinson's monstrous birth followed her excommunication and removal to Rhode Island. Her adversaries understood this course of events as God's judgment against her dissenting opinions and thus as vindication of their own controversial actions in prosecuting and banishing her. Thomas Welde's brief narrative of the Antinomian Controversy insists on the appropriateness of the form God's punishment takes: "And see how the wisdome of God fitted this judgment to her sinne every way, for looke as she had vented misshapen opinions, so she must bring forth deformed monsters; and as about 30 Opinions in number, so many monsters; and as those were publike, and not in a corner mentioned, so this now come to be knowne and famous over all these Churches, and a great part of the world" (214–215). Welde exploits the pun on "misconception" to assert an analogy between Hutchinson's ideas and her offspring. The symmetry his analogy secures between the punishment and the crime lends authority to his interpretation of these strange events.

Although Welde relies most explicitly on the association between heresy (misconceived ideas) and monstrosity (misconceived offspring) to make his case, other beliefs about monstrosity commonly held at the time simultaneously register here. The age-old belief that monsters result from sexual misconduct recalls and seemingly confirms implications made at the trial that Hutchinson's ideas would lead to sexual promiscuity. Welde's analogy also invokes the imagination theory, which attributes monstrous offspring to the harmful influence of a woman's imagination on her womb.[22] The imagination theory relies on widely held characterizations of women's imaginations as potentially unstable, wildly passionate, and dangerous to their procreative function. It opposes intellectual creativity and physical procreativity, prohibiting imaginative or intellectual pursuits for women who would have normal, healthy children. Thus, Welde's analogy also dismisses Hutchinson as an irrational woman even as it casts her as an unwomanly participant in intellectual theological debates.

Welde and Winthrop disseminated the story of Hutchinson's monstrous progeny to establish that her doctrine and her behavior were indeed in error. The multiple registers of monstrosity at play in Welde's pun on "misconception" functioned to consolidate meaning for Welde and Winthrop's representation of the Antinomian Controversy at its resolution. The narrative simultaneously displaces the content of Hutchinson's ideas and her accusations against the clergy and renders her synonymous with her procreativity, making it unnecessary to refute her claims on doctrinal grounds. The narrative reasserts order, putting Hutchinson back into her proper place as a woman and reestablishing the efficacy of visible evidence. In direct contrast to Hutchinson's own disorderly claims about unreliable visible evidence, Hutchinson's monstrous birth delivered an unequivocal confirmation for her adversaries that the condition of the soul is reflected in its visible issue.

The Progeny of Biomedical Science and Technology

Anne Hutchinson believed in absolute divine truth but denied the efficacy of visible evidence in favor of self-knowledge gained through faith. In an inversion of these seventeenth-century disputes over the relevance of visible signs, postmodern recognition of the power-mediated relationships between signs and signification engages representations but rejects notions of foundational truth. Much like Puritan disavowal of heretical claims for the disjunction of signs and signification, U.S. public culture at the end of the twentieth century jealously maintains a signifying system grounded in biology. Puritan traditions of supernatural agency relied on a system of visible signs to ground in divine will a worldview encompassing religious doctrine as well as civil order. In present-day biologically essentialist versions of personal and national identity, the morphologies of human bodies visibly signify the invisible essence of identities, while the nuclear family signifies a civil order based on a natural order provided by the biology of reproductive heterosexuality. Assisted reproduction occupies a critical site in these cultural politics. As technology that produces babies, thereby enabling families, it nonetheless also exposes personhood and family to be legal conventions and social customs rather than natural facts grounded in a discretely bounded human organism or the biological processes governing generation.

Practices including in vitro fertilization, surrogacy, gamete or sperm donation, and cryopreservation circumvent the role of sex in procreation, multiply the contributors to generation, produce extrabodily human reproductive material, and multiply and extend the possibilities for conception and pregnancy resulting from one ovulation and one ejaculation. Thus, surrogacy as well as egg and sperm donation complicate kinship, while more generally, in vitro fertilization denaturalizes the nuclear family by artificially proliferating biological relationships. In addition, assisted reproduction highlights the permeable, indiscrete qualities of reproductive bodies, rendering the natural boundaries of the human body ambiguous. In the narratives provoked by these circumstances, late-twentieth-century permutations of Western traditions of monstrosity provide the conceptual framework and rhetorical strategies to elaborate and respond to assisted reproduction's failure to reproduce the nuclear family and its compromise of the discretely bounded human organism.

For instance, one "celebrated case" presented by C.J.S. Thompson's *Mystery and Lore of Monsters* suggests the tensions that nondiscrete monstrous bodies produce for liberal political theory. In seventeenth-century France, a "double-headed monster" was convicted of murder and condemned to death but not executed "on account of the innocence of one of its component halves."[23] Here the two-headed monster with a consciousness corresponding to each head but only one body commits an extreme antisocial act, but the multiplicity of his embodiment hopelessly frustrates the implementation of penal codes and legal culpability. Likewise, extrauterine conception makes apparent the permeable boundaries of reproductive bodies. As Sarah Franklin describes the dilemma created by extrabodily reproductive material, "An embryo outside the body can only be created by interfering with a woman's body and therefore cannot be called an individual or given civil rights without creating a conflict of interest between two persons over one body—a conundrum that confounds the entire basis of liberal democratic freedoms grounded in notions of individual integrity and autonomy."[24] Of course, this is also the conceptual framework defining the contemporary abortion debate, which articulates a conflict of interest between a pregnant woman and the fetus she is gestating, and this conundrum is shared by the two-headed monster guilty of murder. However, in a 1995 divorce proceeding, assisted reproduction makes a man's property in himself an issue as well.

In 1995 Steven Kass sued his former wife for custody of fertilized eggs cryopreserved since 1993 to prevent her from becoming pregnant against his will with their jointly conceived child.[25] The judge in the case decided in favor of Maureen Kass. He ruled that in the case of in vivo conception, a husband's rights end with ejaculation, refusing to differentiate between in vitro and in vivo conception. The significant difference, though, is that cryopreservation multiplies and extends indefinitely the possibilities for pregnancy resulting from one ejaculation. According to Steven Kass, the decision of the courts violates his procreative autonomy because his former wife could theoretically become pregnant with his child at any time during the remainder of her life. One interesting aspect of this case is that it features the alienable status of sperm in in vivo as well as assisted reproduction. In American culture, female bodies penetrated, inhabited, subsumed, or otherwise ambiguated by another are not unthinkable or even unusual, and the abortion debate has made the fetal personhood conundrum a familiar one. However, the discrete, autonomous male body is a key assumption (usually left unquestioned) informing notions of political agency. While a woman's property in herself has been a hard-won right established only relatively recently, a white man's property in himself is foundational to liberal democracy. The idea that a man's sperm is alienable makes visible the conventional rather than natural status of the autonomous male body that provides the material referent for the abstract individual of liberal democracy.

Aristotle's definition of the parameters for normative procreation also resonates for the age of high-tech assisted reproduction. For Aristotle, "anyone who does not take after his parents is really in a way a monstrosity, since in these cases Nature has in a way strayed from the generic type."[26] In the past, a child's resemblance to its parents, particularly its father, functioned as the sign of legitimate paternity, while a monstrous child failed to reproduce such signs. Currently, resemblance to one's parents continues to signify legitimate lineage. In the following examples, racial identity functions as a visible sign of genetic relationship or the lack thereof, making excess biological relationships produced by assisted reproduction highly visible and undermining the attempt of middle-class, heterosexual married couples to reproduce the exclusive, genetic family unit.

Consider the media account of the following incident. In 1995 a mistake made by a fertility clinic in the Netherlands surprised a white Dutch couple with twins, one white and one of mixed race.[27] A technician reused a pipette containing sperm from a previous fertilization, resulting in twin children with different genetic fathers, one the mother's husband, the other a black man from Aruba previously unknown to the white couple. Certainly, a family consisting of a white married couple and two sons, one white and one of mixed race, could result from circumstances that do not include technological intervention, but these circumstances would not usually elicit media coverage. *Newsweek*'s coverage of this story features a picture of the infant brothers, and the headline below it reads "Twins—with Two Fathers." The combined effect of the headline and the photo functions to sensationalize the family in question. The visual text is provided to create disbelief and to incite readers to continue reading for an explanation, since experiential knowledge dictates to late-twentieth-century audiences that twins cannot be of different races and that two men cannot father one pregnancy. What allows *Newsweek* to render this an extraordinary case and therefore newsworthy is the fact that the brothers are twins, that a technician's error complicated the intended paternity, and that racial difference made the error visibly evident.

Newsweek's story expresses discomfort with two consequences of assisted reproduction highlighted by these circumstances. First, assisted reproduction produces conventional kin relationships through artificial means, potentially undermining the naturalized status of the nuclear family. Second, in vitro fertilization multiplies the contributors to conception to include lab technicians and doctors, and inadvertently in this case, sperm donors, in addition to the heterosexual married couple hoping to produce genetic offspring. Of course, lab technicians and doctors are routinely involved in pregnancy for many women in industrialized nations. However, in vitro fertilization extends that medical management and intervention to conception. This intervention redefines the relationships necessary for conception, and it allows opportunities for human error. It also creates biological relationships only possible through the use of artifice, in this case twins with different genetic fathers.

Similarly, in a 1990 custody case discussed in detail by Valerie Hartouni, in vitro fertilization combined with a surrogacy arrangement multiplied the maternal, biological contributors to generation.[28] Gestational surrogate Anna Johnson, a black woman, sued genetic parents Crispina Calvert, a Filipina woman, and Mark Calvert, a white man, for custody of the resulting infant. The interested parties made opposing claims for a natural, and therefore privileged, relationship to the child constituted by a biological tie. Anna Johnson contributed the biological processes of gestation and parturition, while Crispina Calvert supplied the egg, which was then fertilized with her husband's sperm. Hartouni's excellent analysis of this case discusses how the racialized discourse of welfare reform informed the court's rejection of Anna Johnson's claims to a legitimate maternal relationship.

Race also functions here in an economy of bodies as visual signs. Against

Johnson's claims that she bonded with the infant in utero, Crispina Calvert invoked visual evidence, asserting that the child "looks just like us."[29] Here race visually marks genetic relatedness, as it did in the story of the twins with two fathers, and this racial element makes more pronounced the conventional idea that children generally look like their legitimate, biological parents. Calvert's claim derives its force from an essentialist definition of race as a biological fact of the body that makes identity visible. Her appeal to visual evidence mobilizes to her advantage assumptions about the authority of biological evidence to establish a legitimate maternal relationship in the case of natural reproduction, about identity as a stable essence legible in a person's body, and about procreation as a means by which parents reproduce their own identities by producing offspring.[30]

The mandate of the courts in *Johnson v. Calvert* was to determine which biological, maternal relationship constituted the more natural one. In the absence of medical practices including in vitro fertilization, surrogacy, and gamete donation, the biological contributions to one pregnancy are confined to one woman. Thus, in the past custody disputes over maternal rights have typically occurred between adopted mothers and birth mothers, and the courts have differentiated between the social relationship established by parenting and a biological relationship that was necessarily also genetic. Now medical intervention makes it possible to distribute the genetic and gestational contributions to one pregnancy among more than one woman, allowing more than one woman to claim a biological tie to one child. In the Johnson case, the judge roundly rejected the possibility of joint custody, finding a "three-parent, two-mom claim was a situation ripe for crazy-making."[31] Instead the courts asserted genetic relationship as the natural relationship, despite legal precedent that previously privileged gestation or "the birth tie" as constituting a natural, biological relationship (74). As Hartouni has argued, by deciding against Johnson, a single mother, and against a joint-custody arrangement, and by awarding sole custody to the Calverts, a middle-class, married couple, the courts decided in favor of the family that most closely reproduced the nuclear family. Importantly, the court's decision in favor of the Calverts inverts the relationship between foundational biological facts and derivative social relationships. Here the normative nuclear family functions as the standard used to differentiate among various biological relationships in order to establish legitimate maternity.

As the circumstances presented by "Twins—with Two Fathers" and *Johnson v. Calvert* attest, assisted reproduction complicates generation by multiplying the number of contributors necessary to produce a child. In each case, the representations offered by the media and the courts validate the attempt of married couples to produce their genetic offspring through the intervention of reproductive technologies. What emerges as fantastic and unnatural in these cases is not technological intervention per se. Rather, in "Twins—with Two Fathers" it is the failure to reproduce the desired genetic paternity made visibly evident by one child's racial difference from his parents and his brother. In *Johnson v. Calvert* it is Anna Johnson's claim to share a legitimate maternal relationship with the infant she gestated despite their differing racial identities, which make it visibly evident that the child is genetically related to the Calverts.

Assisted reproduction destabilizes any simple equation of the biological with the natural. Yet the representations of each situation discussed here nonetheless reinvest in the authority of biology to establish what is natural: while the Kass case simply refuses to acknowledge any challenge to the notion of nature that underwrites the liberal rights discourse employed by all parties involved, the other two examples portray the circumstances they describe as the anomalous results of high-tech generation. "Twins—with Two Fathers" reauthorizes the normative nuclear family through commentary that intends to elicit negative responses to assisted reproduction's artificial proliferation of biological relationships, and in the Johnson case the courts exercised the normative authority of the nuclear family.

A Contract with America

Anne Hutchinson's heretical ideas threatened the Puritan concept of their project in the New World. The Puritans believed themselves to be a chosen people fulfilling their covenant with God by building an earthly community of saints. Given the long-standing tradition of locating the United States' national origins in the Puritan colonies, it is not surprising that the notion of a chosen people powerfully informs the concept of America. In one version of what Haraway calls "secular salvation history," Americans are the sanctioned guardians of democracy.[32] In another related national salvation narrative, that of family values, the nuclear family defined as a genetic unit serves as the foundation for and the fulfillment of the American national contract. Such millennial discourse inevitably produces monsters alongside its miracles. Biomedical technologies are frequently rendered miraculous. However, assisted reproduction is also monstrous because it intervenes in an equation of an a priori natural order with the biological facts of procreation, an equation central to some current definitions of civil society. As in the Antinomian Controversy, monstrosity activates multiple registers of meaning simultaneously, a quality that makes the monster a powerful rhetorical figure. Narratives provoked by assisted reproduction invoke various traditions of monstrosity to articulate the epistemological and political dangers posed by biomedical intervention in generation.

Notes

1. Jamie Talan, "Scientist Knew the Promise of Embryo Research," *Newsday*, 30 November 1997, A55.
2. See, for example, Kathleen Kerr and Jamie Talan, "Mixed Blessing," *Newsday*, 30 November 1997, A5, and Dorinda Elliott and Friso Endt, "Twins—with Two Fathers," *Newsweek*, 3 July 1995, 38.
3. Kelly Hurley, *The Gothic Body: Sexuality, Materialism, and Degeneration at the Fin de Siècle* (New York: Cambridge University Press, 1996), 15.
4. See Janet Farrell Brodie, *Contraception and Abortion in Nineteenth-Century America* (Ithaca, N.Y.: Cornell University Press, 1994), and Linda Gordon, *Woman's Body, Woman's Right* (New York: Penguin Books, 1974).
5. Rosemarie Garland Thompson, "Introduction: From Wonder to Error—A Genealogy of Freak Discourse in Modernity," in *Freakery: Cultural Spectacles of the Extraordinary Body*, ed. Rosemarie Garland Thompson (New York: New York University Press, 1996), 3.
6. My thanks to Susan Squier for this observation (personal communication).
7. See the following for historical information on monstrosity: Lorraine Daston, "Marvelous Facts and Miraculous Evidence in Early Modern Europe," *Critical Inquiry* 18, no. 1 (1991): 93–124; Katharine Park and Lorraine J. Daston, "Unnatural Conceptions: The Study of Monsters in Sixteenth and Seventeenth-Century France and England," *Past and Present* 92 (August 1991): 20–54; C.J.S. Thompson, *The Mystery and Lore of Monsters: With Account of Some Giants, Dwarfs and Prodigies* (New York: Macmillan, 1931); Dudley Wilson, *Signs and Portents: Monstrous Births from the Middle Ages to the Enlightenment* (New York: Routledge, 1993).
8. Ambroise Paré, *On Monsters and Marvels* (1575), trans. Janis L. Pallister (Chicago: University of Chicago Press, 1982).
9. Daston, "Marvelous Facts and Miraculous Evidence in Early Modern Europe."
10. Marie-Hélène Huet, *Monstrous Imagination* (Cambridge: Harvard University Press, 1993), 103–124, and Robert Bogdan, *Freak Show: Presenting Human Oddities for Amusement and Profit* (Chicago: University of Chicago Press, 1988), 2.
11. The emergence of biology occurs as part of the reorganizations of Western knowledge that characterize the shift from the classical to the modern episteme. Michel Foucault, *The Order of Things: An Archeology of the Human Sciences* (1966; reprint, New York: Vintage, 1971). Georges Canguilhem makes the connection between industrialization and the demand for standardization within disciplines including medicine. *The Normal and the Pathological* (New York: Zone Books, 1991), 237–238.
12. Bogdan, *Freak Show*, 10–11.
13. J. W. Ballantyne, *Teratogenesis: An Inquiry into the Causes of Monstrosities. History of Theories of the Past* (Edinburgh, 1897); George M. Gould and Walter L Pyle, *Anomalies and Curiosities of Medicine* (Philadelphia, 1897); Franklin P. Mall, "A Study of the Causes Underlying the Origin of Human Monsters," *Journal of Morphology* 19, no. 1 (1908): 3–367.
14. Michael Sappol, "Sammy Tubbs and Dr. Hubbs: Anatomical Dissection, Minstrelsy, and the Technology of Self-Making in Postbellum America," *Configurations: A Journal of Literature, Science, and Technology* 4, no. 2 (1996): 131–183.

15. Steve Jones, *The Language of Genes* (New York: Doubleday, 1993), 226.
16. Donna Haraway, *Modest Witness@Second Millennium.FemaleMan Meets OncoMouse: Feminism and Technoscience* (New York: Routledge, 1997), 175.
17. Amy Schranger Lang, *Prophetic Woman: Anne Hutchinson and the Problem of Dissent in the Literature of New England* (Berkeley and Los Angeles: University of California Press, 1987).
18. See, for example, Andrew Delbanco, *The Puritan Ordeal* (Cambridge: Harvard University Press, 1989), 136–137, and Mary Beth Norton, *Founding Mothers and Fathers: Gendered Power and the Forming of American Society* (New York: Knopf, 1996), 359–400.
19. Welde and Winthrop's narrative of the Antinomian Controversy is included in David Hall, ed., *The Antinomian Controversy, 1636–1638: A Documentary History*, 2d ed. (Durham, N.C.: Duke University Press, 1990), 201–310.
20. Lang, *Prophetic Woman*, 18.
21. Hall, *Antinomian Controversy*, 311.
22. Huet, *Monstrous Imagination*, 1.
23. Thompson, *Mystery and Lore*, 126.
24. Sarah Franklin, "Postmodern Procreation: A Cultural Account of Assisted Reproduction," in *Conceiving the New World Order: The Global Politics of Reproduction*, ed. Faye Ginsburg and Rayna Rapp (Berkeley and Los Angeles: University of California Press, 1995), 337.
25. Ford Fessenden, "Woman Has Custody of Fertilized Eggs: Ex-Spouse's Rights Dismissed," *Newsday*, 20 January 1995, A4.
26. Aristotle, *Generation of Animals*, trans. A. L. Peck (Cambridge: Harvard University Press, 1963), 4:iii, 401.
27. Elliott and Endt, "Twins—with Two Fathers," 38.
28. Valerie Hartouni,"Breached Births: Reflections on Race, Gender, and Reproductive Discourses in the 1980s," *Configurations: A Journal of Literature, Science, and Technology* 2, no. 1 (1994): 73–88.
29. Quoted in Hartouni, "Breached Births," 84.
30. Marilyn Strathern, "Displacing Knowledge: Technology and the Consequences for Kinship," in Ginsburg and Rapp, *Conceiving the New World Order*, 354.
31. Quoted in Hartouni, "Breached Births," 83.
32. Haraway, *Modest Witness*, 44.

Part 3   Fictions

Confessions of a Bioterrorist

CHARIS THOMPSON CUSSINS

Subject Position and Reproductive Technologies

THE FOLLOWING STORY about reproductive possibilities is informed and inspired in virtually every detail by conversations with patients and practitioners in infertility clinics during fieldwork that stretches back intermittently to the late 1980s and by my experiences with people and animals in in situ wildlife conservation (parks and community-based conservation) and ex situ (zoo) animal conservation. The common thread running through these sites and explored in this story is the valuing of reproductions: Who and what gets to reproduce where and under what conditions? Why are resources committed to enhancing some human and nonhuman reproductions and to restricting or obliterating others? The story suggests that what is reproductively subversive or liberatory varies from one situation to another. The story makes an ethical argument for movement beyond a single standpoint and tries to show how one's standpoint and its conditions of transgression allow such movement.

Confessions of a Bioterrorist

Mary, a thirty-something white middle-class mother of two, had a daughter and a son, born almost three years apart, who were both in school now. With a Ph.D. in animal physiology, Mary fell into the "postponed-childbearing" model of the highly educated Western women. Her daughter was born when she was in her first postdoctoral position, "unplanned, but wanted," as she and her husband (married five months before the birth) liked to say. Two years later they embarked on the requisite sibling, and nature obliged by providing a boy. On a whim perhaps, recalling the vagaries and imperatives of contraception in the university years, Mary asked to have her tubes tied at her son's birth.

Her son had been delivered minutes previously by planned cesarean section for the sin of remaining head up in her uterus into the thirty-eighth week of pregnancy. Though woozy from the spinal, Mary understood with utter clarity that he was a boy and that somehow she had done what needed to be done. She lay in the operating room, separated from her opened belly by a sterile blue sheet. From the masked, covered, bowed, and bobbing heads that appeared over the sterile screen she knew that at least some of the layers of her severed abdomen remained to be stitched back together again. "It's now or never," she thought, with pre-sedative lucidity. Mary managed somehow to attract the attention of the crowd on the belly side of the screen. "Wait, I want you to tie my tubes while you're in there." The heads looked up, stilled, featureless in masks. Her husband beside her, cradling the new and swaddled baby, laughed, as if to laugh it off. She turned first to him, overwhelmed with joint love for the baby. A drugged sleep and a fairly successful breast-feed later found her in the recovery ward confronted by a doctor reading from her medical notes; the notes plainly confirmed that she had just had her fallopian tubes tied to prevent future conceptions.

Before her son's birth, Mary had moved from her East Coast postdoc to a large western coastal military town where her husband had taken up a tenure-track position. Her infant daughter began nursery school, and Mary followed up a friend's suggestion and applied for a physiology job in the research department at the world-famous zoo next to the naval hospital. She was hired on a temporary basis on a grant from the Friends of the Zoo. Within a week Mary learned from a business school graduate student who was studying the zoo that it was a marvel in corporate self-reinvention, transforming itself overnight from an unprofitable and cruel relic of U.S. envy for French and English menagerie imperialism to a hugely lucrative modern Noah's ark, saving the world's habitat-deprived creatures from going the way of Cuvier's megatherium. She and Dr. Thomson, a woman about a decade older than herself, had the run of the physiology lab, such as it was. Mary quickly became a reproductive physiologist. She worked with a majority of women colleagues on soft money, only tangentially connected to the university by adjunct positions and shared lecture audiences, only somewhat in day-to-day awe and resentment of their few senior male colleagues who ranked in cyberspace and stability of funding by being such things as worldwide species coordinators for highly endangered captive animal populations. Above all, Mary learned about science in a world where science and technology could not yet be taken off the shelf and were not yet regulated. "Empirical," to a zoo reproductive physiologist, meant that one did not yet know how to *obtain* hippo semen, let alone what temperature it needed to be frozen at or how quickly it could safely be thawed. Technological resources were scarce by university lab standards and correspondingly flexible; the microwave oven was used for isolating DNA from condor eggshell lining as well as for heating one's lunch.

Mary's first five years at the zoo saw her grant renewed, the birth of her son (and the tying of her tubes), and the establishment of the frozen zoo. The frozen zoo came in with rhetorical flourish, vociferously promoted by senior scientists and the zoo administration, and echoed back ratcheted up in the media as the panacea to conservation. By freezing germ plasm in perpetuity, it would buy time for human civilization to decide what they wanted/needed to save and how to save it. It would replace the need for or provide the time to reconstruct lost habitat. It was the obvious successor to the embattled Endangered Species Act, riding high on the wave of favor for a genetic conception of "species." And, it was a prospector's dream come true, banking genetic diversity for posterity/prosperity. No one seemed to be asking who or what would benefit, and the funds came pouring in from an enthusiastic urban public.

Dr. Thomson and Mary, having set up the thing, knew that the reality was rather different from the rhetoric. The frozen zoo was a dingy concrete room filled with a motley selection of cooling devices, liquid nitrogen tanks, and liquid-nitrogen-filled freezers. Most of the freezers looked just like the domestic versions, only with a different coolant, disciplined by frequent liquid nitrogen truck visits to replenish the tanks, careful temperature control feedback mechanisms, and a backup generator. The freezers contained spun and washed sperm specimens in freezing straws, some cell preparations, and a growing number of frozen embryos. And in any case, for all their genetic essentialism, those researchers most excited about banking the genetic resources of wild animals still needed the species intact so as to correlate genes with the desired traits they believed they were banking. The majority of wild animals hadn't even been karyotyped; armadillos were not yet drosophila. There were only two rules for the frozen zoo.

First, there had to be a consensus that the species in question was worth saving. Under the new prospecting biodiversity mentality, that was almost no constraint at all. While the Endangered Species Act had exempted from protection, in fine Orwellian fashion, pests and vermin and certain representatives of the "class insecta," frozen zoos dealt with the pestilence-irrelevant world of suspended animation and genetic diversity. Bioprospectors (those "pure" scientists interested in the priceless genetic resources trapped inside millennia of adaptive organisms, just as much as those who were funded by or worked for Merck and the other pharmaceutical bioprospecting conglomerates) told the policy-making community that we didn't yet know enough;

didn't yet know what would turn out to have been worth saving; couldn't speak with scientific certainty. And so, they argued, to be on the safe side (or to maximize opportunity benefits), the whole lot should be saved. Field biologists, on their side, presented policy makers with algorithms for preserving processes maintaining biodiversity, unique habitats, endemic species, and representative ecosystems. Not enough knowledge to adjudicate said one side; not enough time or resources not to adjudicate said the other.

The only other rule was no hybrids. Hybrids were OK in agriculture and domestic breeds of animals; accessions of agricultural plants and seed banks were, after all, the prototype of ex situ gene and germ plasm conservation, and the DNA of hybridized domesticated animals was well represented in frozen tissue banks around the world. But the zoo was freezing to save endangered species, and Mary and Dr. Thomson were sufficiently constrained by their mission to operate under an absolute moratorium on a sideline in on-site hybridization experiments. The Chicago Zoo was just about to start doing interspecies gestational surrogacy, using common domestic species to gestate the embryos of endangered species, but genetic hybridization was absolutely illicit there too. Sometimes zoo spokespeople said hybrids were not "natural," but zoos were themselves sensitive to the charge of being unnatural. Besides, there were too many countries where historically domesticated and feral stocks had blended to produce eagerly sought-after traits. The powerful business and science bioprospecting constituency pushing the frozen zoo didn't want to lean too heavily on the "no human interference" Western understanding of "natural." Many valuable animals existed in non-Western democracies, where different understandings of nature and unreliable interest in compliance with international standards and treaties on conservation prevailed; the politics were simply too delicate, as all conservationists knew, to get hung up on whether or not something was "natural."

Dr. Thomson and Mary had had little luck with freezing the eggs of the large mammals they were especially interested in, and collecting eggs was a tricky business. Access to eggs meant surgical intervention, and any surgery had to be approved by the ethics committee and have zoo veterinary resources committed to it. In practice this restricted egg collection to opportunistic harvesting, when a female animal was going into surgery for an independent procedure. If the animal was still unconscious when the procedure was over, and Mary had prior committee approval, she would be allowed to excise a small amount of ovarian tissue or to aspirate mature eggs. They used this protocol, too, for sperm collection in large or dangerous animals like rhinos, which were electro-ejaculated at surgery, although in the case of rhinos this added thirty to forty minutes to anesthesia time. Animals kept in fields rather than cages at the zoo were also collected at surgery because it was too difficult to get an animal in a large enclosure to ejaculate at the right place and time. This meant getting approval for ruminants, which was always dicey because you could not fast grazers before surgery and the longer the anesthesia, the more likely they were to regurgitate food at surgery.

Mary and Dr. Thomson frequently joked about the manual, mechanical, and electrical means they had perfected to obtain their bestiary of ejaculates. They discovered the precise stroking required to maximize the sperm entering the vas deferens in pheasants. They indulged the bizarre individuality of the male cheetahs, allowing each his specific object of fixation. Of the hand-reared cheetahs, one liked a human female keeper to be in the cage with him and would not ejaculate into the artificial vagina mounted on the crate containing him unless that keeper was present, and a second needed his favorite stuffed animal toy. Of the cheetahs raised in the zoo in social groups, one could be collected by hand as long as he was moved to an empty female cheetah cage where the smell of estrous hormones was sufficient stimulation.

In a serendipitous linkup, the small reproductive physiology lab became the recipient of weekly charitable donations of ovarian tissue from the local cat and dog spay clinic, and an experimental program of in vitro maturation of immature eggs was begun. If they could reliably get immature eggs to ripen in vitro for the dog and cat family—excellent model species—they would gain invaluable experience and enhance the prospects of being able to ripen eggs to fertilize with fresh or thawed semen on demand. This would massively improve the prognosis for a comprehensive frozen embryo bank. Mary's job had developed its own momentum and research agenda, and she was well satisfied.

After Mary had been at the zoo approximately five years and seen her younger child into preschool, four significant things happened in a short space of time. Together these four things were to take her to an altogether different level of involvement with her work and immerse the so reproductively normal Mary in a labyrinth of other reproductions. First, Mary was assigned to take Professor Jung Yingqian, a representative of the Chinese Academy of Science Biodiversity Committee, around the zoo and its research facilities. Second, Mary went to a lecture on population control and met Gabriela Richards, a professor of sociology. Third, she began informally to collaborate with Eva Avery, an embryologist at a nearby human infertility clinic. And fourth, she was sent by the Nature Conservancy to a cattle-ranching area in southwestern New Mexico to get some reproductive data on an endangered species of quail and a threatened leopard frog.

Professor Jung Yingqian followed her itinerary as planned by the Chinese Academy of Sciences. At fifty-two this was her second overseas assignment since becoming the public relations delegate for the Biodiversity Committee of the academy. The first trip had been eighteen months ago, when she had

been a representative to the 1992 United Nations Conference on Environment and Development in Rio de Janeiro. After a quarter of a century as an
invertebrate zoologist, the change in orientation had been a challenge, but
her immaculate English and diplomatic demeanor won her instant favor. In
Rio, Jung was able to describe a vast country blessed with great biogeographic
richness and an unusually high proportion of endemic and relic species that
had survived in the large areas that had not been affected by the glaciation
of the late Tertiary. The Chinese Academy of Sciences was interested in getting pledges of funding for biodiversity conservation, and Jung carefully
swapped promises of Chinese compliance and monitoring for international
investment. This second trip was a follow-up to the Earth Summit; Jung had
spent six days meeting with government ministers, nongovernmental organizations, and funding institutions in Washington, making good on some of the
pledges made in 1992.

From Washington, Professor Jung flew to California. Mary met her at the
airport and spent the rest of the day taking her around the zoo's research facilities before taking her back to the airport for the night flight out again.
Jung was visiting the zoo because an unprecedented deal was being brokered
between the zoo and the Chinese government. The zoo badly wanted a giant
panda, one of the highest-ranked animals in the world in terms of zoo visitor
appeal. But, as part of the new conservation ethos, they neither wanted nor
stood any chance of getting a panda without in some way claiming to be add-
ing to the long-term thriving of this endangered animal. A deal was taking
shape, and it looked like a pair of captive-born pandas would be delivered to
the zoo shortly, in exchange for more than a million dollars, all earmarked
for Chinese panda conservation and habitat restoration. The pandas were to
be a gift of the Chinese government, and the earmarked money was to be a
gift in turn from the zoo. In this way, the Appendix 1 CITES listing and other
bureaucratic obstacles could be circumvented, and zoo gate receipts and
China's international conservation profile would soar. Professor Jung was acting as an ambassador, checking the facilities out and gauging the level of research and animal welfare at the zoo. She was also, of course, estimating the
trustworthiness of the private sector zoo administration and the soundness of
the deal.

Mary found Professor Jung courteous and interested but gleaned little of
either her person or the state of ex situ biodiversity conservation in China
during their seven hours together. Jung conveyed the Chinese government's
desire that panda germ plasm be collected and stored in the frozen zoo, to
complement China's own national germ plasm banking initiative. The zoo research department's director agreed to this request by signing on a dotted line
over lunch. Mary enjoyed the day's break from her usual routine but thought

little about it afterward. Five months later, however, she received a letter asking her to take responsibility for oversight of the panda germ plasm and cell lines. A Chinese physiologist would be arriving with the pandas to do the cell cultures and any gamete preparations, and Mary (thanks to her personal contact with Professor Jung) was formally requested to become the independent monitor of the well-being of the precious tissue. Her colleagues at the research department at the zoo were amused by the letter and urged Mary to take up her new "policing" role. With good humor, and a genuine feeling of having had some honor conferred on her, Mary accepted the job.

Mary's law enforcement role had no practical consequences whatsoever until the Chinese physiologist had visited and successfully ensconced the panda tissue in the cryobank. From then on, an additional security system was added to the door to the frozen zoo, and Mary was the lone possessor (aside from the zoo director and the Chinese Academy of Sciences) of the combination required to open the lock. The janitor could activate it at six every evening, but no one could get access to the room again the next morning until Mary opened the lock. This was not quite as onerous as it seemed, for the lock could be deactivated electronically via modem from her home. Nonetheless, it changed her relation to her workplace and to the contents of the freezers, instilling in her a combination of proprietary interest and faint disgust at the idea that she was the person keeping out whatever it was that should not be let in. She noticed, but only on reflection, that she accepted security for the germ plasm as readily as she accepted the predominant rhetoric of fear governing her children's movements in her suburban neighborhood, where she had equally little idea from whom or what she was protecting them.

Lectures in the endowed public lecture hall at the zoo were usually book-signing affairs attended by the more earnest and older, wealthier sector of the zoo membership through advance purchase of tickets. A smattering of researchers and students drifted over from the zoo or the university for most of them. Presentations by white women primatologists with worldwide followings for their Edenic lives in the bush compiling soap-operatic genealogies of individual chimpanzees or orangutans were sellout events. Tales of swimming with dolphins or living among elephants were equally popular. Occasionally there would be a lecture on a conservation-related topic that did not directly concern the ecology or natural history of an individual species or ecosystem. One such lecture was given in the fall of 1994 by a prominent Australian conservationist and public policy adviser. Mary attended his lecture on human population control and conservation along with an almost 100 percent turnout of the zoo research division.

The talk began, crescendoed, ended; the audience clapped heartily, and an intermission before questions was announced. The speaker was still standing in the middle of the stage, grinning and swaying with bravado, as Mary got up from her seat. A zoo official hustled him offstage, but his final slogan about the magic bullet of conservation—condoms for humans, of course—hung in the air like something from the nearby naval boot camp: "Elastic is too drastic but plastic is fantastic!" Mary made her way to the ladies' lavatories at the back of the building that only zoo personnel knew about, glad to be missing the usual line. The woman who had been sitting next to her in the auditorium was right behind her. Mary hesitated as she held open the bathroom door for the other woman, and the woman offered an explanation in a British accent. "I've given up waiting for architects of public places to work out that it takes longer to pee if you have to bare your bum first; I always look for someone who knows where they're going, and nine times out of ten there's a loo stashed somewhere else, reserved for insiders." She laughed and smiled all at once and, waiting by the outside door, gestured Mary into the one cubicle. Mary went in, grinning, agreeing, wondering to herself what made her stand out as an insider. They exchanged more smiles as Mary came out and the English woman went in, and Mary decided to take her time washing her hands on the pretext that the woman might need showing back around to the front of the auditorium. Together they walked out of the bathroom and joined the crowd buying plastic glasses of California wine.

The woman's name was Dr. Gabriela Richards, daughter of first-generation Caribbean Londoners, father returned to Jamaica some time ago, mother and aunt still in Battersea. She was the only English black woman in her year to have gotten a graduate place at Oxford, and she was now a lecturer in sociology at University College, London. How long had she been in California, Mary asked. Just a couple of weeks, since the beginning of the academic year. Was she here to stay? No, she was on a one-year fully funded sabbatical to research contemporary American issues in race and ethnicity. Weren't there any race issues in England? Yes, all too many, but a different colonial history and little or no shared national identity—Irish, Pakistanis, Bangladeshis, Sikhs, Caribbean Islanders—but some things were the same, the comparison would be productive. If you were black in the United Kingdom academy, did you have to work on race and ethnicity to get listened to? It helped, but, if you think about it, you can talk about anything under that umbrella, and in the United Kingdom we use umbrellas a lot.

Mary asked Gabriela what she thought of the lecture they had just heard. "Oh, mostly it was predictable, don't you think?" replied Gabriela. "An Aussie male worried sick that the Indonesians would manage in the twenty-first century what the Aborigines never even threatened: dilute the racial purity of low birth rate white Australians and end the illusion of Australia as an outpost Western economy with Western living standards; the underpopulated continent could absorb the human settlement, too, and he knows that." But wasn't he talking generally about protecting animal habitats by restricting human population growth? "If you think so; seems to me human population's nearly always a red herring as a starting place—educate women, work out what ecological role people play in each ecosystem, then we can talk human population numbers—and as he said himself, it's the "ecological footprint" that counts; how much space and resources each person uses up . . . isn't it funny the way men use these primordial metaphors—couldn't you just picture the huge white Western ecological footprint on the dusts of the northern Rift Valley being excavated in some distant millennium by a new family of Leakeys and their black field assistants?" Mary was laughing again, off balance, enjoying herself.

By this time three of Mary's colleagues had joined them, also with plastic glasses of wine in hand. Mary introduced Gabriela, omitting to mention that they had only just met. Mary's boss, the species coordinator for the Przewalski's horse, Professor Walker, was among the three zoo researchers. They were discussing a risky effort to reintroduce the horse into its former range in Mongolia. Mary's colleagues were assessing the prospects for the repatriation given Mongolia's attempts to move to a multiparty political system. The chance to acquire an international profile by being associated with a high-publicity conservation campaign was being fiercely contested by the different potential party candidates. Professor Walker was skeptical about the genuine commitment to the conservation success of the process, though.

He was worried that the Mongolian planes that were not IATA-certified would not be safe for the horses. Elaborating for Gabriela, he said, "Moving animals safely is the stock and trade of zoos; its the one thing we know we do well. But once those horses leave Beijing, that's as far as the zoo's network of expertise penetrates." He said he was worried too that the horses would end up either being corralled in an airplane hangar in Ulan Bator once the foreign press had left town, or be let loose onto the plains only to die out again from being genetically swamped by the domestic and feral horses there with whom they could easily interbreed. He had modeled the number of Przewalski's horses needed to ward off the threat of genetic dilution, but the model relied on the subsequent tracking and contracepting of hybrid horses in the target area. Gabriela, visibly agog, whispered to Mary, "'Repatriation?' 'Contracept?'—are you people the animal division of the INS?" Mary explained to Gabriela that the entire Przewalski's horse population was descended from thirteen ancestral captive individuals and that the zoo kept tabs on the whole pedigree, now thirteen or fourteen generations. "Eat your hearts out, anthropologists," muttered Gabriela. The thousand or so extant horses spread out in zoos around the world were one of the great successes of ex situ conservation; each horse was carefully monitored and match-made according to genetic representation of the four surviving matrilineages. They were one of the species Mary and Dr. Thomson collected semen from by electro-ejaculation at surgery.

The hand bell was being rung to call the audience back to the auditorium for questions. Mary asked Gabriela one last question as they returned to their seats. "Where are you going to be studying this year?" "Well," said Gabriela, "after the conversation we have just had, I think I might try the zoo." "Great," said Mary. During questions they exchanged e-mail addresses on sections of Mary's wine-stained napkin that she pulled out of her pocket.

Gabriela began visiting the zoo research department about once a week, for a morning or afternoon in the lab, or a lecture or veterinary procedure. Sometimes she just watched and listened; occasionally she would ask questions or interview people. Mary and Gabriela always had lunch or a coffee together on these visits and often went through the back entrance of the research buildings into the zoo proper to see the animals. Gabriela was as interested in who came to zoos as in the animals themselves. She commented on the high number of African American and Latino families and pointed out to Mary that all the black girls at the zoo had elaborate plaits or cornrows and barrettes and hair fixtures, not the middle-class (straightened, parted just once, and virtually unadorned) hairstyles worn by the few black girls at Mary's children's school. Gabriela joked to Mary about how subversive it was for her to be coming to see caged animals as an upwardly mobile black. "Like a successful black homeowner going camping in the wilderness for pleasure!" she said. Mary grinned and winced; that was one of the things Mary really enjoyed doing with her husband.

Mary began to decipher a hitherto hidden reality around her in the comings and goings of people. Gabriela in turn was more and more drawn to the interfaces of human skills, technology, and animals that piece by piece built up the facts of Mary's research world. And she was more and more interested in the comparisons and interactions between the ways humans and animals were sorted and valued through access to and constraints on reproductive possibilities. Mary's and Gabriela's main medium of communication was e-mail, and after a month or so of seemly missives, their correspondence became increasingly playful. Mary saved all Gabriela's messages and knew that they were friends.

About the time that they started spending most of their zoo-visiting lunchtimes at the nonhuman primate exhibits, Gabriela started addressing Mary as "the Virgin" in her e-mails. Mary complained vigorously in her response to the first such message, pointing out that she had had no say in her naming and that, anyway, she was not one. Gabriela wrote back that it was an acronym celebrating Mary's daring in deciding in surgical delicto flagrante to contracept herself. Gabriela now used the active verb "to contracept," which the animal researchers used, as often as she could for humans, so as, she said to Mary, to be able to see through the euphemisms of choice that drenched all human discussions of contraception. But, Mary wanted to know, what did the acronym stand for? Already Mary could tell that she was going to let Gabriela get away with this, like everything else Gabriela teased her about. "Virtual Impregnation Required; Gonads Inaccessible Now" came back the one-line response.

Pygmy chimpanzees, bonobo chimps, *Pan paniscus*. The pygmy, or bonobo, chimps were Mary's and Gabriela's favorite animals in the zoo. The "habitat" exhibit was less ghastly than many primate exhibits, and the individuals on display were alternated so as to give each bonobo a break from public human scrutiny. Nonetheless, two or three hours watching these animals confirmed Mary's feeling that, endangerment notwithstanding, captivity and display was inappropriate for this species. The first day they spent on the bench at the bonobo exhibit they watched an oldish-looking male walk off and try to position himself to pee so that he wouldn't lose face with or offend either his fellow bonobos on one side of the glass or the public on the other. "Poor sod," said Gabriela.

The "bonobo bench" became Mary's and Gabriela's locale for serious discussions of reproductions. Gabriela spoke with the primate behaviorists at the zoo and some of the itinerant graduate students and other researchers working on nonhuman primates. She found out that the boundary between what humans and nonhuman primates were supposed to be able to do was still the Holy Grail, and still shifting continuously. Now that language was no longer the separating criterion, the researchers were looking to conscious cognitive and social capabilities that carried eerie echoes of justifications of slavery and colonialism, apartheid and prohibitions on miscegenation to Gabriela: the ability to have abstract thought, to self-represent, consciously to navigate by cognitive maps, to maintain complex social relationships over space and time, to delegate work to other animals and things, to engage in symbolic cultural transmission. Mary tried to convince Gabriela of the social and moral virtues, as well as the truth value, of decreasing the cognitive gap between humans and nonhuman animals. Gabriela in turn tried to make Mary see that if you were going to keep looking for this gap, you had better make sure that all human beings fell on the right side of it, because history showed that it was by no means self-evident that they all would.

Gabriela also spent a morning with the reproductive endocrinologist, Dr. Patten, who was a specialist in great ape and pachyderm fertility. Bemused, Dr. Patten tried to think of compelling examples of great ape infertility, teenage pregnancy, and homosexuality for Gabriela. Mostly, thought Dr. Patten, these were conditions that showed up under stress, in captivity or, in the case of homosexuality, as a means of brokering conflict. The incidence of infertility among the great apes in the wild was so low that primatologists usually measured the end of subadulthood and the beginning of adulthood for females by the onset of the first pregnancy. Captive great apes such as Penny Patterson's sign language–using gorilla, Koko, however, quite often had problems getting pregnant. Many of Biruté Galdikas's ex-captive orangutans were sexually precocious, becoming pregnant while still of an age that was labeled by Galdikas as "adolescence" for the wild orangutans of Kalimantan and leaving little space between subsequent births. And a groundbreaking study had just been done on female/female sexuality among the masterfully reconciliatory bonobos here at the zoo by Franz de Waal and his students. Gabriela thanked Dr. Patten profusely for her time and ran to get Mary. "Drop what you're doing, Our Lady Maria, let's go!"

On the bonobo bench Gabriela talked fast and furious. "It's all there," she told Mary; "all the links are there." "The ethologists thought the problem was anthropomorphism and that the human-centeredness had to be purged when we studied nonhuman primate behavior. And we've been struggling ever since on how to bring back in the knowledge gained by experience of, and empathy with, the apes. But "bias" was never one way only; the zoomorphism was always there too; the traffic had to go both ways and told us what was noble and what pathological; which animals *and* which people were sui generis and so worth caring for . . . " "Hold on, hold on," said Mary. "What's been going on? I'm completely lost. Dr. Patten told you this?" "No, but she told me that the apes enact the sins of modernity too, and do so pace Margaret Mead— did you know that unnatural orangutan upbringings create dysfunctional adolescents who have teenage pregnancies and don't understand optimal birth spacing? Doesn't that sound a bit like a racialized narrative of the reproductive predicament of the urban poor and the developing world that you've heard somewhere before? There's a primatologist who calls these orangutans 'rehabilitants' when she tries to return them to the wild—we blame their social environment, but that environment is nonetheless criminalizing."

"But there's more," Gabriela continued. "I've cracked the problem of how to become a scarce and highly valued reproducer. My great grandparents were owned, and so was their reproduction; their children were chattel, someone else's property. Like cattle or chickens, right? But more flexible. The endangered animals here all have highly valued reproduction; in fact, we even swallow disgust that anyone would place these amazing bonobos in a zoo in the name of the scarcity and value of their offspring to be. We don't ask, 'How did this ape in front of me come to be more precious than my great grandmother?' because the answer is self-evident—or so we think—scarcity of the species. That's the main sorting concept between indentured humans/domesticated animals on the one side and free humans/wild animals on the other, right now. But if you think about human reproduction, we go to extraordinary lengths to enable wealthy infertile couples to reproduce their one or two infinitely precious offspring; well, lo and behold, the most upwardly mobile of all the apes, the quasi language–using Koko of the Palo Alto Hills, turns out to have been infertile and to have needed reproductive technologies. She surpassed my great-granny in recognized cultural capital, and while granny was dropping babies in the sugarcane, of unasked-for paternity, to increase plantation property, Koko was getting the chance to bear an intrinsically valued child, no matter the cost. QED!" Gabriela was ablaze and excited. "And, what's more, it turns out that the Greeks were right about homosexuality and a stable polity; only difference is, if we believe the bonobos, it was the women, not the men, who kept it all together!"

Mary queried and protested, of course, as she always did. She replied that the reproductive politics of endangered species were far more complicated than Gabriela thought; that the hierarchy of animals had its own politics; that hybrid and domestic strains often got the most resources; that many conservationists were more interested in dynamic systems' well-being and process and variety and in their own way were a major force for diversity and could be thought of as the multiculturalists in a field dominated by the often nativist, preservationist types. She also said, thinking of couples she knew who were going through infertility treatments, that seeking medical help for infertility did not at all mean that your reproduction was highly valued or that you had vast resources.

While Gabriela was doing fieldwork at the zoo, Mary started to collaborate with a woman named Eva Avery, embryologist and senior lab technician at a nearby infertility clinic. They met at a Tap Pharmaceuticals–sponsored lecture on the new techniques for maturing unripe human eggs in vitro, which was held at the university Faculty Club. Mary, Dr. Thomson, and Dr. Patten were there in connection with their spay clinic project. Eva was there to get any tips going to help her set up in vitro egg maturation to improve her clinic's egg donation program. If she could freeze ovarian tissue obtained from willing donors at the time of tubal ligation, then she could defrost and mature eggs for donor egg cycles of in vitro fertilization without having to go through the costly process of getting donor's and recipient's menstrual cycles synchronized. It would also relieve the expense and risk to the donor of going to surgery specially for egg retrieval. Like the eggs of other large mammals, ripe human ova were very difficult to freeze and thaw successfully. Eva also had another motivation for acting fast. She had a case of a young woman who was about to undergo chemotherapy. The woman did not have children yet but did not want to lose the chance of having them in the future. As she had no partner in mind at present, the possibility of making in vitro embryos and freez-ing those for future implantation was not there. Eva was hoping successfully to be able to freeze some ovarian tissue for subsequent in vitro egg matura-tion, when the time was right.

Dr. Patten, in her rather gruff manner, introduced herself and Mary to Eva. Dr. Patten had long believed that human infertility clinics and zoo re-productive endocrinologists and physiologists should share expertise, and was she envious of the resources that endocrinologists and embryologists at infer-tility clinics had. The clinic where Eva worked had opened about a year ago and was unique in the area for its huge technical budget. The clinic had been designed especially for infertility procedures and included egg and andrology labs that connected directly to the operating room, and a video linkup that enabled patients in the operating room to watch their gametes and embryos as they were being manipulated in the lab. Dr. Patten began the conversa-tion by "reminding" Eva that the biochemical urinalysis that was a mainstay of choreographing the timing of infertility procedures had been developed for nonhuman animals. "It's not just mice and hamster ova that you got from us." To Mary's surprise, Eva rose to the challenge and offered to come down and look at the facilities at the zoo and see if she had any equipment she no longer needed, or reagents that had passed their human sell-by date that would still be fine for experimenting on spay clinic tissue. She also offered to show Mary, Dr. Thomson, and Dr. Patten around her labs and teach them what she knew about micromanipulation and freezing and let them practice on her teaching microscopes.

Later in the week, at the bonobo bench, Gabriela debriefed Mary. "How come you didn't invite me to the lecture?" "It didn't occur to me that you'd be interested in a Tap Pharmaceuticals event." "But they're going to freeze ovarian tissue with undeveloped follicles in it; and girl's ovaries contain germ plasm from early on in gestation. That means they could use the ovaries of aborted female fetuses and stillborn female fetuses to help menopausal women get pregnant, couldn't they? Did they talk about that? That could really screw up the succession of generations!" Mary assured her that no scientists in America would want to touch anything to do with abortion. "But why?" in-sisted Gabriela; "you could easily imagine it being marketed for right-to-lifers the same as organ donation: 'Your chance to turn death back into the gift of life.' Hey, we could even bank the unripe eggs and racialize and meritocratize them like they do the sperm in sperm banks: 'Sample number 7B: mother never lived, but had she lived, would have been attractive black woman with Nobel prize who played varsity volleyball' . . . " "Stop!" demanded Mary. "No one's going to start farming or raiding abortuses any time soon."

Eva and Mary visited each other fairly frequently. Mary acquired micromanipulation skills that enabled her to insert a single sperm under the zona pellucida of an egg, using a hand-blown micropipette, a high-powered scope, mouth suction, and a little acid tyrodes. Stunning a fast-swimming sperm by thwacking it on the tail with the pipette tip and then sucking it up the pipette tail first was the most difficult skill, and it took several sessions on the teaching scope to get it right. They used "reagents" to practice on, arguing that they were acquiring skills, not experimenting. "Reagents" were patients' gametes that had passed into the "junk" category for such reasons as failure to fertilize, religious objections of source patients to freezing or donation of excess gametes, polyspermic fertilization, necrosis, arrested development. Eva proclaimed Mary proficient and stopped her training the day she got what appeared to be a viable fertilization. Eva destroyed the two pro–nuclei-stage embryos the next morning, despite the temptation to watch them grow. She did not want to dabble in life after death and was rid of the pre-embryos before they entered the "resurrected" category of embryos, with all the legal and moral registrations of the lab that would bring back into effect.

Eva, for her part, acquired access at the zoo lab to cat and dog ovarian tissue and to premises where it was not contravening OSHA or Animal Welfare regulations to work on nonhuman gametes other than frozen mouse or hamster eggs. Eva let Mary have a decent haul of superfluous clinic equipment, in exchange for a day spent doing the cleaning and inventory in preparation for Eva's in vitro lab certification. During the course of that day, Mary found out a little about how Eva had ended up in the field and some possible reasons why she was making a connection with reproductive technologies at the zoo.

Eva was the mother of two girls, born three months apart, because it took Eva a few more cycles than her partner to get pregnant using the rudimentary turkey baster version of artificial insemination that they had both used sixteen years ago. Wanting a family, but not being able to decide who should bear the baby, she and her partner had decided that twins would be fine. The sperm came from a mutual friend, masturbated into sterile specimen cups, in the bathroom at Eva's apartment. The friend liked masturbating and hated the idea of paternity, so what seemed to Eva in retrospect to have been an appallingly risky and low-tech business had gone smoothly. The girls were great, too. Eva had custody of both of the teenagers now, although it was not called that because there had been no contest over where they should go when Eva and her partner split up. The girls wanted to stay put and to stay together.

Eva had been trained as a cytogeneticist and had received the biggest shock of her life when she karyotyped a chimpanzee somatic cell for the first time, in connection with a project for the Center for Disease Control. She had simply not been prepared for the similarity between human and chimp chromosomes. Her daughters' conceptions, and a fervent commitment to safe options for lesbian and gay parenting in the age of AIDS, had subsequently induced Eva to become involved in a local sperm bank, which in turn eventually led to her applying for and accepting a job in an infertility clinic. She was an excellent technician and welcomed the involvement of patients in their treatment. The physician directors of the clinic did not want to lose her, and she enjoyed a large degree of autonomy in the lab.

Gabriela met Eva on a couple of occasions and got on well with her. One evening Eva came down to the zoo labs after work to try a new egg-thawing regimen with Mary. Mary's children were camping with her husband for four days, and so Mary was free to work late. Gabriela came down too, armed with the accoutrements of her latest enthusiasm, a video camera and tripod. Gabriela was going to take some more ethnographic film of Eva and Mary at work, she said. Mary pretended not to notice Gabriela's incorrigible hand in the label scribbled on the spine of the videocassette: "CVS (Cogito Virgo Sum); Parts I and II." CVS was the chorionic villi sampling procedure that Eva had taught Mary a couple of weeks ago. In humans it was used as an earlier diagnostic test for genetic anomalies than amniocentesis. Its advantage was that it allowed "therapeutic abortions" to be carried out in the first trimester of pregnancy, rather than well into the second. Mary and Dr. Thomson agreed to learn how to do it on the zoo animals so as to collaborate with the geneticists, who wanted to establish some baseline data on inherited diseases and inbreeding. Gabriela had filmed the session just because of her fascination with the expression "therapeutic abortion" and the idea of incest— inbreeding—in nonhumans. At the bonobo bench, though, she had later told Mary that she felt as if she had seen the web of constraint and possibility extending into and out of the previously inscrutable, inseparable bodies of mother and fetus; had seen the opening, separating, and attaching of facts and values by linking biological skills and technology to the fetus via its extracted and cultured cells. She couldn't stop thinking about the proliferating trails moving between in utero and ex utero. "Mary, Mary," Gabriela intoned almost plaintively, "what I didn't realize is that there are so many ways to be a Virgin."

Gabriela's filming of the thawing that night became another entry in her anthology of taken virginities; of trails in and out of impregnation and gestation. After they had finished their work, the three women decided to go down into the zoo proper. They used the microwave to reheat some coffee, which they put in a flask, and locking up behind themselves (including relocking the frozen zoo that Mary had deactivated to allow them to work late), they made for the bonobo bench. The bonobos were nowhere to be seen, asleep somewhere probably. The women sat down anyway, and the indefatigable

Gabriela began to talk. As she talked, Mary realized that Gabriela was talking about herself, something that, for all her openness and loquacity, Gabriela rarely did. The dark and the late hour and the privacy of the abandoned public place made for intimacy.

It turned out that Gabriela had a northern European lover waiting for her back in London. She joked to Mary and Eva that she had been so successful in acquiring the academy's baggage of mobility—posh accent, good hair, short fingernails, dowdy clothes—that she had selected herself out of all but a handful of intellectuals in her choice of mate. "I really like him. I'm even into the whole genetic parenting thing; I'd like to make babies with him—or one, anyway. But this is what I'm scared of: you hear of those tricks of nature where a black person and a white person produce a blond-haired child. Of course I'd love the child anyway, but when I think of being a mother to a school-aged child, I imagine a black kid in his suburban school having everything I didn't have, but being able to resist at the same time; you know, a dose of 'in your face' blackness." They were all laughing, and the warmth disarmed Gabriela. "So this is what you two can do for me: can you use your reproductive technologies to engineer a bit of genetic essentialism? Do you think you can make sure my baby is black enough if you grow the embryo in the lab? I'll get Anders to Fed Ex us a few cryovials of semen, and we can have conception without penetration for racial purity, just like those Mongolian horses of Dr. Walker's . . . " Gabriela, Eva, and Mary began speculating about what they would have to do; how long it would be before gene therapy could be deployed in that sort of way; and whether the conglomerate of things that made someone count as black enough in different countries today was the kind of thing that would ever be amenable to therapeutic incision or excision from chromosomes. "The only gene therapy procedures we have at the moment involve biopsying an entire cell from an embryo, and then, if the problem genes are present or if the chromosomes are male in sex-linked diseases, we just throw the embryo away; if they are absent or the embryo is a girl for sex-linked diseases, we go ahead and implant," lamented Eva. "These procedures are not exactly fine-tuned yet."

"Well, that's my Virgin fantasy; what about you two?" said Gabriela, deflecting the intimacy from herself without stifling it. Mary denied having any, but Eva immediately began. "You must know why I'm here so much; what my interest is?" Gabriela and Mary looked nonplussed but sat up in anticipation for the revelation. "You know the micromanipulation techniques we use for severe male infertility that I taught you, Mary? If you think about it, you manually put the sperm inside the egg for fertilization. So we don't need sperm morphology for fertilization anymore; it's just the chromosomes and a few activating proteins, right? What I would really love to do is to take two eggs and fertilize one with the other. Not as the only way to get pregnant; not as parthenogenesis; no cloning; fully normal meiotic recombinant reproduction; just combining two eggs, rather than having to involve sperm. There are some guys who tried it on mice and found that there was a problem with the placenta—but if it becomes possible eventually, I want to know how to do it." Gabriela was impressed. Mary was shocked. "Is it legal?" demanded Mary, "and what responsibility do I have if you've been doing this in my lab?" Eva reassured her; Mary settled into the idea, and the three of them sat quiet for a while, sipping their coffee and mentioning the need to go home as it was getting late.

A scuffling from the bonobo exhibit saw a female bonobo come into view, dimly lit by the night-lights on the visitors' side of the glass. The bonobo peed decorously and disappeared from view again. Mary found the night prowling strangely moving; exactly what she might have done. "That's mine," she said quietly. "Your what?" asked Gabriela. "I've just thought of my Virgin fantasy." "Tell us, Mother of Us All!" exclaimed Gabriela, delighted and fully animated once more. Eva grinned, too, and leaned forward. Mary looked shy, which was normal for her, but began. "Well, I work all day with these highly endangered species, and their gametes and embryos. Meanwhile, my human reproducing is over. But my pituitary hasn't got the message and churns out the same old hormones; I plump up a juicy endometrium every month, of proven fertility, and then shed it in that endless cycle of sapping and waste. I could use that uterine lining for some of the embryos; I could gestate endangered animals; "donor embryo, or gestational surrogacy" as they call it in your field, Eva. I wouldn't kid myself I was being saintly; but that's the whole point about the Virgin, isn't it? You can't know—even if the emissary Gabriela comes to you in your reveries!—which gestations will save the world. The ethics of rearing the baby myself or reintroducing it to zoo bonobos or the wild would be hellish to decide about," Mary continued, fast. "It's the erotics, really, that's the fantasy. Having a bonobo growing inside me out of my own proteins into a different species; the honor of the international VIP guest pregnancy; watching my stomach stretched from the inside by furry hands and feet; breastfeeding an ape child . . . the politics could come later." Gabriela hugged Mary; Eva said "Yuck!"; they all laughed. Mary felt a mixture of exhilaration and embarrassment, for having spoken. "This is wonderful; we have to get all of these down on the camera next week; CVS Part III!" declared Gabriela, dancing with pleasure, as the three women started toward the zoo exit. In fact though, all three of them knew that the fantasies they had just exchanged would not ever become part of Gabriela's ethnographic record; the moment of confession had passed.

Shortly afterward, in early May 1995, a guy with a neatly trimmed beard and cowboy boots came to the zoo, and Professor Walker brought him into the lab to meet Mary. Mary was told that he was a field biologist with the Arizona chapter of the Nature Conservancy. Thinking of what Gabriela would say, she decided that the cowboy boots were part of a uniform that he imagined gave him access to the southwestern rural communities among which he worked. He seemed nice, actually; that disarming and compelling combination of enthusiastic, earnest, and nerdy that characterized many conservation biologists. Why there weren't more prominent women in conservation biology Mary didn't know. The men were outdoors types but feminized in many ways: nontraditional career trajectories, mission scientists, activists for a more just and more interrelated world. Mary was being offered the chance to go and stay on a cattle ranch in southwestern New Mexico for a few days to collect tissue samples from an endangered species of quail and the threatened Chiricahuan leopard frog.

Mary wasn't sure whether to go, but Professor Walker was excited. At something of a juncture in his own life, he was pushing formally and informally for links to be made between the ex situ and in situ conservation communities. "It's the age of unholy alliances," he told Mary in his office that afternoon. "Five years ago the Nature Conservancy would have bought out the cattle ranches those animals are on and left the wildlife in preservationist exclusion to flourish or flounder. Or at least they would have bought conservation easements on the land, exchanging cattle for quail, ranchers for curators. Now this guy is on the same side as the cowboys, working for them, helping them get the science they need to benefit from the wildlife on their land, as a side product of reclaiming their grasslands. Their existence is marginal, and many of them are in debt. They're going for increasing stocking rates of cattle *and* wildlife species, to stop the carrying capacity for *ranchers* dropping to zero and forcing them off the land! A couple of months ago the cowboy president of the group went on TV telling the nation that now that the Soviet Union had fallen, cooperation over land use was possible—we could be witnessing a new era in American politics and history, Mary. Please go. I'd go myself in a shot if it wasn't such a critical time for the Przewalski's reintroduction."

Mary was sitting in the middle of the front bench seat of a truck, about an hour before dawn, driving on a superior version of a dirt road toward the Arizona/New Mexico/Mexican border and Guadalupe Canyon. Breakfast at the ranch where she was staying had been a plethora of fried foods served at 5 A.M., which her sleepy stomach had refused. The tall, gaunt, and handsome rancher who was their host drank milk by the glassful, perhaps to loosen his stiff, cowboy bow legs that, together with his poor hearing, made him seem older than his fifty-nine years; the visitors drank tepid instant coffee. Mary and the two men in the truck were on their way to meet with a local Fitz-carraldo type who pumped considerable land management skills, private money (Mary gathered that he was an heir to some part of a beer fortune), and en-thusiasm into the area. On the way they were going to stop off at a colony of the leopard frogs, where Mary was hoping to get the frog tissue samples she needed. She would also take some samples from the non-native bullfrogs that were preying on the leopard frogs, and the geneticists could give her some hybridization and genetic drift information when she got back. Yesterday she had gone with the TNC guy to set traps and get the quail samples, so things were going well.

The altitude of about five thousand feet gave them a view from the truck in all directions of the desert scrub and tobosa grasslands, the coniferous peaks rising to eighty-five hundred feet, and the canyons and riparian corridors filled with sycamores and cottonwoods, amid the lichen-covered rocky semiarid landscape. Dim shadows and light were cast on one side by the full moon still high in the western sky, and from the other side by the sun not yet up but already lighting the underside of the clouds and the tops of the hills on the eastern horizon. Mary could not remember seeing so much space; it was, as they say, breathtakingly beautiful.

On one side of Mary, at the wheel, sat her cattle-ranching host, Bill. She watched his weathered face, which was just a few inches from hers, remem-bering the tales of mountain lion hunting he had told the night before, at the dinner of more fried meat, which itself had followed an ad lib saying of grace. Suburban Mary had listened to the hunting stories intently, confused by the mixture of killing, love of the animals, and the give and take of the land. What had happened to the Indian and Mexican inhabitants of the area whose photos adorned the ranch walls, Mary wondered, and what role had they played in the ecosystem of the area in previous centuries? Clearly it was a long time since this area had been wilderness, whatever that meant, even though it was so sparsely populated. The land now had so much brush that it only supported one cow per fifty acres, and it took about fifty thousand acres for a family of four to scrape a living off ranching. When Mary heard the stock-ing rates, she understood why the human fertility rates of one or two chil-dren (and in some families, a single girl child—like Professor Jung) were so low. Only the Fitzcarraldo guy had a luxurious third child. Mary should get these people in contact with the Australian population control guru. This was a rural Protestant population that obviously knew how to use condoms or ab-stinence; the land was not productive enough to justify dousing it with many exogenous chemicals, so it was not likely to be infertility caused by contami-nation of the water. On the other side of Mary in the truck sat a board mem-ber of one of the major private funding foundations. He was also a prominent member of the East African conservation community and a pioneer in community-based conservation, it turned out.

Several hours later, but still only the middle of the morning, they were sitting around a table drinking more coffee (this time freshly ground, with hot milk) at the Fitzcarraldo guy's ranch. The frog tissue samples were safely in their Styrofoam containers in the back of the truck. The bearded Fitzcarraldo had shown them the areas that had been burned as part of a let-burn and prescribed burn policy that flew in the face of fifty years of Smoky the Bear "no fire" land management in the United States. The three men had examined the burn, discussed its heat, and marveled at the regeneration of young palatable grasses and seedlings in its wake. By burning lands in rotation, they hoped to improve cattle-stocking rates and fight brush encroachment. To burn systematically, or to rest land from grazing, landowners and federal agencies had to cooperate, so that cattle could be moved off one person's or agency's land and onto another's when necessary.

The second proactive element of the cattle ranchers' group was what they called "grass banking." Gabriela would like that expression, thought Mary; sounds wonderfully pre- (or perhaps post-) capitalist. Grass banking involved the conservation organization buying conservation easements from ranchers, exchanging promises not to develop or subdivide their land in the future, for the lost land value as calculated by land assessors. This hypothetical dollar value was then redeemable for the use of charitably held grasslands where the rancher could graze his or her cattle while resting or burning or reseeding his or her own land. The idea, Mary was told, was that the whole thing could be managed locally, be advantageous to both conservation and the local economy, and be self-sustaining. This did not sound like the usual conservation debates, on which she and her zoo colleagues based their assessments of the dismal future facing biodiversity. It was more than "sustainable use," and it certainly wasn't preservationism. She would have plenty to tell Professor Walker when she returned.

Fitzcarraldo had also shown them his new landing strip and hangar that stood atop a peak immediately behind his house. To build the strip, Fitzcarraldo had simply had the top taken off the mountain. He might as well have topped a boiled egg with a silver spoon, thought Mary, struck by the scale and daring of it all. Mary sat at the table, only half paying attention to the three men. It occurred to her that if she drove out straight after lunch she could return to California a day early. She decided that that was what she would do—call her family from Tucson airport and get in late tonight. Suddenly Mary's attention was brought back to the table. The East African guy was proposing something outrageous, and Fitzcarraldo and Bill were nodding seriously and joining in with their own elaborations. Mary turned a little in her seat to face the East African. The man spoke with the clipped, neutral accent of a descendant of the British colonial elite who had refused himself to take on the more drawling expatriate version of the queen's English and the colonial relations that went with it. He seemed to be making two equally preposterous suggestions.

First, the East African was equating the grass banking to nomadic pastoralism and was inviting representatives of Bill's and Fitzcarraldo's group to come out to East Africa to learn from pastoralists there about drought refuges and intensive but shifting, communal grazing and how to improve cattle-stocking rates by moving cattle with the wildlife migrations. In turn he was suggesting sending some Maasai out to see if they could learn anything from the New Mexican cowboys. Mary was startled by the idea that Maasai would get on the plane to check out some Americans' ranching operations and then flit back again to instruct their novice western counterparts in how to get grass banking right—the combination of modern mobility with traditional land tenure, along with the reverse of the usual direction of flow of expertise and information, was galvanizing. Fitzcarraldo looked about ready to book his next vacation.

Bill was so involved in working out the details of the other suggestion that his East African safari itinerary was temporarily on hold. The other suggestion was that Bill and his neighbors should take delivery of a cargo of elephants. The East African knew a few places where there were too many elephants to be compatible with other land uses and biodiversity—somewhere near Mount Kenya, it seemed. Rather than cull them or have them starve themselves and a lot of the other species that depended on their presence for grass regeneration, he was proposing to ship twenty or so over. He reckoned they could stand the winter cold, coming from the slopes of Mount Kenya, and he guaranteed that they would chomp their way through thousands of tons of unpalatable brush and open up grassland for Bill's cattle. What was more, he was claiming that rhinos or elephants were just what was missing from this landscape. The Pleistocene extinctions and recent overhunting had wiped out the large browsers that this vegetation evolved with and depended on for succession and its variety of habitats. Elephants would fill an empty ecological role and restore diversity-creating dynamism to the system. Mary was reeling. Sending in pronghorn or Coos deer was one thing, or even bringing in some wartime goats to eat what nothing else would eat. But savannah elephants? The most exotic of the exotics! Preservationism was antediluvian; sustainable use had been surpassed, and now it seemed that nativism, too, was out the window. Bill had taken it all on board with absolute equanimity and was wondering aloud whether the nearest airport at Douglas, Arizona, had a strip long enough to land the size of plane that would be required to transport elephants.

Driving herself back down the Geronimo trail toward Tucson, Mary considered the possibility that elephants might be as natural ascending the slopes of the Madrean Sky Islands as those of the Aberdares and Mount Kenya (even if the East African had been exaggerating, to get the ranchers to think adventurously). It was a delightful twist in the annals of appeals to nature to justify conserving one kind of life or another. Mary was beginning to make the links between the ex situ and in situ wildlife conservation that Professor Walker was so keen on and the links between human and nonhuman reproductions that she was learning to track with Gabriela. Whose reproduction was valued and by whom, and whose reproduction was owned and by whom. Ownership and value were enunciated through an intricate articulation of all sorts of possible and partially conflicting utopias, all sorts of potential futures worth caring about and investing in. Resistance and oppression resided in the very same niches, but one had to dare to transgress.

There was a phrase that Gabriela used: "Dare to know." She said it came from Kant and was probably really about a masochistic process of disembodiment required in the act of knowing that had been proposed as an antidote to the off-the-shelf Cartesian version of disembodied knowledge. Gabriela thought it was important because it recognized that knowing was acting and that knowing was tied up with a moral self. What interested Mary was the connection between building a self and daring to know the world. She hadn't thought that much about it, but she suspected that the moral trick in knowing was being able to move to and with other places and points of view. Taken right, that was the true privilege of mobility. Her mistake, her middle-class heritage, was that she had grown up sorting the good from the bad according to a stable self, a static point of moral reference, fallible only insofar as she failed to live up to the standards of the institutions of family, school, church, and a democratic polity that calibrated that point of reference. Working with animals, and more recently, seeing the huge variation and interconnections in human points of view, had slowly shown Mary the arrogance of such moral passivity. You had to have compassion for the bonobo, for the rancher, for the director of the zoo, for the slave owner and the slave, and for the hunter and the hunted. This meant being prepared to have the whole self move, not simply collapsing into the object of study—the sentimental anthropological fantasy of "going native"—or ethnocentrically translating the object of knowledge into your own scheme of things. Compassion didn't stop you from judging or acting; it was the precondition of it.

When the three men had been talking about bringing in exotic animals to increase indigenous biodiversity, Mary remembered Professor Walker's words about "unholy alliances." Her reflections on compassion and the plurality of values it entailed seemed to come full circle. She had been seized by the boldness of the possibility, so graphically elaborated by the East African and Bill, so instantly assimilated and normalized. The principal thing that Mary derived from these two days was that she now had no excuse not to act. Arriving at the Tucson airport, she failed to call home to let her family know that she would be home early.

It is just after midnight, and Mary is parking her car at the zoo, pulling into her place with her headlights already turned off. She has not gone home, and she has let no one know that she is back. She gets out of the car and runs for the outside door to the research department. She lets herself in and heads for her lab. She hastily prepares some equipment and goes back downstairs to the frozen zoo. There she deactivates the Chinese lock and then the regular bolt. She then punches in the combination for one of the freezers. She knows that each time one of the combination numbers is used, the time and date are automatically logged, for security reasons. It is a risk she is willing to take, though; no one but herself and Dr. Thomson ever checks the logs. Using a pair of huge insulated gloves, Mary reaches into the liquid nitrogen and brings out a straw containing four bonobo embryos. She closes up the freezer and the room again and heads upstairs with her precious contraband.

Mary works frantically for the next couple of hours, feeling no fatigue, only a pulsing exultation. The embryos are thawed, her blood is drawn and prepared; the embryos are examined for viability. It is day fifteen of Mary's cycle; she hopes the timing is right. With the bonobo embryos and Mary's serum in petri dishes in the CO_2 hood and the Edwards catheter from Eva's lab ready to go, Mary undresses her lower half, swabs her genital area, and scrubs her hands once more. She takes three painkillers and an antibiotic. Mary then loads the embryos into the catheter, watching her actions through the microscope. She gets onto her makeshift bed—the lab bench with the microscope on it, covered with semisterile disposable sheets they use for the animals. Using a speculum and a mirror to guide her, she inserts the flexible catheter tip into her vagina and gently through the opening of her cervix. She breathes deeply for two or maybe three minutes, before pulling back slightly on the catheter to make sure that it is inserted fully. Everything is OK. Mary exerts pressure on the plunger, releasing the serum containing the bonobo embryos into her uterine cavity. She waits for a further five minutes and then removes the catheter. Without getting up, she shuffles her bottom slightly, so as to be able to look at the catheter tip under the microscope once more. There are no embryos in sight. At least some of them must be inside her. Mary puts down the catheter and lies back to wait. Eva always has the infertility patients stay lying down for two hours after embryo transfer, so Mary does the same.

Mary cannot relax, but she can lie very still. Her mind is racing, almost hallucinogenic; her body is rigid. Elephants and her own children and bonobos and cowboys and Eva's girls and catheters and Maasai warriors and Gabriela and the cheetahs are swirling around her; one moment she is pregnant, the next minute she has lost it all in a monthly bleed; then she is choosing names for her bonobo babies, not knowing what sex they are and in her confusion, unable to remember how to tell the gender; a priest is leaning over her threatening that he cannot baptize them if she doesn't choose a name, but Mary doesn't know how to name them until she can find out which is a boy and which a girl; then she hears the bonobos at the zoo calling her, demanding their baby back, and an INS official is handing out visas to all the bonobos to return to Zaire; they are traveling first class on British Airways, and her babies are wearing diapers and sitting in car seats; then a flight attendant rushes out and says that Mary can come too, and she gets on and sits in economy, listening to the cries of her babies, so that she can go up and breast-feed them whenever they get hungry . . . Mary jolts herself back to the present. She is trying to bring herself back around, to clear her head, like chasing a terrifying nightmare that won't let you go even though you are defying it with obvious signs of being fully awake. Only forty minutes have passed since the embryo transfer. Mary is frightened.

Somehow Mary gets through the next hour and a half. Then she stays on the bench for another forty-five minutes, for good measure. Dawn has long since penetrated the lab, and Mary realizes that she probably has only a few minutes to get dressed and cleaned up before the ever hardworking Californians start to arrive for the day's work. Mary erases the trails of the night's activities as best she can and quietly lets herself out of the back of the building to have a walk. An hour later she returns, unable to be away from the scene of her crime, sure that she will be caught any minute, and only finding peace in being there to witness her own apprehension. Dr. Thomson is pleased that Mary is back at work a day early, and together they put in a thoroughly normal day's work. At home that night, Mary doesn't mention that there had been a change in her travel plans.

The daily routine of the next two weeks takes on a mantric quality. Mary's sleep is troubled, her every waking action the performance of a puppet, herself concealed and living out a wholly distinct and unseen narrative. The normality of everything around her is what passes the time. Mary tells no one that she is now a remorseless criminal (Gabriela had said that she especially liked Mary's Virgin fantasy because white middle-class Mary, keeper of the panda germ plasm, would never in real life know what it was like to be a potential criminal in the eyes of others). And Mary tells no one that she wants more than anything in the world for her bioterroristic act to succeed: she longs to be pregnant.

It is fourteen days after the embryo transfer. Mary has not yet begun to bleed. She has had sex with her husband a few times since the transfer, but she has no reason to doubt the soundness of her tubal ligation; she is certain that if she is pregnant, it is with bonobo, not child. She goes to the bathroom and checks the toilet tissue one last time, just to be sure that there is no blood. There isn't. She drives to work and heads for the cupboard where she and Dr. Thomson stored the things that Eva gave them from her lab. There are some pregnancy strips past their sell-by date; Mary takes one of the strips out of the container, slips it into her pocket, and locks the cupboard back up. In the bathroom at the zoo she holds the strip under a stream of urine and then waits a minute, watching. "One Mississippi, two Mississippi, three . . . " The diagnostic band changes color, faintly at first, and then unmistakably. Mary is ecstatic; terrified; paralyzed. She wants to run out into the corridor and have someone else read the strip, someone else confirm the pregnancy and begin the anticipation with her, but there is absolutely no one; cannot be. Slowly she pulls her panties and jeans back up, looking tenderly, respectfully at her stomach as she does so.

What now? She has to have a plan. She goes to the bonobo bench to think. There are some obvious ground rules. No one must know, not her husband, not Gabriela, so she will have to conduct her life with a degree of privacy that she has had no need for until now. There can be no prenatal care or medical care of any kind, so she must stay healthy by herself. And she must find out all she can about hybrid pregnancies and bonobo babies so that she can be prepared and be a good mother when the time comes. Those are the three ongoing priorities, she decides. The fourth issue is what to do when the baby or babies arrive, if all goes well. There are three options, as she sees it now. There is the Moses solution; she can simply leave the baby on the zoo doorstep in a wicker basket. Or she can have someone take the baby (or take it herself) to somewhere where it has a chance of surviving in the wild. Or she can raise it as her own. Each option is fraught with contradictions and shortcomings; none presents itself as clearly more desirable than the others. She resolves to wait and see how the pregnancy progresses. Watching the early morning play of the bonobo group in front of her, Mary feels herself slowly relax for the first time in two weeks. She stretches out her legs in front of her and rolls her shoulders back, sighing. Four bonobos are in sight in the exhibit, and, for a moment, Mary is completely and utterly happy.

As the weeks pass, Mary manages better than she had anticipated with her three priorities. Telling no one is hard, but not as hard as it might have been, given that she would have had no idea how to begin to tell anyone. She is more anxious that her body will give her away. There is morning nausea, but nothing like as bad as it had been with her other children, which she finds counterintuitive but interesting. She puts salted crackers instead of her usual oatmeal cookies on her early morning tea tray, and no one comments on the difference. Then there is the fact that she is not cycling. The only person who would notice that is her husband. She decides to wait until he does notice, and say nothing in the meantime. About nine weeks into the pregnancy he asks her when she last had her period. She replies, offhandedly, that she isn't sure, a couple of weeks ago, wasn't it? The subject is dropped. And then there are the signs of pregnancy; the bloated tummy and the anticipatory breasts. Mary is slender, and her stomach is still small; in any case bonobo babies are quite a bit smaller than human babies, and gestation is shorter; Mary hopes she is pregnant with a singleton and that she can get through the majority of the pregnancy without her stomach giving her away. Her breasts are somewhat tender and somewhat fuller, but despite appreciative touching from her husband, he does not question.

Mary's health is good, and she ingests daily vitamin supplements and does all the sensible things she can think of like drinking water and taking moderate exercise. She is pleased with her body; how well it is coping, the hardness pressing out between her pelvic bones; the exquisite flutters of movement within her womb. Finding out about hybrid pregnancies in primates has proven a little bit more difficult. In particular, no one seems to be absolutely certain whether labor would be triggered by the fetus or the pregnant mother. Mary is worried about this because a bonobo gestation is about six weeks shorter than a human pregnancy, and her first two children were not born at all prematurely. She will have to make sure there is some oxytocin on hand. Although she is giving it increasing thought, she has made no progress on where she ought to deliver yet and whether she can seek help at that time.

At the end of September, about eighteen weeks into the pregnancy, Mary is invited to a going-away party for Gabriela. Relations with Gabriela have been a little distant lately. Gabriela has stopped coming to the zoo, in a mad rush to write up her data before returning to the United Kingdom. For her part, Mary has barely answered Gabriela's recent e-mails, addressed with unfailing tenderness to some epithet or other for the Virgin. Gabriela's messages used to fill Mary with pleasure and excitement, but they now invoke such an extreme longing to bring Gabriela into her secret and her crime that she can hardly get beyond the Hail Mary's and Ave Maria's. The message inviting Mary to the going-away party starts "La Virgen con el Niño!" Alone in front of her computer screen, Mary bursts into tears. "Gabriela cannot be leaving," her sobs say; "Gabriela is my midwife, my partner in crime; if she goes, it will be unbearable." Nonetheless, Mary RSVPs in a lighthearted manner. On Friday evening she instructs a baby-sitter on her children's food likes and dislikes, as she and her husband change into party clothes, and the children dance outlandishly to getting-ready music. Mary is in the bathroom wearing just pantyhose and bra, when her husband runs his hand over her belly, commenting on its firmness. For a second, Mary is stock-still, dreading, knowing that like this she could not lie to him. But he does not ask; just kisses her between her shoulder blades. She has learned in the last few months not to follow every comment with an explanation; a hard lesson for Mary, but one that is standing her in good stead in her need for privacy. As her husband leans down to pull his socks on, Mary longingly traces the outline of his bending torso with her eyes. Never has she has she been so separated from him. The party is lively, and Mary dances it away, hardly constrained by her condition. She drinks enough wine to be able to bid Gabriela an effusive farewell without breaking down.

A month later Mary receives a fax from the Chinese Academy of Sciences. The physiologist will be back in two weeks' time to check on the panda germ plasm and to take some more tissue samples. Within the course of a single week Mary reencounters the Chinese physiologist and the East African conservationist. Professor Walker had invited the East African to spend a day at the zoo on his next trip to the United States. He and three senior African research scientists spend a whole day at the zoo, including attending a lab meeting and trying out the new laser DNA sequencer that had been a gift to the zoo. There is still an annual ten-thousand-dollar servicing fee, and it still costs a few hundred dollars to run thirty-six samples, though, so the Africans are not convinced that they want one themselves; in any case the verdict is not in on what role phylogenetics should play in in situ conservation. The East African does not really remember Mary, but the sight of him reminds her of the conditions of mental clarity that had precipitated her pregnancy, this time completely disorienting her. She returns to the lab bench and picks up some work. "Routine, normality," she repeats to herself, one hand adjusting the scope and the other cradling the underside of her belly.

Early December Mary comes into work to find everyone in an uproar. The Chinese Academy of Sciences is concerned that there had been a break-in to the frozen zoo back in May. The physiologist apparently Xeroxed the security records before returning. No one has been able to account for the entry into the room or the freezer. Dr. Thomson asks Mary to let her into the frozen zoo. Fifteen minutes later Dr. Thomson has completed an inventory of the freezer and has found four bonobo embryos missing. Professor Walker is strutting and fretting. Mary looks stunned, which she does not have to feign. Then she asks to see the records and the inventory sheets for herself. They fax official reassurances to the Chinese that they are looking into it with every possible means at their disposal and will not let it happen again.

Toward the end of the afternoon Mary notices Dr. Thomson looking at her. Dr. Thomson asks her who she thinks could have broken in. Mary detects that this is not an innocent question; but neither is it an accusatory one. It is a question of someone for whom a solution is starting to dawn but who is not ready yet to follow the solution to its logical conclusion. Mary turns the question around to Dr. Thomson. They come up with nothing. As Mary is leaving, Dr. Thomson asks Mary if she has gained a little weight recently, to which Mary replies that she doesn't think so particularly, but that she doesn't keep track of those kinds of things. In fact, Mary has only gained a handful of pounds, and in her loose clothes she certainly doesn't look obviously pregnant, but her waist has thickened and her stomach is rounded. Mary realizes that it is only a matter of time until Dr. Thomson can no longer refrain from putting the pieces together. That night Mary tells her husband and children that she has to go the following week for a ten-day research trip back to Arizona and New Mexico. This is the first time that she has lied blatantly and implausibly. She says that she will be back before Christmas and will call frequently. Her husband is surprised but so busy with his own end-of-term commitments that he simply complains about the increasing demands of her job and asks her to do the Christmas cards before she leaves. Mary tells Professor Walker and Dr. Thomson that she is going on a family holiday.

Mary leaves work the following Monday with a suitcase in the car and still no idea what she will do in the next few days. To lend some plausibility to her departure, she has a plane ticket to Tucson and a booking at a cheap hotel near the airport. Arriving at Tucson and checking into the hotel, she decides that Tucson was as good a choice as any. She has rarely seen a more anonymous place, and she can easily drive into the hills, even go back to the quails and frogs if she feels like it. The next few days are some of the emptiest Mary can remember spending. She sleeps a lot, although quite fitfully, eats in one or other of the appalling hotel restaurants, and takes walks up and down and behind the row of hotels and service entrances to the airport. She writes intensely ordinary holiday letters to her family and her in-laws and once-a-year friends and phones home every other night, inventing tales of leopard frogs that stand in as bedtime stories for the children.

Mary also tries to plan. The bonobo inside her is moving all the time now, and she knows that it only has a week or two until it is due by bonobo dates. She lies in the bath or in bed for long periods of time thinking about her condition, fantasizing more than she has ever done before, free to caress and touch herself. On the night of 22 December, a day before she is due to return to California, Mary experiences her first light Braxton-Hicks contractions. At first she is not sure, but in the middle of the night she definitely feels the uterine tightening again. She glances at the ampoule of oxytocin from Eva's that she has been carrying around with her, which is just visible in her open wash bag by the basin. Seems like she will not need to set up an IV after all. At four o'clock in the morning she wakes up again, suddenly petrified. What the hell is she doing? What happens if she hemorrhages? Who will assist at the delivery? What will the baby need? Who will cut the umbilical cord? Frantic, she pulls her handbag toward her and switches on the light. She reaches for the phone and calls Gabriela in London, where it is the middle of the day.

Luckily Gabriela is in. "Gabriela?" says Mary, "can you talk?"

"Maria, is that you?" says Gabriela, taken aback, and instantly modifying her usual jocularity to anxious concern. "What's the matter, what's going on? Where are you? Of course I can talk."

Mary begins before she can give in to the urge just to hang up. "I did it, Gaby. The Virgin fantasy thing. I broke into my own frozen zoo and stole the bonobo germ plasm; I'm wanted back at the zoo or will be any day now, and my family thinks I'm on a research trip. Gab—I think I'm about to go into labor, and I don't know what to do." Mary is crying and choking. "But Gaby, it isn't all bad; the pregnancy is unbelievable . . . "

Gabriela is aghast. "Mary, are you serious? You did it? When!? But Mary, the Virgin can't be a bioterrorist! Tell me you're joking . . . "

"Gaby, don't you get it? She *was* a bioterrorist, a Middle Eastern one . . . " Mary is clearer now, pragmatic, but still desperate. "What should I do? I fly back to California tomorrow, and I've probably got a good twenty-four hours before labor proper. Please help me."

Gabriela is thinking fast. "I'm getting the first plane that's available. I'll be with you as soon as I can. In the meantime you have to call Eva. She will do the delivery. We'll take it from there."

"O.K.," says Mary, overcome with fatigue following on the relief that Gabriela has come through, that she has understood and is coming to be with her for the birth. "But Gaby, its going to be Christmas Eve; Eva's clinic will be closed."

"All the better; Eva has the keys and can let us in. Just call her now, and then call me straight back. I will speak to her too. Tell her everything. And I'll get there as soon as I can. Tell your family you will be back on Christmas day; if they protest, shower them with love and hang up. There's no bed in Bethlehem for you, Mary, but we will make absolutely sure that you have a couple of decent midwives and access to an operating room."

Note

All characters in this story are fictional. I thank L. Anderson, embryologist and lab technician at a southern California infertility clinic, for her fascinating tutorials in and outside the clinic. I also thank equid geneticist A. Oakenfull for her introduction to the wonders of zoo reproductions, and O. Ryder for his openness; also conservationist D. Western for an incomparable apprenticeship in community-based wildlife conservation in East Africa and the United States. Above all, I thank A. Lintz, dear friend and brilliant sociologist, for her insights on race, class, reproduction, and gangsters and for the exquisite compassion she shows all her subjects, both human and nonhuman.

Immaculate Mothers and Celibate Fathers

RICHARD NASH

Where Did We Come From, and Where Are We Going?

A STARTLING FRISSON IN Charis Thompson Cussins's "Confessions of a Bioterrorist" animates my reading of the story. That is hardly surprising, for the story is built on, indeed insists on, the rhetorical effects of alienating, disorienting, even "shocking" juxtapositions. Central to the story's effect is its reinscription of the traditional nativity story of Christianity as a parodic tale of interspecies gestation: the biblical Mary was, the protagonist of this story discovers, "a Middle Eastern bioterrorist." What fascinates me is the way in which the narrative's obvious concern with the touchstones of postmodern radical politics (feminism, environmental conservation, animal rights activism, reproductive rights, and the like) keeps turning back to Enlightenment positions, albeit inflected in new ways. I want to look at a single moment at the heart of Cussins's narrative and explore how that moment carries us back to fundamental concerns underwriting Enlightenment anxieties of reproductive technologies, racial politics, species differentiation, and the formation of political action. Does Cussins's story mark a break with our heritage of a collective fantasy of idealized modernity, or does it rather illustrate the impossibility of imagining beyond the limits of that fantasy?

I am referring to the interpolated, tripled "confession" contained within the story's ostensible titular "confession." Halfway through the narrative, the three main characters assemble in the San Diego Zoo after closing time, so that Gabriela can film Mary and Eva attempting "a new egg-thawing regimen." Afterward, they sit and talk at what has become their favorite gathering spot, the bench in front of the bonobo exhibit. The text underlines that this conversation is unique, and it loads the conversation with the cloistered trappings of the confessional: "As she talked, Mary realized that Gabriela was talking about herself, something that, for all her openness and loquacity, Gabriela rarely did. The dark and the late hour and the privacy of the abandoned public place made for intimacy."

In this intimate setting the women divulge three distinct confessions, fantasies of possible alternative futures that nourish and motivate each of them. For Gabriela, who confesses first, the fantasy is the familiar dream of eugenics: the desire for genetic manipulation to facilitate an essentialized racial purity. For Eva, the dream is, despite her disclaimers, the familiar quest for single-sex reproduction, without the encumbrances of heterosexual conjugation. Mary's concluding fantasy is to violate the species taboo of Leviticus 20:15–16 and bring forth "alter," rather than "after," her kind. Each of these dreams is marked by a particular orthodoxy of postmodern radical politics. While Gabriela desires the eugenicist's essentialized racial purity, it is with a particularly postmodern ironic twist: she wants to guarantee her child "a hefty dose of 'in your face' blackness." Similarly, Eva's desire is not Frankenstein's parthenogenetic dream that dispenses with women but a gynocentric reproductive fantasy: "What I would really love to do is to take two eggs and fertilize one with the other . . . just combining two eggs, rather than having to involve sperm." She makes it sound as easy as breakfast. Mary's, of course, is the most complex, for instead of providing a particular ironic postmodern spin to a traditional patriarchal protectionist fantasy, hers directly violates traditional taboo. Even here, however, the fantasy has a clearly articulated precedent: Donna Haraway's statement "indeed, I have always preferred the prospect of pregnancy with the embryo of another species."[1] This confessional moment on the bonobo bench not only draws the three women into an unspoken confederacy but does so by labeling a familiar triad on which radical politics seeks to destabilize Enlightenment patriarchy: race, gender, species.

"Confessions of a Bioterrorist" is Latourean fiction woven from the multiple strands of networks, accidental affiliations, interactions across variations in scale, and dynamic interplay of human and nonhuman actors that characterize Latour's description of science in action. Science, here, is not the purified work of the lab set apart from the world it seeks to know but is rather woven into and out of the lives of its practitioners. The story's premise contradicts Latour's third guarantee of the Modern Constitution: "Nature and Society must remain absolutely distinct: the work of purification must remain absolutely distinct from the work of mediation" (Latour 1993, 32). The explicit violation of taboo at the narrative's climax completes a description of scientific practice in which this idealized separation is followed *only* in theory.

Cussins's story dramatizes Latour's thesis that the dream of the modern requires both the complicity of "hybrids and networks" in the construction of "pure" knowledge *and* the disavowal of such complicity.[2]

One story we can tell of the rise of modern science foregrounds concerns with purity, hybridity, and reproductive technologies in a narrative that (like Cussins's) centers around a bonobo. The first bonobo to reach England alive came ashore late in 1697 or early in 1698. He was entrusted to the care of England's foremost anatomist, Dr. Edward Tyson, who performed a complete anatomy after his death in April 1698. The ensuing work, published in an expensive folio volume with elaborate plates, under the auspices of the Royal Society, became a foundational work in the field of comparative anatomy. On the basis of this work, Tyson's biographer, Ashley Montagu, writes: "No man has ever been more truly the founder and father of his subject than Tyson has been of Primatology" (Montague 1943, 399).

This claim is odd in at least two ways: Tyson died in 1708, half a century before Linnaeus coined the term *primate* to describe humans and other apes; at the time of his death, Tyson's admittedly celebrated study of his hybrid human/nonhuman actor was overshadowed by Tyson's even more celebrated celibacy. This vaunted sexual purity was identified with the purity of his knowledge claims.[3] An anonymous account of Tyson's life, published in *A Compleat History of Europe . . . For the Year 1708*, comments on both his celibacy and the sudden nature of his death: "This learned Physician having never been married, but I may say, devoted himself to Caelibacy . . . [death] overtook him suddenly, and in an Instant, deprived him of Life, on Sunday the first of August, about five in the Evening, as he was pleasantly Conversing with a Gentlewoman his patient in her Apartment" ("An Account of the Life and Writings of Dr. Edward Tyson" 1709, 404).[4] Constructing Tyson as a paragon of science requires him to sacrifice human bodily pleasures for the more refined and solitary pleasures of the mind.[5]

In the peculiar reproductive technology of "pure" science, Tyson's celibacy qualifies him as the father of a discipline whose subjects will be named only a half century after his death, a conception almost as immaculate as any ever dreamed of in Cussins's "Confession." Moreover, Tyson mobilized his description to construct the bonobo beneath his knife as nonhuman and nonape. Tyson concluded that his creature was a pygmy, but in a confession of his own, he announces that he framed that conclusion not as the result of his scientific discoveries but as the precondition to their existence: "I must confess, I could never before entertain any other Opinion about [pygmies], but that the whole was a Fiction, and as the first Account we have of them, was from a Poet, so that they were only a Creature of the Brain, produced by a warm and wanton Imagination, and that they never had any Existence or Habitation elsewhere" (Tyson 1699, "Phil. Essay," 1). Tyson's anatomy of "a pygmie" allows him to "discover" the "real," nonhuman basis for the fabulous tales of poets. His anatomy was so convincing that well after human pygmies in central and southern Africa had been encountered by Westerners, their existence continued to be discredited.

The "creature[s] of the Brain, produced by a warm and wanton Imagination" that Tyson will reveal to be monstrous representations of a quasi-human hybrid sound very much like contemporary descriptions not of the fanciful productions of poets but of the monstrous reproductions of teratogeny. By Tyson's time the doctrine of the prenatal influence of the imagination had entrenched itself as the compelling explanation for monstrous birth, and the excited maternal imagination was the established reproductive technology for the generation of monsters.[6] When, in 1726, Mary Toft was said to have given birth to rabbits, some doubted the story from the beginning, some were taken in, and most were of a divided opinion, alternating between the poles of belief and disbelief. Critical to deciding the truth of her account, as Dennis Todd remarks, was the perceived relationship between species difference and reproductive potential:

> Douglas's ultimate rejection of Mary Toft's claim should not be taken
> as evidence that he doubted the doctrine of the influence of the
> imagination. He chooses his words with great care: "I begin by
> declaring it to have been always my firm Opinion, that this Report
> was false; in the First Place, because I could never conceive the
> Generation of a perfect Rabbit in the *Uterus* of a Woman to be
> possible, it being contradictory to all that is hitherto known, both
> from Reason and Experience, concerning the ordinary, as well as
> extraordinary Procedure of Nature, in the Formation of a *Foetus*"
> (*Advertisement*, 3). The important word here is "perfect," and
> Douglas's point is that a human cannot give birth to "an entirely
> different Species" (38). (Todd 1995, 284 n. 29)

The pygmies Tyson encountered in Pliny and other classical authors are identified as monstrous, unnatural impossibilities that, like the monstrous productions in nature, are to be accounted for as the offspring of a wanton imagination, "a creature of the brain." Correcting the errors of the poets and the excesses of imagination leads Tyson to identify the "real" pygmy of nature in the bonobo brought back to England. The painstaking anatomy that follows this creature's death is mobilized on behalf of fixing his identity as a natural pygmy, neither human, from whose anatomy he differs in thirty-four ways (94–95), nor ape, from whose anatomy he differs in forty-eight ways (92–94). The liminal status of Tyson's pygmy between human and ape at once naturalizes the monstrous pygmy created by the wanton imagination of poets and stabilizes that figure in a natural order that insists on species purity. Like Douglas, who will maintain "that a human cannot give birth to 'an entirely different Species,'" Tyson also insists that his pygmy is to be accorded its own species: "Now not withstanding our *Pygmie* does so much resemble a *Man* in many of its Parts, more than any of the *Ape-kind*, or any other *Animal* in the world that I know of: Yet by no means do I look upon it as the Product of a *mixt* Generation; 'tis a *Brute-Animal sui generis*, and a particular *Species* of *Ape*" (Tyson 1699, 2).

As an anatomist, Tyson found the ape most closely approaching the human on an imagined "chain of being," or *scala natura* (Dougherty (1995), 66). Tyson's principal criteria were functionalist, and his comparative anatomy presented a strong case that the material form of his "pygmie" more closely approximated the functional requirements of the human form than any other species in the natural world. Naturalists tended to differ from anatomists in minimizing the importance of the ape's material approximation of the human form, in favor of a ranking of animal nature that emphasized the perceived uniqueness of human mental activity. In this version, the ape mimicked man, but without reason, while other animals approached man much more closely in their rational capacity. For neither naturalist nor anatomist did such proximity translate into anything approaching evolutionist logic. Although the chain of nature needed to be complete, each link was imagined to be utterly distinct and independent; species was fixed.

Thus, despite the appearance of disagreement between naturalists and anatomists, their shared assumption of species fixity meant that where sexual activity crossed species lines it would be marked by the inability to reproduce.[7] Against the vulgar superstition that apes were the result of a "mixt generation" between man and beast, Tyson insisted on the species integrity of his pygmy. Yet even while Tyson presented his anatomy to the Royal Society as material evidence of that animal that, "coming nearest to Mankind; seems the Nexus of the Animal and Rational," the body was on display in Moncress's coffeehouse for a shilling a view as "a MONSTER, wonderful to behold, being human upward and bruit downward," in the tradition of mixed generation. The exemplary cases of "hybridous" mixed generation for Enlightenment taxonomy were the mule and the hinny, the offspring of a jackass and a mare, and a stallion and a female ass, respectively. Although such "hybridous" breeding was in some instances possible, the offspring was marked by an inability to reproduce. Thus, species identity was preserved by an inheritable capacity to reproduce.

Throughout the eighteenth century, as Europeans sought to identify their relation to those creatures we now identify as "nonhuman primates," narratives of such hybridous couplings signal anxiety over the limits of species identity in the absence of an evolutionary model. Since Darwin, the dominant metaphor for primate relations is one of kinship, and the anxieties surrounding debate over evolution almost invariably reveal themselves in the rhetoric of family, blood, resemblance, and so forth. As Piet de Rooy has pointed out, this led in the case of Herman M. Bernelot Moens "to the conclusion that 'humans and anthropomorphic apes are literally blood relatives.' This in turn suggested that, just as in the case of related animals like horses and donkeys, or hares and rabbits, hybrids between these apes and man must be possible" (de Rooy 1995, 195). For Moens, a follower of Haeckel, the goal was to realize such a potential and prove empirically the possibility of "a missing link." For the eighteenth century, however, such hybridous fantasies offered not evidence of evolutionary continuity but either confirmation or refutation of a putative species distinction between man and ape.

James Burnett, Lord Monboddo, maintained the minority view that these creatures were what he sometimes termed an "infantine" variety of the human species. For him, the narratives of returning travelers that testified to the reality of such hybridous couplings constituted evidence not of evolutionary kinship but of a shared species identity. Among the many arguments he offers for species kinship between humans and orangutans is the testimony of a Swedish traveler, Keoping (trusted by Linnaeus), who claims to have seen "a child of an Oran Outan by a woman" (Monboddo 1779, 133n). While such stories operated anecdotally, they were so frequently cited that it is difficult to encounter a discussion of primate speciation conducted by an Enlightenment philosopher that does not retail at least one narrative of hybridous reproduction; although a certain amount of repetition is encountered, it is surprising how many variations of this single story exist. Londa Schiebinger has noted that there are multiple variations on this story but one motif seems paradigmatic: "In these accounts it is invariably the male ape who forced himself on the human female. To my knowledge there was not one account in this period of a female ape taking a man or even of intercourse between a female ape and a male human" (Schiebinger 1993, 95).

Even though Schiebinger is right to stress the near ubiquity of the gendered configuration of the hybrid coupling, a rule-proving exception may be found in an incident that forms the crucial moment of self-identification in *Gulliver's Travels*. There, Gulliver, who has until this moment strenuously denied any connection to the bestial Yahoos, tells us he was bathing in a river when "a young female Yahoo . . . inflamed by desire . . . came running with all speed and leaped into the water within five yards of the place where I bathed. . . . She embraced me after a most fulsome manner" (Swift 1941, 250). This event is a "mortification" to Gulliver, "for now I could no longer deny that I was a real yahoo in every limb and feature since the females had a natural propensity to me as one of their own species" (250).[8] While I do not wish to discuss Swift's satire in too great detail here, from the text's opening pun on "masturbation," Gulliver's alienation from his fellow humans has been signaled among other ways through sexual innuendo, a point not lost on his friend Alexander Pope, whose minor epistle on the occasion of the publication of *Gulliver's Travels* ("Mary Gulliver to Capt. Lemuel Gulliver") responds in kind: "*Where sleeps my Gulliver? O tell me where?/*The Neighbors answer, *With the Sorrel Mare.*"[9] Better known, however, than the species-confounding assault in Gulliver's fourth voyage is a related moment in the second voyage.

Anticipating King Kong, Gulliver in Brobdingnag (where everything is twelve times the scale we are accustomed to) is seized by an ape and carried, like Fay Wray, to the top of a tall building. Before he is rescued, he must suffer the trauma of being force-fed by the maternal male primate: "He took me up in his right Fore-foot, and held me as a Nurse does a Child she is going to suckle; just as I have seen the same Sort of Creature do with a Kitten in *Europe*" (106). Although this scene has provided considerable material for biographical and psychoanalytic critics (Swift, a posthumous child, had been abducted by his nursemaid while an infant), Todd notes that Gulliver's allusion refers to an interspecies drama staged as public spectacle that Swift is likely to have witnessed in London. Ned Ward's *London Spy* contains a description of the show alluded to; in our own time, a comparable spectacle is the children's picture book *Koko and Her Kitten*.[10] Penny Patterson has been faulted for anthropomorphizing Koko, and Cussins's story slyly alludes to Koko's reproductive difficulties aping those of her affluent human alter egos. Swift's narrative, with its ironic overtones, conceals as much as it reveals about Swift's own attitude: Is Gulliver a helpless human in the hands of a giant beast, or does the narrative remind us of a kinship between nurturer and nurtured, desired and desiring? Whatever Swift's attitude, the display Ned Ward described shares the same visual economy as the one Penny Patterson promotes in *Koko and Her Kitten*: viewers are fascinated by the mix of similarity and difference in another primate's appearance, especially as that creature's behavior seems to reproduce our "nature."

In the Enlightenment, the two tracks of that response corresponded to a fundamental divergence over questions of species and taxonomy that separated anatomists like Tyson from naturalists like Buffon. Despite what seems both general similarity and specific difference at a level of anatomical function, specific behaviors, like domesticating, or parenting, a kitten, seem at times to reproduce "human nature." In some cases, such as the elephant, the consolation of significant anatomical difference could license narratives of dramatic similarity in nature; Buffon includes several anthropomorphic stories of elephant behavior. Where anatomical resemblance threatens with a monstrous similarity, however, those narratives become more dangerous, particularly when the human nature being approximated is already dangerously carnal. Among the ways that Tyson's pygmy resembled humans more than apes, or apes more than humans, Tyson notes, pertaining to reproduction, only that "the Orang-Outang or Pygmie differ'd from a Man, and resembled more the Ape and Monkey-kind . . . in having no pendulous *Scrotum*" (94).

This observation was almost immediately challenged on the basis that Tyson's subject was by his own account an infant, but within Tyson's narrative it is easy to discern a logic for inclusion: "Whether the *Testes* being thus closely pursed up to the Body, might contribute to that great *salaciousness* this *Species* of *Animals* are noted for, I will not determine: Tho' 'tis said, that these *Animals*, that have their *Testicles* contained within the Body, are more inclined to it, than others. That the whole *Ape*-kind is extremely given to *Venery*, appears by infinite stories related of them" (42). Without relating all of them (he has previously cited some), Tyson proceeds to an account from Licetus "of a Woman who had two Children by an *Ape*" (42). Tyson's discussion, though it is careful in language ("I will not determine") unites anatomical findings with traditional lore regarding sexual appetite. According to this tradition, women were more salacious than men because their organs of generation were folded inward and consequently were warmer. Thus, the celibate anatomist can find in the body of an infant bonobo a material justification for a species distinction that naturalizes human behavior as modest and ape behavior as salacious, while linking that species distinction to a gender distinction that identifies women with apes. He then illustrates that finding with a classical narrative uniting woman and ape in salacious coupling, even though the reproductive success promised by the narrative contradicts the very species distinction he is seeking to affirm.

Acknowledging Tyson's very real contribution to scientific knowledge should not blind us to some of these ironies in his work. If there is to be a progressive component to Enlightenment science, then surely the past three hundred years have dispelled many of the myths and presuppositions that Tyson was willing to countenance, even as he set out to discredit the fables of pygmies. Such an ironic reading enables us to locate Tyson's contribution to our knowledge of primate identities and reproductive technologies as both empirically sanctioned and socially constructed. Ultimately, this is the sort of reading practice that Cussins's story facilitates. "Confessions of a Bioterrorist" reads our knowledge of primate identities and reproductive technologies ironically in offering us an ironic liberation narrative. Her story is not so much a manifesto but an intervention, educating us as ironic readers, enabling a different construction of "Enlightenment" science.

During the last decade of his life, Tyson did more than any person in England to ameliorate the living conditions of the inmates of Bedlam, who, before his tenure at the hospital, were on display to paying customers in the manner of a human zoo. Despite vastly different sexual politics and valorizations of critical terms like "purity" and "hybrid," within their respective historical moments, Cussins and Tyson each mobilize science in the service of a narrative of hope and liberation. Both are interested in what they consider to be a regenerative politics of human identity, and each of them turns to considerations of primate identities and reproductive technologies. "Confessions of a Bioterrorist" ironizes the triumvirate of race, gender, and species that governs our Enlightenment reproductive practices. The tripled confession at the center of the story imagines alternative futures that might arise from an alternative reproductive technology. But what at first seems so revolutionary comes increasingly to resemble the Enlightenment ideology that produced it. Just as Cussins's story embraces its fictional genre, insisting on the liberatory mode of imaginative construction, Tyson's narrative repeatedly reminds us of its factual status, its commitment to truth and verification. Yet, as we read Tyson now, we cannot (for all the solid material science of that work) escape the awareness of the fictional and legendary component of the work; at the same time, our reading of "Confessions" is repeatedly interrupted by our recognition of the factual potential of that story: this is an eminently plausible network of affiliations.

The cloning of an adult mammal in the spring of 1996 challenged popular opinion and glossed Eva's explicit disavowal of cloning in the midst of her confession. Eva's fantasy of "combining two eggs" is identified "not as parthenogenesis; no cloning." Popular discussions of cloning often involve some laboratory version of Calvin and Hobbes's "transmogrifier," in which some object is placed in a box and then two identical objects walk out. The "cloning" of Dolly, on the other hand, involved the nuclear transfer from a mammary gland cell of a six-year-old Finn Dorset ewe in the last trimester of pregnancy to an enucleated oocyte of a Scottish Blackface ewe, who served as host during a 148–day pregnancy. The reproductive technology that generated Dolly is not the direct egg-scrambling recipe imagined by Eva but does perhaps more closely resemble that technology than the popular representation of cloning suggests.[11] Moreover, her delivery closely approximates Gabriela's fantasy for racially pure offspring of an interracial partnership; the product of cell tissue from a Finn Dorset ewe and Scottish Blackface ewe bears none of the racial markings of the Blackface surrogate mother but "displayed the morphological characteristics of the breed used to derive the nucleus donors and not that of the oocyte donor."[12] The cloning of Dolly might well be thought of as a reproductive technology in the service of generating racially purified offspring from an interracial, same-sex female lamb coupling.

And that brings me back to consider how the tripled terms of Enlighten-

ment breeding practices (race, sex, and species) that "Confessions of a Bioterrorist" wishes us to reimagine continue to line up in relation to those key-
words "purity" and "hybrid." What was constructed as "natural" can be charted
quite simply: with regard to species, hybridous interaction is sterile and taboo, purity must be observed; with regard to race, both absolute purity and
unrestrained hybridity are characterized as dangerous, an occasional hybrid
cross within a pure stock is valorized; with regard to sex, purity (whether in
the form of celibacy, onanism, or same-sex coupling) is barren, and only a hybrid cross can reproduce.

I am not, even remotely, self-aware at a cellular level. Yet I try to be self-
aware. In part, that awareness takes the form of recognizing my identity in
relation to apparently stable categories of race, sex, and species. Of these, race
is the most obviously unstable category, but an emerging and developing literature on intersexed identity points to the problematics of assuming a stable
sexual binarism. While only a Gulliver could confuse horses and humans, genetic research indicates a closer kinship between humans and bonobos than
between zebras and horses. The lines between species must be drawn by someone and exist nowhere in nature. Cussins has written a story that, by insisting on the proliferation of alternative possibilities, challenges the valorization
of clarity, purity, and Enlightenment idealized in the figure of the celibate father of primatology, Edward Tyson. What her project shares with Tyson's, and
what continues to offer the greatest hope in the Enlightenment project that
has come to be known generically as science, is a commitment to the importance of self-awareness as a mechanism for regenerative, liberatory politics.[13]

I am finishing production of this essay on Father's Day, and my overwarm
imagination is generating hybrids.[14] What I envision is a continuation of
Cussins's narrative, one in which the various hybrids alluded to in this essay
continue their proliferation. In my continuation, Mary has given birth to her
bonobo, and as humans often do for their human progeny, she has acquired a
pet to serve as playmate. Although this pet will function in many ways (as
such pets often do) like a doll, unlike the feline pet Ned Ward described being nursed by a monkey in eighteenth-century London or the kitten nurtured
by Koko in late-twentieth-century California, this pet is a Finn Dorset lamb
from Scotland, the first mammal since Christ conceived by no earthly father.
Like many mothers with their human offspring (and like at least one maternal chimp named Washoe), Mary will introduce her child to language. In part,
she will experiment with teaching a sign system similar to that which the
bonobo Kanzi has been studying in Atlanta; but like many human mothers,
she will also repeat, and in some cases modify, traditional nursery rhymes to
reinforce the lessons in language acquisition. Every night, I imagine, she will
croon to her child their favorite rhyme:

Mary has a little lamb
Whose fleece is white as bone:
No dad she had, one black-faced mum,
Your Dolly is a clone.

Notes

1. Haraway 1989, 377. Haraway's statement is made in her discussion of Octavia Butler's articulation of the fantasy in her xenogenesis trilogy: *Dawn* (1987), *Adulthood Rites* (1988), and *Imago* (1989), all published by Warner Books.
2. On this subject, see Young 1995. A quick glance at Samuel Johnson's *Dictionary of the English Language* (1758) reveals the fairly narrow use of *hybrid* relative to the proliferating cognates of that word's Latourean playmate, *purification*. *Hybrid* and all its cognates appears only once, is given a single definition, and is supported by one quotation from the naturalist John Ray: "Hybridous, Begotten between animals of different species." From *pure* to *purity*, Johnson defines twenty-one related terms, offering for them a total of fifty-four definitions, supported by illustrative quotations from forty-nine texts.
3. The poet Elkanah Settle was inspired (if that is the word) to rhapsodize in a threnody on the occasion of his death: "Nor Wonder ne'er by Beauty Captive led,/ No Bridal Partner ever shared his bed./No, to the blinder God no Knee e'er paid,/ To great MINERVA his whole Court he made" (Settle 1708, 8).
4. "An Account of the Life and Writings of Dr. Edward Tyson" 1709. In an age notorious for innuendo, when "to converse" held connotations of sexual intimacy that no longer obtain ("to have commerce with a different sex," Johnson's *Dictionary*), it is tempting to read reports of Tyson's celibacy as compromised by the circumstances of his sudden demise. But for both his anonymous biographer and Elkanah Settle, Tyson's celibacy was important as testimony to his devotion to science. Cf. Haraway 1989, 33.
5. Settle's verse paragraph opens with the defining synecdoche for science ("Such the lost HEAD we mourn") and concludes with the consequent rejection of domestic happiness: Tyson hears only the Apollonian music of learning, "Musick so much beyond the poorer Cries/of unharmonious Cradle Nurseries" (8). Cf. Schiebinger 1989.
6. "The doctrine was so well established by the early eighteenth century, in fact, that it had overshadowed all other explanations of the causes of monstrous birth, and it was turned to almost automatically to account for a wide variety of anomalies and malformations" (Todd 1995, 47).
7. See Salisbury 1994, 85, and Young 1995, 7–9. I would note the particular "semiotic relationship" between species identity and sexual reproduction, in which each term was available to serve as a sign for the other. Thus, species identity could be signaled by sexual reproduction, and species difference could be signaled by the failure of such union. At the same time, barrenness (or even a purported diminishing of reproductive potential over time) could signal species difference. Young discusses how this semiotic relationship was read differently by monogenesists and polygenesists in construction of racial identities. The logic of this relationship is powerfully self-defeating: only successful reproduction can signal species identity, but the presumption of species difference prohibits the sexual interaction that would test that identity.
8. I have encountered two similar stories in wire service reports. In 1981, "an orangutan grabbed and kissed a naked woman who was about to take a bath in a river

in Borneo"; in 1993, "an orangutan ambushed a French tourist as he was strolling in a Malaysian park on Borneo and stripped him naked."

9. Pope 1963, 486–488.

   In the opening paragraph of *Gulliver's Travels*, Gulliver describes his family, education, and apprenticeship to a surgeon named James Bates. He runs through most of the permutations for alluding to this apprenticeship before his final reference, which triggers his desire to leave his family and go to sea: "But my good Master Bates dying . . . "

10. Ward's description is fulsome: "At last out comes an Epitome of a Careful Nurse, drest up in a Country Jacket, and under her Arm a Kitten for a Nurslin, and in her contrary Hand a piece of Cheese; down sits the little Matron, with a very Motherly Countenance, and when her Youngster mew'd, she Dandled him, and Rock'd him in her Arms, with as great Signs of Affection as a Loving Mother could well show to a disorder'd Infant; then bites a piece of Cheese, and after she had mumbled it about in her Mouth, then thrust it in with her Tongue into the Kittens, just as I have seen Nasty Old Sluts feed their own Grand children" (Ward 1924, 173).

11. By the way, some things never change. "Dolly" was named by her male observers after Dolly Parton, in recognition of the cell nucleus's tissue of origin. One can only wonder what naming practice would have been invoked had Dolly been male.

12. Wilmut et al. 1997, 811.

13. Like the implications of Wilmut's experiments in reproductive technologies in Edinburgh, "Confessions of a Bioterrorist" provokes us to reimagine our construction of "natural" reproduction in the network charted by "race," "sex," "species," "purity," and "hybridity." Such provocation is, I think, valuable just as it was three hundred years ago when Tyson challenged received constructions of "mixt generation" and the teratogenous prenatal influence of excited imagination. Our various subject positions are constituted (at least in part) by a relationship between race, sex, and species, and it is a natural constraint as well as a social construction. If current science is less interested in the relatively clumsy terminology of Enlightenment science and more focused on transformations at the cellular level, it does not alter the fact that both reproductive technology and primate classification are tools of self-definition, operating in the borderlands of natural constraint and social construction. We cannot, nor should we try to, do away with our understanding of the natural constraints on individual identity, but we should change our mythologies that mobilize those identities.

14. One final irony: it is now almost a year since I wrote this sentence. A Mother's Day has come; another Father's Day rapidly approaches. As the reproductive technology of academic publication approaches conclusion, I find that just over a month ago, on 13 April, Dolly became a mommy via traditional reproductive technologies.

Steps Toward a Millennial Imaginary

GABRIELE SCHWAB

Reproductive Fantasies in Cussins's "Confessions of a Bioterrorist"

Fantasies about alien impregnation and cross-species offspring, genetic engineering and freak mutations, embryo swapping and cloning, sperm banks and cryonic preservation abound at century's end, bespeaking a cultural imaginary simultaneously fascinated and horrified by the possibilities of reproductive technologies. Reproduction is one of the most sensitive issues in an ecology in which overpopulation is a major threat to the survival of the planet. Ironically, reproduction itself is all about survival—the survival of a species, or, more specifically, our species, because we humans are the only ones with the power to implement reproductive technologies. Fantasies about sex and survival that challenge the boundaries of "natural" reproduction quickly accumulate allegorical meaning and cultural capital. The market value of such fantasies is linked to the fact that the fertility rates in industrial countries are decreasing at an alarming rate while the threat of global overpopulation persists at a worldwide scale. But the ramifications of millennial fantasies of technological human reproduction reach beyond their merely pragmatic compensatory role, bespeaking fundamental changes in the cultural and biological fabric of the planet at large. The most nightmarish scenarios contain alien abductions, enforced genetic engineering, gene trading, and impregnation by aliens. More tangible nightmares take place closer to home in today's flourishing fertility clinics. Doctors (most prominently the infamous trio at the University of California–Irvine) play God by swapping eggs and embryos without consent or (in the documented case of a gynecologist from another state) impregnate unknowing women with their own sperm.

Compared with such real and imagined nightmares, Cussins's "Confessions

232

of a Bioterrorist" seems almost tame at first glance. In a pointedly understated, matter-of-fact tone the narrator relates the story of Mary, a thirty-something-year-old middle-class mother of two with a Ph.D. in animal physiology. During her study of primate development, Mary breaks into a frozen zoo bank to steal embryos from an endangered primate species, the bonobo, and then impregnates herself without the knowledge of her family. "Confessions of a Bioterrorist" thus presents us with yet another version of the manifold "primate visions" that Donna Haraway's brilliant book of the same title has exposed as a pervasive feature in modern biopolitics. I will therefore use Haraway's reflections on simians and aliens to frame my own reading of Cussins's story.

While "Confessions of a Bioterrorist" is a fiction about reproductive possibilities, the author informs us that it is "inspired in virtually every detail by conversations with patients and practitioners in infertility clinics during fieldwork that stretches back intermittently to the late 1980s and by my experiences with people and animals in in situ wildlife conservation (parks and community-based conservation) and ex situ (zoo) animal conservation" (189). We might, then, read "Confessions of a Bioterrorist" as an imaginary ethnography based on fieldwork in two different places—infertility clinics and zoos or wildlife parks—which are linked by their "valuing of reproductions." The author introduces the story by asserting quite emphatically that reproduction is politics, nature, identity; past, present, and future. Witnessing reproduction under experimental conditions therefore contributes to the politics of reproduction, the reinvention of nature, and the conservation of "identity." It assists in the engineering of the species' future by conserving the gene pool inherited from the past or by manipulating its present manifestations.

Telling a fictional story in response to her own fieldwork, Cussins takes literally what Haraway calls the "thinking of scientific practice as storytelling."[1] The story of a scientist who acts out cultural fantasies about the object of her study, the primates, foregrounds how such fantasies pervade scientific imagination, pointing to a phantasmatic surplus of the social construction of science. Mary's story attains its relevance because, owing to their evolutionary proximity to humans, primates continue to function as allegorical figures in the cultural imaginary. Both fascinated and repelled by this proximity, popular culture and popular scientific storytelling feature primates as objects to test the boundaries of "the human" and to mirror phantasms of origin, animal nature, and human difference.

Moreover, Haraway's *Simians, Cyborgs, and Women* reveals the striking connections in the cultural imaginary between the figures of the primate, the cyborg, and the alien as three icons in the gendered and sexualized social construction of nature, science, technology, and culture. Reading Cussins's story in the context of these connections, I will contrast her reproductive fantasy of a woman who bears a simian with that of a woman who bears alien offspring. Haraway ends both *Primate Visions* and *Simians, Cyborgs, and Women* with a brief reading of Octavia Butler's *Xenogenesis* series, a science fiction written by an African American feminist who imagines a future kinship between humans and aliens. The vicissitudes of forced reproduction, crossbreeding, biodiversity conservation, and genetic engineering provide the dramatic scenery for this narrative, which is, primarily, about agency in reproduction. Haraway's approximation between primatology and Butler's science fiction provides a framework for placing Cussins's fantasy in the context of reproductive technologies and contested reproductions.

Both Butler's and Cussins's stories about monstrous reproductions challenge the boundaries of what we perceive as human—a challenge that reflects an increasing separation in contemporary high-tech cultures of the human from the natural. The "natural" itself has, as Cussins argues, become a highly contested category: "The powerful business and science bioprospecting constituency pushing the frozen zoo didn't want to lean too heavily on the 'no human interference' Western understanding of 'natural.' Many valuable animals existed in non-Western democracies, where different understandings of nature and unreliable interest in compliance with international standards and treaties on conservation prevailed; the politics were simply too delicate . . . to get hung up on whether or not something was 'natural'" (192).

This bracketing of the "natural" deeply affects the practice of animal research, ethnography, and fieldwork. Cussins's imaginary ethnography is framed as a metafiction, enfolding the story of a fictional ethnographer—Mary, the bioterrorist—who challenges the boundaries of fieldwork in her own way. Mary claims that her professional ethics is more radical than the familiar nostalgia of going native: "This meant being prepared to have the whole self move, not simply collapsing into the object of study—the sentimental anthropological fantasy of 'going native'—or ethnocentrically translating the object of knowledge into your own scheme of things." Instead of a mere fusion with her object of study, Mary pursues a transgression of self-boundaries perceived as a moving out of herself: "Compassion didn't stop you from judging or acting; it was the precondition of it" (211).

For Mary, the compassionate move outward results in an act that recalls the psychological dynamics of cannibalism: she literally "incorporates" the object of her study. Instead of eating it, she places it into her womb. In cannibalistic incorporations the other continues to live inside the cannibal, passing on his strength and other desired properties. Native people have even turned the anthropological phantasm of cannibalism around, blaming anthropologists for cannibalistic appropriations, thus insinuating that the cannibal desire to incorporate the object is not alien to the practice of fieldwork. Equally, it is not new to frame as fieldwork imaginary ethnographies that record reproductive technologies and alien reproduction. Butler's trilogy *Xenogenesis* is a science fiction imagining the cultural contact between the last humans who survived a nuclear holocaust and the Oankali, alien colonizers who try to save the earth's genetic pool in order to enrich and diversify their own. Humans and aliens observe each other like ethnographers, collecting information in order better to understand and cope with their mutual difference. In her precontact life before the nuclear holocaust, Lilith, the leading human protagonist, was majoring in anthropology. With bitter irony she now alludes to herself as a fieldworker when she is forced to bear cross-species children for the Oankali: "I suppose I could think of this as fieldwork—but how the hell do I get out of the field?"[2] Interestingly, the Oankali also provide a literal image of fieldwork's cannibal inclinations. They live their cannibal desire by "tasting" others with their tongues or tentacles, thereby creating intimate contact as well as conveniently collecting knowledge and genetic information. Both Butler's and Cussins's postmodern vision of "cultural contact" thus casts their fieldworkers as liminal figures with fluid boundaries toward their objects of study. In a similar vein, Donna Haraway concludes at the end of her analysis of Butler's *Xenogenesis* series in *Simians, Cyborgs, and Women*: "Anthropologists of possible selves, we are technicians of realizable futures. Science *is* culture."[3]

What these women ethnographers record, then, is the site of alien reproduction of children—be it one of a cross-species child of human and alien (Oankali) origin or one of a bonobo primate born to a human mother. Recording and witnessing the other—alien or primate—growing in one's own body and, in the case of Lilith, merging with one's own genes, forces one to experience the very boundaries of the species. Lilith's child is, as Haraway reminds us, "the child of five progenitors, who come from two species, at least three genders, two sexes, and an indeterminate number of races."[4] Imagining that alien invasions or human technologies make it possible for women to bear such others raises the most complex and complicated problems that contemporary biopolitics and bioethics must face in an age of reproductive technologies.

Bearing offspring from another species is also an experience that challenges the boundaries of human bonding. After becoming pregnant without consent, Lilith rejects the alien side of her own children: "But they won't be human. That's what matters," she exclaims, whereupon her alien mate responds, "The child inside you matters."[5] Mary, the bioterrorist, by contrast has become pregnant of her own will, fertilizing herself with a stolen bonobo embryo. Yet, is it the "primate child" inside her that matters? Cussins leaves this dilemma unresolved—just as Butler does not resolve the emotional and ethical dilemma that Lilith faces in relation to her alien child.

The recording of Mary's pregnancy is a tale of fantasy and regression, utopia and repression. Withdrawing to a Tucson hotel, she fantasizes "more than she has ever done," all the while writing "intensely ordinary holiday letters to her family and her in-laws" (217). About to give birth, Mary calls her friend Gabriela and confesses to have done the "Virgin fantasy thing" of impregnating herself with stolen bonobo germ plasm. "Confessions of a Bioterrorist" ends with the "Angel's" laconic response: "There's no bed in Bethlehem for you, Mary, but we will make absolutely sure that you have a couple of decent midwives and access to an operating room" (218).

Elevating the bonobo to a Christ figure, this last sentence leaves the reader with her own "primate visions." In contrast to the orthodox narrative of the holy birth of Jesus Christ, the bonobo springs from an "unholy alliance." What will happen to the little monkey born in a virgin birth to a human mother? If the bold allusion to the Christ figure is any indication, we may assume that the humans will end up killing the bonobo. But then we might also speculate about the bonobo becoming a savior figure. Would he (assuming he shares Christ's gender) try to save the humans from themselves and their own hubris? A kind of inverted Darwinism is, of course, implied throughout the story. The evolutionary telos can be turned around by technological means. Could Mary's bonobo be the first of a new species of human-born bonobo who would lead humans back to a primordial primate life, forsaking the very technology that has facilitated their coming into existence?

But Cussins's fantasy is not technophobic. Utopian bioterrorist, Mary would rather adhere to Andrew Ross's "Chicago Gangster Theory of Life" than to a narrative of nostalgic return to primate life in the trees of Eden.[6] Cussins therefore aptly includes "gangsters" when she thanks A. Lintz for her "insights on race, class, reproduction, and gangsters and for the exquisite compassion she shows all her subjects, both human and nonhuman" (219). In this respect, Cussins story counters the conventional narrative of primatology as Haraway defines it: "Primatology is about primal stories, the origin and nature of 'man,' and about reformation stories, the reform and reconstruction of human nature. Implicitly and explicitly, the story of the Garden of Eden emerges in the sciences of monkeys and apes, along with versions of the origin of society, marriage, and language."[7] "Confessions of a Bioterrorist" features a woman's willful renunciation of the Garden of Eden. A satirical inversion of the origin of species, Mary's primal story tells of the reconstruction of animal nature within human bounds. Defying both biological and cultural boundaries of reproduction, Mary's terrorist act could be judged as an outrageous denial of, if not ultimate rebellion against, the binarism of human and animal that lies at the very origin of culture and its distinction from nature. Blasphemously mocking the Christian myth of virgin birth, she exposes in grotesque distortion the most fundamental terms according to which this distinction aligns the female with nature: nature, the body, the primitive, animal, and female are all subjected to a confusion of boundaries. It is high-tech science that allows Mary to merge with a primitive animal, thus defying nature in feigning a grotesque act of "solidarity" (which she defines as compassion) with the other of man, the primate. Her own body becomes the stage for questioning her culture's obsession with this primate other in its attempt to separate itself from the natural, the animal, and the primitive. The fact that Cussins ends her story before the primate's birth marks its existence as a monstrous, unspeakable reality. If, as Haraway believes, the primal stories about monkeys are also about the origin of language, we may truly wonder what language Mary's bonobo will speak? Most likely it will remain—as it does in the story—an unnameable, deprived of language and agency.

The problem of agency is raised in the subtitle of Cussins's story: "Subject Position and Reproductive Technologies." Who has agency in the age of reproductive technologies, and who has the power to decide about reproduction? The issue is ethical as well as political. Technological reproduction is about making and inventing the future and about the (re)production of imaginable human and nonhuman selves. But it is also about the specter of gangsters and terrorists arrogating the right to decide "who and what gets to reproduce where and under what conditions" (189). Cussins's protagonist, Mary, has appropriated this choice for herself—the bonobo is a "baby" of choice. Mary's biopolitics is "in your face," a terrorist act performed by a split mind. The woman who lives her female fantasy of a virgin birth remains split from the one who calls home to her human children every night and writes intensely ordinary letters. Cussins defers the ethical dilemma to the readers. If reproduction is, as Cussins suggests, about politics, nature, and identity, then what does the bioterrorist's story tell us about these issues? To the degree that reproductive power is shifted to the institutional apparatus of technological reproduction, agency is taken away from the women who have traditionally borne the offspring. This lack of agency, in turn, will invite yet unimagined abuses of power, including the anti-institutional appropriation of power by "bioterrorists"—an anxiety that has recently surfaced in the media in relation to the debates about the cloned Scottish sheep. From this perspective, Mary's bioterrorism could be perceived as a travesty of anarchist resistance and feminist assertion. While she depended on her husband to conceive and bear her human children, nobody but she gets to decide whether she bears an embryo of primate origin. And if reproduction is "nature," then nature would certainly not facilitate the development of a primate embryo in a female body—unless it appeared "natural." If reproduction is identity, then how is Mary's identity affected by bearing primate offspring? And what happens to the bonobo's "identity"? How does this birth alter the identity of the human species? Traditionally—and well before Darwinism—monkeys have been perceived as the animal most closely related to humans. Occupying a liminal space between nature and culture, primates in the cultural imaginary often gain the status of being "almost human." Mary's pregnancy with the bonobo, however, only drives home how firmly the boundaries between the species are nonetheless established. While films in which women primatologists raise and nurture baby monkeys like human children are blockbusters and thrive on the market value of a primate primitivism, the fact that a woman chooses to bear a primate embryo and give birth to a little bonobo turns her into a monster.

Monsters are beings who violate the boundaries of what is conventionally defined as "human." *The American Heritage Dictionary* distinguishes between different types of monsters according to the specificity of their boundary violation: "1. A creature having a bizarre or frightening shape or appearance. 2. An animal or plant having structural defects or deformities. 3. A fetus or infant that is grotesquely abnormal. 4. A very large animal or object. 5. One who inspires horror or disgust."[8] It is interesting to compare the boundary violation in Lilith's alien child with that of Mary's bonobo. Oankali children combine human and alien features. Their most striking physical difference consists in sensory tentacles that can appear anywhere on the body. Some Oankali have gray tongues with deadly stingers. Most humans instinctively react by finding them ugly and frightening, and they certainly inspire horror and disgust in those who have not yet been in intimate contact with them. Appearing like humans with structural defects or deformities, they recall those other monsters, the mutants. The Oankali's "deformities," however, endow them with capacities that far exceed that of their human counterparts: their senses show a much higher development, and they have the ability to correct genetic defects and heal their own or other bodies from most injuries. (They can, in other words, prevent the development of monsters!).

By contrast, Mary's bonobo will display the familiar shape and appearance of a simian and most likely be free of defects or deformities. It is, however, a "fetus or infant that is grotesquely abnormal" and therefore inspires horror and disgust—not because of its own physical properties but because of its location inside the womb of the wrong species. The boundary violation lies here, in a lack of respect for the boundaries of the species—an act perceived as bioterrorism. Mary, however, sees her transgression of the boundaries of the species as a form of compassion toward the object of study. In its most radical form, such a compassion would require that one substitutes an anthropocentric or even "species-centered" ethic with a biocentric ethic.[9] If it is true that, as Haraway claims, "decolonization forced white western scientists to restructure their bio-politics of self and other, native and alien," then this process also requires the development of a new ethics related to the changing biopolitics.[10] And yet, can one derive a biocentric ethic from an act of bioterrorism?

And how far will this compassion extend once the Bonobo is born? More important, how will Mary "externalize" it into a communal world? Interestingly, during her pregnancy Mary rather regresses to a narcissistic involvement with herself. She all but forgets about the being growing inside of her, resorting instead to fantasizing and giving herself pleasure freely. Far from inhabiting a space of deterritorialization in which she experiences a Deleuzian "becoming animal," she remains in a space of normality that appears all the more monstrous precisely because it depends on the utter repression of what is about to happen. To a certain extent, we as readers remain suspended in that space as well. Mary seems to be too mundane to be radical, too monstrous to be real. We relate to her story as a "thought experiment" rather than a powerful fiction. But as such, this experiment confronts us with yet another "realizable future"—that of cross-species fertilization of humans.

Cussins's "primate vision" raises more questions than it answers. If reproduction is past, present, and future, are the primates as the distant past of the humans perhaps also their future? Literalizing questions about reproductive technology in an outrageous visual fantasy, "Confessions of a Bioterrorist" insists that we will no longer be able to ignore the far-reaching implications of postmodern reproductive biopolitics. The work of humans in the age of technological reproduction requires a radical rethinking of the boundaries of nature and culture as well as the boundaries of what we define and experience as "human." Reproductive technology has become culture, and we are technicians of our own futures. Responding to the threats and challenge of such technology, reproductive fantasies and fictions belong to what Donna Haraway calls the "survival literature in global, nuclear culture."[11]

While "Confessions of a Bioterrorist" can be read as a response to late-twentieth-century primatology, Butler's *Xenogenesis* series is explicitly conceived as a postnuclear holocaust survival fiction. Survival literature harbors savior figures and fantasies of redemption. Similarly, the main protagonist in *Adulthood Rites*, the second book of Butler's *Xenogenesis* series, is figured as a "construct human"—offspring of human and alien parents—who takes it upon himself to save the human race by granting them reproductive rights under condition of their relocation to Mars. There they will be allowed to reproduce even under the risk that they only use this right once again to destroy themselves. Cussins provides the rhetorical framework for a savior narrative with her story of the virgin birth, but the bonobo can at most be a pitiful savior figure. Rather than a narrative of redemption, Cussins presents us with a tale of the technological gothic. The little bonobo is not King Kong, the failed primate savior, but the unnamed and unnameable product of his "mother's" monstrous transgression. In him we encounter the unnameable monster of reproductive technologies.

"Science fiction is a territory of contested cultural reproduction in high-technology worlds," writes Haraway.[12] The science fiction discussed here is primarily about contested biological reproduction. It engages cultural fantasies generated by the fact that technology has begun to appropriate the territory of biological reproduction. How we address questions raised by such science fiction will determine the identity, the boundaries, and the heteronomy of our species. It will equally affect others we choose to destroy or allow to reproduce—be it in their natural environment, an animal conservation site, or an in vitro cylinder; be it in a body of their own or an alien species. Thus it may well be a primate of woman born that renders the human body into the alien object as which it already figures in many discourses of science and technology. The body as the last remnant of "nature" becomes as alien as the species it harbors—be it a bonobo embryo from a frozen zoo or an alien from outer space.

The primate and the alien are liminal figures in the cultural imaginary, marking the boundaries between the human and the nonhuman. In the age of their own possible technological reproduction, humans can no longer figure these boundaries as a distinction between nature and culture. Fictions that challenge and redraw those boundaries therefore work toward setting new terms for the traffic between nature and culture—a traffic in which humans are reconfigured from the perspective of primate and alien visions.

Notes

1. Donna Haraway, *Primate Visions: Gender, Race, and Nature in the World of Modern Science* (New York: Routledge, 1989), 8.
2. Octavia E. Butler, *Dawn*, book one of the *Xenogenesis* series (New York: Warner Books, 1987), 91.
3. Donna Haraway, *Simians, Cyborgs, and Women: The Reinvention of Nature* (New York: Routledge, 1991), 230.
4. Ibid., 227.
5. Butler, *Dawn*, 263.
6. Andrew Ross, *The Chicago Gangster Theory of Life: Nature's Debt to Society* (New York: Verso, 1994).
7. Haraway, *Primate Visions*, 9.
8. *The American Heritage Dictionary*, 2d College Ed. (Boston: Houghton Mifflin, 1982).
9. For a discussion of the expansion of ethics from anthropocentrism to speciesism and biocentrism, see Roderick Nash, *The Rights of Nature: A History of Environmental Ethics* (Madison: University of Wisconsin Press, 1989).
10. Haraway, *Primate Visions*, 7.
11. Ibid., 3.
12. Ibid., 5.

Conclusion

E. ANN KAPLAN
SUSAN SQUIER

The essays in this volume explore a range of "reproductive technologies" from the specifically biomedical to the broadly sociocultural. The volume opens and concludes with assisted reproductive technology, used as treatment for human infertility and for zoological conservation. Along the way, essays also explore the practices of cosmetic and transsexual surgery that people use to reproduce a certain biological physique. Commercial film, popular fiction, and journalism reproduce dominant images; but avant-garde fiction, film, and video reproduce a network of subjectivities, relationships, and practices so as to break the monopoly of experts: these aesthetic modes can give direct testimony about the varied oppressive effects of the experts' practices.

This collection includes a range of disciplines and genres with essays that study the transformative knowledge and practices that transgress established boundaries. We have labeled this transgression "playing Dolly" to allude to Ian Wilmut's accomplishment in cloning the Finn Dorset ewe. The disciplinary monopoly that constructs solid boundaries between different kinds of expert knowledge is breaking down, just as the other kinds of boundaries (of gender and genre, of species and generation) are being eroded. Essays in this volume explore the kinds of feminist scholarship that can emerge at such a moment of boundary breakdown. But what of the future? How will "playing Dolly" reconfigure knowledge and practices in the years to come?

We can begin to answer these questions if we turn to the 10 March 1997 issue of *Time*, which superimposes on its cover photo of identical sheep the caption "Will There Ever Be Another You? A Special Report on Cloning." Published in response to the cloning of Dolly, the issue covered the full range of news the event generated, beginning with a "Special Report: The Age of Cloning" and then providing assessments of the event's technological, ethical, financial, and psychological implications. But, interestingly, following these expert assessments and still under the subcategory "Science," the volume featured a work of fiction, Douglas Coupland's short story "Clone, Clone on the Range." Coupland, best known for his fictional definition of Generation X, weighs in on the Dolly story with a work, carefully labeled "science fiction," that is closer to satire than science. The story's first sentence sets the tone: "Back when the first news of successful human cloning was announced, humanity was split into two irreconcilable camps: those who said, 'How demonic!' and those, like myself—beloved and durable film star Corey Holiday—who said, 'Hey! Where do I send my money?'"

Vivian Sobchack observes, in her essay in this volume, that "cinema is cosmetic surgery . . . and cosmetic surgery is cinema, creating us as an image we not only learn to enact . . . but also must—and never can—live up to." Coupland's short story extrapolates from those age-extension properties shared by cinema and cosmetic surgery an even more powerful site of rejuvenation, tracing movie star Corey Holiday's search for an entrepreneur in "retail cloning" who can help him hold back age. Echoing the agribusiness-reproductive technology link that Charis Cussins's short story explores, Holiday's search leads him to "an exclusive (naturally) cow-based Saskatchewan cloning spa—a spa combining the best of Saskatchewan's cattle country with Canada's lax cloning laws." There he has himself cloned five times: the embryos are to be gestated in the "superior cattle with modified immune systems" who were being used there as the "cross-species surrogate of choice." However, cattle rustlers abscond with the surrogate cows, and only after the media cooperates and gives the embryo stealing top billing on the evening news does Holiday find his stolen embryos. When the story ends, we learn that Holiday has left Hollywood. Instead, he and his movie star wife, Lori, have dedicated their lives "to fighting embryo poaching. Us and our 10 beautiful children: Cori, Korrie, Corry, Korey, Korrey, Laurie, Lorrie, Lurey, Lorrey and Lorri."

Written in response to the riveting news story of Dolly's cloning, Coupland's work of fiction recapitulates a number of the themes explored by authors in this volume who wrote before Wilmut's feat: these themes include the links between medical and agribusiness uses of reproductive technology; the traffic between biological, cinematic, surgical, and financial modes of reproduction; the remarkable speed with which striking biological innovations are normalized, whether it's human surrogacy, gamete donation, cloning, or xenosurrogacy. Finally, with its inclusion in the Time section on science, Coupland's short story illustrates the crossover effect of avant-garde fiction in this time of increasing boundary breakdowns. Like Charis Cussins short story in this volume, "Clone, Clone on the Range" enacts a generic version of the resistance it narrates with its tale of the clonal father who pledges his life to fighting "cattle rustlers," film stars and financial magnates who are cornering the market on "life."

Works Cited

Abu-Lughod, Lila. "The Romance of Resistance: Tracing Transformations of Power through Bedouin Women." In *Beyond the Second Sex: New Directions in the Anthropology of Gender*, ed. Peggy Sanday and Ruth Goodenough, 311–337. Philadelphia: University of Pennsylvania Press, 1992.

"An Account of the Life and Writings of Dr. Edward Tyson." In *A Compleat History of Europe*. London, 1709.

Akheter, H., et al. "A Five Year Clinical Evaluation of Norplant Contraceptive Subdermal Implants in Bangladeshi Acceptors." *Contraception* 47, no. 6 (1993): 569–582.

The American Heritage Dictionary. 2d College Ed. Boston: Houston Mifflin, 1982.

Antrowitz, Barbara, and Pat Wingert. "The Norplant Debate." *Newsweek*, 15 February 1993, 37.

Aristotle. *Generation of Animals*. Translated by A. L. Peck. Cambridge: Harvard University Press, 1963.

Ballantyne, J. W. *Teratogenesis: An Inquiry into the Causes of Monstrosities: History of Theories of the Past*. Edinburgh, 1897.

Balsamo, Anne. *Technologies of the Gendered Body: Reading Cyborg Women*. Durham, N.C.: Duke University Press, 1996.

Barrett, Michelle. *Women's Oppression Today*. Rev. ed. London: Verso, 1980.

Baudrillard, Jean. *The Transparency of Evil: Essays on Extreme Phenomena* [1990]. Translated by James Benedict. London: Verso, 1993.

Beck, Ulrich. *Risk Society: Towards a New Modernity* (London: Sage Publications, 1992).

Begley, Sharon. "The Baby Myth." *Newsweek*, 4 September 1995, 38–47.

Berenson, A. B., and C. M. Wiemann. "Patient Satisfaction and Side Effects with Levonorgestrel Implant (Norplant) Use in Adolescents Eighteen Years of Age or Younger." *Pediatrics* 92, no. 2 (1993): 257–260.

BKKBN (Indonesian National Family Planning Coordinating Board). *The Muslim Ummah and Family Planning in Indonesia*. Jakarta, Indonesia: BKKBN, 1993.

Blackwood, Evelyn. "Senior Women, Model Mothers, and Dutiful Wives: Managing Gender Contradictions in a Minangkabau Village." In *Bewitching Women, Pious Men: Gender and Body Politics in Southeast Asia*, ed. Aihwa Ong and Michael Peletz, 124–158. Berkeley and Los Angeles: University of California Press, 1995.

Blank, Robert, and Janna C. Merrick. *Human Reproduction, Emerging Technologies, and Conflicting Rights*. Washington, D.C.: Congressional Quarterly Press, 1995.

Bogdan, Robert. *Freak Show: Presenting Human Oddities for Amusement and Profit*. Chicago: University of Chicago Press, 1988.

Boyer, Paul. *By the Bomb's Early Light: American Thought and Culture at the Dawn of the Atomic Age.* New York: Pantheon, 1985.

Brenner, Suzanne. "Why Women Rule the Roost: Rethinking Javanese Ideologies of Gender and Self-Control." In *Bewitching Women, Pious Men: Gender and Body Politics in Southeast Asia,* ed. Aihwa Ong and Michael Peletz, 19–50. Berkeley and Los Angeles: University of California Press, 1995.

———. "Reconstructing Self and Society: Javanese Muslim Women and 'the Veil.'" *American Ethnologist* 23, no. 4 (1996): 673–697.

Brodie, Janet Farrell. *Contraception and Abortion in Nineteenth-Century America.* Ithaca, N.Y.: Cornell University Press, 1994.

Bruckner, Pascal. *The Divine Child: A Novel of Prenatal Rebellion.* Translated by Joachim Neugroschel. Boston: Little, Brown & Co., 1994.

Butler, Judith. *Bodies That Matter: On the Discursive Limits of Sex.* New York: Routledge, 1993.

Butler, Octavia E. *Dawn: Xenogenesis.* New York: Warner Books, 1987.

———. *Adulthood Rites: Xenogenesis.* New York: Warner Books, 1988.

———. *Imago: Xenogenesis.* New York: Warner Books, 1989.

Butzel, Henry M. "The Essential Facts of the BABY M Case." In *On the Problem of Surrogate Parenthood,* ed. Herbert Richardson, 7–20. Symposium Series, 25. New York: Edwin Mellen Press 1987.

Canguilhem, Georges. *The Normal and the Pathological.* New York: Zone Books, 1991.

Chaloupka, William. *Knowing Nukes: The Politics and Culture of the Atom.* Minneapolis: University of Minnesota Press, 1992.

Charlesworth, Max. *Bioethics in a Liberal Society.* Melbourne: Cambridge University Press, 1993.

Chasseguet-Smirgel, Janine. *Creativity and Perversion.* London: Free Association, 1985.

Chesler, Phyllis. *Sacred Bond: The Legacy of Baby M.* New York: Simon and Schuster, 1988.

Cohen, Margot. "Success Brings New Problems." *Far East Economic Review* 151, no. 16 (18 April 1991): 48–49.

Crossette, Barbara. "A Third-World Effort on Family Planning." *New York Times,* 7 September 1994, 8.

Croxatto, H. B. "Norplant: Levonorgestrel-Releasing Contraceptive Implant." *Annual Medicine* 25, no. 2 (1993): 155–160.

Cullins, V. E. "Injectable and Implantable Contraceptives." *Current Opinion in Obstetrics and Gynecology* 4, no. 4 (1992): 536–543.

———. "Preliminary Experiences with Norplant in Inner-City Populations." *Contraception* 47, no. 2 (1993): 193–203.

Cussins, Charis. "Producing Reproduction: Techniques of Normalization and Naturalization in Infertility Clinics." In *Reproducing Reproduction: Kinship, Power, and Technological Innovation,* ed. Sarah Franklin and Helena Ragoné, 66–101. Philadelphia: University of Pennsylvania Press, 1998.

Daston, Lorraine. "Marvelous Facts and Miraculous Evidence in Early Modern Europe." *Critical Inquiry* 18, no. 1 (1991): 93–124.

Debord, Guy. *The Society of the Spectacle* [1967]. Detroit: Black and Red Press, 1983.

Deegan, Mary Jo. "The Gift Mother: A Proposed Ritual for the Integration of Surrogacy into Society." In *On the Problem of Surrogate Parenthood,* ed. Herbert Richardson, 91–106. Symposium Series, 25. New York: Edwin Mellen Press, 1987.

de Lauretis, Teresa. "Signs of Wa/onder." In *The Technological Imagination: Theories and Fictions,* ed. Teresa de Lauretis, Andreas Huyssen, and Kathleen Woodward. Madison, Wis.: Coda Press, 1980.

———. *Technologies of Gender: Essays on Theory, Film, and Fiction.* Bloomington: Indiana University Press, 1987.

Delbanco, Andrew. *The Puritan Ordeal*. Cambridge, Mass.: Harvard University Press, 1989.

de Rooy, Piet. "In Search of Perfection: The Creation of a Missing Link." In *Ape, Man, Apeman: Changing Views since 1600*, ed. Raymond Corbey and Bert Theunissen, 195–209. Leiden: Department of Prehistory, Leiden University, 1995.

Doane, Mary Ann. "Technophilia: Technology, Representation, and the Feminine." In *Body/Politics: Women and the Discourses of Science*, ed. Mary Jacobus, Evelyn Fox Keller, and Sally Shuttleworth, 103–176. New York: Routledge, 1990.

Dougherty, Frank. "Missing Link, Chain of Being, Ape and Man in the Enlightenment: The Argument of the Naturalists." In *Ape, Man, Apeman: Changing Views Since 1600*, ed. Raymond Corbey and Bert Theunissen, 63–71. Leiden: Department of Prehistory, Leiden University, 1995.

Duden, Barbara. *The Woman Beneath the Skin: A Doctor's Patients in Eighteenth-Century Germany*. Cambridge: Harvard University Press, 1991.

———. *Disembodying Women: Perspectives on Pregnancy and the Unborn*. Cambridge: Harvard University Press, 1993.

Dwyer, Leslie. "Spectacular Sexuality: Nationalism, Development, and the Politics of Family Planning in Indonesia." In *Gender Ironies of Nationalism: Sexing the Nation*, ed. Tamar Mayer. New York: Routledge, forthcoming.

"Elizabeth." "A Surrogate's Story of Loving and Losing." *U.S. News and World Report*, 6 June 1983, 77.

Elliott, Dorinda, and Friso Endt. "Twins—with Two Fathers." *Newsweek*, 3 July 1995, 38.

"Ending Child Labour." *Economist*, 30 January 1993, 26–27.

Englemann, George J. "The Increasing Sterility of American Women." *Journal of the American Medical Association* 37 (1901): 890–897.

Epstein, Julia, and Kristina Straub. "Introduction: The Guarded Body." In *Body Guards: The Cultural Politics of Gender Ambiguity*, ed. Julia Epstein and Kristina Straub, 1–28. New York: Routledge, 1991.

Escobar, Arturo. *Encountering Development: The Making and Unmaking of the Third World*. Princeton, N. J.: Princeton University Press, 1995.

Evans-Pritchard, E. E. *Witchcraft, Oracles, and Magic among the Azande*. New York: Oxford University Press, 1937.

"Family Planning Participants Spurn Comfy Contraceptives." *Jakarta Post*, 12 July 1996, 2.

Felski, Rita. "Fin de Siècle, Fin de Sex: Transsexuality, Postmodernism, and the Death of History." *New Literary History* 27 (1996): 337–349.

Ferguson, James. *The Anti-Politics Machine: "Development," Depoliticization, and Bureaucratic Power in Lesotho*. Minneapolis: University of Minnesota Press, 1994.

Ferzacca, Steve. "In This Pocket of the Universe: Healing the Modern in a Central Javanese City." Ph.D. diss. University of Wisconsin at Madison, 1996. See abstract in *Dissertation Abstracts International* 57, no. 6 (December 1996): 2545A.

Fessenden, Ford. "Woman Has Custody of Fertilized Eggs: Ex-Spouse's Rights Dismissed." *Newsday*, 20 January 1995, A4.

Findlay, Stephen. "Birth Control." *U.S. News & World Report*, 24 December 1990, 58–64.

Fineman, Martha A. and Martha T. McClusky, eds. *Feminism, Media, and the Law*. London and New York: Oxford University Press, 1997.

Fleming, Anne Taylor. *Motherhood Deferred: A Woman's Journey*. New York: G. P. Putnam's Sons, 1994.

Foucault, Michel. *The Order of Things: An Archeology of the Human Sciences*. 1966. Reprint, New York: Vintage, 1971.

Frank, M. L., A. N. Poindexter, M. L. Johnston, and L. Bateman. "Characteristics and

Attitudes of Early Contraceptive Implant Acceptors in Texas." *Family Planning Perspective* 24, no. 5 (1992): 208–213.

Franklin, Sarah. "Fetal Fascinations: New Dimensions to the Medical-Scientific Construction of Fetal Personhood." In *Off-Centre: Feminism and Cultural Studies*, ed. Sarah Franklin, Celia Lury, and Jackie Stacy, 190–213. London: Harper-Collins, 1991.

———. "Postmodern Procreation: A Cultural Account of Assisted Reproduction." In *Conceiving the New World Order: The Global Politics of Reproduction*, ed. Faye Ginsburg and Rayna Rapp, 323–345. Berkeley: University of California Press, 1995.

———. "Making Miracles: Scientific Progress and the Facts of Life." In *Reproducing Reproduction: Kinship, Power, and Technological Innovation*, ed. Sarah Franklin and Helena Ragoné, 102–117. Philadelphia: University of Pennsylvania Press, 1998.

Freud, Sigmund. "The Predisposition to Obsessional Neurosis." In *Collected Papers*, vol. 2, ed. Ernest Jones, 122–132. Translated by Joan Riviere. London: Hogarth and the Institute of Psycho-Analysis, 1959.

Geertz, Clifford. *After the Fact: Two Countries, Four Decades, One Anthropologist.* Cambridge: Harvard University Press, 1995.

Geertz, Hildred. *The Javanese Family: A Study of Kinship and Socialization.* Prospect Heights, Ill.: Waveland Press, 1961.

Gelman, David, and Daniel Shapiro. "Infertility: Babies by Contract." *Newsweek*, 4 November 1985, 74–76.

Ginsberg, Faye. "The 'Word-Made' Flesh: The Disembodiment of Gender in the Abortion Debate." In *Uncertain Terms: Negotiating Gender in American Culture*, ed. Faye Ginsberg and Anna Lowenhaupt Tsing, 59–75. Boston: Beacon, 1990.

Gledhill, Christine, ed. *Home Is Where the Heart Is: Studies in Melodrama and the Woman's Film.* London: British Film Institute, 1987.

Goldberg, David Theo. *Racist Culture: Philosophy and the Politics of Meaning.* Oxford: Blackwell, 1993.

Good, Byron. *Medicine, Rationality, and Experience: An Anthropological Perspective.* New York: Cambridge University Press, 1994.

Gordon, Linda. *Woman's Body, Woman's Right.* New York: Penguin Books, 1974.

———. "Some Policy Proposals: Reproductive Rights for Today." *Nation*, 17 September 1987, 230–232.

Gould, George M., and Walter L. Pyle. *Anomalies and Curiosities of Medicine.* Philadelphia, 1897.

Greenhalgh, Susan. "Controlling Births and Bodies in Village China." *American Ethnologist* 21, no. 1 (1994): 3–30.

Grogan, D. "Little Girl, Big Trouble: A Surrogate Birth, a Divorce, and a Tangled Custody Fight Mean an Uncertain Future for a Child Known Only as Tessa." *People*, 20 February 1989, 36–41.

Guinzburg, Suzanne. "Surrogate Mothers' Rationale." *Psychology Today* (April 1983): 79.

Gupta, Nelly E., and Frank Feldinger. "Brave New Baby." *Ladies Home Journal* 106, no. 2 (1989): 140–141.

Hall, David, ed. *The Antinomian Controversy, 1636–1638: A Documentary History.* 2d ed. Durham, N.C.: Duke University Press, 1990.

Haraway, Donna. *Primate Visions: Gender, Race, and Nature in the World of Modern Science.* New York: Routledge, 1989.

———. *Simians, Cyborgs, and Women: The Reinvention of Nature.* New York: Routledge, 1991.

———. *Modest Witness@Second Millennium.FemaleMan Meets OncoMouse: Feminism and Technoscience.* New York: Routledge, 1997.

Hartmann, Betsy. *Reproductive Rights and Wrongs: The Global Politics of Population Control.* Boston: South End Press, 1995.

Hartouni, Valerie. "Breached Births: Reflections on Race, Gender, and Reproductive Discourses in the 1980s." *Configurations: A Journal of Literature, Science, and Technology* 2, no. 1 (1994): 73–88.

Hatley, Barbara. "Theatrical Imagery and Gender Ideology in Java." In *Power and Difference: Gender in Island Southeast Asia,* ed. J. Atkinson and S. Errington, 177–207. Stanford, Calif.: Stanford University Press, 1990.

Hausman, Bernice. *Changing Sex: Transsexualism, Technology, and the Idea of Gender.* Durham, N. C.: Duke University Press, 1995.

Heidenreich, Linda. "A Historical Perspective of Christine Jorgensen and the Development of a Construct." Paper presented at the First International Congress on Cross-Dressing, Sex, and Gender, California State University at Northridge, 1995.

Henrikson, Margot. *Dr. Strangelove's America: Society and Culture in the Atomic Age.* Berkeley: University of California Press, 1998.

Hessert, S. William, Jr. "Distinguished Speaker: Dr. Ian Wilmut." *State College* (March 1998): 31.

Hobart, Mark, ed. *An Anthropological Critique of Development: The Growth of Ignorance.* New York: Routledge, 1993.

Huet, Marie-Hélène. *Monstrous Imagination.* Cambridge: Harvard University Press, 1993.

Hull, Terence. "Population Growth Falling in Indonesia." *Bulletin of Indonesian Economic Studies* 27, no. 2 (1991): 137–143.

Hurley, Kelly. *The Gothic Body: Sexuality, Materialism, and Degeneration at the Fin de Siècle.* New York: Cambridge University Press, 1996.

International Bank for Reconstruction and Development (IBRD). *Population and the World Bank: Implications from Eight Case Studies.* Washington, D.C.: IBRD Operations Evaluation Department, 1992.

International Bank for Reconstruction and Development (IBRD), Indonesia. *Family Planning Perspectives in the 1990s.* Washington, D.C.: IBRD, 1990.

Jameson, Fredric. Foreword to Jean-François Lyotard, *The Postmodern Condition: A Report on Knowledge.* Translated by Brian Massumi. Minneapolis: University of Minnesota Press, 1984.

———. *Postmodernism: Or, the Cultural Logic of Late Capitalism.* Chapel Hill, N.C.: Duke University Press, 1990.

Johnson, Samuel. *Dictionary of the English Language: in which the words are deduced from their originals [etc.].* London, 1755.

Jones, Steve. *The Language of Genes.* New York: Doubleday, 1993.

Jorgensen, Christine. *Christine Jorgensen: A Personal Autobiography.* New York: Bantam Books, 1968.

Kane, Elizabeth. *Birth Mother.* New York: Harcourt Brace, 1988.

Kaplan, E. Ann. *Motherhood and Representation: The Mother in Popular Culture and Melodrama.* London: Routledge, 1992.

———. *Women and Film: Both Sides of the Camera.* New York: Routledge, 1983.

Kaplan, Tracy, and John Johnson. "District Defends School Clinic Offering Norplant Contraceptive." *Los Angeles Times,* 26 March 1993, B3.

Kasule, J., T. Chipato, A. Zinanga, M. Mbizvo, and J. Maigurira. "Norplant in Zimbabwe: Preliminary Report." *Central Africa Journal of Medicine* 38, no. 8 (1992): 321–324.

Keeler, Ward. "Speaking of Gender in Java." In *Power and Difference: Gender in Island Southeast Asia,* ed. J. Atkinson and S. Errington, 127–152. Stanford, Calif.: Stanford University Press, 1990.

Kennedy, Ian. *Animal Tissue into Humans: A Report by the Advisory Group on the Ethics of Xenotransplantation*. London: Her Majesty's Stationery Office, 1996.

Kerr, Kathleen, and Jamie Talan. "Mixed Blessing." *Newsday*, 30 November 1997, A5.

Kimbrell, Andrew. *The Human Body Shop: The Engineering and Marketing of Life*. San Francisco: HarperSanFrancisco, 1993.

King, Sherry, and Elaine Fein. "'I Gave Birth to My Sister's Baby.'" *Redbook* (April 1986): 34–38.

Kirkman, Maggie, and Linda Kirkman. *My Sister's Child*. Ringwood, Victoria: Penguin Books, 1988.

Kolata, Gina. *Clone: The Road to Dolly and the Path Ahead*. New York: Morrow, 1998.

Kuttner, Robert. "Columbia/HCA and the Resurgence of the for-Profit Hospital Business. Pts. and and 2. *New England Journal of Medicine* 335, no. 5 (1996): 362–367; no. 6 (1996): 446–451.

Lacayo, R., and W. Svoboda. "Is the Womb a Rentable Space?" *Time*, 22 September 1987, 36.

Lang, Amy Schranger. *Prophetic Woman: Anne Hutchinson and the Problem of Dissent in the Literature of New England*. Berkeley and Los Angeles: University of California Press, 1987.

Laqueur, Thomas. "Orgasm, Generation, and the Politics of Reproductive Biology." In *The Making of the Modern Body: Sexuality and Society in the Nineteenth Century*, ed. Catherine Gallagher and Thomas Laqueur, 1–41. Berkeley: University of California Press, 1987.

Lasker, Judith N., and Susan Borg. *In Search of Parenthood: Coping with Infertility and High-Tech Conception*. London: Pandora, 1989.

Latour, Bruno. *Science in Action: How to Follow Scientists and Engineers Through Society*. Cambridge: Harvard University Press, 1987.

———. *We Have Never Been Modern*. Cambridge: Harvard University Press, 1993.

Laws, Glenda. "Tabloid Bodies: Aging, Beauty, and Health in Popular Discourse." Paper presented at "Women & Aging: Bodies, Cultures, Generations," Center for Twentieth Century Studies, University of Wisconsin–Milwaukee, April 1996.

Lerner, Sharon. "The Price of Eggs: Undercover in the Infertility Industry." *Ms.* (March–April 1996): 28–34.

Ludovici, Anthony. *Lysistrata, or Woman's Future and Future Woman*. London: Kegan Paul, Trench, Trubner, & Co., 1924.

Luker, Kristin. *Abortion and the Politics of Motherhood*. Berkeley: University of California Press, 1984.

Lyotard, Jean-François. *The Postmodern Condition: A Report on Knowledge*. Translated by Brian Massumi. Minneapolis: University of Minnesota Press, 1984.

Malcolm, Andrew H. "Steps to Control Surrogate Births Stir Debate Anew." *New York Times*, 26 June 1988, A1.

Mall, Franklin P. "A Study of the Causes Underlying the Origin of Human Monsters." *Journal of Morphology* 19, no. 1 (1908): 3–367.

Markoutsas, Elaine. 1981. "Women Who Have Babies for Other Women." Condensed from *Good Housekeeping* (April 1981). *Reader's Digest* 119 (August 1981): 71.

Marrs, Richard. *Dr. Richard Marrs' Fertility Book: America's Leading Fertility Expert Tells You Everything You Need to Know about Getting Pregnant*. New York: Dell, 1997.

May, Elaine Tyler. *Homeward Bound: American Families in the Cold War*. New York: Basic Books, 1988.

McDougall, Joyce. *Theatres of the Mind: Illusion and Truth on the Psychoanalytic Stage*. London: Free Association, 1986.

McKay, Shona. "A Media Judgement on Surrogate Birth." *Maclean's*, 14 February 1983, 41.

McNicholl, Geoffrey, and Masri Singarimbun. *Fertility Decline in Indonesia*. Yogyakarta: Gadjah Mada University Press, 1986.

McPherson, C. B. *The Political Theory of Possessive Individualism: Hobbes to Locke.* Oxford: Clarendon Press, 1962.

Melamed, Elissa. *Mirror, Mirror: The Terror of Not Being Young.* New York: Linden Press, 1983.

Meyerowitz, Joanne. "Sex-Change and the Popular Press: Historical Notes on Transsexuality in the United States, 1930–1955." *GLQ* 4, no. 2 (1998): 145–158.

Mills, Karen. "'I had My Sister's Baby.'" *Ladies Home Journal* (October 1985): 20–23.

Mingay, Jane. "The Furor over Surrogate Motherhood." *Maclean's,* 5 July 1982, 18.

Mitchem, Carl, and Robert Mackey. *Philosophy and Technology.* New York: Free Press, 1972.

Monboddo, James Burnett, Lord. *Ancient Metaphysics, Volume Third, Containing the History and Philosophy of Man.* Edinburgh, 1779.

Monroe, Jonathan. "Poetry, the University, and the Culture of Distraction." *diacritics* 26, nos. 3–4 (Fall–Winter 1996): 3–30.

Montagu, M. F. Ashley. *Edward Tyson, M.D., F.R.S., 1650–1708, and the Rise of Human Comparative Anatomy in England.* Philadelphia: American Philosophical Society, 1943.

Montgomery, Peter. "Should Surrogate Motherhood Be Banned?" *Common Cause Magazine* (May/June 1988): 36–38.

Muller, Hermann. *Out of the Night: A Biologist's View of the Future.* London: Victor Gollancz, 1936.

Muller, Stephen, et al. "National Institutes of Health Final Report of the Human Embryo Research Panel." 27 September 1994.

Murphy, Julie. "Egg Farming and Women's Future." In *Test Tube Women: What Future for Motherhood,* ed. R. Arditti, R. Dueilli Klein, and Shellen Minden, 68–75. London: Pandora Press, 1984.

Musallam, B. F. *Sex and Society in Islam.* Cambridge, U.K.: Cambridge University Press, 1983.

Nadel, Alan. *Containment Culture: American Narratives, Postmodernism, and the Atomic Age.* Durham, N.C.: Duke University Press, 1995.

Nash, Roderick. *The Rights of Nature: A History of Environmental Ethics.* Madison: University of Wisconsin Press, 1989.

Neff, David. "How Not to Have a Baby: Surrogate Mothers May Create a New Class of Breeder Women and Further Confuse the Family Unity." *Christianity Today,* 3 April 1987, 14–15.

Neumann, Peter, Soheyla D. Gharib, and Milton C. Weinstein. "The Cost of a Successful Delivery with In Vitro Fertilization." *New England Journal of Medicine* 331, no. 4 (1994): 239, 242.

"Norplant: A Three-Year Report." *Glamour* (July 1994): 154–157.

Norton, Mary Beth. *Founding Mothers and Fathers: Gendered Power and the Forming of American Society.* New York: Knopf, 1996.

Nye, David E. *American Technological Sublime.* Cambridge: MIT Press, 1994.

Oudshoorn, Nelly. "A Natural Order of Things? Reproductive Science and the Politics of Othering." In *Future/Natural: Nature, Science, Culture,* ed. George Robertson, Melinda Mash, Lisa Tucker, Jon Bird, Barry Curtis, and Tim Putnam. Routledge: New York, 1992.

Pace, Brian, and Micaela Sullivan-Fowler, eds. "JAMA 95 Years Ago." *Journal of the American Medical Association* 276, no. 14 (1996): 1120.

Paré, Ambroise. *On Monsters and Marvels* [1575]. Translated by Janis L. Pallister. Chicago: University of Chicago Press, 1982.

Park, Katharine, and Lorraine J. Daston. "Unnatural Conceptions: The Study of Monsters in Sixteenth- and Seventeenth-Century France and England." *Past and Present* 92 (August 1981): 20–54.

Pateman, Carole. *The Sexual Contract*. Stanford, Calif.: Stanford University Press, 1988.

People Today, 5 May 1954.

Petchesky, Rosalind. *Abortion and Woman's Choice: The State of Sexuality and Reproductive Freedom*. New York: Longman, 1984.

———. "Foetal Images: The Power of Visual Culture in the Politics of Reproduction."
In *Reproductive Technologies: Gender, Motherhood, and Medicine*, ed. Michelle
Stanworth, 57–80. Minneapolis: University of Minnesota Press, 1987.

———. "Fetal Images: The Power of Visual Culture in the Politics of Reproduction."
In *Theorizing Feminism: Parallel Trends in the Humanities and Social Sciences*, ed. June
C. Herrmann and Abigail J. Stewart, 401–423. Boulder, Colo.: Westview Press,
1994.

Piotrow, Phyllis T., Katherine A. Treiman, Jose G. Rimon III, Sung Hee Yun, and Benjamin V. Lozare. *Strategies for Family Planning Promotion: World Bank Technical Paper Number 223*. Washington, D.C.: World Bank, 1994.

"Planning for the Future: Norplant, A Contraceptive Option for Young Women." Grady
Memorial Hospital Patient Education Media Services Dept., 1992.

Pope, Alexander. "Mary Gulliver to Capt. Lemuel Gulliver." In *The Poems of Alexander
Pope*, ed. John Butt. New Haven, Conn.: Yale University Press, 1963.

"Pregnant Drinkers Face a Crackdown." *New York Times*, 24 May 1998, 16NE.

Prosser, Jay. *Second Skins: The Body Narratives of Transsexuality*. New York: Columbia
University Press, 1998.

"Psychiatrist Testifies in Black Surrogate Mom's Favor." *Jet Magazine*, 29 October 1990,
9.

Purvis, Andrew. "A Pill That Gets under the Skin." *Time*, 24 December 1990, 66.

Qadir Djaelani, H. Abdul. *Keluarga Sakinah*. Surabaya, Indonesia: PT Bina Ilmu, 1995.

"Radical Prophylaxis." *Time*, 29 November–5 December 1992, 23.

Ragoné, Helena. *Conception in the Heart*. Boulder, Colo.: Westview Press, 1994.

Rapp, Rayna. "Constructing Amniocentesis: Maternal and Medical Discourses." In
Uncertain Terms: Negotiating Gender in American Culture, ed. Faye Ginsberg and
Anna Lowenhaupt Tsing, 28–42. Boston: Beacon, 1990.

Raymond, Chris Ann. "In Vitro Fertilization Enters Stormy Adolescence As Experts
Debate Odds." *Journal of the American Medical Association* 259, no. 4 (1988): 464.

Richards, Louise. "Giving the Gift of Life." *Ladies' Home Journal* 106, no. 2 (1989):
22–23.

Robertson, John A. *Children of Choice: Freedom and the New Reproductive Technologies*.
Princeton, N.J.: Princeton University Press, 1994.

Robins, J. Max. "A New Wrinkle in Video Technology." *TV Guide* (Los Angeles Metropolitan Edition), 28 September–4 October 1996.

Robinson, Kathryn. "Choosing Contraception: Cultural Change and the Indonesian
Family Planning Program." In *Creating Indonesian Cultures*, ed. Paul Alexander.
Sydney: Oceania Publications, 1989.

Ronell, Avital. "A Disappearance of Community." In *Immersed in Technology: Art and
Virtual Environments*, ed. Mary Anne Moser et al. Cambridge: MIT Press, 1996.

Ross, Andrew. *The Chicago Gangster Theory of Life" Nature's Debt to Society*. New York:
Verso, 1994.

Rothman, Barbara Katz. *Recreating Motherhood: Ideology and Technology in a Patriarchal
Society*. New York: Norton, 1989.

Rowland, Robyn. *Living Laboratories: Women and Reproductive Technologies*.
Bloomington: Indiana University Press, 1992.

Salisbury, Joyce. *The Beast Within: Animals in the Middle Ages*. New York: Routledge,
1994.

Sappol, Michael. "Sammy Tubbs and Dr. Hubbs: Anatomical Dissection, Minstrelsy, and the Technology of Self-Making in Postbellum America." *Configurations: A Journal of Literature, Science, and Technology* 4, no. 2 (1996): 131–183.

Sarne, Michael, dir. *Myra Breckenridge*. United States, 1970.

Schiebinger, Londa. *The Mind Has No Sex?*. Cambridge: Harvard University Press, 1989.

———. *Nature's Body: Gender in the Making of Modern Science*. Boston: Beacon, 1993.

Schmidt, Matthew, and Lisa Jean Moore "Constructing a 'Good Catch,' Picking a Winner, " in *Cyborg Babies: From Techno-Sex to Techno-Tots*, Robbie Davis-Floyd and Joseph Dumit, eds. New York: Routledge, 1998.

Sears, Laura, ed. *Fantasizing the Feminine in Indonesia*. Durham, N.C.: Duke University Press, 1996.

Settle, Elkanah. *Threnodium Appolinare; A Funeral Poem to the Memory of Dr. Edward Tyson*. London, 1708.

Shaaban, M. "Experience with Norplant in Egypt." *Annual of Medicine* 25, no. 2 (1993): 167–169.

Silver, Lee. *Remaking Eden: Cloning and Beyond in a Brave New World*. New York: Avon, 1977.

Sirlin, David Harley. "Christine Jorgensen and the Cold War Closet." *Radical History Review* 62 (Spring 1995): 136–165.

Smyth, Ines. "The Indonesian Family Planning Program: A Success Story for Women?" *Development and Change* 22 (October 1991): 781–805.

Smith, Lynn, and Nina J. Easton. "The Dilemma of Desire." *Los Angeles Times Magazine*, 26 September 1993, 24–42.

Sobchack, Vivian. "Revenge of *The Leech Woman*: On the Dread of Aging in a Low-Budget Horror Film." In *Uncontrollable Bodies: Testimonies of Identity and Culture*, ed. Rodney Sappington and Tyler Stallings, 79–91. Seattle: Bay Press, 1994.

———. "Scary Women: Cinema, Surgery, and Special Effects." In *Figuring Age: Women, Bodies, Generations*, ed. Kathleen Woodward. Bloomington: Indiana University Press, 1998.

Solomon, J. Fischer. *Discourse and Reference in the Nuclear Age*. Norman: University of Oklahoma Press, 1988.

Soufoulis, Zoë. "Exterminating Fetuses: Abortion, Disarmament, and the Sexo-semiotics of Extraterrestrialism." *diacritics* 14, no. 2 (1984): 47–59.

———. "Interdictions, Intersections, Interfacing: Women, Technology, Art, and Philosophy." Julian Branshaw Memorial Lecture, Sydney, Australia, 1993.

Sourbut, Elizabeth. "Gynogenesis: A Lesbian Appropriation of Reproductive Technologies." In *Between Monsters, Goddesses, and Cyborgs: Feminist Confrontations with Science, Medicine, and Cyberspace*, ed. Nina Lykke and Rosi Braidotti, 228–229. Atlantic Highlands, N.J.: Humanities Press International, 1996.

Squier, Susan. *Babies in Bottles: Twentieth-Century Visions of Reproductive Technology*. New Brunswick, N.J.: Rutgers University Press, 1994.

———. "Fetal Subjects and Maternal Objects: Reproductive Technology and the New Fetal/Maternal Relation." *Journal of Medicine and Philosophy* 21 (1996): 515–535.

———. "Interspecies Reproduction: Xenogenic Desire and the Feminist Implications of Hybrids." *Cultural Studies* 12, no. 1 (1998): 360–381.

Stack, Carol. "Different Voices, Different Visions: Gender, Culture, and Moral Reasoning." In *Uncertain Terms: Negotiating Gender in American Culture*, ed. Faye Ginsberg and Anna Lowenhaupt Tsing, 19–27. Boston: Beacon, 1990.

Stanworth, Michelle. "Birth Pangs: Contraceptive Technologies and the Threat to Motherhood." In *Conflicts in Feminism*, ed. M. Hirsch and E. Fox Keller, 288–304. New York: Routledge, 1990.

———, ed. *Reproductive Technologies: Gender, Motherhood, and Medicine*. Minneapolis: University of Minnesota Press, 1987.

Stone, Sandy. "The *Empire* Strikes Back: A Posttranssexual Manifesto." In *Body Guards: The Cultural Politics of Gender Ambiguity*, ed. Julia Epstein and Kristina Straub, 280–304. New York: Routledge, 1991.

Strathern, Marilyn. *Reproducing the Future: Anthropology, Kinship, and the New Reproductive Technologies*. Routledge: New York, 1992.

––––––. "Displacing Knowledge: Technology and the Consequences for Kinship." In *Conceiving the New World Order: The Global Politics of Reproduction*, ed. Faye Ginsburg and Rayna Rapp, 346–336. Berkeley: University of California Press, 1995.

"Sure-Fire Birth Control, for Five Years." *U.S. News & World Report*, 12 November 1990, 15.

Swift, Jonathan. *Prose Works of Jonathan Swift*. Vol. 11. Edited by Herbert Davis and Irvin Ehrenpreis. Oxford, U. K.: Shakespeare Head Press, 1941.

Talan, Jamie. "Scientist Knew the Promise of Embryo Research." *Newsday*, 30 November 1997, A55.

Thom, Mary. "Dilemmas of the New Birth Technologies." *Ms.* (May 1988): 70'72.

Thompson, C.J.S. *The Mystery and Lore of Monsters: With Account of Some Giants, Dwarfs, and Prodigies*. New York: Macmillan, 1931. Published as *The History and Lore of Monsters*. London: William and Morgate, 1996.

Thompson, Rosemarie Garland. "Introduction: From Wonder to Error—A Geneology of Freak Discourse in Modernity." In *Freakery: Cultural Spectacles of the Extraordinary Body*, ed. Rosemarie Garland Thompson, 1–19. New York: New York University Press, 1996.

Tifft, Susan. "It's All in the (Parental) Genes." *Time*, 5 November 1990, 77.

Todd, Dennis. *Imagining Monsters: Miscreations of the Self in Eighteenth-Century England*. Chicago: University of Chicago Press, 1995.

"Transsexuality: The Postmodern Body and/as Technology." *Exposure: The Journal of the Society for Photographic Education* 30, nos. 1–2 (fall 1995): 38–50. Revised in Susan Stryker, *Ecstatic Passages: A Postmodern Transsexual Memoir*. New York: Oxford University Press, forthcoming.

Travis, J. "Dolly Had a Little Lamb." *Science News* 153 (1998): 278.

Treichler, Paula A. "Feminism, Medicine, and the Meaning of Childbirth." In *Body/Politics: Women and the Discourses of Science*, ed. Mary Jacobus, Evelyn Fox Keller, and Sally Shuttleworth, 113–138. New York: Routledge, 1990.

Turim, Maureen. "Viewing/Reading *Born to Be Sold: Martha Rosler Reads the Strange Case of Baby S/M* or Motherhood in the Age of Mechanical Reproduction." *Discourse* 13, no. 2 (1991): 32.

Turner, Victor. *The Ritual Process*. Chicago: Aldine, 1969.

Tyson, Edward. *Orang-Outang, sive Homo Sylvestris: or, the Anatomy of a Pygmie compared with that of a Monkey, an Ape, and a Man. To which is added, a Philological Essay Concerning the Pygmies, the Cynocephali, the Satyrs, and Sphinges of the Ancients* [1699]. London: Dawsons, 1966.

United States Agency for International Development (USAID). *AID's Role in Indonesian Family Planning: A Case Study with General Lessons for Foreign Assistance*. Washington, D.C.: USAID AID Program Evaluation Report Number 2, 1979.

Wallace, Mike. *Mike Wallace Interviews*. April 1959. Audiotape recording in author's possession of televised broadcast.

Ward, Ned, *The London-Spy Compleat*. Edited by Ralph Straus. London: Casanova Society, 1924.

Wells, Jeffrey. "Mirror, Mirror." *Entertainment Weekly*, 12 April 1996.

Whitehead, Mary Beth. *A Mother's Story*. New York: St. Martin's Press, 1989.

Wigley, Mark. "Prosthetic Theory: The Discipline of Architecture." *Assemblage* 15 (1991): 7–29.

Wills, David. *Prosthesis*. Stanford, Calif.: Stanford University Press, 1995.

Wilmut, I., et al. "Viable Offspring Derived from Fetal and Adult Mammalian Cells." *Nature* 385 (27 February 1997): 810–813.

Wilson, Dudley. *Signs and Portents: Monstrous Births from the Middle Ages to the Enlightenment*. New York: Routledge, 1993.

Wolf, Diane. *Factory Daughters: Gender, Household Dynamics, and Rural Industrialization in Java*. Berkeley and Los Angeles: University of California Press, 1992.

"Woman Charged in Fetus Death." *Centre Daily Times*, 10 September 1994, 10A.

Woodward, Kathleen. "Youthfulness as a Masquerade." *Discourse* 11, no. 1 (Fall–Winter 1988–1989): 133–134.

Xiao, B. L., S. J. Gu, S. L. Wang, P. D. Zhu, and S. Q. Shi. "Norplant and the Levonorgestrel IUD in Chinese Family Planning Programmes." *Annual Medicine* 25, no. 2 (1993): 155–160.

Yaqub, Memon Reshma. "The Double-Edged Sword of Norplant." *Chicago Tribune*, 24 January 1993, sec. 6, 11.

Young, Robert J. C. *Colonial Desire: Hybridity in Theory, Culture, and Race*. New York: Routledge, 1995.

Notes on Contributors

ANNE BALSAMO is a senior research scientist at Xerox PARC. She was the former director of the Graduate Program in Information Design and Technology at Georgia Institute of Technology, where she also taught courses in science, technology, and culture. Her first book, *Technologies of the Gendered Body: Reading Cyborg Women*, investigates the technocultural construction of the gendered body through its engagement with a range of new biotechnologies. Her next book investigates emergent New Media formations.

CHARIS THOMPSON CUSSINS is assistant professor in the departments of Sociology and Women's Studies at the University of Illinois, Urbana-Champaign. Her most recent publications include "Quit Sniveling Cryo-Baby: We'll Work Out Which One's Your Mama!" in *Cyborg Babies: From Techno-Sex to Techno-Tots*, edited by R. Davis-Floyd and J. Dumit (Routledge, 1998), and "Primate Suspect: On Suspicion and Some Varieties of Science Studies," in *Close Encounters: Primates, Science, and Scientists*, edited by S. Strum and L. Fedigan (Chicago University Press, 1999).

LESLIE DWYER recently completed a dissertation in anthropology at Princeton University, focusing on discourses of sexuality, gender, and modernity among Indonesian Muslims. She has been the recipient of research grants from Fulbright, the American Association of Asian Studies, and the MacArthur Foundation, as well as fellowships from the Charlotte Newcombe Foundation and the Institute for Advanced Study. Her current research focuses on tourism and sexuality in Bali.

DION FARQUHAR is a political theorist, poet, and prose fiction writer. She teaches (as an adjunct) in Women's Studies programs in New York and Santa Cruz, including Hunter College and the New School Graduate Faculty. The mobile and garrulous gametes about which she writes for this volume are insisting on a book of their own, to tell of the scandals, provocations, and recuperations that they continue to engender. She has enthusiastically agreed to try and fit them in.

E. ANN KAPLAN is professor of English and comparative literature at the State University of New York at Stony Brook, where she also founded and directs the Humanities Institute. Kaplan has written and lectured internationally on literary and film theory and practice, psychoanalysis, postmodernism, and, most recently, postcolonialism and multicultural women's films. Her feminist and cultural studies research focuses on the female body and psychology, women's changing historical roles, social practices, and representations. Her many books include *Women and Film: Both Sides of the Camera, Motherhood, and Representation, The Mother in Popular Culture and Melodrama*, and, most recently, *Looking for the Other: Feminism, Film, and the Imperial Gaze*. Kaplan's new research is on aging and diversity.

PAMELA L. MOORE is a medical journalist and editor in Denver, Colorado. She received her Ph.D. from the State University of New York at Stony Brook. Her edited collection, *Building Bodies*, was published by Rutgers University Press in 1997, and she was a contributor to the *Literature, Arts, and Medicine Database* at http://endeavor.med.nyu.edu/lit-med.

RICHARD NASH is an associate professor of English at Indiana University, where he specializes in eighteenth-century literature and literature and science. Currently working on a book, with the tentative title "Wild Enlightenment," on the figure of the wild man in literature and science during the long eighteenth century, he has published on subjects as diverse as eighteenth-century mathematics and twentieth-century representations of gorillas.

GABRIELE SCHWAB teaches English and comparative literature at the University of California–Irvine, where she also serves as director of the Critical Theory Institute. Her most recent books are *Subjects without Selves: Transitional Texts in Modern Fiction* (Harvard University Press, 1994) and *The Mirror and the Killer-Queen: Otherness in Literary Language* (Indiana University Press, 1996). Currently she is working on a book entitled "Imaginary Ethnographies." She is also editing a collection of essays related to a current project at the Critical Theory Institute entitled "Forces of Globalization."

VIVIAN SOBCHACK is associate dean and professor of film and television studies at the UCLA School of Theater, Film, and Television. She was the first woman elected president of the Society for Cinema Studies. Her work focuses on film theory and its intersections with philosophy and cultural studies, genre studies of American film, and studies of electronic imaging. Her books include *Screening Space: The American Science Fiction Film* (Rutgers University Press, 1997) and *The Address of the Eye: A Phenomenology of Film Experience* (Princeton University Press, 1992), and she has edited the anthology *The Persistence of History: Cinema, Television, and the Modern Event* (Routledge, 1996). Currently she is completing a forthcoming collection of her own essays called *Carnal Thoughts: Bodies, Texts, Scenes, and Screens.*

KAY TORNEY SOUTER is senior lecturer in English at La Trobe University, Melbourne, Australia. She teaches feminist, body, and post-Kleinian psychoanalytic studies and is an editor of *Hysteric: Body/Medicine/Text.* She is the author of a number of articles on medical narrative, the representation of reproductive technology, and the reading of childhood trauma.

SUSAN SQUIER is Julia Gregg Brill Professor of Women's Studies and English at the Pennsylvania State University, where she teaches science studies, feminist theory, and modern British literature. She is the author of *Babies in Bottles: Twentieth Century Visions of Reproductive Technology* (Rutgers University Press, 1994) and *Virginia Woolf and London: The Sexual Politics of the City* (University of North Carolina Press, 1985), coeditor of *Arms and the Woman: War, Gender, and Literary Representation* (University of North Carolina Press, 1989), and the editor of *Women Writers and the City: Essays in Feminist Literary Criticism* (University of Tennessee Press, 1984).

SUSAN STRYKER is affiliated with the History Department of Stanford University and holds a Social Science Research Council postdoctoral fellowship in human sexuality studies. She has written extensively on transgender issues for both scholarly and popular audiences and recently edited a special issue of the queer studies journal *GLQ* devoted to the emerging field of transgender studies. Her book *Ecstatic Passages: A Postmodern Transsexual Memoir* is forthcoming from Oxford University Press.

KARYN VALERIUS is teaching composition for the Freshmen Learning Community in Science at the State University of New York at Stony Brook. She is writing a dissertation on monstrosity to complete doctoral work in English at Stony Brook. She has published an essay on assisted reproduction entitled "Genetic Essentialism: Race, Class, and the Politics of Reproduction" in the journal *Consumption, Markets, and Culture* 1, no. 3 (1997).

ANGELA WALL is currently a Brittain Fellow at the Georgia Institute of Technology in Atlanta and teaches classes on cultural studies of gender, science, and technology. She is completing a doctoral dissertation titled "Managing Motherhood: The Reproductive Body in Contemporary Culture" in the Modern Studies Program at the University of Wisconsin, Milwaukee. Her work on postmenopausal motherhood is forthcoming in *Wild Science* (Routledge).

JOHN WILTSHIRE is a reader in English at La Trobe University, Melbourne, Australia, where he teaches in the fields of literature and medicine, psychoanalysis and gender studies. He is the author of *Samuel Johnson in the Medical World* (Cambridge University Press, 1991), *Jane Austen and the Body* (Cambridge University Press, 1992), and, with Paul A. Komesaroff, *Drugs in the Health Marketplace* (Arena, 1995). With Philipa Rothfield and Kay Torney Souter, he edits *Hysteric: Body, Medicine, Text*.

Index

abortion, 119, 202, 204
 and conflict between woman and
  fetus, 179–180
 and ignorance, 75–76n.7
 and natural "facts," 74–75n.6
 Norplant as alternative to, 69–70
 prohibited by Islam, 50
 and scapegoating, 60
 and subsequent surrogacy, 119,
  132n.22
Abraham, patriarch, 117
abstinence, 67
"acceptor clubs," Indonesian, 49
adoption, giving child up for, and
  subsequent surrogacy, 132n.22
adultery
 by fictional mother, 123–124,
  133n.30
 and monstrous birth, 174
 symbolic, surrogacy as, 119
Adulthood Rites (Butler), 239
advertising, for assisted–reproduction
  technologies, 81, 83–85
Advisory Group on the Ethics of
  Transplantation (Britain), 111
ageism, 148, 153
agency
 in reproduction, 234, 237
 technological, 89
agitprop, 133n.33
 and video melodrama, 126
AIDS, 78n.29. *See also* HIV
 and sexual liberation discourses, 162
Aigen, Betsy, 3, 120
aliens
 abductions by, 232

impregnation by, 232, 235
 as liminal figures, 240
Althusser, Louis, 97n.6
Amazing Equal Pay Show, The (film),
  133n.33
American Fertility Society, 81
American Medical Association (AMA),
  and abortion, 75n.7
American Society for Reproductive
  Medicine, 12–13n.1
amniocentesis, 74n.5
Anderson, L., 218n
"angelic mother," 123
anger and desire, 148–149
Annas, George, 82
Antinomian Controversy, 176–178, 183
ape-man hybrids, 225
apes. *See also* primates
 as allegorical figures, 233
 sexuality of, 200, 201, 227, 230–231n.8
apostasy, and monstrous birth, 174
"Aristotelian vs. Heideggerian Approach
  to the Problem of Technology, The"
  (Hood), 89–90
Aristotle, 96
articulation, 91, 93
artificial insemination, 19, 118, 133n.28,
  203
artificial/natural boundary, 18
Ashley, Kawana, 101, 105, 111, 113
assisted reproduction, 11, 17
 and assisted replication, 101–115
 and fear of monstrosity, 172–184
 transsexuality as, 161
assisted-reproduction technologies
  (ART), 81

Fantastic Voyage (film), 106
fantasy
    cultural, of transsexuality, 161–166
    as productive mode, 173
Farquhar, Dion, 6, 17–32, 93, 258
fatherhood
    gestational, 130–131
    as mere gamete contribution, 102
Federal Trade Commission, 84
    and fertility advertising, 94
Felski, Rita, 162
femininity, discourse of, on egg donation, 24
feminist studies, and technology, 88–90
Fertility Clinic of Northern New Jersey, 85
fertility clinics, 232
    profitability of, 82
Ferzacca, Steve, 54n.5
fetal alcohol syndrome, 114n.4
fetal/maternal boundary, 102
    and embryo research, 108–111
fetal-protection agenda, 115n.20
fetal visualization techniques, 103, 105
fetus
    "at risk," 8
    miscarried, 174
    and mother as antagonists, 101, 107, 179–180
    personhood of, 74n.6, 95, 111, 180
    public, 175
    quickening of, 103, 104, 114n.11
    as subject, 101
    subjectivity of, 108, 113
    symbiosis with mother, 29
fiction, 11–12, 241
    as resistance, 5–6
film, *see* cinema
"Fin de Siècle, Fin de Sex" (Felski), 162
First Strategic Group, 84
"five precepts," Indonesian state doctrine of, 44
Foucault, Michel, 127–130, 131, 169
fragmentation of motherhood, 93–94
Franklin, Sarah, 74n.6, 179
freak shows, 174, 175
freedom, reproductive
    and financial access, 77n.16
    rhetoric of, 65
Freixas, Laura, 115n.20
Freud, Sigmund, 104, 108, 149
fusion, dyadic, vs. Oedipal tension, 138

gamete intrafallopian transfer (GIFT), 34n.18, 118
gamete traffic, 6, 7, 13n.9, 17–32, 94
    bidirectional politics of, 25
    and gender difference, 19–21, 32
    and gender routing, 23–25
    scandal of, 21–23, 25–26
Geertz, Clifford, 47
gender
    construction of, 10–11
    and division of labor, 97n.6
    and gamete traffic, 19–21, 23–25, 32
    grounded in flesh, 170
    and modernism, 169
    politics of, 47
    semiotic codes of, 168–169
    transsexuality's challenge to, 160
"Gender and Technology" conference (SUNY Stony Brook, 1996), 2, 4
gene banks, 192
Generation X (Coupland), 242
"genetically unfortunate," 175
genetic engineering, 234
    enforced, 232
Genetics and IVF Institute, 85
gene trading, 232
genitalia, male, as norm, 76n.16
George VI, death of, 160
Gerike, Ann, 146
germ plasm conservation, 192
gestation
    of human embryos in animals, 109–110
    and subject formation, 102–103
Ginsberg, Faye, 74–75n.6
Girl Scouts, Indonesian, 47
God
    chosen people of, 177, 183
    and the legitimation of surrogacy, 131n.10
    monstrous births as judgment from, 174
    personal relationship with, 177
"going native," 211, 234
Goldberg, David Theo, 104, 113
Goldberg, Whoopi, 133n.28
Gone With the Wind (film version), 125
Gordon, Linda, 133n.29
Goslinga-Roy, Gillian M., 127–130, 131, 131n.1, 132–133n.27, 132n.11, 133n.31, 133n.38
gossip, 49
grace, state of, and good deeds, 176